# The Pacific Coast League

## 1903–1988

## Bill O'Neal

**EAKIN PRESS** ★ Austin, Texas

*For my aunt,*
*Ann O'Neal Tinkle*
*An artist and poet who taught me*
*her love of books.*

FIRST EDITION

Copyright © 1990
By Bill O'Neal

Published in the United States of America
By Eakin Press
An Imprint of Eakin Publications, Inc.
P.O. Drawer 90159      ★      Austin, TX 78709-0159

ISBN 0-89015-776-6

**Library of Congress Cataloging-in-Publication Data**

O'Neal, Bill, 1942–
    The Pacific Coast League, 1903–1988 / Bill O'Neal.
        p.   cm.
    Includes bibliographical references.
    ISBN 0-89015-776-6 : $14.95
    1. Pacific Coast League — History. I. Title.
GV875.P33054   1990
796.357′64 — dc20                                                          89-48395
                                                                                 CIP

# Contents

Foreword      v

Preface and Acknowledgments      vii

1903–1909:   Birth of the Coast League      1

1910–1919:   Decade of Dynasties      19

1920–1929:   The Golden Age of the Coast League      35

1930–1939:   The PCL During the Depression      57

1940–1949:   Baseball on the Coast During
and After the War      78

1950–1959:   Decade of Change      101

1960–1969:   More Change      119

1970–1979:   Prosperity Returns to the PCL      134

1980–1989:   Coast League Comeback      147

Nicknames      168

Ballparks      171

Pacific Coast League Cities      178

*Albuquerque,* 179

*Calgary,* 186

*Colorado Springs,* 189

*Dallas,* 191

*Denver,* 192

*Edmonton,* 195

*Eugene,* 198

*Fort Worth,* 200

*Fresno,* 201

*Hollywood,* 203

*Honolulu,* 210

*Indianapolis,* 215

*Las Vegas,* 216

*Little Rock,* 219

*Los Angeles,* 222

*Mission (San Francisco),* 230

*Oakland,* 233

*Ogden,* 239

*Oklahoma City,* 241

*Phoenix,* 243

*Portland,* 247

*Sacramento,* 255

*Salt Lake City,* 262

*San Diego,* 269

*San Francisco,* 274

*San Jose,* 282

*Seattle,* 284

*Spokane,* 289

*Tacoma,* 293

*Tucson,* 300

*Tulsa,* 305

*Vancouver,* 307

*Venice,* 312

*Vernon,* 313

Pacific Coast League Records                                    318
    Annual Standings, 318        Most Victories, 335
    Playoff Results, 328         Winning Percentage, 336
    All-Star Games, 329         Most Strikeouts, 338
    PCL Presidents, 331         Lowest ERA, 339
    Batting Champions, 331      30-Game Winners, 340
    Home Run Champs, 332      200 Victories, 340
    RBI Leaders, 333           Most Valuable Players, 340
    Stolen Base Leaders, 334    PCL Hall of Famers, 341
    .400 Hitters 335            Lifetime Records, 342
    50 Home Runs, 335        Season Records, 342

Bibliography                                                    345
Index                                                          351

# Foreword

I first became associated with the Pacific Coast League in 1970 as executive vice-president and general manager of the Portland Beavers, following twenty years as an American League executive. Later, as owner and president at Portland, I moved the club to Spokane before being selected to succeed Roy Jackson as PCL president in 1979. While working for the past two decades in the historic Coast League, I have witnessed increasing fan support for the fine quality of baseball played by our clubs.

During my tenure as league president, the PCL has moved into Edmonton and Calgary, bringing the number of Canadian franchises to three. We also have introduced PCL baseball to glamorous Las Vegas, and most recently to beautiful Colorado Springs. In every city families are flocking to the ballparks to enjoy the Coast League version of America's national pastime, and club officials are striving to provide wholesome, inexpensive entertainment in a comfortable setting.

Fans in thirty-three cities have embraced Coast League baseball throughout the twentieth century, thrilling to the exploits of talented hitters and pitchers for almost nine decades. It is my hope that baseball buffs will find the unique flavor and history of the PCL recaptured in Bill O'Neal's book, and that fans will continue to enjoy Coast League ball in the years to come.

BILL CUTLER
Pacific Coast League President

# Preface and Acknowledgments

The Pacific Coast League holds a unique position among baseball circuits. For decades the PCL maintained the longest schedule in baseball, and the astounding statistical achievements which resulted have been a delight to study. The PCL was the only minor league to be granted Open Classification status. The circuit made a serious effort to become a major league, and for decades many players genuinely preferred to ply their trade in the PCL rather than in the big leagues of the East. The Coast League established a mystique that still can be identified today, a mystique I discovered while researching in the past and present cities of the PCL. I visited streamlined new stadiums, charming old ballparks, and city blocks where historic playing fields long ago were replaced by commercial buildings. In public libraries I pored through tattered game programs and fading newspaper accounts and magnificent photographs of teams and players and ballparks of seasons gone by. In the ten current PCL stadiums I had the pleasure of interviewing club officials, veteran fans, and players, and in other locations I was privileged to share the reminiscences of retired players and their wives. During the course of a rich and enjoyable research experience I became indebted to numerous past and present Coast Leaguers.

I owe a special debt of gratitude to PCL President Bill Cutler, who has offered strong support from the inception of this project. In addition to providing miscellaneous information and an illuminating interview, Bill arranged generous financial assistance from the PCL which made it possible for me to travel thousands of miles to research in almost three dozen PCL cities and to acquire scores of photographs. Bill Cutler is a knowledgeable and gentlemanly baseball executive, and without his cooperation it would have been impossible to complete this volume.

W. Lloyd Johnson, executive director of the Society for American Baseball Research, provided me with a great deal of encouragement regarding this project, as well as numerous tips regarding research sources. The National Baseball Hall of Fame in Cooperstown supplied me with a large amount of essential materials, and I am especially indebted to Gary Van Allen, assistant file manager, for his prompt and meticulous responses to my requests.

In Carthage I enjoy the friendship of two former Coast League players. Joe Vitter, an infielder with both the San Francisco Seals and the Missions, granted me several interviews, and his charming wife, Eleanor, allowed me to utilize the scrapbooks she has compiled. Jon Perlman, who has pitched for the Phoenix Firebirds and Colorado Springs Sky Sox during the 1980s, reflected with fascinating insight upon his experiences in the contemporary PCL. Jon's lovely wife, Dana, also offered valuable thoughts about the role of modern players' wives. Joyce Chapman, Mary Rose Johnson, and Barbara Bell of the M. P. Baker Library at Panola College provided me with their usual cooperation in utilizing interlibrary loan and similar library services. I am deeply grateful to Karon Ashby, mathematics instructor at Carthage High School, for helping me to computerize the statistical section and miscellaneous other items. I owe a special debt to Ted Leach, talented sports editor of the *Panola Watchman*, who generously assisted me in assembling photographs.

Mariana York of Hubbard, Texas, is the widow of Tony York, an infielder for the Los Angeles Angels, Seattle Rainiers, and San Diego Padres during the 1940s and early 1950s. Following a lengthy interview at her home, Mrs. York graciously permitted me to carry off her voluminous scrapbooks, photograph collection and other memorabilia, and I cannot adequately express my appreciation for her gracious cooperation.

Tim Phillips, a baseball historian from Dallas, initiated contact with me and generously provided last-minute information. At the Fort Worth Public Library, Max Hill expertly guided me through the vast collection of the Local History and Genealogy Department.

I struck PCL gold in California, first at Sacramento's City Library and at the California State Library, where staff members offered invaluable assistance as I investigated the rich resources of their libraries. A day later, I benefitted from the expertise of William W. Sturm, librarian in charge of the Oakland History Room in the Oakland Public Library, where impressive newspaper and photographic materials about Bay Area baseball are on file. I also was ably assisted by staff members of the San Francisco Public Library.

Club officials of the San Jose Giants and staff members of the San Jose Public Library aided me in investigating local baseball history. In Fresno, I was given decisive assistance by Linda Sitterding, reference librarian of the Fresno County Free Library.

I telephoned and corresponded with Richard Beverage of Placentia, California. Mr. Beverage is a leading authority on the Coast League, and I drew heavily upon his definitive books, *The Angels* and *The Hollywood Stars*. I am indebted to another Coast League expert, Dick Dobbins of Alamo, California, who provided me with precise answers to a number of PCL mysteries I encountered. Ken Stadler of Agoura, California, author of the highly informative *The Pacific Coast League, One Man's Memories*, was most gracious in a telephone interview.

Will Henry of Encino, a gifted western novelist who also was an enthusiastic fan of the Hollywood Stars during the 1940s and 1950s, shared many amusing reminiscences with me during a series of telephone conversations. Statistician William J. Weiss from San Mateo promptly provided me with the complete official PCL figures for 1987. Bruce Ericson of San Diego generously suggested several unsuspected research avenues.

I was greatly aided in Tacoma by the dynamic Stan Naccarato, president and GM of the Tigers, by Frank Colorusso, assistant GM, and by Brian Kamens of the Tacoma Public Library and J. Michael Kenyon, who possesses an encyclopedic knowledge of and longtime affection for the Coast League. In Seattle, I was aided by Kathryn Sheldon of the Seattle Public Library and by Gary Waddingham, author of the nostalgic *The Seattle Rainiers, 1938–1942*. Tom Lipe, general manager of the Spokane Indians, provided background information about his club.

Joe Buzas, genial owner and president of the Portland Beavers, granted me a fascinating interview and the loan of numerous photos from the team scrapbooks. Also of assistance were John Christensen, Beavers radio announcer and director of public relations, business manager Mike Parker, and Phil Anez, director of marketing and sales. During a game, I was introduced to Beavers superfan Alice Spackman, who has avidly followed Coast League ball since 1944 and who reminisced with me at length. Steve Halburg courteously guided me through the impressive photographic and file resources of the Oregon Historical Society in Portland. Bob Beban, president and GM of the Eugene Emeralds and a former PCL umpire, contributed a candid and informative interview.

In Tucson, I received welcome assistance from Lori Davisson and Reva Dean of the Arizona Historical Society, and by Tom Cutler, Toros account executive. Tommy Gonzales, longtime stadium superintendent of the Muni in Phoenix, shared his rich recollections with me.

Pat McKernan, president of the Albuquerque Dukes, gave invaluable impetus to this project and loaned me rare materials from his office. I also was assisted by Mark Rupert, Dukes director of administration, and by staff members of the Albuquerque Public Library. In Colorado Springs, Fred Whitacre, outgoing GM of the Sky Sox, provided me with a cordial interview.

I was treated with great courtesy in Las Vegas, and I am indebted to Larry Koentopp, president and GM of the Stars. Assistant GM Don Logan, director of public relations Bob Blum, and office personnel Kery Koentopp and Jeanette Lynn.

In Salt Lake City Ron Kendall of the Trappers' staff was extremely cooperative, and I am grateful to staff members of the Ogden Public Library. I was aided in Oklahoma City by staff members of the Metropolitan Library System and by '89ers maintenance personnel. Wayne McCombs, who is compiling a history of professional baseball in Tulsa, graciously responded to last-minute queries.

In Canada, I was the recipient of considerable hospitality. Laurie Roberts and Chris Middlemass of the Vancouver Public Library were cheerfully helpful. I gleaned a great deal of information from Canadians vice-president and GM Stu Kehoe, and from assistant GM Dick Phillips, and from dedicated fan Norm Gloag. Calgary Cannons GM John Dittrich opened his team's extensive photographic files to me and provided exceptional courtesies. Owner and president Russ Parker was generous with his time at a late hour, and I enjoyed an informative conversation with Cannons fan Bill Tanguay. I received assistance from the staff of the Edmonton Public Library and from Trappers secretary Elaine Ell, and club President Mel Kowalchuk made himself available for an interview during a flurry of game activities.

My daughters, Lynn, Shellie, Berri and Causby, provided welcome companionship during a long research trip. We enjoyed a number of PCL games together, and they were uncomplaining troopers throughout a succession of hard drives. Berri and Causby were especially helpful during an extensive photocopy session at the Oakland Public Library, while Lynn and Shellie proofread the manuscript with their customary patience and expertise. My wife Faye offered numerous tips on grammar and style, and generously overlooked my time-consuming immersion in the Coast League.

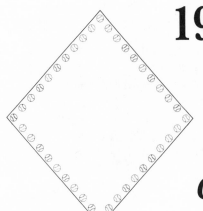

# 1903–1909

## *Birth of the Coast League*

The California gold rush introduced baseball to the Pacific Coast, and the Eagles of San Francisco, organized in 1859, afforded the first regular competition for pick-up teams. In 1862 the Pacifics were organized in San Francisco and frequently challenged the Eagles, to the delight of sporting enthusiasts and gamblers. The first enclosed ballpark on the Pacific Coast was built in San Francisco at 25th and Folsom Streets, and the Eagles hosted the Wide Awakes of Oakland in the inaugural game, a 37–23 victory for the home team on November 26, 1868. In 1869 the first professional club, the barnstorming Cincinnati Red Stockings, visited the West Coast and walloped the Pacifics, 66–4 and 35–4.

During the post-Civil War era, baseball proliferated in California, and keen rivalries developed between teams representing different cities. The California League was organized in 1885 with three clubs from San Francisco and one from Sacramento. Soon afterward the California State League was formed with a trio of San Francisco teams and one from across the Bay in Oakland. These leagues would play for a time, disband, then reorganize a season or two later, usually with clubs from other California cities. As the years passed, these teams played increasingly better ball, players became more accomplished, and a growing number of athletes

1

from the West began to play for the major league teams of the East. And at the conclusion of the major league seasons, eastern professionals regularly barnstormed through Texas, Arizona, California, and other western locales where the climate permitted winter baseball.

The California League of 1898 boasted teams from eight communities: San Francisco, Oakland, Sacramento, Santa Cruz, San Jose, Stockton, Fresno and Watsonville. Normally the circuit was composed of just four to six teams, while it was sometimes referred to informally as the "Pacific Coast League." Clubs from northwestern cities such as Portland and Seattle often traveled south to compete in California. These communities, along with other cities from the Northwest that would some day play in the PCL, placed professional clubs in the Pacific Northwest League, which was organized in 1892.

Visiting major league teams long had snapped up the most promising minor leaguers they played against, if possible without compensation to minor league club owners. This problem increased after 1901, when the American League established itself as a major league and competed aggressively with the National League for the best available talent. In September 1901 minor league presidents assembled in an emergency meeting in Chicago and formed the National Association of Professional Baseball Leagues. The primary purpose of the National Association was to prevent minor league rosters from being raided by the American and National leagues, but soon other operating procedures were established to regulate the minors, including a strict reserve clause prohibiting minor leaguers from jumping to other minor league clubs. Minor circuits were divided into A, B, C, and D classifications, depending upon the population of member cities, experience level of players, and size of team rosters and salary totals. Any minor league which failed to unite with the National Association was termed an "outlaw" circuit, and all leagues operating with the National Association were called members of "Organized Baseball."

Both the California League and the Pacific Northwest League were members of the National Association when the 1902 season began. The Pacific Northwest League of 1902 was made up of Portland, Seattle, Tacoma, Spokane (each of these cities would eventually field teams in the Pacific Coast League), Butte and Helena, while the California League completed 1902 with San Francisco, Los Angeles, Oakland, and Sacramento. But after one season, members of the California League determined to expand their league significantly. For the 1903 season, San Francisco, Los Angeles, Oakland, and Sacramento, along with Portland and Seattle, would compete as the Pacific Coast League outside Organized Baseball.

The Class C Pacific Northwest League angrily protested that their territorial rights in Portland and Seattle — rights assigned by Organized Baseball through the National Association — had been violated, but the PCL was not a member of the National Association. Deciding to fight expansion with expansion, executives of the Pacific Northwest League established clubs in the PCL's strongest cities, San Francisco and Los Angeles. The circuit changed its name to the more suitable "Pacific National League," and team officials even sacrificed certain star players to San Francisco and Los Angeles in an effort to compete more successfully with the PCL in these key cities. The president of the American Association, Thomas J. Hickey, and the president of the Western League, Michael H. Sexton, traveled to the West Coast as representatives of the National Association. Hickey and Sexton attempted to settle the growing conflict, but to no avail.

During the 1903 season there was head-to-head competition between the two leagues, with games scheduled on the same afternoons in Los Angeles and San Francisco in ballparks almost adjacent to each other. The Pacific Coast League proved more popular among Californians, and the Pacific National League franchises in Los Angeles and San Francisco folded during the season. Tacoma and Helena also disbanded, and Portland transferred to Salt Lake City; only four of the eight clubs which began 1903 in the Pacific National League managed to finish the schedule.

The original PCL clubs brought most of their 1902 players to the inaugural season of what would become referred to simply as the "Coast League." The early owners (like most of today's owners) were civic-minded baseball enthusiasts who often lost money as club backers. In the first years of the Coast League there were no major league affiliations. Minor league clubs were locally controlled, and owners were not obligated to promote their players to the major leagues, although frequently the difference between a profit or loss was the sale of a promising athlete to a big league team.

In the early years of the PCL, rosters numbered only 14 or 15 players. Clubs carried four pitchers, each of whom was expected to work all nine innings of every start. There were no relief specialists — the ace of the staff would be brought in between starts to salvage close games. Not infrequently a pitcher would hurl two games when a doubleheader was scheduled on "his" day. Because there were only one or two substitutes on early rosters, the speediest and best-hitting pitchers often were called upon to play in the outfield. Player-managers were utilized by almost all clubs, and because of the long PCL schedules, one of the few backup players always was a catcher.

For years PCL teams scheduled more than 200 games per season. The season ran eight months or more, from March through November, or even into early December. Balmy weather permitted schedules of up to 225 games, while major leagues scheduled 154-game seasons. Coast League players were compensated for long schedules, and since major leaguers were paid miserly salaries, many PCL athletes chose to stay in the West. Not only was it possible to earn as much or more for a season of Coast League play — the weather was generally better much of the year than in big league cities in the East, and travel conditions also were more favorable. In the Coast League it soon became customary for a team to move into a city for a seven-game series beginning on a Tuesday. There would be a single game beginning at mid-afternoon daily on Tuesday through Saturday, with a doubleheader on Sunday. Monday was a travel day, and travel was by train. A team would be on the road for two weeks, then have a two-week home stand (by contrast the major leagues would play three- or four-day series, and travel schedules and home stays were irregular).

The first Coast League ballparks boasted substantial wooden grandstands and plank fences, with general admission prices set at 25¢. Wooden outfield bleachers brought seating totals up to several thousand, but when important games caused overflow crowds, standing-room-only sections were created by roping off areas down the outfield lines or in the outfield against the fence. Fair balls which bounded into roped-off areas were ground rule doubles. Bases were canvas sacks, similar to what is used today, but home "plates" were fashioned of wood and imbedded in the ground. Usually there was only one clubhouse, for the home team. Visiting clubs dressed in their hotel rooms, and after a game undressed and bathed back at the hotel.

*The first day of the first season, Monday, March 9, 1903, in Sacramento. The opposing Sacramento and Oakland teams paraded in open automobiles to the ballpark to drum up a crowd. The Sacts beat Oakland, 7–4.*

— Courtesy California State Library, Sacramento

Attired in their uniforms, teams frequently were paraded through the streets in open automobiles to the ballparks, in an effort to drum up attendance. Until 1930 there were no night games, but games were started as late in the afternoon as possible so that businessmen could attend (of course, there has always been a delicious sense of hooky about going to ball games during work hours, and many businessmen needed little encouragement to slip away to the ballpark). It was the duty of umpires to keep the game moving at a fast pace, so that play would not have to be suspended because of darkness. Hurlers were not allowed to dawdle between pitches, there were few pitcher substitutions to slow the action, low-scoring contests were common throughout the dead-ball era, and games usually were completed within an hour and a half or less. On July 30, 1905, Los Angeles and Oakland reeled off a doubleheader in just one hour and 38½ minutes. Both games lasted nine innings, the first being played in 47½ minutes, the second in 51 minutes. Games of the period were crisply played and enthusiastically attended, and when the Pacific Coast League opened play in 1903, baseball truly was America's national pastime.

From the opening season the Coast League boasted numerous excellent players, many with major league experience or promising futures, and many from California or other PCL cities. For example, the 1903 Los Angeles Angels boasted an outfielder from San Diego in his second year of pro ball; Gavvy Cravath would spend five seasons with the Angels, then in an 11-year big league career he would twice hit .341 and six times he would win or share the National League home run crown. Pitcher Joe Corbett, a native of San Francisco, had been 24–8 with the 1897 Baltimore Orioles. First baseman Pop Dillon was a major league veteran, Harry Spies had caught for two National League teams, and 41-year-old center fielder Dummy Hoy had spent 11 seasons roaming big league outfields. Ace hurler Doc Newton, already an experienced major leaguer, would pitch a total of eight years in the big time, and Dolly Gray would go on to pitch three seasons for Washington.

On opening day, Los Angeles hosted Seattle at Chutes Park. Doc Newton started and the Angels won a pitchers' duel, 2–1. The talented Angels went on to establish a PCL record by winning their first 15 games. Los Angeles dominated the circuit throughout the season, claiming the *only* winning record of the year, an impressive 133–78 mark. Doc Newton (35–12) recorded the most victories and the highest winning percentage, and on November 8 pitched the Coast League's first no-hitter, a 2–0 win over Oakland in which he also issued no walks. Warren Hall (32–18), Joe Corbett (25–17), and Dolly Gray (25–20) also pitched superbly. First baseman Pop Dillon (.360 with 43 stolen bases) hammered out the team's highest batting average, while pitcher Joe Corbett (.336) was the only other Angel to hit above .294. Pop Dillon became a fixture in Los Angeles as a player and manager through 1915, when he was 42, although he played sparingly during his last few seasons.

The first PCL batting champ was Seattle center fielder Harry Lumley, whose average (.387) would not be matched until 1923. Sacramento shortstop Dan Shay (.244 with 83 steals) was the stolen base champ. Twenty players stole 40 or more bases, and Sacramento established the all-time season record with 422 steals. Seattle's Jim Hughes (34–15) was right behind Newton in victories, while Portland's John Thielmann (18–7) tossed three one hitters. Oakland pitcher Oscar Graham (27–26) established all-time marks by issuing 234 bases on ball and hitting 49 batters, and on

April 7 Seattle hurler John Hickey put himself in the PCL record book by walking 13 hitters in a game against San Francisco.

Following its successful inaugural season, the Pacific Coast League was wooed by Organized Baseball. American and National League officials made the long train journey to San Francisco to persuade PCL president Eugene F. Bert and other Coast League executives — J. Cal Ewing was a key figure — to join the National Association. American League president Ban Johnson, National League president H. C. Pulliam, and Ned Hanlon were instrumental in arranging for the PCL to become a part of Organized Baseball as a Class A circuit. (The Class C Pacific National League concluded operations in 1904 with just three teams. The California State league continued to operate as an outlaw circuit for a few more seasons, also attempting to go head-to-head with PCL teams in California cities. California League rosters were appreciably bolstered late each year when big league players at the close of the major league seasons would sign on, but in 1907 the PCL prevailed upon the National Association to disallow this practice.) Also in the off-season, the Sacramento franchise was transferred to Tacoma. And hoping to avoid the lack of interest caused by the Los Angeles runaway of 1903, club owners decided to divide the long season into two halves, with the winners of each half competing for the pennant in a postseason playoff series.

But Tacoma won the first half of the season, which lasted from March 24 through July 24, then apparently won the second half, July 26 through November 27. Los Angeles, however, challenged Tacoma's second half title. Although Tacoma (64–48) won more games in the second half than LA (60–45), the winning percentage was the same (.571). Furthermore, Los Angeles claimed that a tie game involving Tacoma should be played off, and if the Tigers lost, the Angels would be the second half winners. There was confusion among the fans, but President Bert announced that Tacoma had won the pennant outright. Nevertheless, managers Mique Fisher of the Tigers and Jim Morley of the Angels decided to stage a nine-game playoff series, beginning November 30. One game ended in a tie, Tacoma won five games, and Los Angeles won four.

Tacoma's Truck Egan (.311 with 25 homers) repeated as home run king in 1904, while Seattle again provided the batting champ, left fielder Emil Frick (.337). Once more Doc Newton (39–17) notched the most victories and highest winning percentage,

*The Tacoma Tigers, 1904 PCL champs. Shortstop Truck Eagan (top left) was the home run king in 1903, 1904 and 1905, and the batting champ in 1907. Righthander Orvie Overall (second row, second from left) won 32 games for the champs, then went up to the big leagues.*

— Courtesy Tacoma Public Library

while establishing the all-time record for wins in a season. Robert Keefe (34–15) and Orval Overall (32–25) of Tacoma were workhorses for the league champions, while Oakland's James Buchanan (33–20) and San Francisco's James Whalen (32–23) were other mound standouts. For the second year in a row, Portland's Isaac Butler lost an all-time record, 31 games, and Portland established a permanent record with 136 season losses.

On the opening day of 1904, Los Angeles first baseman Pop Dillon was prohibited from playing by the league president because he had been purchased by Brooklyn, and Dillon went on to play the entire season for the National League club. Baseball's most notorious first baseman, Hal Chase, performed for LA in 1904 (.279), then began a controversial 15-year big league career featuring his superb gifts as a fielder and his proclivity to throw games for gamblers. Seattle center fielder George Van Haltren, whose 17-year major league career dated back to 1887, came to bat 941 times (he collected 253 hits for a .269 average), an all-time record, and Seattle established a team record with 7,623 at-bats.

**Opening Day**

*Season openers always featured a flag-raising ceremony, this one at San Francisco's Recreation Park in the early years of the Coast League.*
— Courtesy California State Library, Sacramento

Coast League opening days, like those in other baseball circuits, have featured parades, celebrities, politicians, pre-game banquets, brass bands, special events, and expectant crowds. Governors, mayors, boxing champs, prominent preachers, and — especially in LA and Hollywood — movie stars have thrown out the first ball. In earlier years, players in uniform would be driven to the ballpark in open touring cars; today skydivers parachute into Tacoma's Cheney Stadium. At Sacramento's 1930 opener, 11,000 fans watched General William E. Gillmore, commander of the Army Air Corps, pitch the first ball to Mayor C. S. H. Bidwell. The ball was dropped from an army plane by parachute, and City Manager James Dean tried to hit it with a bat.

On Opening Day 1904, umpire Jack McCarthy appeared in San Francisco sporting a new-fangled chest protector, which soon would become common with catchers (who previously positioned themselves far behind the plate) as well as with umpires. Pre-game presentations to managers and players have included floral horse-

(continued)

shoes for good luck. Heavyweight champ Jim Jeffries participated
in LA's opening day festivities in 1908; pioneer auto racer Barney
Oldfield was on hand in LA in 1916; and Esther Williams threw
out the first ball for the Angels in 1949.

In 1912 the auto parade through San Francisco boasted 24
"machines," but the next year 100 autos formed the caravan
through Portland. There were 15,000 fans in San Francisco in 1912
to watch 27 Seals players "in bright new uniforms" and 25 members of the Oaks' roster march in from center field to home plate.
For years San Francisco Mayor James Rolph, Jr., regularly threw
out the first ball, and when he later became governor of California
he happily handled the same duties at Sacramento. In the 1918
opener, Mayor Rolph won a new suit by throwing a baseball further than Chief of Police White. And in 1922 Oakland policemen,
on hand to regulate the opening day crowd, engaged in a bitter al-
tercation among themselves.

James Whalen pitched 11 scoreless innings to end the 1904
season, then opened 1905 with four shutouts to establish the all-
time Coast League record of 47 consecutive scoreless innings. Late
in the year, William Tozer of Los Angeles (22–15) set the record
for one season by twirling 44 consecutive shutout innings. San
Francisco's Whalen went on to lead the league in victories (32–25),
including a no-hitter, while LA's Dolly Gray (30–16) posted the
best winning percentage. Tacoma's Robert Keefe (30–22) was a
30-game winner for the second year in a row and also pitched a no-
hitter. The other no-hitter of 1905 was twirled by Sea Lion Hall
(23–27), who pitched another hitless game in 1906. (Eli Cates of
Oakland threw a no-hitter in 1906 and another the following season.) On July 8, 1905, Seattle's Charles Shields (20–24) struck out
19 Portland batters, a single-game mark that twice has been tied.

The split-season concept again was employed in 1905, and defending champ Tacoma won the first half as shortstop Truck
Eagan (.278 with 21 homers) won his third straight home run title.
But Los Angeles took the second half, behind batting champ Kitty
Brashear (.303), returned first sacker Pop Dillon (.272 with 53
steals), and stolen base king Larry Schlafly (77 steals), who pulled
off an unassisted triple play from his second base position. Thus another Angels-Tigers nine-game postseason series was set up, this
time to decide the pennant. Despite impressive on-field success
during the first half, financial difficulties forced the Tacoma franchise to shift operations to Sacramento for the last part of the sea-

*Baseball at Tacoma's Athletic Park.*
— Courtesy Tacoma Public Library

son, and the club nosedived to last place. In the playoffs, Los Angeles proceeded to win five of the first six contests to claim the flag, but the two teams played four more exhibition games to generate a little additional income.

During the first three seasons of PCL play, numerous all-time fielding records were set, including several negative marks. Gloves were small and flimsy, and playing surfaces were rough. Uncertain fielding conditions of the day caused the inclusion of columns for Putouts, Assists, and Errors in box scores, and with the long Coast League schedules, vast totals of miscues were inevitable. In 1904 Seattle shortstop Russell Hall piled up a record 119 errors, and that same season Portland shortstop Charles Zinssar — normally an outfielder — established a record by making five boots in one game. Portland committed a record-setting 669 errors during 1904, thereby setting the PCL's worst fielding percentage (.929). On May 20, 1903, Oakland committed 15 errors against Seattle, a mark that has never since been equalled. LA second baseman George Wheeler made 78 bobbles in 1903, a record unwillingly matched by Oakland second sacker George Cutshaw in 1910. In 1903 Oakland center fielder William O'Hara made 45 errors, an

---

**"Dear Sir . . ."**

During the first years of the Pacific Coast League, games were officiated by a solitary umpire. Even after a second official began to be assigned to games in 1908, it was the function of the plate umpire to announce starting batteries to the crowd until PA systems were installed in ballparks. Standing at home plate, the umpire would face the grandstand, shout "Ladies and gentlemen . . ." through a megaphone, and call out the starters.

On November 8, 1905, Portland and Oakland squared off for a Wednesday afternoon game in miserable San Francisco Bay weather. Both clubs were suffering through the latter stages of losing seasons, and only one fan turned out for the meaningless contest. The umpire faced the solitary spectator, lifted the megaphone, and proclaimed, "Dear Sir . . ."

---

all-time record for outfielders, and that same year Oakland's catcher, Si Gordon, also muffed 45 chances and set the all-time mark for receivers. Doc Newton won 39 games for LA in 1904, thereby establishing the all-time victory standard — but he also committed a record 28 errors.

On a more positive note, in 1905 Portland catcher Larry McLean established a record with 892 putouts, and Seattle catcher Ralph Freary was credited with seven assists in a single game, a mark tied in 1908 by Los Angeles receiver Ted Easterly. Oakland right fielder Wilbur Murdock unleashed 63 assists in 1903, the all-time record by an outfielder, and during the same year Sacramento second sacker Perle Casey handled a record 1,337 chances and 700 putouts. In 1905 Sacramento's Tom Sheehan set a mark for PCL third basemen with 345 putouts, and on August 6 Portland shortstop Jake Atz handled a single-game record 10 putouts. During the 1905 season San Francisco, which played a record 230 games from March 30 through December 17, chalked up the most putouts — 6,284 — and most chances — 9,350 — in PCL history.

Two weeks after the start of the 1906 season, at 5:30 on the morning of April 18, a massive earthquake devastated San Francisco, killing about 700 citizens and destroying more than 28,000 structures — including the Seals' baseball park. Within two days, the National Association appealed to all member leagues to raise funds for the relief of the PCL. That same day the National League made a $1,000 contribution, while in the American League on April 29, New York and Philadelphia netted nearly $6,000 with an exhibition in New York — the first major league Sunday game ever played on Manhattan Island. On Monday, May 14, executives of the PCL met to decide whether or not to discontinue operations. At the urging of Eugene F. Bert and J. Cal Ewing, Coast League owners determined to play out the schedule.

Compounding a difficult situation, Los Angeles owners found it financially impossible to maintain their club, and turned the franchise back to the league. President Bert promptly arranged for the league to support the club until new owners could be found. Soon a number of LA businessmen purchased stock and reorganized the Los Angeles baseball club on a sound basis. During this touch-and-go period, Angels players accepted substantial pay cuts so that the club could continue to operate. Indeed, throughout the league owners felt forced to ask players to take salary reductions or be released. Several players tried to jump their contracts, but the National Association prohibited anyone signed to a PCL contract to play with any team in Organized Baseball.

When the dust settled from the earthquake, J. Cal Ewing, who owned both the San Francisco and the Oakland clubs, shifted the Seals' "home" schedule to Oakland. Indeed, Ewing regularly had scheduled Oakland weekday games for more populous San Francisco. But 300,000 San Franciscans now were homeless, and 65,000 of them moved across the bay to Oakland, almost doubling that city's population and significantly strengthening the Oaks' local base of support. PCL president Eugene F. Bert moved the league offices from San Francisco to 1007 Broadway Street, Oakland.

The split-season format of the past two years was abandoned by PCL owners, and the best team of 1906 proved to be Portland. Portland outfielder Mike Mitchell (.351) was the batting and home run champ, but his meager total of six roundtrippers was the smallest total of any PCL homer king. Seattle righthander Rube Vickers (39–15 with 408 strikeouts in 526 innings) turned in a remarkable season, matching Doc Newton's victory record, leading the league in winning percentage, and establishing all-time records for strikeouts and innings pitched.

In 1907 the dynamic J. Cal Ewing, who had declined to serve as the PCL's first president, accepted leadership of the league and held the position for three years. Fresno had replaced the troubled

*The Portland Beavers, 1906 PCL champs. Manager-outfielder Walter McCredie (top left) led the Beavers to five pennants, while outfielder Mike Mitchell (top, fourth from left) was the 1906 batting and home run leader.*

— Courtesy Ted Leach

Tacoma-Sacramento franchise for 1906, but finished last and dropped out of the league. Seattle, far removed from California, also withdrew from the PCL to play in the nearby Northwestern League. For the next two years, therefore, Cal Ewing would preside over a four-team Coast League — Los Angeles, San Francisco, Oakland, and Portland — and in both seasons the Angels dominated the circuit. Four-team leagues were not unusual in that period, and when the National Association created a new classification in 1908, the PCL was one of three circuits to be elevated to the top status.

The 1907 Angels were led by Dolly Gray (32–14), who paced the league in victories and winning percentage, by first sacker Pop Dillon (.304), and by outfielders Walter Carlisle (.259 with 39 stolen bases and a league-leading 14 home runs) and Gavvy Cravath (.303 with 10 homers and 50 stolen bases), a five-year Angels' veteran who would go up to the Boston Red Sox in 1908. Carlisle cracked three of his homers on August 18 against Oakland (but the Oaks won, 7–4), the first time a Coast Leaguer hit three round-trippers in one game. Batting champ Truck Eagan (.335, 10 HRs,

*LA Angels, 1907 PCL champs. Outstanding players were pitching leader Dolly Gray (top right), popular Pop Dillon (next to Gray), talented Gavvy Cravath (next to Dillon), and home run champ Walter Carlisle (number 11).*

— Courtesy Ted Leach

31 SBs) had moved to Oakland and remained one of the league's primary offensive performers.

An appreciative crowd of 5,000 attended the doubleheader victory that ended LA's 1907 season, and the championship players were presented with bouquets. A strong nucleus returned to Los Angeles in 1908 and the Angels flew to their fourth PCL flag (one disputed) in seven seasons. It was the heart of the dead-ball era, featuring the hit-and-run, base stealing, sacrifice bunting, one-run ball games and low batting averages. For three years the Coast League batting champ hit below .300: Portland first baseman Babe Danzig in 1908 (.298); San Francisco outfielder Henry Melchior in 1909 (.298); and San Francisco infielder-outfielder Hunky Shaw in 1910, with the lowest average (.281) ever to top the PCL. A good pitching staff was the key to winning championships, and in 1908 the Angels boasted veterans Dolly Gray (26–11), Walter Nagle (24–10), and Frank Hosp (20–15).

With the long PCL schedule, the four members of the 1907 and 1908 circuit played each other 65 to 70 times per season, which dulled fan interest. In 1909 the league expanded back to six teams,

*San Francisco's 1907 second-place team.*
— Courtesy Ted Leach

with Sacramento rejoining the PCL as well as Vernon, a small suburb of Los Angeles. It was thought Vernon would attract LA fans when the Angels were out of town, and through the years Vernon would play many games in the Los Angeles ballpark when the Angels were on the road.

San Francisco put together its first championship team in 1909, headed by hitting titlist Henry Melchior and a superb mound corps which starred Frank Browning (32–16) and Cack Henley (31–10). From July 1 through July 5 San Francisco hurlers pitched 48 straight innings of shutout ball against Sacramento. Frank Browning led the league in victories and reeled off 16 consecutive wins. The record-setting streak began with complete games against Oakland on June 10 and 11 and included four shutouts, a no-hitter, and a 5–4 triumph over the Angels and Walter Nagle — in 19 innings on June 23. Nagle (18–9) had the satisfaction of halting Browning's magnificent string with a 2–1 victory on August 15.

Cack Henley posted the league's best winning percentage, crowning his season with a 24-inning shutout in Oakland on June 8. In one of baseball's most notable pitching duels, Henley locked horns with the Oaks' Long Jim Wiggs (19–23). Wiggs allowed 11

*San Francisco's first PCL pennant-winners, 1909.*
— Courtesy California State Library, Sacramento

hits in 24 innings, walked six, and struck out 13. Henley whiffed only six, but he issued merely one base on balls and gave up just nine hits. After 23 scoreless innings, San Francisco finally scored an unearned run; the error was made by Tyler Christian, a pitcher (18–17) who played the entire game at second base. Henley blanked Oakland in the 24th for a sensational 1–0 triumph. The game was played in three hours and 35 minutes. San Francisco's second baseman was Kid Mohler, who participated in two double plays. Mohler played with Seattle in 1904, with San Francisco from 1905 through 1912, and with Sacramento in 1914; 14 years in the Coast League, 25 seasons in pro ball — as a *left*handed second baseman!

Another classic pitching performance of 1909 was turned in by Portland's Alex Carson (29–20) on July 22, a 10-inning, 1–0 no-hitter over Los Angeles. Carson yielded no walks, and the only base runner came on an error by the shortstop after Alex had retired 23 men in a row. Carson only struck out one batter, but just two balls were hit to the outfield — 17 Angels were retired on ground balls and 12 on pop-ups. Portland's William Tozer (31–12) had his best year in 1909, and he was ably backed by Fred Harkness (29–20) and Ray Garrett (25–19).

The first seven years of the Pacific Coast League had been a resounding success. The PCL played baseball's longest schedule, competing leagues had been vanquished, the Coast League was one of the top three circuits in the National Association, and West Coast fans were able to enjoy the performance of talented players. As Organized Baseball entered the second decade of the twentieth century, the artistic and financial potential of the Coast League brimmed with promise.

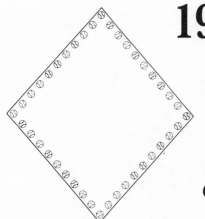

# 1910–1919

## *Decade of Dynasties*

In the same way that Los Angeles had claimed four of the first six Coast League flags, the PCL's second decade likewise would be dominated by dynasties. Portland won four of the decade's first five pennants, San Francisco flew the PCL flag in 1915 and 1917, Los Angeles won two titles in three years, and for three consecutive seasons Vernon posted the best record in the league. Club owners still were free to keep players as long as they liked — unless major league purchase offers proved too tempting — and many professional athletes preferred conditions in the Coast League, for reasons already described. Rosters tended to be stable, therefore; when a minor league team found a winning combination, a string of successful seasons often resulted.

Portland's manager was Walter McCredie, who had led the 1907 club to the city's first pennant, and who would skipper the 1910, 1911, 1913 and 1914 champs. The 1910 titlists could manage only a .218 team batting average, but the best mark in the league was posted by San Francisco — a dead-ball .226 — and Hunky Shaw won the hitting crown by batting merely .281. The emphasis was on pitching, and Portland boasted Gene "Rubber" Krapp (29–16), Bill Steen (23–17), and southpaw Sylveanus Augustus Gregg (32–18).

*Portland southpaw Vean Gregg was 32–18 in 1910, leading the PCL with 14 shut-*
*outs (including two in one day) and 376 strikeouts.*

— Courtesy Ted Leach

Vean Gregg had a magnificent season, leading the league with 376 strikeouts and establishing a PCL record with 14 shutouts. Gregg took the mound for a Sunday doubleheader against Sacramento, blanked the Sacts 4–0 in the first game, then won a 1–0 pitchers' duel in the five-inning second contest. Three days later Gregg threw a regulation 1–0 shutout over Los Angeles (Portland's powerful staff blanked LA for 48 consecutive innings while setting a record of 88 scoreless innings from October 6–16). Gregg tied John Thielman's 1903 record by hurling three one-hitters during the season, and on September 2 he downed the Angels 2–0 with a no-hitter. During the no-hitter, Gregg whiffed eight consecutive batters, beginning with the last hitter in the sixth through the first batter of the ninth, and George Wheeler was the sole strikeout victim to hit a foul ball.

The best winning percentage of 1910 was recorded by Oakland's John Lively (13–15), and Walter Moser (31–20) provided the staff with a formidable one-two punch. San Francisco ace Cack Henley led the league in victories (34–19) while working a record 312 innings without relief from March 30 through August 23. Henley's teammate, Frank Miller (20–15), twirled a no-hitter against

---

**Odd Endings**

With two out in the seventh inning of a game between Sacramento and Vernon on August 27, 1910, Tiger pitcher Alex Carson waved his bat at strike three. The Sacramento players trotted toward their bench as Carson strolled to the mound. But the catcher had dropped the third strike and neglected to throw to first, instead tossing the ball toward the pitcher's mound. Tiger manager Hap Hogan shouted to Carson to run to first base. But Sacramento outfielder Ed Van Buren, who had reached the infield, alertly snagged the ball and threw to his first baseman, finally closing the inning.

At the close of the 1913 season in Oakland, the Oaks trailed Sacramento by a wide margin in the bottom of the ninth. A local high school catcher named Muskowitz was sent to the plate and delivered a single to right in his first professional appearance. Sacramento players, with victory assured, held back and, as the crowd cheered him on, Muskowitz stole second, third and home.

---

Vernon. On Sunday morning, May 15, Miller won the first game of a doubleheader over Oakland. The two teams trooped across the bay, Miller loosened up again, then pitched another complete game victory over the Oaks.

On opening day in 1911, San Francisco drew 9,000 fans, while 7,000 attended in Los Angeles. Portland had sold Vean Gregg and Gene Krapp to Cleveland, but the defending champions produced an even more balanced pitching staff in 1911. Bill Steen (30–15), who led the league in victories and winning percentage, Elmer Koestner (25–15), Tom Seaton (24–16), and Ed Henderson (21–12) recorded 100 of the team's 113 wins. Center fielder Buddy Ryan won the batting and home run titles (.333 with 23 homers), and with an improved offense, Portland clinched a second straight pennant.

Harry Sutor of San Francisco was the 1911 strikeout king (22–22 with 339 Ks in 365 innings), and he pitched a 1–0 no-hitter over Oakland. Oakland's ace was fireballing southpaw Harry Ables (22-11), who had been a six-year Texas League star, setting the circuit's all-time strikeout record (325) in 1910. Ables no-hit the Angels in 1911, and he would dominate the league the next year. Another 1911 no-hitter was recorded on July 5 over Sacramento, a 1–

*The 1911 batting and home run champ was Portland center fielder Buddy Ryan (.333 with 23).*

— Courtesy Ted Leach

0 triumph by Portland's Ferdinand Henkle in his first game as a professional. On September 10 Portland's Elmer Koestner and Sacramento's Jack Fitzgerald (20–17) dueled for 24 innings. Koestner gave up one run on 12 hits, Fitzgerald yielded one run on 10 hits, and after three hours and 45 minutes, the 1–1 marathon was called because of darkness.

The 1911 stolen base champ was Oakland second baseman George Cutshaw (90 steals), but on July 26 San Francisco outfielder Putt Powell reached first base, then stole second, third and home. A more spectacular feat was pulled off by Vernon center fielder Walter Carlisle on July 19 during a game with Los Angeles. With the score tied in the ninth inning, Vernon starter Al Carson walked the first two Angels, Charles Moore and George Metzger. Harry Stewart came in from the bullpen, but Los Angeles third sacker Roy Akin hit the first pitch on a line over second base for an apparent single. The hit-and-run sign was on, and Moore and Metzger were at full speed by the crack of the bat. But Carlisle, playing close in a style being popularized by Red Sox center fielder Tris Speaker, sprinted in and snared the ball with a diving catch. Carlisle scrambled to his feet, touched second base for out number

*Portland's Bill Steen led the PCL in victories with a 30–15 record.*
— Courtesy Ted Leach

*Tom Seaton was 24–16 for Portland's 1911 pennant winners.*
— Courtesy Ted Leach

*Young Roger Peckinpaugh played shortstop for Portland's 1911 champs, then went on to star for 16 years in the American League.*

— Courtesy Ted Leach

two, then trotted to first to complete the unassisted triple play. Admiring fans from Los Angeles as well as Vernon presented a diamond-studded gold medal to Carlisle. The next season Roy Akin played third for Waco on the Texas League, and on May 9 he pulled off an unassisted triple play himself.

In 1912 Oakland interrupted Portland's title monopoly with the Oak's first PCL pennant. Oakland first baseman Gus Hetling (.297 with 33 steals) was named Most Valuable Player in the league by a group which gave him a Chalmers automobile (a Chalmers was the era's prize for a major league MVP). Harry Ables (25–18 with 303 strikeouts in 363 innings) led the league in victories (LA's Charles Chech, 25–14, tied his total), strikeouts, walks and innings pitched. On Friday morning, October 25, Ables shutout the Angels, 10–0, in his home park. The teams traveled to San Francisco for the afternoon game, and Ables blanked LA, 2–0, in seven innings (darkness halted play), to complete an iron-man doubleheader shutout. (Ables may have damaged his left arm — he never had another winning season, and retired in 1915 at the age of 31.)

Oakland's William Malarkey (20–11) posted the league's best

*Lefthander Hub Pernoll was 23–16 for Oakland in 1911.*

— Courtesy Ted Leach

## Timing the Players

On May 14, 1912, during a Tuesday afternoon game between Portland and Vernon, one Wild Bill Ruess, "known all over the state of California as an accurate timer," clocked the speed of various base runners and situations. Ruess measured how long it took to throw the ball to first from second, short, and third, and how long it took a fly ball to reach a fielder's glove. Runners were timed going from home to third, from home to second, and, of course, from the batter's box to first. Vernon's speedy center fielder, Walter Carlisle, who stole 76 bases and turned in an unassisted triple play during the season, sprinted to first base in the fastest time of the day, $3^1/_5$ seconds.

*Sunday morning, September 3, 1911, at Freeman's Park in Oakland. Oaks' left-hander Harry Ables is on the mound against Portland. Ables was 22–11 with a no-hitter in 1911, then led the league with 25 victories and 303 strikeouts in 1912.*

— Courtesy Oakland Public Library

winning percentage, and in a Sunday morning game against San Francisco on June 30, he pitched no-hit ball for nine innings before giving up a safety in the 10th. But because of a time limit imposed in order to move the second game across the bay, the scoreless tie was called at the end of 10. Oakland led the PCL in team hitting, outfielder Bert Coy would be the home run king for the next two years, and second baseman Bill Leard was the 1912 stolen base champ. Portland first sacker William Rapps victimized Oakland with an unassisted triple play on September 14, but the Oaks dealt out most of the punishment in 1912, outlasting Vernon for the flag by a game.

Vernon's franchise was moved by owner Peter Maier to Venice, another suburb of Los Angeles, on the seacoast. Otherwise the league remained stable in 1913, and Walter McCredie led Portland back to the throne room. Strikeout leader Bill James (24–16, with 215 Ks) and Irv Higginbotham (21–14) headed a solid pitching staff, and Portland registered the league's best team batting average. Second place Sacramento led the PCL in home runs with a dead-ball total of 47, while Portland's entire championship squad

*Oakland, 1913. William Malarkey, standing at left, was 25–16 for the last-place Oaks. Bert Coy (number 15) was the home run champ for the second year in a row. Bill Leard (18) stole 70 bases, and the previous year he led the PCL with 80 steals.*

— Courtesy Ted Leach

hit just 27 roundtrippers. Base running remained a far more important offensive weapon than power hitting. Los Angeles led the circuit with a total of 406 stolen bases, then went on to a 12-year career in the National League.

In 1914 Portland took a second consecutive pennant for the second time. Catcher Gus Fisher (.355) led the team in hitting — but not the league, since he played in "only" 139 games of a schedule exceeding 200 contests. Outfielder Ty Lober was the PCL home run champ with a grand total of nine roundtrippers, and second baseman W. K. Rodgers (.292 with 71 steals) was the stolen base king. For the third year in a row, Portland's slickest-fielding infielder was shortstop-second baseman Dave "Beauty" Bancroft, who would move up to the Philadelphia Phils in 1915 en route to a Hall of Fame career. Irv Higginbotham (31–20 in 60 games and 418 innings) led the league in victories, games and innings pitched as Portland won its fourth flag of the decade.

San Francisco's Skeeter Fanning (24–18 in 1914, after posting the most victories in 1913 with a 28–15 record) no-hit the championship Portland club on October 25, 1914. Oakland in-

*Sacramento, 1913. John Williams (number 4) was 17–7, William Shinn (13) hit .302 with 71 stolen bases, and Duke Kenworthy (14) would be the 1916 batting champ.*

— Courtesy Ted Leach

fielder Jack Ness stole second, third and home in the fifth inning of a game against Venice on July 10. Five days earlier Oakland stole 13 bases against Sacramento, which remains the PCL record for thefts in a single game. Los Angeles outfielder Harry Wolter, a six-year big league veteran who was a native of Monterey, won the batting title in 1914 (.328), then repeated the next year (.359). Los Angeles lefty Slim Love, who hailed from Love, Mississippi, won the PCL's first ERA crown in 1914 with the lowest mark (1.56) that has been recorded to date. Love came back to win again in 1915 (1.95 ERA with a 23–15 record in 59 games), then he went up to pitch for five years in the American League. LA's Jack Ryan (24–11) posted the league's best winning percentage of 1914 — and his team's second-highest batting average (.320).

Sacramento suffered through a losing season in 1914. Attendance became so poor that the club folded early in September. But the league took over the franchise and moved it to San Francisco, calling the team the Missions. For years Oakland had played as many as five weekday games in San Francisco when the Seals were

*In 1901 a diamond and grandstand went up at Vaughn Street, and in 1912 the facility was expanded to a capacity of 12,000. The Vaughn Street Park hosted PCL baseball until it was razed in 1955.*

— Courtesy Ted Leach

on the road, and the same arrangement was made for the Missions during the last months of the season.

Bill Lane, who had operated a minor league team in Salt Lake City since 1911, purchased the Mission franchise and moved it to Utah's capitol city for 1915. Lane's Salt Lake City Bees would never win a PCL pennant, but Bonneville Park was compact and a baseball would carry like a rocket in the arid atmosphere. In 11 seasons in the league, the Bees would win the team hitting title nine times, and fans were entertained by numerous remarkable batting feats. After two seasons in Venice, Peter Maier decided to move his franchise back to Vernon for the 1915 season, and the Venice ballpark was dismantled and transported to Vernon along with the team.

San Francisco won the 1915 pennant, behind home town natives Spider Baum (30–15), Harry Heilmann (.364), and Ping Bodie (.325 with 19 homers). Bodie's season propelled him back to the big time, where he totaled nine years as an American League outfielder. Although Heilmann played only 98 games at first base he led the league in errors, but a .342 lifetime big league batting average would carry him to the Hall of Fame. A career minor leaguer (19 years, 325–280), Baum pitched for Los Angeles, Sacramento, Vernon, Venice, San Francisco, and Salt Lake City in the PCL. During 15 Coast League seasons, he was a 20-game winner eight times, but 1915 was his finest year. Baum recorded 261 victories in the PCL, a total exceeded only by Frank Shellenback.

After a disappointing rookie season with the Chicago Cubs, James Johnston was back in the PCL for 1915, this time with Oakland. The fleet outfielder again led the Coast League in stolen bases (.348 with 82 SBs), then returned to the big leagues to stay. On September 8, 1915, Salt Lake City first baseman Bunny Brief (.363 in 82 games) somehow played an entire game against Vernon without recording a single putout. Salt Lake City's Lefty Williams (33–12 with 294 Ks in 419 innings) led the PCL in victories, strikeouts and innings. Williams went on to the Chicago White Sox, but after totaling 45 victories in 1919 and 1920, his promising career was ended by the Black Sox scandal. Future Hall of Famer Stan Coveleskie (17–17 in 64 games) led the league in games pitched while toiling as a starter-reliever for Portland.

A 1916 opening day crowd of 16,212 watched Los Angeles defeat Vernon behind the three-hit pitching of Jack Ryan. Ryan (29–10) went on to lead the league in winning percentage, and the Angels went on to bring LA its only pennant of the decade. Portland's Allen Sothoron (30–17) recorded more victories than any other PCL pitcher, Vernon's Art Fromme (23–14, 1.92 ERA) was the ERA champ, and the Bees' Paul Fittery (29–19 with 203 strikeouts in 448 innings and 65 games) led the league in strikeouts, innings and games pitched. San Francisco's Skeeter Fanning twirled his second PCL no-hitter against Vernon on June 23, and Oakland's Bill Prough pitched 10 hitless innings in a scoreless duel with San Francisco on June 4. Prough finally surrendered a hit in the 11th, yielded no hits during the next three innings, then gave up a hit in the 15th, 16th and 17th innings before being removed for a pinch hitter in the bottom of the 17th. Oakland finally won the game, 1–0, in the last of the 18th.

Oakland second baseman-outfielder Duke Kenworthy (.314) was the first righthanded batting champ since 1908, and, aided by the friendly confines of Bonneville Park, Bunny Brief (.314 with 33 homers) walloped the greatest number of home runs yet recorded in a Coast League season. In 1916 Portland outfielder Bill Lane

---

**Bad Luck Baserunners**

On July 20, 1916, Portland second baseman W. K. Rodgers pulled off the PCL's fourth unassisted triple play in a game against Salt Lake City. The two runners caught off base were Billy Orr and Buddy Ryan.

Five years later Orr and Ryan both were playing for Sacramento when the Coast League recorded its fifth unassisted triple play. This time Salt Lake City was in the field, and shortstop Harry Sand turned the triple dip. The luckless Sacts baserunners were none other than Billy Orr and Buddy Ryan.

---

(.276 with 56 SBs) won the first of his four PCL stolen base titles. Unfortunately, Oakland seemed to benefit little from the exploits of Lane and Kenworthy; the Oaks lost 136 games, tying Portland's record for greatest number of losses.

Shortly after the 1917 season opened, the United States entered World War I. With a martial spirit, Coast Leaguers seemed unusually combative. On May 13 in Los Angeles, for example, there was a bench-clearing brawl during the second extra-inning game of a hotly-contested doubleheader. On June 18 San Francisco pitcher Indian Smith walloped Oakland catcher Dan Murray with a bat; but during the last week of the season San Francisco visited Oakland, and Murray thrashed Smith to secure revenge. A more serious problem was financial, caused by wartime travel restrictions and distraction among fans. On June 6 the league cut expenses by cutting rosters to 16 players, and there was growing talk that faraway Portland would be dropped from the league in favor of Sacramento.

Los Angeles made a determined effort to win a second consecutive pennant, but San Francisco finally edged the Angels for the 1917 championship. San Francisco was sparked by Spider Baum (24–17) and outfielders Mike Fitzgerald (.324 with 51 steals) and Biff Schaller (.314 with 51 steals) — and by Eric Erickson (31–15 with a 1.93 ERA and 307 strikeouts in 62 games and 444 innings). Erickson, a 22-year-old native of Sweden, was the first PCL hurler to win the pitcher's Triple Crown — most victories and strikeouts, and lowest ERA — and he also led the league in games and innings pitched.

Salt Lake City third sacker Maurice Rath (.341) became the

first switch hitter to win a Coast League batting title, and Bees outfielder Jack Tobin (.331) led the league in hits and runs scored,
then went up to the St. Louis Browns to resume a 14-year big
league career. Oakland native Irish Meusel (.311 with 69 steals)
was the stolen base champ, then he went on to star for 11 years
(.310 lifetime average) in the National League. But his younger
brother Bob followed Irish into the PCL, banged out Vernon's best
average (.337) in 1919, then went on to a decade of stardom (.309
lifetime) with the New York Yankees in the same outfield with
Babe Ruth.

Sacramento re-entered the league in 1918 as a replacement for
Portland, which was dropped because of wartime travel problems.
Although 8,000 fans attended the season opener at San Francisco,
the excitement level was somewhat low because people were more
concerned about the war. Fan indifference continued despite a
close pennant race between Los Angeles and Vernon, and attendance lagged severely. Furthermore, a number of players were now
wearing military uniforms because of enlistment or the draft. The
draft applied to able-bodied men between the ages of 21 and 31,
and pressure was increasingly felt by healthy young athletes to become a part of the war effort. Secretary of War Newton Baker ordered a "work or fight" directive, pronounced in the spring of 1918
by the Army's Provost Marshal, Gen. Enoch Crowder. Baseball executives appealed for exemptions similar to those issued to actors
on the grounds that public entertainment was necessary, and considerable discretion was left to individual draft boards. But local
boards felt compelled to demonstrate patriotism, and boards in
California and Utah — the two states in which the 1918 PCL operated — ruled that baseball players were subject to the "work or
fight" order.

League directors held an emergency meeting on Saturday,
July 13, in Los Angeles. It was decided to halt play after the Sunday doubleheaders, but Vernon and Los Angeles were neck-and-
neck (after the doubleheaders the Tigers were 58–44, while LA
stood 57–47). A best-five-of-nine playoff series between LA and
Vernon was announced, with the winner to be awarded the 1918
championship. The Angels took five of the first seven contests to
claim their second pennant in three years (but PCL records always
have acknowledged Vernon as the 1918 champ).

With each team playing only about 100 games in 1918, season

statistics were uncharacteristically modest. LA spitballer Doc Crandall (16–9) and Tiny Leverenz (16–5) of Salt Lake City tied for the lead in victories. Vernon's Jack Quinn, the ERA champ (1.65), also won the strikeout title with just 99 Ks. San Francisco's Art Griggs (.378 with 12 homers) won the hitting crown and tied for the home run lead with Salt Lake City first baseman Earl Sheely (.300).

With the war over and fan interest renewed, the Coast League rebounded strongly in 1919, expanding to eight teams for the first time. Portland and Seattle were readmitted to the circuit, and each of the eight clubs made money on the season. On Sunday, April 20, 11,224 fans attended a morning game in Oakland with the Seals, and at the afternoon game in San Francisco 12,621 came to the ballpark. On the same day in Los Angeles approximately 25,000 attended a similar doubleheader between the Angels and Vernon. Vernon and LA staged another wire-tight pennant race, with the Tigers finally prevailing by 1¹/₂ games.

Doc Crandall (28–10) of the Angels again led the PCL in victories, while teammate Curly Brown (25–8 with a 2.03 ERA) was the ERA and percentage titlist. Strikeout champ Bill Piercy (26–18 with 163 Ks), who had tossed a no-hitter in 1915, enjoyed his best season with Sacramento. Vernon's key pitchers were Wheezer Dell (25–16), Art Fromme (20–7), and Happy Joe Finneran (14–4). Dazzy Vance (10–18 for Sacramento) was not impressive in his only season in the PCL; he moved to the Southern Association for the next two years, but at the age of 31 he finally went up to Brooklyn and was the National League stikeout king for seven consecutive seasons.

Salt Lake City outfielder Bill Rumler (.362) won the hitting title, teammate Earl Sheely (.305 with 28 homers) again paced the league in home runs, and Oakland's Bill Lane won his second stolen base crown. Wahoo Sam Crawford (.360) led the PCL in base hits; a 19-year big league veteran (.309 lifetime) he played the last four seasons of his career with Los Angeles.

The Coast League had emerged from the difficulties of World War I stronger than ever, and the circuit prepared to charge into the 1920s with eight clubs and a solid reputation for baseball excellence. Pitching had dominated play since 1903, with sustained performances that had exhibited remarkable stamina and talent. But rising batting averages and the feats of Earl Sheely and other sluggers presaged a new era of exciting offensive displays.

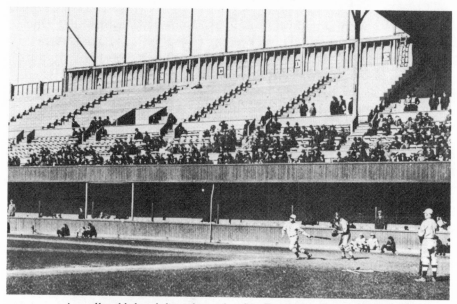

*A small, cold, but dedicated crowd at San Francisco's Recreation Park.*
— Courtesy Ted Leach

*During a 22-year career, outfielder Chester Chadbourne logged 10 PCL seasons while playing for Portland, Oakland, and Vernon.*
— Courtesy Ted Leach

# 1920-1929

## The Golden Age of the Coast League

Baseball overcame the problems posed by World War I only to face a far greater threat when it was revealed that members of the Chicago White Sox had worked with gamblers to throw the 1919 World Series. Since the late nineteenth century professional baseball at every level had attracted keen gambling activity, from casual betting between local fans in minor league bleacher sections to big-time bookies in major league cities. A significant reason for scoreboards which relayed inning-by-inning results of all league games and for telegraphed marquee progress reports of out-of-town contests was to keep gamblers posted with up-to-the-minute information.

Recognizing that public confidence in the national pastime had been shaken by the Black Sox scandal, major league owners appointed Federal Judge Kenesaw Mountain Landis as Commissioner of Baseball and gave him sweeping powers. The uncompromising Landis banned eight Black Sox players from professional ball and otherwise crusaded to purify baseball's image.

As part of the general cleanup the Coast League came to grips with allegations that several 1919 games had been thrown by crooked players. The PCL's new president, William H. McCarthy of San Francisco, conducted a careful investigation, resulting in the

*Until radio broadcasts became commonplace, baseball fans and gamblers avidly gathered outside newspaper buildings to view play-by-play results.*

— Courtesy Tacoma Public Library

suspension of Salt Lake City outfielders Harl Maggart and Bill Rumler, the 1919 batting champ, hurlers Tom Seaton (25–16 with Portland in 1919) and Casey Smith (17–19 with San Francisco), and Vernon first baseman Babe Borton (.305). Criminal charges were brought before a Los Angeles grand jury in October 1920, but Borton counterattacked by claiming that Vernon had won the 1919 pennant by bribing opposing players. Although the accused athletes were cleared of charges on a technicality, McCarthy unequivocally resolved the gambling scandal by expelling from PCL play all players suspected of wrongdoing. McCarthy thus established a strong precedent for other baseball executives through his tough and straightforward manner of dealing with gambling scandals, and he cleared the atmosphere for the Coast League to fully participate in the baseball boom of the 1920s.

The eager quest for a good time that was one of the characteristics of the Roaring Twenties resulted in an enormous growth of spectator support for sports. Baseball capitalized with a livelier ball and the home run heroics of Babe Ruth. The emphasis on scoring a single run with bunting, base stealing, the hit and run, and sacrifice flies disappeared beneath a barrage of extra base clouts. Baseball entered the Golden Age of sports with a flurry of home runs, and fans responded enthusiastically as batting averages and ERAs soared.

During the 1920s Coast League spectators witnessed three batters hit over .400, Tony Lazzeri wallop 60 homers two years before Babe Ruth turned the trick in the big leagues, RBI totals that far exceeded 200, and other unprecedented offensive perform-ances which set numerous all-time PCL records. The most as-tounding hitting feats came from Salt Lake City, but San Francisco managed to win four pennants during the decade. Some of the fin-est of all career minor leaguers played in the PCL during the 1920s, not to speak of an impressive array of future big league stars. Re-flecting the prosperity of the Coast League was the fact that the 1920s would be one of the most stable periods in circuit history; the only franchise movement came in 1926, an adjustment that im-proved and solidified the PCL.

In 1920 Vernon became the first Coast League team to fly three successive pennants, following a tight race with Seattle, Los Angeles, and San Francisco. The Tigers boasted a fine pitching staff, headed by Wheezer Dell (27–15), strikeout leader Willis Mitchell (25–13), and Frank Shellenback (18–12). It was Shellen-back's first year in the PCL, although he already had pitched two seasons of pro ball, including two stints with the Chicago White Sox. Shellenback would spend the rest of his career in the Coast League: 1920–24 with Vernon, 1925 with Sacramento, 1926–35 with Hollywood, and 1936–38 with San Diego. In 19 PCL seasons, he became the circuit's all-time winner with a 295–178 record (in all he was 315–192 as a minor leaguer, along with an 11–15 Amer-ican League mark). He led the Coast League in victories in 1919 (26–12) and 1932 (26–10), but enjoyed his best season in 1931 (27–7).

Salt Lake City first baseman Earl Sheely (.371 with 33 hom-ers) won his third straight home run crown and added the batting championship. Oakland righthander Buzz Arlett (29–17 with a 2.89 ERA in 427 innings) led the league in victories and innings pitched. Arlett led the PCL in games pitched in 1919 (22–17 in 57 games) and again in innings in 1922 (25–19) before his arm went dead — probably from overwork — when he was 24. A switch hit-ter, he promptly converted to the outfield. After five years as one of its premier hitters, he produced astronomical batting averages and boomed out a barrage of doubles, triples, homers and RBIs.

## RUSSELL "BUZZ" ARLETT

| Year | G    | IP    | W    | L   | BB  | SO  | ERA  |
|------|------|-------|------|-----|-----|-----|------|
| 1918 | 21   | 153   | 4    | 9   | 43  | 34  | 2.70 |
| 1919 | 57*  | 348   | 22   | 17  | 112 | 79  | 3.00 |
| 1920 | 53   | 427*  | 29*  | 17  | 134 | 105 | 2.89 |
| 1921 | 55   | 319   | 19   | 18  | 115 | 101 | 4.37 |
| 1922 | 47   | 374*  | 25   | 19  | 112 | 128 | 2.77 |
| 1923 | 28   | 125   | 4    | 9   | 47  | 34  | 5.76 |

| Year | G   | R   | H   | 2B  | 3B  | HR  | RBI  | SB  | BA   |
|------|-----|-----|-----|-----|-----|-----|------|-----|------|
| 1923 | 149 | 76  | 147 | 31  | 5   | 19  | 101  | 9   | .330 |
| 1924 | 193 | 122 | 229 | 57  | 19* | 33  | 145  | 24  | .328 |
| 1925 | 190 | 121 | 244 | 49  | 13  | 25  | 146  | 26  | .344 |
| 1926 | 194 | 140 | 255 | 52  | 16  | 35  | 140* | 26  | .382 |
| 1927 | 187 | 122 | 231 | 54* | 7   | 30  | 123  | 20  | .351 |
| 1928 | 160 | 111 | 205 | 47  | 3   | 25  | 113  | 10  | .365 |
| 1929 | 200 | 146 | 270 | 70* | 8   | 39  | 189  | 22  | .374 |
| 1930 | 176 | 132 | 223 | 57  | 7   | 31  | 143  | 8   | .361 |

At the age of 32, Arlett played his only big league season, with the Philadelphia Phils (.313, 18 HRs, 72 RBIs). For the next three years, he led the American Association in home runs, and when he finally retired, he had established himself as the best switch hitter in minor league history, with a .341 lifetime average and 432 homers.

Arnold "Jigger" Statz played with Los Angeles in 1920, the first of 11 seasons he would put in with the Angels. A fleet, hard-hitting center fielder, Jigger also played with four big league teams, but he was a Coast Leaguer through 1942, and he established numerous all-time PCL offensive records. Herman Pillette, eventually nicknamed "Old Folks," also made his Coast League debut in 1920. He pitched for seven teams during a Coast League career that lasted for 23 seasons, along with three years (1922–24) as a Detroit Tiger, and he won 226 PCL games. Another debut came on the last day of the 1920 season, when the Angels inserted their 14-year-old batboy, Jimmy Reese, to play an inning at second base. Later Reese played second with the Yankees (he roomed with Babe Ruth) and Cardinals, before returning to the Angels for four seasons (1933–36); he also played PCL ball with Oakland (1925–29) and San Diego (1937).

Los Angeles came from back in the pack to win the 1921 pennant on the last day of the season. San Francisco led the standings most of the year, but late in the season the Angels won 12 in a row, took six games of an eight-game series with San Francisco, then trounced hapless Portland (51–134, .276) in the season's final series to claim the championship. The Angels had a strong pitching staff, including Doc Crandall (24–13), ERA champ Vic Aldridge (20–10, 2.16), and Art Reinhart (15–5), who led the league in winning percentage. A hard-hitting outfield sparked the offense: Wahoo Sam Crawford in right (.318 with 103 RBIs); center fielder Jigger Statz (.310 with 52 stolen bases); and left fielder Dixie Carroll (.292 with 45 steals and a league-leading 22 triples).

Vernon's Wheezer Dell (28–14) compiled the most victories in 1921, while Paul Fittery (25–14, 164 Ks) won his second strikeout crown. Lefty O'Doul (25–9) and John Crouch (25–15) of San Francisco, and Oakland's Harry Krause (24–13) also had excellent seasons. The home run leader was Salt Lake City second baseman Paddy Siglin (.344 with 22 homers), and in a July 4 contest against Sacramento he became the first Coast Leaguer to hit two roundtrippers in one inning. In one game, Bees shortstop Henry Sands (.320) pulled off an unassisted triple play.

Late in the season William K. Wrigley, majority stockholder in the Chicago Cubs, purchased the Los Angeles Angels. The independent owners of the PCL had maintained only loose ties with major league teams. But the Wrigley family would own the Angels until 1957, and as the years passed Coast League teams, like other minor league operations, would develop closer affiliations with big league clubs. PCL teams, however, had their own farm clubs in the lower minors, and the circuit would maintain a greater degree of independence than any other minor league, eventually making a strong bid for major league status.

San Francisco, after faltering late in the 1921 season, acquired a new manager, Dots Miller, who had been a National League infielder from 1909 through 1921 and who would lead the Seals to back-to-back pennants in 1922 and 1923. The Seals' success, however, almost was overshadowed by brilliant individual performances. Vernon challenged strongly in 1922, sparked by southpaw Jakie May. May had pitched ineffectively for the St. Louis Cardinals from 1917 through 1921 (10–25). But with Vernon in 1922 he became the second Coast Leaguer to win the pitcher's Triple Crown (35–9, 238 Ks, 1.84 ERA). Wheezer Dell (23–17 with a no-

---

### Strange Happenings In Oakland

On April 28, 1923, Oakland led Salt Lake City, 5–3, but in the ninth inning the Bees filled the bases with two out. When Paul Strand, the best hitter in the league, came to bat, Oaks manager Ivan Howard instructed pitcher Harry Krause to issue an intentional walk. Howard's daring strategy worked, because with the score now 5–4, the next hitter, Joe Wilhoit, flied out to end the game.

Later in the season, on July 21 in Oakland, Portland's leadoff man, William Rodgers, hit the first pitch of the game for a homer. In the bottom of the ninth, Oaks pitcher Ray Kremer hit the *last* pitch of the game for a homer to lift his team to a 4–3 victory.

---

hitter), Bill James (21–12), and Jess Doyle (20–15) gave Vernon four 20-game winners, and third baseman Red Smith (.349 with 101 RBIs) led a high-scoring offense.

San Francisco was even better, leading the league in team hitting and runs scored. The Seals' roster boasted eight batters who hit above .300, and in 1923 the club compiled a .319 average. There were other fine offensive performances in 1922: Salt Lake City player-manager, Duffy Lewis (.362, 20 HRs, 108 RBIs), who had spent 11 years as an American League outfielder; Seattle outfielder Brick Eldred (.354 with 131 RBIs); Los Angeles first baseman Art Griggs (.338, 20 HRs, 129 RBIs); and Seattle outfielder Bill Lane (.285 with 166 runs and 60 steals), who led the league in runs scored and won his third stolen base title. In 1923 Duffy Lewis (.358, 28 HRs, 115 RBIs) and Brick Eldred (.353, 71 doubles, 116 RBIs) again were impressive, and so were outfielders Pete Schneider (.360, 19 HRs, 110 RBIs) of Vernon and Ray Rohwer (.325, 37 HRs, 135 RBIs) of Seattle, among many other fine hitters.

But the offensive standout of both 1922 and 1923 was Salt Lake City outfielder Paul Strand. Like Buzz Arlett, Strand spent the early years of his career as a pitcher, including three seasons with the Boston Braves (7–3). Following military service in World War I he switched to the outfield, and he was purchased by Salt Lake City in 1921 (.314). In 1922 the Pacific Coast League first began to tabulate Runs Batted In, and Strand won the first two RBI titles — plus much more. He dominated Coast League pitching, winning back-to-back Triple Crowns. Strand was awesome in

---

**Super Slugfest**

In an era of astounding offensive performances, the most pro-lific explosion occurred, of course, in Salt Lake City on May 11, 1923. Although Vernon would finish in last place in 1923, the Ti-gers were inspired by the cozy confines and dry air of Bonneville Park, drubbing the Bees, 35–11. Vernon collected 33 hits, while Tiger pitcher Wheezer Dell yielded 15 hits and 5 walks but coasted to an easy victory. Three Salt Lake City pitchers could come up with just one strikeout against the red-hot Tigers.

Records established included most runs scored in a game (46) and most homers (11). Vernon set the following club records: most runs (35), most homers (9), most total bases (67), and most RBIs.

Tiger right fielder Pete Schneider (.360 on the season) went on a tear, blasting five homers and a double. Schneider tied the record for most homers in an inning and set six individual marks: most at bats (8), most runs scored (6), most home runs (5), most grand-slam homers (2), most total bases (22), and most RBIs (14). In his last time up, Schneider drilled what looked like his sixth home run, but the ball failed to clear the fence by inches, and he settled for a two-bagger. Schneider hit just 14 other homers during the season. A native of Los Angeles, Schneider broke into the big leagues at the age of 18 in 1914 as a pitcher with Cincinnati. He won 20 games in 1917, but his arm went dead two years later, and he spent the last decade of his career as a minor league outfielder.

---

1922 (.384, 28 HRs, 138 RBIs), leading the league not only in bat-ting average, homers and RBIs, but in hits (289) as well. The next year (.394, 43 HRs, 187 RBIs) Strand's numbers were even higher, and he also led the PCL in runs (180) and set the all-time record in Organized Baseball for hits (325). Strand went up to the Philadel-phia Athletics in 1924 (.228), but soon he was back in the minors. Although he would retire after the 1928 season, Strand put in two final years in the Coast League, playing for Portland in 1926 (.326) and 1927 (.355).

The Triple Crown heroics of Strand and Jackie May were not enough to keep San Francisco out of the PCL throne room. Al-though San Francisco had won only three pennants in the first two decades of the PCL, the Seals finally put together a team that would win three flags in four years, 1922, 1923, and 1925. Vernon offered a year-long challenge in 1922, but San Francisco won the title during the season's final series, with Oakland. The Seals successfully defended their crown, running away with the 1923 flag. The 1924 race went down to the final day, as San Francisco, Los Angeles, and Seattle each had a shot at the pennant. Seattle was victorious over Portland, while San Francisco lost to Oakland, and Los Angeles was beaten by Vernon. But the powerful Seals roared back in 1925, taking first place early in the season and establishing one of the best records (138–71) in PCL history, while hitting .315 as a team.

San Francisco's dynasty was established with a nucleus of major league-quality players who were with the club for years, along with a few athletes who put in a spectacular season or two before moving up to the big leagues:

Bert Ellison — A first baseman who had played five years for the Detroit Tigers, Ellison was appointed manager in 1923 and led the team to two pennants. He hit .306 in 1922, .358 with 129 RBIs in 1923, .325 with 160 RBIs in 1925, and .381 with 35 homers in the non-championship year of 1924.

Gene Valla — The left fielder in 1922, he took over center field the following year, batting .333, .334 and .333 during the pennant seasons, as well as .367 in 1924,

Hal Rhyne — A shortstop, Rhyne hit .285, .296 and .315 for the titlists, then went to the National League for the next seven years.

Pete Kilduff — A five-year veteran of the National League, Kilduff at second base formed, along with Rhyne, a slick double-play combination (the Seals led the PCL in fielding in 1922, 1924 and 1925). During the pennant seasons Kilduff hit .287, .328, and .306 with 20 homers and 126 RBIs.

Sam "Slam" Agnew — Agnew had caught for seven years in the American League. As a Seal he hit .337, .312 and .325 for the titlists. He was spelled behind the plate during these seasons by Archie Yelle, a three-year veteran of the American League, but Yelle could not hit with Agnew's prowess.

Willis Mitchell — A southpaw (who hit righthanded — .308 in 1925), Mitchell had pitched 11 seasons for Cleveland and Detroit. Although he was 34 when the title run began, he was 24–7, 10–9 and 20–8 for the champions, and he went 28–15 to lead the PCL in victories in 1924.

Robert "Speed" Geary — A righthander (who hit lefthanded), Geary had pitched three years in the big leagues, and was a 20-game winner in each of the championship seasons: 20–9, 21–11, and 20–12.

Doug "Buzz" McWeeney — A righthander who would put in eight years in the major leagues, McWeeney was a key contributor to each of the pennant-winning mound staffs: 15–7, 20–9, and 20–5.

Jim "Death Valley" Scott — A nine-year veteran of the American League, Scott was 34 in 1922, but he went 25–9, then sagged to 11–9 in 1923 (although one of his 1923 victories was a no-hitter).

Paul Waner — As a 20-year-old rookie, Waner hit .369 for the 1923 champions, and batted .356 in 1924. An expert at handling a bat, Waner liked to shoot for the foul lines, either getting extra bases or a foul ball, and often opening up the power alleys as outfielders cheated toward the foul lines. Waner sparked the 1925 champs, leading the league with a .401 average and 75 doubles, while driving in 130 runs. Paul's younger brother Lloyd broke in with the Seals in 1925, hitting .250 in 31 games, Paul and Lloyd would go on to Hall of Fame careers, and Paul would win three National League batting crowns.

Jimmy O'Connell — The center fielder for the 1922 champs, O'Connell hit .335 and was sold to the New York Giants for $75,000.

Willie Kamm — The third baseman in 1922, Kamm was sold to the White Sox for $100,000 after batting .342 with 20 homers and 124 RBIs. Kamm was the first minor leaguer to be sold for six figures. At Willie Kamm Day on October 15, San Francisco fans collected $1,019.72 to purchase Kamm a diamond ring.

Ed Mulligan — A veteran big league outfielder, Mulligan took over at third in 1923, hitting .329 and handling the hot corner for the 1925 champs as well.

Frank "Turkeyfoot" Brower — After completing five years in the American League, Brower played right field for the 1925 champs, pounding out a .362 average with 36 homers and 163 RBIs.

Tim Hendryx — An eight-year American League veteran, Hendryx roamed the outfield for the 1923 and 1925 pennant winners, batting .339 and .303.

Joe Kelly — An outfielder who hit .333 in 1922 and .348 the next year.

From 1922 through 1925 the Seals averaged 122 victories per year, with their best performance coming in 1925 (138–71 with a .641 winning percentage, the highest figures in franchise history). Although the roster during this dynastic period featured an unusually large number of former or future major leaguers, PCL games always showcased several participants who would see or had been to the big time, and most Coast League seasons exhibited men who would become authentic big league stars.

The 1924 Seattle pennant-winners starred veteran Coast Leaguers Brick Eldred (.351), Vean Gregg (25–11), Ray Rohwer (.325 with 33 homers), and Bill Lane (.336 with 45 steals), who won his fourth stolen base crown. Lane would retire after the 1926 season, having stolen 468 bases in the PCL, an all-time record. Other stars of 1924 included three Portland players: home run champ James Poole (.353 with 38 homers); third sacker Frank Brazill (.351 with 36 homers); and 21-year-old catcher Mickey Cochrane (.333 in 90 games), who would move on to the Athletics the next year and carve out a Hall of Fame career. Oakland righthander George Boehler (26–21 with 216 Ks in 396 innings), who had pitched for three big league clubs, led the PCL in innings pitched and strikeouts. On Friday, July 18, Boehler hurled two complete game victories over the Angels, and he would win three strikeout titles in four years.

In 1924 Salt Lake City hit .327 as a team for the second consecutive season (the 1923 mark was a fraction of a percentage point higher, and established the all-time Coast League record. Player-manager Duffy Lewis (.392 with 28 homers) set the pace by winning the batting championship, and 11 other players hit over .300. The 1924 Bees scored the most runs in PCL history (1,416), cracked the most doubles (556), and banged out the most RBIs (1,294). On Friday, May 16, Salt Lake City walloped six homers, while Vernon hit five, matching the single-game record total. During a record-setting series with San Francisco at Bonneville Park from Tuesday, May 20, through Sunday, May 25, the two clubs exploded for 264 hits, including 38 home runs. The Saturday slugfest accounted for 54 base hits and 99 total bases. Seals player-manager Bert Ellison went 25 for 37, including ten home runs — five in the Sunday doubleheader. Portland second baseman Ernest McCann established a single-game record by rapping out seven singles against Salt Lake City.

Salt Lake City's team average dropped to a mere .321 in 1925, but shortstop Tony Lazzeri salvaged the Bees' reputation for power hitting. In an age of unprecedented batting exploits, the 21-year-old native of San Francisco excited the baseball world with his 1925 slugging feats (.355, 202 runs, 60 HRs, 222 RBIs). Lazzeri set the

---

**PCL vs. The American Association**

Following the 1919 season St. Paul, champions of the American Association, traveled to Los Angeles to challenge the Vernon Tigers, PCL champs, in a best-of-nine series. The hard-fought postseason exhibition went the full nine games before powerful Vernon won the deciding contest.

Five years later St. Paul, following another championship season, headed west again to take on the Coast League victors in Seattle. Rain caused two days of postponements, then St. Paul won the opening game, The skies opened again for three successive days, and club officials called off the water-logged series. The following year, 1925, San Francisco and Louisville locked horns in the postseason, with the Seals prevailing, five games to four.

---

all-time PCL standards for home runs, RBIs and runs scored, and he clouted 60 homers two years before Babe Ruth equalled the feat. Lazzeri was purchased by the Yankees, and he was the star shortstop the year that Ruth hit 60.

Lazzeri's magnificent season almost overshadowed the remarkable performance of batting champion Paul Waner (.401 with a record 75 doubles), Lefty O'Doul (.375 with 191 RBIs and a 19-for-21 streak against Vernon), Frank Brazill (.394, 29 HRs, 155 RBIs), Ray Rohwer (.334, 40 HRs, 153 RBIs), George Boehler (23–25 with 278 Ks in 417 innings), who won his second consecutive strikeout title, and LA's Charley Root (25–13), who would go on to pitch for the Cubs for the next 16 years.

Although Sacramento lost a record-setting 17 straight games, Vernon finished last in 1925, for the second time in three years. The Maier family decided to sell their franchise to former league president William H. McCarthy of San Francisco, who re-created the Mission club. The plan was to repeat the brief experiment of 1914, placing the Missions in Recreation Park while the Seals were out of town. And now that Los Angeles only had one team, Bill Lane decided to move his club to the nearby movie capitol, Hollywood. Salt Lake City had proved to be too small to offer Lane a suitable profit, and other Coast League owners, happy to be relieved of travel expenses to Utah, approved the transfer of the Bees. Late in 1925 the Angels had moved into a magnificent new park, 22,000-seat Wrigley Field, and Lane arranged to rent the stadium

*In 1925 future Hall of Famer Paul Waner (right) led the PCL with a .401 average and a record-setting 25 doubles. Bert Ellison (left) was the 1924 RBI leader and, along with Gene Valla (center), was a feared slugger for the Seals during the 1920s.*
— Courtesy Oakland Public Library

for his team while the Angels were on the road. For the next several seasons, therefore, the Coast League's largest two cities would support two teams apiece and offer continuous play to local baseball fans.

The Missions finished third in their first season, featuring the stolen base champ, outfielder Evar Swanson (.316 with 43 steals), and pitchers Old Folks Pillette (21–16) and Bert Cole (29–12), who led the league in victories. James Elliott of Seattle (26–20 with 203 Ks) was the strikeout king, as George Boehler spent the year in Brooklyn. Portland outfielders Bill Bagwell (.391) and Elmer Smith (.336, 46 HRs, 133 RBIs) led the PCL respectively in hitting and home runs, while Oakland's Buzz Arlett (.382, 35 HRs, 140 RBIs) was the RBI titlist. Mission outfielder Ike Boone (.380, 32 HRs, 137 RBIs) made his first appearance in the Coast League, then went up to the Chicago White Sox — but the PCL would see the lefthanded slugger again.

Despite such fine players from opposing clubs, Los Angeles had put together a team which would be the class of the Coast League in 1926. Vowing to buy a club that would bring a champi-

*Wrigley Field, opened late in the 1927 season, cost over one million dollars and was a minor league showplace for the Angels.*

— Courtesy California State Library, Sacramento

onship to new Wrigley Field, Angels leadership revamped the team throughout the off-season. Jigger Statz was brought back to Los Angeles from the Cubs, and in addition to a brilliant hitting performance (.354 with a league-leading 291 base hits and 18 triples), he made just two errors in 199 games in center field. Key acquisitions included star third baseman Frank Brazill (.336, 19 HRs, 111 RBIs) and pitcher Earl Hamilton (24–8). The pitching staff also boasted ERA leader Elmer Jacobs (20–12, 2.20), 39-year-old Doc Crandall (20–8), and Wayne Wright (19–7), and totaled 127 complete games.

LA's championship roster was decimated in 1927 as several star players went to the big leagues, and the Angels plummeted to last place, despite the efforts of Brazill (.327) and outfielders Art Jahn (.343 with 146 RBIs) and Dick Cox (.345). Portland's Elmer Smith (.368, 40 HRs, 141 RBIs) won his second consecutive home run crown in 1927, and Lefty O'Doul of the Seals (.378, 33 HRs, 158 RBIs, 40 SBs) was the stolen base leader. Forty-year-old Harry Hooper, a famous American League outfielder (1909–25), came out of retirement to help the Missions (.284 in 78 games); the future Hall of Famer was a native of the Bay area, but this was his only

*Portland, 1927. Elmer Smith (seated, second from left) hit 40 homers for his second consecutive home run title. Paul Strand (standing, third from left) won back-to-back Triple Crowns in 1922 and 1923. Dudley Branom (standing sixth from right) hit .374, and shortstop Bill Cissell hit .323 and was purchased by the White Sox for $123,000.*

— Courtesy Portland Beavers

appearance in the Coast League. Portland shortstop Bill Cissell (.323) was purchased by the Chicago White Sox for $123,000, and he went on to play nine seasons for five big league clubs. In an August 20 game against Hollywood, Sacramento outfielder Ray Rohwer (.334) came up six times without an official at-bat (he walked once, was hit by a pitch, and was credited with four sacrifices); his record was not matched until 1985.

Oakland won the 1927 championship, the club's first pennant since 1912. The offense was sparked by the redoubtable Buzz Arlett (.351, 30 HRs, 123 RBIs, and a league-leading 54 doubles). Oaks first baseman John Fenton (.278 with 110 RBIs) stroked three triples in an October 1 game with San Francisco, establishing a PCL record that has been tied three times. The key to the Oaks' title was a fine pitching staff, led by George Boehler (22–12), who had returned from a season in Brooklyn to record his third PCL strikeout title and to lead the circuit in victories. Pudgy Gould (17–5) had the league's best winning percentage (in 1919, while pitching for

*Recreation Park, San Francisco, on opening day of the 1927 season. San Francisco native Gus Suhr, left, hit 27 homers and drove in 118 runs, and would play 11 seasons of big league ball.*

— Courtesy Oakland Public Library

Salt Lake City, he had recorded two complete game victories over Seattle in an August 3 doubleheader). Wilbur Cooper was effective (15–12), following 16 years in the big leagues in which four times he had been a 20-game winner. Forty-year-old Harry Krause (15–6) recorded yet another good season. A San Francisco native, Krause pitched for five seasons in the American League (37–26), put in three years with Portland (1913–15), and was an Oakland mainstay for 12 seasons (1917–28), before closing his career with the Missions in 1929. He won 300 minor league games, including a 249–220 PCL record. His victory total was the third highest in Coast League history, and his best years came in 1914 (22–18), 1917 (28–26), 1921 (24–13), and 1922 (21–19).

The 1927 batting and RBI champ was big Smead Jolley (.397, 33 HRs, 163 RBIs). Jolley began his career as a righthanded pitcher, but his obvious hitting talents soon placed him in the outfield as one of the most feared lefthanded sluggers in minor league history (.366 lifetime average, along with a .305 mark in 473 big league games). Jolley first appeared in the Coast League with San Francisco in 1925 (.447 in 38 games), played regularly in 1926

*The legendary slugger Smead Jolley (.366 lifetime) led the PCL in hitting and RBIs in 1927 (.397, 33 HRs, 163 RBIs). The next year he won the Triple Crown (.404, 45 HRs, 188 RBIs), and added a third batting title in 1938 (.350).*

— Courtesy Bill McIntyre

(.346, 25 HRs, 132 RBIs), then won the first of three PCL batting titles in 1927.

Jolley roared to an even better season the next year, corraling the first of two Triple Crowns (.404, 309 hits, 45 HRs, 188 RBIs) and leading the league in hits. Jolley's phenomenal season propelled the Seals to their fourth pennant of the decade and himself to the American League for the next four years. Jolley had an outstanding supporting cast, as the Seals pounded out the league's highest batting average (.308) and the most home runs (182). Outfielder Earl Averill, on the eve of a Hall of Fame career, had broken in impressively with San Francisco in 1926 (.348, 23 HRs, 119 RBIs), was almost as good the next year (.324, 20 HRs, 116 RBIs), and after his 1928 performance (.354, 36 HRs, 173 RBIs, and a league-leading 178 runs) he was purchased by the Cleveland Indians for a reported $50,000.

Other key players included outfielder Roy Johnson (.360 with 20 homers), first baseman Hollis Thurston (.347 with 24 homers), first sacker Gus Suhr (.314, 22 HRs, 133 RBIs), and shortstop Hal Rhyne (.312 with 106 RBIs). Southpaw Dutch Ruether, after pitching for 11 years in the big leagues, led the PCL in victories and winning percentage (29–7), and he hit so well (.316 in 72 games) that he frequently was used as a pinch hitter. Elmer Jacobs (22–8, 2.56) again was the ERA champ, and Walter Mails (20–12) rounded out an excellent top three.

Mission outfielder Evar Swanson (.346 with 49 steals) won his second stolen base crown, and veteran big leaguer Earl Sheely hit explosively (.381, 21 HRs, 128 RBIs) while playing first base for Sacramento. Sacramento's best pitchers were Ray Keating (27–10) and Louri Vinci (23–11), who would lead a strong challenge for the 1928 pennant. Oakland's double-play combination, shortstop Lyn Lary (.314) and second baseman Jimmy Reese (.247), were purchased by the New York Yankees for $100,000. Lary enjoyed a 12-year career in the big leagues, Reese was left in Oakland for more seasoning, but after he raised his batting average 100 points in 1929 the Yankees brought him up.

Prior to the 1928 season, league owners, keenly aware of the negative effects on attendance by Oakland's 1927 runaway, decided to resurrect the split-schedule format, with a seven-game playoff at the end of the season between the two winners. San Francisco easily won the first half and coasted to the PCL's best record. But Sacramento tied the Seals for the second half lead, and a special three-game series was ordered. Sacramento won two straight games to set up the scheduled playoff, but San Francisco took four games out of the first six. A $20,000 purse was provided for the top four teams: the Seals took home $9,000, Sacramento collected $6,000, third-place Hollywood earned $3,000, and the fourth-place Missions claimed $2,000.

Henry Williams of Los Angeles, president of the PCL since 1924, asked 21 sportswriters to vote on an honorary All-Star team:

| | |
|---|---|
| 1B | Earl Sheely, Sacramento (.381) |
| 2B | Johnny Kerr, Hollywood (.301) |
| 3B | James McLaughlin, Sac. (,310) |
| SS | Lyn Lary, Oakland (.314) |
| SS | Dudley Lee, Hollywood (.273) |
| LF | Roy Johnson, SF (.360) |
| CF | Earl Averill, SF (.354) |
| RF | Smead Jolley, SF (.404) |
| Ut. | Hollis Thurston, SF (.347) |
| C | John Bassler, Hollywood (.300) |
| P | Dutch Ruether, SF (29–7) |

---

**The Stars Go Airborne**

A landmark event in the history of professional sports occurred on Sunday, July 15, 1928. The Hollywood Stars, preparing
to conclude a series in Seattle with the customary doubleheader,
were due to open a home series on Tuesday. The Cascade Limited
from Portland would take the Stars to Los Angeles on time, but no
train connection to Portland could be made by Sunday evening.

Hollywood owner Bill Lane had accompanied the Stars on the
trip, and he decided to send half of his team out of town on Saturday with the equipment baggage. Lane persuaded about half of his
men to play the Sunday doubleheader, then fly 150 miles to Portland. Air travel in 1928 held a certain element of risk, but the Stars
played on Sunday, then flew safely to Portland in time to catch the
Cascade Limited. Although regular flights by sports teams was
many years away, the Hollywood Stars of the Coast League had
become the first professional club to travel by plane.

---

Ike Boone, back in the Coast League after a poor season with
the White Sox, missed an All-Star berth despite a fine hitting performance (.354). But there would be no doubt about his credentials
in 1929. Roaming the outfield for Portland, he won the Triple
Crown with the highest season average so far recorded in the Coast
League (.407, 55 HRs, 218 RBIs). His astounding numbers also included a league-leading 323 hits, and 523 total bases, the most *ever*
accumulated during a season of professional ball. Boone went on an
even greater rampage in 1930 (.448 with 22 homers and 96 RBIs in
just 83 games), but he was sold to Brooklyn before mid-season.
Boone, who had hit .402 as the batting champ of the 1923 Texas
League, did not end his career until 1936, when he was 39. He hit
.319 in 455 big league games, and his .370 mark in 1,857 minor
league games established the all-time career record.

Smead Jolley also had a remarkable season in 1929 (.387, 35
HRs, 159 RBIs), and so did Gus Suhr (.381, 51 HRs, 177 RBIs),
who led the league with 196 runs, one more than Boone. Suhr
played first base in every inning of San Francisco's 202 games. A
San Francisco native, Suhr played with the Seals from 1925
through 1929, then launched an 11-year big league career. Among
other outstanding hitters were LA's Earl Webb (.357, 37 HRs, 164
RBIs) and Wally Berger (.335, 40 HRs, 166 RBIs), and Oakland

*In 1929 18-year-old Lefty Gomez won 18 games for the Seals, then went on to a Hall of Fame career with the Yankees.*

— Author's collection

infielder John Vergez (.323, 46 HRs, 165 RBIs). LA infielder Fred Haney (.292 with 56 steals) won the first of four PCL stolen base crowns. On July 4 Seals infielder Babe Pinelli, an eight-year big league veteran, walloped two grand-slam home runs against Seattle, tying Pete Schneider's single-game record.

Future Yankee star Lefty Gomez recorded a good season (18–11) for San Francisco even though he was just 18, while 42-year-old Doc Crandall (11–13) retired after an illustrious career (249–163 in the minors, 101–62 in the big leagues) in which he was a 20-game winner five times in the Coast League. The strikeout leader in 1929 was Oakland's Howard Craghead (21–12, 190 Ks), and Hollywood's Frank Shellenback (26–12) led the league in victories and winning percentage. But the Missions boasted the PCL's best pitching staff, which starred Bert Cole (24–12), who again was used as a pinch hitter (.324 in 77 games), and Old Folks Pillette (23–13), who tossed a no-hitter against Seattle.

The Missions charged to a commanding lead in 1929, but just before mid-season the owners decided to stimulate the pennant race and attendance by again utilizing the split-schedule device (indeed, paid admissions had reached record totals in 1928, and in

---

### Tragedy Off the Field

In 1928 the Hollywood Stars had been considered daredevils for boarding a rickety airplane in order to make a train connection, but automobile travel was almost as dangerous on the primitive highways of the day. At the end of spring training in 1929, a carload of Portland players crashed while returning from San Diego, and outfielder Denny Williams was killed. Shortly before the season opened, righthander Clyde Nance of the Missions died when his car overturned. And just after the 1929 playoffs, Hollywood outfielder Bill Albert was fatally injured when his auto collided with another car.

---

1929 almost two million tickets were sold in PCL parks). The Missions were declared first-half champions, then went on to post the best overall record of the season. San Francisco, led by Smead Jolley, recorded the year's second-best mark, but failed to make the playoffs.

Sparked by a high-octane offense, Hollywood edged the Missions for the second-half title. The formidable Stars' lineup included slick-fielding first sacker Mickey Heath (.349, 38 HRs, 156 RBIs), third baseman Russ Rollings (.324), longtime big league catcher Hank Severeid (.415 with 72 RBIs in just 79 games), and outfielders Elias Funk (.384, 13 HRs, 125 RBIs), Cleo Carlyle (.347, 20 HRs, 136 RBIs), and Bill Rumler (.386, 26 HRs, 120 RBIs). Rumler, of course, had been suspended from PCL play during the gambling scandals of 1920. But Bill Lane kept him on the reserve list for eight years, and when Rumler received a pardon from Organized Baseball he was invited to spring training with Hollywood. Although 37 years old, Rumler still swung a powerful bat. He nailed down the right field position, and notched the highest average of any regular on the team.

The star of the 1929 playoff series was spitballer Frank Shellenback, who not only had led the league in wins but also had been an excellent pinch hitter (.322 with 12 homers in 70 games). The Missions won the first two games in San Francisco's Recreation Park. But in the last game in San Francisco, Shellenback pitched and hit (one homer, two singles and three RBIs) the Stars to a victory. Back in Los Angeles Shellenback tied the fourth game in the ninth with a pinch hit home run, and the Stars evened the series

*A career .370 hitter in the minor leagues, Ike Boone terrorized PCL pitchers for four seasons. In 1929 he walloped 323 hits and won the Triple Crown (.407, 55 HRs, 218 RBIs).*

— Courtesy Ted Leach

with a tenth-inning victory. Hollywood took the series lead with another win the following day, then Shellenback pitched his team to the championship in the sixth game, adding yet another home run.

By the end of the 1920s, the Coast League had established a unique position for itself in Organized Baseball. Los Angeles and San Francisco were big-time cities, larger and more attractive than many major league cities of the East. During the pitcher-dominated dead-ball years, strong-armed PCL hurlers had piled up incredible totals of victories, innings pitched, etc. The 1920s had brought an offensive explosion, and the long Coast League schedule allowed sluggers to whack out sensational numbers of homers, doubles, triples, and RBIs. Astronomical batting averages and high-scoring games brought record-breaking crowds to the ball parks. One of the primary appeals of baseball for the dedicated fan is watching the same players on a daily basis, learning an athlete's strengths and weaknesses and quirks, anticipating his performance in various situations, and becoming familiar with the chemistry of the team.

This pleasure is largely unavailable in the minor leagues today, but for several decades Coast League teams could exhibit the same players season after season. Fan identity with talented players, an extremely high quality of play, and the stability of a strong eight-team circuit sometimes prompted Coast League owners to refer condescendingly to the major leagues as "the Eastern leagues."

# 1930–1939

## *The PCL During the Depression*

During the Great Depression numerous minor league clubs folded, and entire circuits were forced to disband. The Coast League, however, continued to enjoy solid franchise stability and an excellent caliber of play. The PCL lowered admission prices (in 1932 general admission seats went down to 50¢ across the league, and reserved seat fares also were reduced), and there was a general belt tightening across the circuit. But the sensational offensive performances of the 1920s were maintained through the 1930s, and a splendid array of baseball talent was exhibited in ballparks throughout the Coast League.

Joe DiMaggio, for example, played three years for San Francisco, while Ox Eckhardt won four batting titles and took his place alongside such legendary minor league superstars as Smead Jolley and Ike Boone. San Francisco claimed two pennants during the decade, Los Angeles won three, and the 1934 Angels proved themselves to be the greatest team in Coast League history. Throughout minor league baseball, night play in lighted parks and the Shaughnessy playoff system were introduced during the 1930s to stimulate attendance. The Coast League embraced these innovations, and despite the Depression the 1930s proved to be a successful era in PCL history.

57

Artistically, purists always have insisted that night games, especially under inferior minor league lighting, have ruined baseball. Fastballs are more difficult to see and hit, players' daily routines are upset when day games follow night games, or vice versa, and athletes' performances are affected by fatigue. But working people found it more convenient to attend night games, and the marked rise in attendance rendered it mandatory for Depression-era ballplayers to adjust. During the National Association winter meeting late in 1929, Des Moines of the Western League announced its intention to play Organized Baseball's first night game. But Des Moines opened on the road, and a Western Association team, Independence, Kansas, beat the Iowa club to the punch by playing under makeshift arclights on April 28, 1930. Other minor league clubs quickly followed suit, and even though the big leagues conservatively refrained from staging a night contest until 1935, every minor league park where light towers were installed enjoyed an immediate jump in attendance.

The Coast League's first night game was staged in Sacramento on Thursday, May 22, 1930. Plans were announced to install lights in every park except San Francisco, and Phil Wrigley proclaimed his intention to put up "the best incandescent lighting money can buy" in Wrigley Field. Indeed, Wrigley Field's two home teams, Los Angeles and Hollywood, each won half of a split schedule, played an all-LA championship series, and produced a total season attendance exceeding 850,000 (the St. Louis Browns and Cardinals, playing in the Browns' Sportsman's Park, failed to draw that many fans in 1930 for major league baseball). The Angels pulled in a crowd of 17,000 for their first night game, on July 22, and it was immediately decided to schedule all weekday games at night. And when the Angels and Stars played a crucial seven-game series in September, almost 80,000 fans crowded into Wrigley Field.

Los Angeles won the first half of the 1930 schedule, and Hollywood took the second half, posted the best record of the season, then won the playoff series for the second year in a row. Jim Turner (21–9 with a .342 batting average) and Frank Shellenback (19–7) were the best Star pitchers, and every regular except shortstop Dudley Lee (.275) hit over .300. Although Bill Rumler was 42, he terrorized opposing pitching (.353 with 82 RBIs in 95 games) until a broken ankle ended his PCL career. Jesse Hill, a magnificent

USC athlete with letters in football, track and baseball, was signed by Bill Lane following his graduation in May and was a sensation in the outfield and at the plate (.356), smashing a home run off the first pitch he saw as a professional (a pinch hit homer against LA on June 4). Outfielder Dave Barbee, purchased by Lane from Seattle in June, became the 1930 home run champ (.325, 41 HRs, 155 RBIs). First baseman Mickey Heath (.324, 37 HRs, 136 RBIs) set a record with 12 consecutive hits against the Missions on September 2, 3 and 4. Second sacker Otis Brannon (.307 with 130 RBIs), outfielders Cleo Carlyle (.326) and Harry Green (.329), and catchers Hank Severeid (.367) and Johnny Bassler (.365) were other members of one of the most lethal lineups in Coast League history. The Stars averaged almost 13 runs per game in the playoff series, overcoming a six-run deficit in Game Two to win, 14–12, and pounding the Angels 22–4 in Game Four.

LA's lineup also boasted seven regulars who batted over .300, including outfielders Wes Schulmerich (.380, 28 HRs, 130 RBIs), Jigger Statz (.360) and Johnny Moore (.342, 26 HRs, 101 RBIs), first baseman Ray Jacobs (.304, 20 HRs, 130 RBIs), shortstop Carl Dittmar (.310, 14 HRs, 125 RBIs), and third sacker Fred Haney (.312 with 52 steals), who won his second consecutive stolen base crown. San Francisco first baseman Earl Sheely, who had been the home run leader while with Salt Lake City in 1918, 1919 and 1920, and who had won the 1920 batting championship, returned to the PCL after eight seasons in the big time and led the Coast League in hitting and RBIs (.403, 29 HRs, 180 RBIs). Batting .403 earned Sheely another year in the big leagues (he had a .300 lifetime average for nine major league seasons), then he came back to the PCL, this time with the Angels.

Oakland outfielder Buzz Arlett (.361, 31 HRs, 143 RBIs), after 13 years with his home town club, went to the Phillies for his only major league season (during his prime Oakland owners had refused to sell Arlett for less than $100,000, so Buzz had starred year after year for the Oaks). Another Oakland native, catcher Ernie Lombardi, had played superbly for the Oaks in 1928 (.377), 1929 (.366), and 1930 (.370), then went to the National League for a Hall of Fame career. San Francisco native Frank Crosetti was a standout at shortstop for the Seals in 1930 (.334, 27 HRs, 113 RBIs), and after another good season he would spend 17 years in the New York Yankee infield. Outfielder Irvin Hufft recorded a

*Earl Sheely (in suit, showing a first baseman's mitt to a Seattle batboy) led the PCL in 1930 with a .403 average and 180 RBIs.*

— Courtesy Mariana York

banner season (.356, 37 HRs, 178 RBIs) for the Missions, and Portland second baseman William Rhiel (.348) pulled off the sixth — and last, to date — unassisted triple play in the PCL, against Seattle on September 21. In the ninth inning of a June 12 game against Hollywood, Seattle's Louis Alameda (.296) and Robert Holland (.332, 20 HRs, 141 RBIs) each stole home, an unprecedented feat in the PCL which was not repeated until 1961.

Ed Baecht of the Angels led the league in victories and ERA (26–12, 3.23). Veteran righthander Jimmy Zinn tied for most wins (26–12) and twirled a no-hitter against Sacramento. Zinn, who also was a good pinch hitter and outfielder, played a total of 105 games for San Francisco in 1930 and hit .326 (he was a .301 lifetime hitter in the minors, and .283 in 76 big league games). He had pitched five years in the major leagues (13–16) and was in his 16th season as a pro when he signed with the Seals in 1930. He won 295 minor league games, hurled in the PCL for six seasons, and pitched his last professional games when he was 44. An even more impressive minor league hurler, southpaw Tony Freitas (342–238, plus a 25–33 big league mark), led the Coast League in winning percentage (19–6) while toiling for Sacramento in 1930. His career began in 1928 and lasted until 1953, when he was 22–9 for Stockton in the California League at the age of 45. Freitas was 228–175 in the Coast League, and he was a 20-game winner six consecutive years (1937–42) for Sacramento. Sacramento's Fay Thomas (20–19, 228 Ks) was the 1930 strikeout king.

Despite the Depression, paid attendance in 1930 totaled 1,673,123. League owners, however, had never been satisfied with the split-season device, and announced that the 1931 schedule would be played through to a championship, and that it would be reduced to 26 weeks. But Hollywood, playoff champs the last two seasons, roared to a commanding lead in 1931 and threatened to make the race a runaway. Reluctantly league owners decided by telegraphic vote again to resort to a split schedule. With Depression conditions more severe in 1931, and the novelty of night ball worn off, attendance dropped across the league, prompting owners once more to proclaim that the split schedule no longer would be used.

Longtime Hollywood manager Oscar Vitt had lost only slugging first baseman Mickey Heath to the big leagues from his 1930 championship club. Spitballer Frank Shellenback (27–7) and right fielder Dave Barbee (.332, 47 HRs, 166 RBIs) led the Stars to another fine season. Barbee repeated as home run champ, and not only did Shellenback enjoy his finest season from the mound, he won three games with home runs (.285 and 9 homers in 49 games, including 13 pinch hit appearances). Shellenback completed 35 of 36 starts, won his first five games of the year after winning his last 14 decisions of 1930, then, following a loss, won 15 consecutive starts — 34 victories in 35 decisions (his 15 straight wins fell one short of Frank Browning's league record of 16, set in 1909). The only reason he did not go to the major leagues is because spitballs had been outlawed since 1920. Hollywood catchers Hank Severeid (.347) and Johnny Bassler (.354) again were deadly at the plate, and so were outfielders Jess Hill (.318) and Cleo Carlyle (.320).

Hollywood easily won the first half title in 1931, but injuries devastated the club, and the Stars suffered a losing record in the second half. San Francisco surged to the second half lead with the season's best record, then beat Hollywood in four straight to claim the championship. The Seals hit for the highest team average (.314) in the league, while banging out a record-setting 114 triples. The attack was led by first baseman James Keesey (.358 with 113 RBIs), shortstop Frank Crosetti (.343 with 143 RBIs), infielder

Robert Johnson (.334), and outfielders Foy Frazier (.327) and Prince Henry Oana (.345, 23 HRs, 161 RBIs), one of the first Hawaiians to become successful in professional baseball.

Star of the San Francisco pitching staff was Sam Gibson (28–12, with a 2.48 ERA and 204 Ks in 337 innings). The 32-year-old righthander had pitched in the big leagues for four seasons and had played in three other minor circuits before coming to the PCL in 1931. He broke in spectacularly, winning the pitcher's Triple Crown and also leading the league in innings pitched. Gibson was purchased by the New York Giants. After one season (his major league record ended at 32–38), he was back in the PCL with Portland. Gibson returned to San Francisco in 1934, pitching for the Seals until 1944, then spending 1945 with Oakland. Although his Coast League debut proved to be his best season in 27 years as a pro, he was a 20-game winner six times with San Francisco. In 1942, at the age of 43, Gibson was 20–12 with the fifth-place Seals, and he was 227–140 (.619) during his Coast League years. Gibson last pitched when he was 50 in the Georgia-Alabama League, finishing with a minor league record of 302–200.

Ox Eckhardt, a righthanded outfielder who hit from the left side, won his first Coast League batting crown in 1931 (.369). Until 1928 when he was 26, Eckhardt had only played two games of pro ball in his native Texas. But he hit .376 in the Western Association, then moved to Seattle in 1929 (.354), before winning the Texas League batting title in 1930 (.379). In 1931 he was purchased by the Missions, and during his five years with the club he would win four Coast League batting championships.

Portland outfielder Ed Coleman (.358, 37 HRs, 183 RBIs) was the 1931 RBI leader. LA's Jigger Statz had one of his finest years in 1931 (.332, 141 runs, 107 RBIs and 45 steals), scoring the most runs, batting in over 100 runs for the only time in his 24-year career, and winning the first of three PCL stolen base titles. But three Angel pitchers issued a record-setting eight walks in a single inning of play against Hollywood on September 4. And last-place Seattle established an all-time Coast League record by turning 239 double plays. Weak teams always have more double-play opportunities, because there are more men on base while they are in the field.

In 1932 the Coast League established a Most Valuable Player award. Fittingly, Angels center fielder Jigger Statz, who would play more Coast League games and set more lifetime records than any other player, won the first official MVP award. Statz enjoyed one of his best seasons (.347 with 153 runs), again leading the league in runs scored while fielding superbly. Ox Eckhardt started the season with the Boston Braves, but he was given eight pinch hitting opportunities, and he returned to the Mission franchise in time to play 134 games and win his second straight batting crown (.371). Seattle first baseman George Burns (.354 with 140 RBIs) was the RBI champ, while Seattle second sacker Fred Muller (.282, 38 HRs, 121 RBIs) won his first home run championship. On July 9 in a game against Portland, Sacramento third baseman Alex Kampouris exploded for a record seven RBIs in a single inning. Oakland infielder Babe Pinelli, a native of San Francisco who had logged eight years in the big leagues and who had played for four Coast League clubs, retired after a good season (.307) to become a PCL umpire, and after three years he was hired by the National League as an ump.

Hollywood fielded another fine team, led by catcher Johnny Bassler (.357), center fielder Cleo Carlyle (.346, 16 HRs, 106 RBIs), and the redoubtable Frank Shellenback (26–10), who again led the league in victories and completed 35 of 36 starts. The Stars were in first place for more than a month, and challenged for the lead throughout the season.

But Portland, which had not won a pennant since 1914, led the league in hitting and fought off all competition to take the championship. For the first time in league history — except for the war-shortened season of 1918 — a pennant-winning pitching staff did not boast a single 20-game winner. But future big league third baseman Pinky Higgins (.326, 33 HRs, 132 RBIs), outfielder Louis Finney (.351), and first sacker James Keesey (.309 with 122 RBIs) sparked a powerful offense.

Offense remained a key feature in 1933. Ox Eckhardt battered Coast League pitching for the highest average in circuit history (.414 with 143 RBIs and a league-leading 315 hits) and his third consecutive batting crown. Hollywood's Fred Haney (.317 with 63 steals) won his third stolen base title, and Oakland outfielder Frenchy Uhalt (.350 with 62 steals) was right behind.

Perhaps the most remarkable performance was turned in by 18-year-old rookie Joe DiMaggio (.340, 28 HRs, 169 RBIs). A noted amateur player in San Francisco, Joe had played three games for the Seals at shortstop at the end of 1932 on the recommendation

*Ox Eckhardt (.367 lifetime) won PCL batting titles in 1931 (.369), 1932 (.371), 1933 (.414), and 1935 (.399). His .414 average and four hitting crowns are all-time Coast League records.*

— Courtesy Ted Leach

of older brother Vince (.270 in 59 games). Switched to the outfield in his first full season, Joe led the Coast League in RBIs and assists — and he hit safely in an incredible 61 consecutive games. On May 28, 1933, in the second game of a doubleheader against Portland, DiMaggio cracked a double, and the record-setting streak continued through July 25. In 10 of these games DiMaggio stroked three hits, once he collected three doubles and a single, and during the streak he batted .405, with 16 doubles, six triples, and 11 homers. Joe finally was held hitless in five times at bat on July 26 by Oakland's Ed Walsh, Jr., who pitched a no-hitter against the Seals three weeks later. Throughout the streak attendance was boosted (a boon to Coast League cities in the grip of the Depression) as fans flocked to ballparks to see the amazing rookie.

DiMaggio injured a knee in 1934 and played in just 101 games, but still hit .341. Fred Haney (.306 with 71 steals) won his fourth stolen base crown, but Ox Eckhardt (.378) missed the batting title by five percentage points. Hollywood catcher Johnny Bassler continued to batter the ball (.351), and so did Seattle outfielder

Art Hunt (.306, 30 HRs, 128 RBIs) and Hollywood's Smead Jolley (.360).

In 1933 Hollywood's mound corps had four 20-game winners, Archie Campbell (22–15), Frank Shellenback (21–12), Tom Sheehan (21–13), and Vance Page (20–15). The next year Hollywood's only 20-game winner was Joe Sullivan (25–11), while San Francisco's LeRoy Herrmann (27–13) and Sam Gibson (21–17) were other standouts of 1934.

The Coast League was dominated in 1933 and 1934 by Los Angeles. Former big league outfielder Jack Lelivelt was hired as Angels manager at mid-season of 1929, and by 1933 he had built the team into an invincible machine. Third baseman Gene Lillard (.307, 43 HRs, 149 RBIs) was the PCL's home run champ. First sacker Jim Oglesby (.313, 20 HRs, 137 RBIs) hit in 41 consecutive games, a feat overshadowed by Joe DiMaggio. Former batboy Jimmy Reese (.330) held down second base, and center fielder Jigger Statz (.325) was flanked by Tuck Stainback (.335, 19 HRs, 148 RBIs) in right and Marv Gudat (.333, 10 HRs, 113 RBIs) in left. Curveballer Dick Ward (25–9) and Fay Thomas (20–14) were excellent pitchers, but the league's Most Valuable Player was big Buck Newsom (30–11, with 212 strikeouts in 320 innings in 56 games). The colorful righthander led the league in victories, strikeouts, games and innings pitched, won 15 decisions in a row, and went on to hurl in the big leagues until he was 46.

The 1933 Angels won the pennant with a 114–73 (.609) record, but the loss of Newsom, Ward and Stainback to the big leagues posed question marks for the next year. But six regulars returned in 1934: Oglesby (.312, 15 HRs, 139 RBIs) Reese (.311), Lillard (.289, 27 HRs, 119 RBIs), shortstop Carl Dittmar (.294), Gudat (.319 with 125 RBIs), and Jigger Statz (.324 with 61 steals and a league-leading 13 triples). Stainback was replaced in right by Frank Demaree, who would average .299 in 12 big league seasons. Demaree was named MVP of 1934 after winning the Triple Crown (.383, 45 HRs, 173 RBIs, along with 41 stolen bases) with one of the most magnificent performances in Coast League history.

With the departure of Newsom and Ward, Fay Thomas, who had won his last seven games of 1933, became the ace of the staff (28–4, 204 Ks). Thomas led the league in victories and strikeouts while establishing the highest winning percentage (.875) of any PCL pitcher to have 20 decisions. He won his first 15 games in

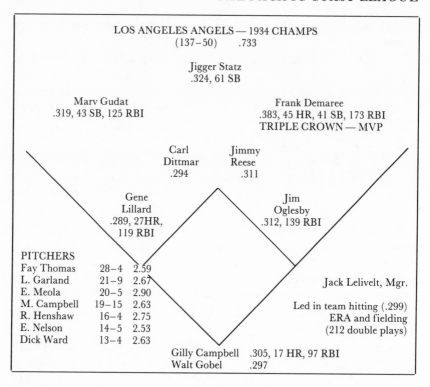

LOS ANGELES ANGELS — 1934 CHAMPS
(137–50)    .733

Jigger Statz
.324, 61 SB

Marv Gudat                                          Frank Demaree
.319, 43 SB, 125 RBI                                .383, 45 HR, 41 SB, 173 RBI
                                                    TRIPLE CROWN — MVP

Carl          Jimmy
Dittmar       Reese
.294          .311

Gene                          Jim
Lillard                       Oglesby
.289, 27HR,                   .312, 139 RBI
119 RBI

PITCHERS
Fay Thomas      28–4    2.59
L. Garland      21–9    2.67
E. Meola        20–5    2.90          Jack Lelivelt, Mgr.
M. Campbell     19–15   2.63
R. Henshaw      16–4    2.75          Led in team hitting (.299)
E. Nelson       14–5    2.53                ERA and fielding
Dick Ward       13–4    2.63              (212 double plays)

Gilly Campbell   .305, 17 HR, 97 RBI
Walt Gobel       .297

1934, giving him a record 22 consecutive victories. Thomas threw a
sinking forkball, but his infield was more than capable of handling
grounders. The Angels led the league in fielding and double plays.

As customary, Los Angeles opened the season with a two-week
home stand, and the Angels bolted to a 23–5 record. Later the
team won 20 of 22 games, prompting a league-wide demand to divide the season. At the end of the first half, the Angels were 66–18
and had an 18½-game lead over second-place Mission. During the
26-week season the Angels won 23 of 26 series, and coasted to the
pennant with a record of 137–50 (.733), the best figures in Coast
League history.

Since Los Angeles easily won both halves there would be no
championship playoff, but owners devised a postseason series between the Angels and an All-Star team from the other seven clubs.
The best-of-seven series was played in Los Angeles, and the All-
Stars were selected by a newspaper ballot of the fans. LA won the
first game, but the All-Stars then took two in a row. The champions rallied to sweep a Sunday doubleheader, then won the sixth

---

### All-Stars vs. The Angels

Mythical Coast League dream teams had been written up in newspapers in past seasons, but the first PCL All-Stars to play lost four of the six postseason games to the magnificent 1934 Angels. The Angels used the same batting order that had carried them to the pennant, while injuries prevented Joe DiMaggio and Seattle second baseman Andy Harrington from playing with the All-Stars.

| *LA Lineup* | | *All-Star Roster* | |
|---|---|---|---|
| Jigger Statz | CF | Babe Dahlgren, Mission | 1B |
| Jimmy Reese | 2B | Al Wright, Mission | 2B |
| Marv Gudat | LF | Jose Coscarart, Seattle | 3B |
| Frank Demaree | RF | Fred Haney, Hollywood | 3B |
| Jim Oglesby | 1B | Jim Levey, Hollywood | SS |
| Gilly Campbell | C | Ox Eckhardt, Mission | OF |
| Gene Lillard | 3B | Smead Jolley, Hollywood | OF |
| Carl Dittmar | SS | Art Hunt, Seattle | OF |
| | | Louis Alameda, Mission | OF |
| *All-Star Games in* | | John Bassler, Hollywood | C |
| *Wrigley Field:* | | Larry Woodall, SF | C |
| LA — 6 | All-Stars — 4 | Joe Sullivan, Hollywood | P |
| LA — 2 | All-Stars — 5 | Herman Pillette, Seattle | P |
| LA — 7 | All-Stars — 9 | LeRoy Herrmann, SF | P |
| LA — 13 | All-Stars — 7 | Sam Gibson, SF | P |
| LA — 3 | All-Stars — 0 | Clarence Mitchell, Mission | P |
| LA — 4 | All-Stars — 3 | Dutch Ruether, Seattle | Mgr. |

---

game and the series. Perhaps the finest team in minor league history, the 1934 Angels had beaten the best that the rest of the PCL could offer.

Depression conditions and the dominance of the Angels caused attendance once more to drop in 1934. In hope of stimulating larger crowds, league owners voted to shorten the season by two weeks — the 174-game schedule would be the shortest since war-shortened 1918 — and changed the seven-game, week-long series format to two series per week, one of four games and one of three. (Later the league would return to the familiar week-long format, with Mondays for travel.) For years PCL roster sizes had been 25, the same number as major league clubs carried. Coast League teams were required to carry 20 veterans and were permitted to have only five rookies. In 1935 however, rosters were reduced to 21, including 16 veterans, as a cost-cutting device. Apparently these measures worked, because there was a general improvement in attendance — except in Hollywood — and for most clubs 1935 was the best year since the Depression began.

Los Angeles retained most of the players from the 1934 champions, but Fay Thomas (St. Louis Browns) and Frank Demaree (Cubs) went to the big leagues. The Angels won the first half title, but sagged badly during the second half, then lost the playoff series. But first sacker Jim Oglesby (.350, 24 HRs, 132 RBIs) enjoyed another fine season, Jigger Statz (.330 with 53 steals) won his second stolen base crown, and third baseman Gene Lillard (.361, 56 HRs, 147 RBIs) blasted his way to another home run title with the best performance of his long career.

The Missions' Ox Eckhardt, in the last of his six seasons in the PCL, won his fourth batting crown (.399). Hollywood's Smead Jolley (.372, 29 HRs, 128 RBIs) also would leave the league at the end of the year, but he would return for a last hurrah. Mission right-hander Walter "Boom-Boom" Beck, who would pitch for six big league teams sporadically from 1924 through 1945, led the PCL in wins and strikeouts (23–18 with 202 Ks).

Joe DiMaggio had recovered from knee troubles to lead San Francisco to the 1935 pennant. (Convinced that he was sound, the New York Yankees had purchased his contract for $25,000, but they wanted him to play with the Seals in 1935 for more seasoning.) DiMaggio just missed the batting title (.398, 173 runs, 18 triples, 34 HRs, 154 RBIs), but led the PCL in RBIs, runs scored, triples, and outfielder assists, and was named Most Valuable Player. Sam Gibson (22–4) and Win Ballou (18–8) headed the Seals' mound staff. San Francisco won the second half, posted the league's best record, and handily defeated the Angels in the playoffs.

After the season W. C. Tuttle, a well-known magazine writer and a baseball enthusiast from Encino, was elected PCL president, and he moved league headquarters from San Francisco to Los Angeles, where he was given offices in the tower at Wrigley Field. The league decided to adopt the Shaughnessy Plan for 1936. Already employed successfully by many minor leagues, the Shaughnessy Plan called for a full season of play, followed by three postseason playoff series. The opening round would pit the team with the best season record against the fourth-place team, while the second- and third-place clubs played each other; the winners of these series then

*Two of the PCL's most famous alumni, Ted Williams and Joe DiMaggio, broke into pro ball as teenagers with their home town teams. Williams played for the Padres in 1936 (.271) and 1937 (.291). DiMaggio was in three games for the Seals in 1932, hit in 61 consecutive games in 1933 (.340 with a league-leading 169 RBIs), injured a knee in 1933 (but still hit .341), then led the PCL in RBIs again in 1934 (.398, 34 HRs, 154 RBIs).*

— Author's collection

### Now Pitching . . . Joe E. Brown!

On the last day of the 1935 season at Wrigley Field, the Missions led Hollywood 14–7 with two out and nobody on in the bottom of the ninth. Comedian Joe E. Brown, a baseball enthusiast, came to the mound for the Stars to pitch to Harry Ruby. Brown called in the outfielders and positioned them in front of him as protection from line drives, but then whiffed Ruby to close out the year.

faced each other in the finals. The Coast League would deduct one cent from each regular season admission around the circuit until a fund of $10,000 had been accumulated. At the end of the season the players on the first-place team would split $2,500; $5,000 would be divided 60–40 by the clubs in the playoff finals; and $2,500 would be divided equally by the two losing teams in the playoff opener.

Despite the Depression, there had not been a franchise move in the PCL since 1926, when Vernon went to San Francisco and Bill Lane brought his club from Salt Lake City to Los Angeles. Lane had experienced difficulties over the rental terms for Wrigley Field, and his fee had been doubled for 1936. Furthermore, Hollywood's first losing season since 1926 had seen admissions plummet to fewer than 90,000. Lane, who had suffered financial losses for three years, determined to leave LA. After investigating other locations, Lane decided upon San Diego, which offered a ballpark and other inducements. Numerous parties thought a move from Los Angeles (population 1,500,000) to San Diego (a border town of 200,000) was doomed to failure. But San Diego tied for second place in 1936, made the playoffs, and totaled almost as many paid admissions as the city's population.

During his first summer in San Diego, Bill Lane signed a 17-year-old pitcher and slugger out of Herbert Hoover High School, Ted Williams. The skinny (6'3, 145 pounds) Williams struck out during his first professional appearance, a pinch hitting try against the Seals, but Lefty O'Doul promptly tried to buy his contract. Williams continued his incessant batting practice, and by the end of the season he was San Diego's left fielder (.271). The next year he enjoyed a solid performance (.291, 23 HRs, 98 RBIs). Lane sold him to the Red Sox, he won the American Association Triple Crown while playing for Minneapolis in 1938, then went to Boston and became one of baseball's greatest hitters.

Frank Shellenback was San Diego's player-manager in 1936, and although he was no longer a front-line pitcher (6–7 in 15 games), he still could handle a bat (.351 in 31 games). Second baseman Bobby Doerr (.342) paced the league in hits and assists, and sparked San Diego to a playoff berth. Oakland's playoff team was headed by Wee Willie Ludolph (21–6), who was voted MVP. Sluggers Art Hunt (.316, 30 HRs, 105 RBIs) and Fred Muller (.305, 30 HRs, 105 RBIs) tied for the home run title and, along with Louis Koupal (23–11) and Kewpie Doll Dick Barrett (22–13), led Seattle into the playoffs.

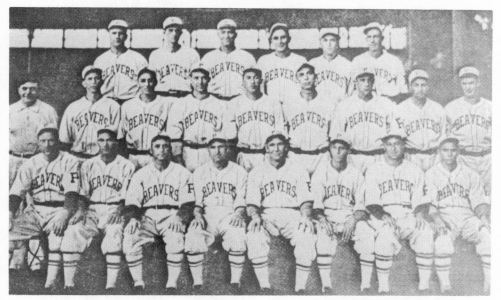

*Portland Beavers, 1936 champs. Outfielder Moose Clabaugh (top right) hit .317 with 112 RBIs, Bill Posedel (middle row, second from left) was 20–10, Fred Bedore (middle, fourth from right) hit .337 with 100 RBIs, John Frederick (middle, second from right) hit .353 with 103 RBIs, and George Custer (middle right) was 25–13. Manager Bill Sweeney (seated, fourth from right) won pennants with LA in 1943 and 1944, and submariner Ad Liska (seated, second from right) won 198 games during 14 seasons with Portland.*

— Courtesy Ted Leach

But Portland was to prove the Cinderella team of 1936. Although the Beavers had won the 1932 pennant, the club nosedived to last place in 1934. George Custer (25–13) posted the most victories of 1936 and added a .306 batting average, while Bill Posedel (20–10) would be especially effective in the playoffs. The Beavers had a knack for dramatic, late-inning surges behind an offense which starred outfielder Moose Clabaugh (.317, 20 HRs, 112 RBIs) and outfielder-first baseman John Frederick (.352). Portland fought its way to the league's best record, then nailed down the championship by winning the PCL's first Shaughnessy Playoffs.

The playoffs caused a dilemma among owners the next year. Sacramento, led by MVP Art Garibaldi (.327, 18 HRs, 23 SBs, 106 RBIs) and Tony Freitas (23–12), charged from last place in 1936 to the league's best record in 1937. But San Diego finished third,

*Barnacle Bill Posedel was 20–10 with Portland's 1936 pennant winners. He went 21–12 the next year, then was purchased by Brooklyn. Barnacle Bill returned to the PCL in 1947 with Seattle (12–8).*

— Courtesy Mariana York

behind Jim Chaplin (23–15) and strikeout leader Manny Salvo (19–13 with 196 Ks), then won eight games without a defeat in the playoffs. San Diego downed Sacramento in the first four games of the opener, then repeated the feat against Portland in the finals. PCL owners thereupon decided that in the future the team that finished the long regular schedule in first place would be declared league champions, while the playoff winners would be awarded the President's Cup and a cash bonus. The players' purse was increased to $12,500. The first-place team would receive the pennant and $2,500; the playoff winner would receive the President's Cup and $5,000; the runner-up would take home $2,500; and the other two playoff teams would earn $1,500 apiece.

Seattle's Art Hunt (.312, 39 HRs, 131 RBIs) repeated as home run and RBI leader in 1937. Sad Sam Gibson (19–8) of San Francisco led the PCL in winning percentage, and manager Lefty O'Doul inserted himself as a pinch hitter 44 times with outstanding results (.386). Although Vince DiMaggio had joined Joe in the big leagues, younger brother Dominic first put on a Seals uniform in

---

**Let 'Em Fight!**

During a 1937 game at San Francisco, Seals catcher Vince Monzo and Missions infielder Joe Vitter, who had played for the Seals earlier in the season, came up swinging after a close play at the plate. PCL President William C. Tuttle had spread the word that on-field fights should not be broken up, and play halted as members of both teams formed a ring and let the gladiators slug it out. When Vitter scornfully invited Monzo to put his face mask back on, the catcher removed his chest protector and shinguards.

The fight went on for several minutes, until three policemen came down from the stands and separated the pugilists. Monzo had a black eye and Vitter sported a knot on his forehead, but when the game resumed neither player was ejected! That evening Monzo and Vitter, who had been friends when both wore Seals uniforms, visited a bar and amiably settled their differences.

---

1937 (.306). After two more fine seasons, Dom became the third DiMaggio brother to reach the major leagues.

An important franchise move occurred prior to the 1938 season. Throughout the Depression the Missions had enjoyed little success on the field. Owner Herbert Fleischaker, a San Francisco brewer, suffered considerable business losses, and with the help of the league he transferred his club to Hollywood. Angels officials were reluctant to rent Wrigley Field, but finally agreed to let the new Stars use the stadium for one year. Gilmore Field opened in Hollywood in 1939, and local interests bought the club. Glamorous Hollywood was back in the PCL for the first time with its own ballpark.

At the age of 36 Smead Jolley returned to the Coast League, splitting the 1938 season between Hollywood and Oakland, winning his third PCL batting title (.350). The big outfielder had a solid season with Oakland in 1939 (.309), then closed out his legendary career by winning the hitting and RBI crowns of the Class B Western International League in 1940 (.373, 25 HRs, 181 RBIs) and 1941 (.345, 24 HRs, 128 RBIs). While posting a lifetime average of .366, Jolley had won seven batting titles in four leagues.

Speedy outfielder Frenchy Uhalt played minor league ball for 22 years (1928–49), including 20 seasons for Oakland, Hollywood and San Francisco of the PCL. As center fielder for the new Holly-

*In his 23-year career Tony Freitas won 342 minor league games, including 228 in the PCL. For six seasons, 1937–42, he was a 20-game winner for Sacramento.*

— Courtesy Ted Leach

wood Stars, he enjoyed his finest season in 1938 (.332 with a league-leading 32 stolen bases). San Francisco outfielder Ted Norbert won the first of four PCL home run crowns (.284, 30 HRs, 163 RBIs), and he added the RBI title as well. Seals player-manager Lefty O'Doul, now 41, cracked pinch hit home runs in both games of a Sunday doubleheader against Seattle on May 29. O'Doul was the first Coast Leaguer to accomplish this feat, although Joe Gordon matched his performance in 1952.

Frank Shellenback finally closed his 22-year playing career (315–192, plus 11 major league victories). The tall spitballer had pitched in the Coast League since 1920 (295–178, .624), establishing all-time records for most victories, highest winning percentage among the 12 PCL pitchers who would win more than 200 games, most innings pitched (4,185), and most complete games (361). San Diego's Manny Salvo (22–9, 191 Ks) won his second straight strikeout crown, and Seattle's Kewpie Dick Barrett hurled two complete game victories in a September 19 doubleheader over Sacramento. Dick Ward of San Diego had a poor season, but he pitched the game of his career on August 30 against Los Angeles.

Ward tossed no-hit ball for 12²/₃ innings, and finally settled for a two-hit shutout, beating the champion Angels 1–0 in 16 innings.

The best pitcher of the year was Fred Hutchinson (25–7 with a 2.48 ERA and a .313 batting average), a 20-year-old rookie who paced the PCL in victories, winning percentage and ERA in his first year of pro ball. Hutchinson led Seattle into the playoffs and was named MVP. Seattle had been acquired by dynamic Emil Sick, who erected a new stadium, hired Jack Lelivelt as manager, and rapidly built the club into a dynasty.

But Los Angeles won the 1938 pennant, behind first baseman Rip Russell (.318, 21 HRs, 114 RBIs), third sacker Charles English (.303, 19 HRs, 143 RBIs), second baseman Eddie Mayo (.332), and center fielder Jigger Statz (.317), who led the league in runs scored — at the age of 41! The best pitchers were Fay Thomas (18–8) and former slugger Gene Lillard (16–10), who had switched to pitching a year earlier and who was headed for a 20-win season until he broke an ankle.

But the Angels were defeated in the opening round of playoffs by the Sacramento Solons. San Francisco, led by Ted Norbert, Dom DiMaggio (.306), and Sad Sam Gibson (23–12 with a .314 batting average and nine pinch hitting efforts), reached the playoff finals. Solon lefthanders Tony Freitas (24–11) and Bill Walker (17–12) each won four games in the playoffs, and Sacramento claimed the 1938 President's Cup.

The next year Los Angeles threatened to repeat as pennant winners by reeling off a record 19 consecutive victories from April 2 through April 21. Former Gashouse Gang star Rip Collins had been purchased to play first base (.334, 26 HRs, 128 RBIs), and he led the league in home runs and RBIs. But Rip's performance tailed off during the latter half of the season, and his 26 homers made up the lowest championship total since 1923, while every previous RBI titlist had knocked in more than 128 runs. Jigger Statz (.311) became the fifth player in Coast League history, and the first man since 1923, to hit two homers in one inning. There was solid pitching from Julio Bonetti (20–5, including a complete game victory which required merely 66 pitches!), Ray Prim (20–17), and Fay Thomas (17–13), but Statz broke a thumb and there were other injuries that helped account for a drop to third place.

San Diego outfielder Dom Dellesandro won the batting title (.368) and Most Valuable Player Award; although his team failed

*Spencer Harris played 28 years, establishing the all-time minor league career records for runs, hits, doubles and total bases. He was in the PCL for eight seasons; in 1939 he hit .339 for Hollywood.*

— Courtesy Ted Leach

to make the playoffs, Dellesandro went up to the Cubs. Oakland second baseman Hugh Luby (.283) played in each of the Oaks' 176 games, and he did not miss a game through 1943; he went up to the New York Giants in 1944, but by then he had established a record of 866 consecutive games. ERA leader Sam Gibson (22–9, 2.24), shortstop Harvey Storey (.351), outfielders Dom DiMaggio (.360) and Ted Norbert (.305, 25 HRs, 105 RBIs), and 45-year-old manager Lefty O'Doul (.400 in 25 games) paced the Seals to a playoff berth.

Jack Lelivelt, who had skippered the magnificent Angel teams of 1933 and 1934, brought the 1939 flag to Seattle. Stolen base champ Jo Jo White (.287 with 47 steaks), shortstop Alan Strange (.335), first baseman George Archie (.330), and outfielder Edo Vanni (.325) led a strong offense. Hal Turpin (23–10) paced the league in victories, while Dick Barrett (22–15), Paul Gregory (18–11), and Les Webber (17–7) rounded out a pennant-winning pitching staff. For the second year in a row, Seattle lost the opening round of playoffs, but the Rainiers had just begun their championship run.

Sacramento again recorded the league's lowest team batting average — and again rode a strong mound corps to the playoff title. Jim Chaplin died during spring training, but the slack was taken up by strikeout leader Tony Freitas (21–18 with 172 Ks), Tom Seats (20–10), and relief ace Ira Smith (12–4).

Attendance totaled 2,199,270 in 1939. Many promotions now were in use which admitted kids free, but paid admissions were 1,662,800 — double that of 1936. Some of the juice that was injected into baseballs during the 1920s had been drained off by the late 1930s, as indicated by declining home run and RBI totals. But players continued to swing from the heels and exciting offense would remain a PCL trademark. Seattle had begun one of the PCL's greatest dynasties, while Sacramento was strengthened by becoming part of the massive farm system of the St. Louis Cardinals. Hollywood became the minor leagues' most glamorous franchise, as local stockholders included such film luminaries as Bing Crosby, Barbara Stanwyck, Gary Cooper, Cecil B. DeMille, and Robert Taylor, and fans flocked to new Gilmore Field to ogle movie stars as well as baseball stars. The Coast League had emerged from the Great Depression stronger than ever, but soon the circuit would have to face the uncertainties of a second World War.

# 1940–1949

## Baseball on the Coast During and After the War

By the beginning of the 1940s, World War II was under way in Europe. For a couple of seasons it was business as usual in the Coast League. Seattle continued its dynastic performance and talented athletes played superbly before enthusiastic crowds. Most minor leagues disbanded after the United States entered the war, but the PCL continued to operate, although there was a dropoff of the quality of play and of fan support. After the war, however, the Coast League led the minors in an incredible resurgence of baseball popularity. Indeed, on-field performances and attendance reached such impressive levels that owners and league officials launched a determined effort to obtain major league status. The league was so stable that the 1940s would be the only decade in PCL history in which there were no franchise movements. And only during the 1940s has the Coast League staged four-team playoffs every year; six times the team that finished first went on to win the playoffs as well. After Seattle relinquished its stranglehold on the throne room, Los Angeles won three pennants and San Francisco claimed four consecutive playoff titles.

Although the Coast League was dominated in 1940 by the Seattle Rainiers, Coast League pitching was dominated by Lou "The Mad Russian" Novikoff. In 1939 after leading the Three-I League

*Lou "The Mad Russian" Novikoff blasted his way to the Triple Crown in 1940 (.363, 41 HRs, 171 RBIs).*

— Courtesy Mariana York

in hitting (.367) the year before, Novikoff won the Texas League batting title (.368), then finished the season by tearing apart the PCL (.452 with 8 homers and 37 RBIs in 38 games). A notorious bad ball hitter, he walloped everything thrown at him in 1940 (.363, 41 HRs, 171 RBIs), winning the Triple Crown and also leading the league in hits (259), runs (147) and total bases (438 — a mark that has not been surpassed since 1940). After sparking the Angels to a second-place finish, Novikoff was purchased by the Chicago Cubs for $100,000.

Seattle southpaw Kewpie Dick Barrett (24–5) led the PCL in victories, strikeouts and winning percentage, and righthander Hal Turpin (23–11) was another outstanding member of a fine mound corps. Offensive leaders were first sacker George Archie (.324) and outfielder Jo Jo White (.295 with 35 steals). The Rainiers easily repeated as pennant winners. The year before, the club had been defeated by the Angels in the playoff opener after winning the flag, but in 1940 Seattle downed Oakland and Los Angeles to cop the playoff title.

The 1941 race was tighter, but Seattle outlasted a hard-hitting Sacramento club to become the first team since Vernon (1918–20)

*"Kewpie Doll" Dick Barrett was a mainstay of the Seattle dynasty. He was a 20-game winner seven times from 1935 through 1942. In 1940 he was 24–5 and in 1942 he was 27–13.*

— Courtesy Mariana York

to finish in first place three years in a row. Again the Rainiers were led by Dick Barrett (20–12) and Hal Turpin (20–6), and again the team also won the playoff series. Sacramento, behind player-manager Pepper Martin (.322), led the league in hitting, finished second in the pennant race, and battled until the seventh game of the playoff finals before bowing to Seattle. Third baseman Don Gutteridge (.309 with 46 steals) was the stolen base champ, and southpaw Wally Hebert (22–10) pitched artfully. But Sacramento's star was righthander Yank Terry (26–8, 2.31 ERA, 172 Ks), who won the pitcher's Triple Crown, was named MVP, then was purchased by the Boston Red Sox.

A 1941 innovation was the Coast League's first mid-season All-Star Game, played in San Francisco on Tuesday, July 29. The first major league All-Star contest had been staged in 1933. The mid-summer exhibition had become a highly popular event, stimulating numerous minor leagues to begin their own All-Star contests. The Coast League featured dream teams selected from the northernmost franchises and from the southern clubs. Attendance was a healthy 9,556, as the South defeated the North, 3–1.

The 1941 season had its tumultuous side. Broadway Bill Schuster, a fiery shortstop for Seattle and Los Angeles, was involved in several on-field altercations. In June Angels hurler Julio Bonetti, who had broken in with the club with a sparkling 20–5 record in 1939, was banned permanently from baseball after being accused by private detectives of receiving a large sum of money from a gambler. Bonetti frequented race tracks, and quite likely was being paid winnings on horse races by a bookie. He hired a lawyer but could not win reinstatement; shattered, Bonetti died at the age of 41 in 1952. In July 1941 Eddie Mayo, crack third baseman for the Angels, was suspended for one year by PCL President William C. Tuttle for allegedly spitting in the face of umpire Ray Snyder. Mayo fought his suspension more successfully than Bonetti, winning exoneration in September.

Important negotiations occurred through the 1941 season. St. Louis Browns owner Don Barnes had decided to move his franchise to Los Angeles. Phil Wrigley finally agreed to sell the Angels and Wrigley Field for $1,000,000. Sportsman's Park in St. Louis, owned by Barnes but used for home games by the Cardinals as well as the Browns, would be sold to the Cards to raise part of the LA purchase price. Scheduling and travel details were planned, and Barnes acquired sufficient votes from fellow owners to approve the move. The transfer question was the first agenda item for the American League on the opening day of the winter meetings of 1941 — Monday, December 8. But on Sunday, of course, the Japanese attacked Pearl Harbor, plunging the United States into war and baseball into uncertainty. The American League promptly voted down the Browns' transfer request. The movement of major league ball to one of the flagship cities of the Coast League would have exerted profound effects upon the PCL — and did in 1958, when Los Angeles and San Francisco both joined the National League.

During the weeks following Pearl Harbor there were concerns throughout Organized Baseball that there would be no professional play in 1942, and along the West Coast the possibility of Japanese attack put the PCL season in particular doubt. But Commissioner Landis formally queried President Roosevelt about the status of baseball, and FDR, a fan since boyhood, felt that professional baseball would be a needed diversion during wartime. On January 14, 1942, the President notified Landis by letter that Organized Baseball should be continued for the benefit of American morale. Coast League clubs began planning for spring training, and on March 24 Lieutenant General John DeWitt granted formal military permission for the circuit to open play. There were restrictions on night games, and on August 20 night contests were forbidden, a military restriction that would be continued during the 1943 season.

Enlistments and draft calls had comparatively little effect on baseball's manpower pool in 1942. Seattle returned many fine players from its championship roster, including ace pitchers Dick Barrett (27–13, 1.72 ERA, 178 Ks) and Hal Turpin (23–9, 2.07 ERA). Barrett and Turpin ranked one-two in the league's ERA race, and Kewpie Dick won the pitcher's Triple Crown. Turpin hurled a one-hitter over San Diego, while the 36-year-old Barrett enjoyed his finest season, winning 20 games for the seventh time in eight years. (Barrett spent the next three seasons in the National League, then pitched in the PCL until 1950. He won 325 games in the minors, including 234 PCL victories, and he set the all-time Coast League strikeout record — 1,866.) The Rainiers' offense could manage just 21 home runs the entire season and Seattle finished third, breaking its string of three consecutive pennants. But the experienced Rainiers rallied to defeat first-place Sacramento in the postseason opener, then downed LA in the finals to win a third successive playoff title.

Portland finished last for the fourth straight year, but Beaver outfielder Ted Norbert (.378, 28 HRs, 99 RBIs) won his third home run crown and only batting title. San Francisco's Robert Joyce (22–10) and Sam Gibson (20–12) again pitched impressively, and so did San Diego's Wally Hebert (22–15) and Jack Salveson (24–12), who hurled two complete game victories over Seattle in a September 20 doubleheader. The second All-Star contest was held in Hollywood, where Gilmore Field had become a popular gathering place for movie celebrities, and the South won a 1–0 pitchers' duel.

Los Angeles battled Sacramento to the wire for the 1942 pennant. The Angels were led by reliable southpaw Ray Prim (21–10), defending batting champ Johnny Moore (.347), third sacker Eddie Mayo (.307 with a club-high 110 RBIs), and slick-fielding first baseman Eddie Waitkus (.336). In 1949 while enjoying a fine season with the Phillies, Waitkus was badly wounded by an infatuated girl, an incident which inspired Bernard Malmud to write *The Natural*.

Pepper Martin molded the Solons in his scrappy image. Southpaw Tony Freitas (24–13) and righthander Sylvester Donnelly (21–10) provided a deadly pitching duo. Catcher Ray Mueller (.297 with 102 RBIs) was voted Most Valuable Player, outfielder Buster Adams (.309, 27 HRs, 107 RBIs) led the team in homers and RBIs, and former Angels slugger Gene Lillard was brought in to provide late-season batting punch (.340 in 29 games). In the last series of the year, the Angels came to Sacramento expecting to clinch the pennant. Needing to take three games out of seven, Los Angeles quickly won the first two games, and held a three-run lead in the eighth inning of the third contest. But Buster Adams and Ray Mueller hit back-to-back homers to lead a come-from-behind victory. Freitas tied the series the next day, and Gene Lillard whacked an 11th-inning, pinch hit homer to win Saturday's game. The season would end with Sunday's doubleheader, and LA still could win the pennant with a single victory. The Angels took a 5–0 lead in the first game, but Adams and Mueller again walloped back-to-back homers and Freitas nailed down another come-from-behind win in relief. Now warmed up, Freitas kept pitching and turned in a four-hitter in the nightcap to give Sacramento its fifth straight victory and its first Coast League pennant.

By 1943 manpower requirements of the armed forces were cutting deeply into baseball rosters, and transportation restrictions also made it difficult to organize minor league ball. The number of minor leagues plummeted from 31 in 1942 to just 10 in 1943, and only 10 circuits would operate in 1944. The Coast League continued play; indeed, despite the absence of night ball attendance was healthy, an endorsement of President Roosevelt's theory that baseball would be a needed diversion for war industry workers. In 1943 the PCL eliminated the All-Star Game and cut back its schedule to 22 weeks, not commencing play until April 17, which was the latest opening date in league history. For once the Coast League played a schedule close to the professional norm, 155 to 158 games apiece (until 1961 the major leagues scheduled 154 games per season, and most minor leagues tried to set up comparable schedules). Rosters were unstable in 1943, not only because of military demands but because the best players who remained in the Coast League were prime candidates to fill depleted major league lineups. For the next three seasons, Coast League fans would watch a great many older players (44-year-old player-manager Charlie Root was Holly-

*LA Angels, 1943 champs. Ted Norbert (top right) won four home run titles, and the 1942 batting crown (.378). Charles English (middle row, fourth from right) and Rip Russell (middle row, second from right) also were feared sluggers.*

— Courtesy Ted Leach

wood's best pitcher at 15–5 in 1943), as well as rookies who would have been too young and green (15-year-old catcher Bill Sarni, a star at Los Angeles High School, played 33 games for the Angels in 1943) to handle the level of pre-war PCL play. During the war years, it also was necessary to take slight shortcuts in the manufacture of baseballs, which further reduced offensive production (in 1943 Seattle hit just 15 home runs as a team, Oakland totaled 17 and San Diego collected 18, while San Francisco merely managed 14 the next year, Sacramento 16 and San Diego 17).

Los Angeles dominated the Coast League in 1943, setting a record early in the season by playing 21 games without a defeat (there was one tie during the string). Late in June the Angels hosted second-place San Francisco, won six contests of the seven-game series, then coasted to the pennant. Managed by Bill Sweeney, Los Angeles finished 21 games ahead of the Seals with a brilliant record (110–45, .710), while leading the league in team hitting and fielding, and setting a standard for fewest strikeouts in a season (390). Right fielder Andy Pafko, on the eve of a long major league career, won the batting and RBI crowns (.356, 18 HRs, 118

RBIs) and was named Most Valuable Player while center fielder John Ostrowski (.282, 21 HRs, 82 RBIs) was the home run champ. Red Lynn (21–8) led the league in victories, Jodie Phipps (17–5) posted the best winning percentage, and Paul Gehrman (20–7), Ken Raffensberger (19–11) and Don Osborn (10–1) also were especially effective.

Despite the efforts of ERA leader Alphs Brazle (11–8, 1.69) and stolen base champ Oral Burnett (.275 with 32 steals), last-place Sacramento established records for fewest victories and lowest winning percentage (41–114, .265). Although the Rainiers had lost most of their dynasty players, Seattle finished third and stunned pennant-winning LA with a four-game sweep in the playoff opener. San Francisco, behind outfielders Harry Steinbacher (.318 with 105 RBIs) and Frenchy Uhalt and pitchers Robert Joyce (20–12) and A. P. Epperly (16–5), won the first of four consecutive playoff titles.

In 1944 although LA's championship roster was decimated by promotions and the military, Bill Sweeney somehow fashioned another pennant winner. Young Bill Sarni returned to serve as backup catcher; Rip Russell, who had retired to stay on his California farm rather than go to the Phils, was persuaded to play first base (.315 with a club-high 17 homers); the Cubs released Ray Prim, who again became the Angels' ace (22–10 with a 1.70 ERA). Ted Norbert was picked up and placed in left field (.289); longtime hitting star Johnny Moore was acquired to fill as an outfielder and pinch hitter (.325). Sweeney fit the pieces together with an expert hand and the Angels repeated as PCL champs for the third time in franchise history.

In the early games of 1944, hitting was anemic throughout the league. PCL officials finally admitted that the baseballs were 1942 vintage and had been in storage. New baseballs were acquired, but the quality was poor and hitting results remained disappointing. Oakland's Les Scarsella won the batting crown with the lowest average (.329) since 1916; he played first base and outfield, he posted a 1.75 ERA and a 3–1 record in 67 innings as a lefthanded pitcher, and he was named MVP for his versatility. Hollywood left fielder Frank Kelleher (.329 with a league-leading 29 homers and 121 RBIs) missed the Triple Crown by a fraction of a percentage point (Scarsella hit .32886 to Kelleher's .32854).

Night games returned in 1944, and so did a double dose of the

*Hollywood Stars, 1944. Frank Kelleher (top, fourth from right) led the PCL in hom-
ers and RBIs, and missed the batting title by a fraction of a point. Babe Herman
(middle, far left) starred for Seattle in 1925, spent 12 years in the big league, then
ripped the ball for Hollywood from 1939 through 1944 (.346 in '44). Longtime Cub
star Charlie Root (middle row, center).*

— Courtesy Ted Leach

All-Star Game. As if to make up for 1943, when the exhibition was
not staged, there were two All-Star contests on Monday, August 7,
1944. One game was held in Hollywood, the other in San Francisco, and teams representing the South won both contests.

During this dead-ball season pitching dominated play. Sacramento southpaw Clem Dreisewerd (20–9, 1.61) was the ERA
champ. For the second year in a row, San Diego righthander Frank
Dasso (20–19 with 253 Ks) was the strikeout king. Marino Pieretti
(26–13 with 8 shutouts), Ad Liska (18–9), and southpaw Roy Helser (20–16) pitched Portland into the playoffs. Playoff champion
San Francisco was led by Robert Joyce (21–20), Ray Harrell (20–
18), and lefthander Tom Seats (25–13). Seats pitched two of his six
shutouts on the same day in an August 6 doubleheader (6–0, then
3–0 in the seven-inning nightcap) over Sacramento. The only other
Coast League pitchers ever to have hurled two shutouts in one day
were Vean Gregg (1910) and Harry Ables (1912).

The military demand for baseball players reached its greatest

*A longtime PCL shortstop, Johnny O'Neill enjoyed his best year when he hit .315 for Portland's 1945 champs.*

— Courtesy Mariana York

heights in 1945, as public criticism of healthy young men in baseball uniforms prompted draft boards to reclassify athletes who previously had been deferred. But even as the quality of play declined still further because of the scarcity of good players, the popularity of the game rose. The war in Europe ended early in the season, and fighting in the Pacific stopped before the end of play in 1945. The number of minor leagues increased from 10 to 12 in 1945, and attendance jumped as war-weary Americans felt a victorious uplifting of spirits and flocked to ballparks throughout the country. Last-place Hollywood enjoyed an attendance of 362,000 in 1945, and seventh-place Los Angeles hosted 350,000. It was the only time in the history of the PCL that two LA franchises brought up the bottom of the standings in the same year. The Coast League again staged two All-Star games on Monday, July 16. The South won in Los Angeles, but the North finally emerged triumphant, 13–3, in Portland — it was the first time in six tries that a northern team had won a PCL All-Star contest. Cumulative attendance for the two games was 11,285, as opposed to 7,924 in 1944, a 42 percent increase. The league lengthened the 1945 schedule back to 180-plus games.

*Jo Jo White starred for Seattle's superb clubs from 1939 through 1942, won the 1945 batting crown for Sacramento (.355), then returned to Seattle as manager.*

— Courtesy Mariana York

Portland outdueled Seattle for the 1945 pennant on the strength of a deep pitching staff which featured Ad Liska (20–12), Burt Pulford (20–11), and Joe Helser (20–14). San Diego starter-reliever Vallie Eaves (21–15 with 187 Ks in 52 games) was the strikeout champ and one of nine 20-game winners in the league. But the best pitcher in the PCL was Seals righthander Robert Joyce (31–11 with 35 complete games and a 2.13 ERA), the first 30-game winner since Buck Newsom in 1933. Joyce led the league in victories, winning percentage, complete games, innings pitched and ERA. The 30-year-old Californian propelled San Francisco to a third successive playoff championship, and was named the PCL's Most Valuable Player.

Another great player, 49-year-old Herman "Old Folks" Pillette, retired after the 1945 season. His 29-year career had started in 1917 and included a record 23 seasons in the PCL. He pitched for Portland, Vernon, Mission, Seattle, Hollywood, San Diego and Sacramento, compiling a 226–235 Coast League mark. His son, Duane, soon followed him to the PCL, then pitched in the big leagues from 1949 through 1956.

Batting champ Jo Jo White (.355 with 40 steals) sparked Sac-

*A former Yankee infielder, Joe Buzas played for Seattle in 1946 and 1947. Now he is well into his fourth decade as a baseball executive, operating 66 minor league clubs. Currently he is president and owner of the Portland Beavers.*

— Courtesy Mariana York

ramento to a playoff berth, along with Guy Fletcher (24–14) and stolen base leader Gene Handley (.307 with 56 thefts). Ted Norbert, now wearing a Seattle uniform, won a record fourth home run crown with a modest season (.258, 23 HRs, 109 RBIs).

Baseball men sensed the tremendous thirst for recreation in postwar America. Major league attendance would jump by 71 percent in 1946, and the number of minor leagues rose from 12 in 1945 to 42 the next year. PCL President Clarence "Pants" Rowland petitioned other minor leagues regarding the intention of his circuit to attain big league status, then at the winter meetings in December 1945, the American and National leagues were asked to recognize the Coast League as a third major league. The main point of this request was to permit the PCL, the most independent of all minor leagues (only Los Angeles was owned by a major league club), to be free from the major league draft and to be able to option Coast League players to the other Triple A circuits without losing title to them. Major league owners soon denied the request, but promised to reconsider the proposal in the future. Coast Leaguers continued to refine the idea, shaping a plan for a five-year period as an inde-

## Mr. Coast League

Frank Joseph O'Doul was born in San Francisco in 1897. Reared in Frisco's tough Butchertown, he became an outstanding lefthanded pitcher with a keen batting eye. Big and strong at the age of 20, he pitched for Des Moines in the Western League, then moved up to the Seals for his second professional season. He went 12–8 in 1918 and appeared in 22 games as a pinch hitter or runner. O'Doul spent 1919 and 1920 with the New York Yankees, but he pitched in just eight innings in two seasons, although he played occasionally as an outfielder or pinch hitter.

Back in San Francisco for the 1921 season, he notched a 25–9 record and hit .338 in 74 games. He was promoted back to the Yankees, but played in just eight games in 1922, then spent 1923 on the Red Sox bench. O'Doul returned again to the PCL in 1924, determined to become a full-time outfielder. The experiment was a roaring success. He hit .392 for Salt Lake City in 1924, then .375 in 1925, leading the Coast League in at-bats (825), hits (309) and triples. The franchise moved to Hollywood in 1926, and O'Doul hit .338. In 1927 he was back with San Francisco, batting .378 and stealing 40 bases; he led the league in hits and runs scored, and was named Most Valuable Player.

At the age of 31 he went back to the big time, spending the next seven seasons with the New York Giants, Philadelphia Phils and Brooklyn Dodgers. In 1929 he won the National League batting championship with a .398 mark, and established a league record with 254 base hits. He hit .383 in 1930, and won another NL batting title in 1932 by hitting .368. In 970 major league games he had a lifetime batting average of .349.

He returned once more to San Francisco as player-manager of the Seals in 1935, appearing in 68 games and leading his team to the PCL championship. O'Doul restricted himself to a pinch hitting role, rattling out a .386 average in 44 games in 1937 when he was 40, although he pitched in five games in 1939 and 1940. Off the roster after 1940, he appeared as a pinch hitter once in 1944 and once the next season. Although he wanted to become a big league manager, Seals owner Paul I. Fagan kept him by paying O'Doul more than he could make in the majors, $45,000 to $50,000 per year.

Beginning in 1943 O'Doul produced four consecutive playoff winners, and the Seals made six consecutive playoff appearances, 1943–48. He was named Seals vice-president in 1948,

(continued)

and his colorful, outgoing personality made him enormously popular with San Francisco fans. But the franchise finally entered a
decline, and following a last-place finish in 1951, O'Doul left the
Seals after 17 years as manager. He managed San Diego for the
next three seasons, winning a pennant in 1954 after a tight race
with Hollywood. In 1955 he managed Oakland, then moved with
the franchise to Vancouver the next year, rapping out a single in a
final pinch hitting appearance — at the age of 59. O'Doul wrapped
up his managerial career with Seattle in 1957, but until his death in
San Francisco in 1969, he traveled around — usually clad in green
suits and sport coats — as a genial ambassador for PCL baseball.

---

pendent circuit, during which time stadiums would be expanded to
major league standards. Since Sacramento and perhaps Portland
might prove unable to support major league ball, Denver, Houston
and Dallas were considered as possible replacement cities. After
five years the PCL would be recognized as a third major league.

The leading advocate of this plan was wealthy San Francisco
owner Paul I. Fagan, who went to great expense to transform Seals
Stadium into a magnificent facility. The Seals' minimum salary
was set at $5,000, the major league minimum, and Fagan paid his
stars and manager Left O'Doul more than they could earn in the
major leagues. The Seals' clubhouse was sumptuously outfitted,
hotels and restaurants were first class on road trips, the team took
spring training in Hawaii in 1946, and the Seals became the first
minor league team to travel regularly by plane. Fagan urged fellow
PCL owners to follow his example, but most men lacked his wealth,
and other clubs would be unable to maintain major league standards and San Francisco's independence, factors which in future
years would prove fatal to the attempt to become a third big league.

San Francisco stormed to the 1946 pennant behind the brilliant performance of Larry Jansen (30–6 with a 1.57 ERA, second
lowest in league history), who led the PCL in victories, winning
percentage, complete games, innings and ERA, and who became
the Coast League's last 30-game winner (the next year Jansen was
21–5 with the New York Giants). The Seals' greatest challenge
came from second-place Oakland, now managed by Casey Stengel.
Oaks first baseman Les Scarsella (.332, 22 HRs, 91 RBIs in 121
games) did not qualify for the batting championship, but won an
unprecedented second MVP award. Oakland beat the Angels in a

*Seattle Rainiers, 1946. Lou Novikoff is seated at far right.*
— Courtesy Mariana York

seven-game playoff opener, but the Seals won the finals, capping their championship season with their fourth straight playoff title.

San Francisco drew an astounding 670,563, establishing a minor league club record for a single season. When the All-Star Game was played in San Francisco on August 19, more than 13,000 fans watched the Seals defeat stars of the other seven teams, 7–0. When Oakland came across the bay for a key series, the seven games attracted a record attendance of 111,622. Oakland also had excellent attendance, Los Angeles pulled in over 501,000 paid admissions, the Hollywood Stars' totals were even higher, and league attendance was an eye-popping 3,718,716.

The next year was even better, as San Francisco and Los Angeles staged a neck-and-neck pennant race. Attendance figures were phenomenal: San Francisco (640,643) almost matched the previous year's total; Los Angeles drew a record number (622,485); fourth-place Oakland (590,327) was impressive; Seattle (548,368) and Hollywood (500,327) pulled in large crowds despite losing records; and even last-place San Diego (353,951) enjoyed enviable numbers. Attendance across the league (4,068,432) set a National Association record, and when Los Angeles hosted the All-Stars on

*Seattle third baseman Hillis Layne won the 1947 batting title (.367).*
— Courtesy Mariana York

August 11, another record (19,851) was established. The Angels and Seals finished the schedule in a dead heat, and a one-game playoff was set for Wrigley Field. The Angels won, 5–0, before 22,996 fans — with thousands more turned away. LA and Hollywood enjoyed a combined attendance comfortably exceeding 1,100,000, a fact which could not fail to impress major league executives. President Rowland continued to press for the five-year plan, but the big leagues eventually would move to the West Coast in the manner intended for 1942 — transfer of existing franchises to key Coast League cities, rather than accepting the PCL as a third major circuit.

Seattle third baseman Hillis Layne (.367) was the 1947 batting champ, while San Diego outfielder-first sacker Max West (.306, 43 HRs, 124 RBIs) won his first home run and RBI titles (there would be more from the ex-big leaguer). Lou Novikoff had his final big season (.325, 21 HRs, 114 RBIs) with Seattle, and Hollywood first baseman Tony Lupien (.341, 21 HRs, 110 RBIs and 40 steals) was named MVP.

Despite greatly improved offensive production, there were several notable pitching performances. Forty-year-old Tommy

*Infielder Tony York played for LA in 1944, Seattle from 1946–50, and Sacramento in 1951. He hit .297 in 1949.*

— Courtesy Mariana York

Bridges, a Detroit Tiger star for 16 seasons, posted the Coast League's best ERA (7–3, 1.64 ERA in 13 games) and tossed a no-hitter for Portland against the Seals. Although listed in contemporary sources as the ERA champ, Bridges only pitched 104 innings, and today the PCL *Record Book* proclaims San Francisco's Robert Chesnes (22–8, 2.32 ERA) as the 1947 ERA winner. Angels left-hander Cliff Chambers (24–9 with 175 Ks) led the league in wins and strikeouts. Chambers pitched a five-hit shutout to defeat San Francisco and clinch the pennant playoff for Los Angeles. Casey Stengel again guided Oakland into postseason play, and his Oaks beat arch-rival San Francisco in the opening round. But in the finals the Angels downed Oakland in five games, giving Los Angeles — winners of more pennants than any other Coast League team — the only playoff title in the history of the franchise.

In 1948 Stengel led Oakland to its first pennant in 21 years. There was a tight flag chase with Lefty O'Doul's Seals, led by batting champ Gene Woodling (.385, 22 HRs, 107 RBIs) and first baseman Mike Rocco (.300, 27 HRs, 149 RBIs). San Francisco's best pitchers were Con Dempsey (16–11 with 171 Ks and a 2.10 ERA), the strikeout and ERA leader, and southpaw Bill Werle

*Four of Casey Stengel's "Nine Old Men" who helped bring the 1948 pennant to Oakland. Left to right: Ernie Lombardi, Billy Raimondi, Cookie Lavagetto and Dario Lodigiani.*

— Courtesy Oakland Public Library

(17–7). But Stengel's team featured the "Nine Old Men," experienced big leaguers such as 40-year-old Oakland native Ernie Lombardi, longtime National League infielder Cookie Lavagetto (.304 in 86 games), and former American League home run champ Nick Etten (.313, 43 HRs, 155 RBIs). There were talented youngsters such as 20-year-old Billy Martin (.277), and Stengel juggled his 25-man roster incessantly, perfecting the masterful style that would bring him a succession of pennants with the New York Yankees. Stengel also had a deep pitching staff which included Ralph Buxton (13–3), reliever Floyd Speer (12–3), and southpaws Earl Jones (13–6) and Aldon Wilkie (11–6). The Oaks nosed out San Francisco by two games, then went on to win the playoff title.

Los Angeles also made the 1948 playoffs, behind outfielders Cliff Alberson (.329, 34 HRs, 103 RBIs) and Ed Sauer (.305, 16 HRs, 121 RBIs), and righthanded victory leader Red Lynn (19–10). Aside from the war-shortened season of 1918, it was the first year in PCL history that the league had failed to produce a 20-game winner. Seattle, under player-manager Jo Jo White, battled all the way to the playoff finals. Defending batting champ Hillis

*The September 1947 cover of the* Pacific Coast Baseball News, *a publication of several pages featuring stories and photos about the PCL.*

— Courtesy Mariana York

Layne (.342) had another fine season for the Rainiers, and Kewpie Dick Barrett (15–13) pitched a seven-inning perfect game against Sacramento on May 16. San Diego outfielder-first baseman Jack Graham (.293 with 48 homers and 136 RBIs in just 138 games) was the home run champ and won the newly established Charles E. Graham Award as MVP. The RBI title went to Hollywood left fielder Gus Zernial (.322, 40 HRs, 156 RBIs), who walloped home runs in four consecutive at-bats against San Diego on May 13 and 19, then cracked two homers in one inning against Sacramento on June 6.

The 1948 All-Star Game, won by a southern team over the northern stars, was held in San Francisco before a fine crowd of 14,210. San Francisco again led the league in attendance (606,563), and Oakland also drew well (552,072). But these totals were down from the previous year, while Los Angeles (576,372) and sixth-place Hollywood (416,725) experienced serious drops in paid admissions. Overall, PCL attendance was down more than 400,000 from 1947. Los Angeles and Hollywood had begun televising home games late in 1947 and increased their TV schedules in 1948 and 1949. Televised baseball soon would have a devastating effect on

## PORTLAND "LUCKY BEAVERS"–1948

*Portland's 1948 club featured 1946 batting champ Harvey Storey (middle row, second from right), veteran hurler Ad Liska (bottom, second from right), former Detroit Tiger star Tommy Bridges (middle row, second from left), and future big league pitcher Duane Pillette (top row, center), who was the son of longtime PCL hurler Herman Pillette.* — Courtesy Portland Beavers

*For years Seattle owner Emil Sick sent out large, handsome, color holiday cards centered around his ball club.*

— Courtesy Mariana York

## The PCL's First Black Players

*One of the PCL's first black players, Artie Wilson, won the 1949 batting title (.348).*

— Courtesy Oakland Public Library

Jackie Robinson played for Montreal of the International League in 1947 (batting champ — .349), then became the first black in the big leagues with Brooklyn in 1948. During the latter year catcher John Ritchey, a lefthanded hitter, signed with San Diego (.323 in 103 games), thus becoming the first black to play in the Coast League. The next year Ritchey (.257 in 112 games) was joined on the San Diego roster by outfielder Artie Wilson, a lefthanded batter from the Negro American League. Wilson played 31 games with the Padres before being dealt to Oakland for the remainder of the year. Playing in a total of 165 games, Wilson led the PCL in hitting and stolen bases (.348 with 47 steals). Also in 1949 righthander Booker McDaniels pitched for last-place Los Angeles (8–9 in 18 games). San Diego employed future major league star Minnie Minoso (.297 with 22 homers) in 1949, along with the legendary Negro League slugger Luke Easter. The 6'4½, 240-pound first baseman was 34, but he pounded out a .363 average with 25 homers and 92 RBIs in just 80 games, and Easter was quickly pro-

(continued)

moted to the Cleveland Indians (and he would play professional ball until he was 49). In 1950 Minnie Minoso (.339, 20 HRs, 30 SBs, 115 RBIs) was joined in San Diego by RBI leader Harry Simpson (.323, 33 HRs, 156 RBIs). The next year Sacramento's Bob Boyd (.342 with 41 steals) was the stolen base leader, and in 1952, while playing for Seattle, he was the batting champ (.320). By this time there were numerous blacks in the PCL, and they have starred in every season for the past four decades.

minor league attendance. But the Coast League enjoyed a slight increase in attendance in 1949 (90,000), while the number of minor leagues moved up to 59 and paid attendance throughout the minors reached an all-time high of nearly 42,000,000.

Prior to the 1949 season, Hollywood switched its major league affiliation from the Chicago White Sox to the Brooklyn Dodgers. Brooklyn had a splendid farm system built by Branch Rickey, and the Dodgers had corralled so many talented players that they needed another Triple A club in order to give top prospects adequate playing time. Hollywood won the 1949 pennant, and remained a power franchise until leaving the Coast League nine years later. Fred Haney was hired as manager of the Stars, and his stable of players included MVP Irv Noren (.330, 29 HRs, 130 RBIs), third sacker Jim Baxes (.287, 24 HRs, 108 RBIs), veteran slugger Frank Kelleher (.253, 29 HRs, 90 RBIs), righthander Pinky Woods (23–12), and ERA leader Willard Ramsdell (18–12, 2.60). Hollywood beat out Oakland for the flag by a five-game margin, then defeated Sacramento and San Diego in postseason play to become the fourth consecutive pennant-winner also to win the playoffs.

Now managed by Charlie Dressen, Oakland led the league in team hitting and produced the batting champ, infielder Artie Wilson (.348 with 47 steals), who also won the stolen base title, and who played for San Diego early in the season. San Diego led the league in homers (187), and lefthanded slugger Max West (.291, 48 HRs, 166 RBIs) won the combined homer-RBI title for the second time, while drawing a record 201 walks from wary pitchers. Padres infielder Al Rosen (.319) and speedy outfielder Minnie Minoso (.297) were on their way to impressive big league careers. Jesse Flores led San Diego's mound staff (21–10), while other quality pitching performances around the league came from Seattle's Guy Fletcher (23–12) and Charles Shanz (22–17), Portland's Harold

Saltzman (23–13), and San Francisco's Con Dempsey (17–11 with 164 Ks), who was the PCL strikeout king for the second year in a row.

The 1940s had been an exciting decade, a period of unprecedented stability and on-field play which alternated from dominance by hitters to dominance by pitchers, then again by hitters. The dead-ball pitchers era came while the PCL overcame the difficulties imposed by World War II and provided a welcome distraction for the war industry workers and off-duty military personnel of the West Coast. In the postwar years there was an offensive explosion fueled by a host of talented returning players. The PCL enjoyed unprecedented prosperity and manuevered to become a western major league, unaware that the 1950s would bring fundamental changes to baseball's most successful and prestigious minor league.

# 1950–1959

## Decade of Change

The 1950s brought the most revolutionary changes in the entire history of the Pacific Coast League. Attendance continued to decline severely, a trend common to all minor leagues. By the end of the decade there were only 21 minor leagues (there were 59 in 1949), and total attendance in the minors dropped from 42,000,000 in 1949 to 12,000,000 in 1959. The PCL found it impractical to continue to try to secure major league status, although for six seasons the circuit was granted a unique "Open" Classification. In 1958 the two largest PCL cities, Los Angeles and San Francisco, acquired National League teams, and the fundamental structure of the circuit was destroyed. The Coast League would never be the same.

Before the opening of the 1950 season, San Francisco owner Paul I. Fagan, frustrated that his efforts to elevate the PCL to major league status had been ignored by big league executives, warned that the circuit might pull out of Organized Baseball and operate independently. Commissioner Happy Chandler met with Fagan to reassure him that the major leagues would address the concerns of the Coast League, and at the end of the season it was announced that a new AAAA classification might be conferred on the PCL.

In an effort to increase shaky attendance, the 1950 schedule

---

### Rookie Homers on First Pitch

On June 24, 1950, Dave Melton, a 21-year-old shortstop who had just been signed off the campus at Stanford University by San Francisco, reported to the Seals at Gilmore Field in Hollywood. Arriving too late to take batting practice, he donned a uniform and watched as the Stars built an 8–4 lead behind the pitching of right-hander Jack Salveson, who would go on to win the ERA title. But in the ninth inning, with a runner on base, Melton was sent up to pinch hit. A lefthanded batter, Melton promptly walloped Salveson's first pitch to the opposite field, 360 feet over the left field fence for a home run. Although the Seals lost to Hollywood, 8–6, Melton had the satisfaction of homering off the first pitch he saw in Organized Baseball.

---

was expanded to 200 games. It was the first time since 1930 that the Coast League had played 200 games, but total attendance dropped despite the extra games, and the PCL never again would stage a schedule of such length. The All-Star Game, played at Sacramento before the smallest crowd (6,424) since 1944, was discontinued. Prior to the start of the 1950 season, it was decided to eliminate the Shaughnessy Playoffs, which had been in effect since 1936.

Skippered by Charlie Dressen, Oakland outlasted San Diego for the 1950 pennant. Oaks outfielder George Metkovich (.315, 24 HRs, 141 RBIs) was named MVP, and the team led the league in hitting behind a host of productive batters, including Earl Rapp (.347, 24 HRs, 147 RBIs) and pitcher Allen Gettel (23–7, with a .348 average in 54 games). San Diego, paced by outfielders Minnie Minoso (.339, 20 HRs, 115 RBIs, 30 steals) and Harry Simpson (.323, 33 HRs and a league-leading 156 RBIs), along with Jack Graham (.293, 33 HRs, 136 RBIs), featured a potent offense which topped the PCL in homers. Hollywood left fielder Frank Kelleher (.270, 40 HRs, 135 RBIs), was the home run champ, and on April 16, Sacramento first baseman Steve Souchak (.292, 25 HRs, 99 RBIs) cracked home runs in the seventh, eighth and ninth innings against the Angels. Angels outfielder Frank Baumholtz (.379 with 254 hits) was the batting champ, and he was the last Coast Leaguer to rap out more than 250 hits in a season.

After sporting new pinstripe uniforms in their season opener on Tuesday, March 28, 1950, the Hollywood Stars unveiled a rev-

*In 1950 the Hollywood Stars attempted to introduce shorts as a uniform innovation designed to improve speed. Left to right, Ed Saner, Glen Moulder and Audy Skurski.*

— Courtesy Ted Leach

olutionary sartorial innovation a few days later. On Saturday, April Fools' Day, the Stars came out attired in pinstriped shorts, complemented by knee socks and rayon T-shirts. The crowd was astounded, but manager Fred Haney insisted that the Stars would be speedier, and the team proceeded to win eight of their first nine in shorts. Haney had determined upon the experiment after watching a British soccer team on tour. Opposing players were openly scornful, and even though the Stars continued to wear the shorts on weekends and holidays, after three years the uniform briefs discreetly vanished.

In 1951 the schedule was reduced to 168 games, and the traditional seven-game series was discarded for the greater variety of three- and four-game series. PCL directors decided to reinstate the Shaughnessy Playoffs, although the three seven-game series would be reduced to best-two-of-three in the opening round and best-three-of-five in the finals. Seattle won the 1951 pennant over Hollywood, then went on to defeat the Stars, three games to two, for the playoff title. After the season the Coast League again rejected the Shaughnessy Plan, and there would be no further playoff series in

*The grandstand at Seals Stadium was not covered.*
— Courtesy Oakland Public Library

the PCL until 1963, when the circuit split into two divisions. It also was decided to return to the familiar week-long, seven-game series.

Seattle's 1951 champions were led by outfielder Jungle Jim Rivera (.352, 20 HRs, 112 RBIs), who won the batting title and the MVP award. The Rainiers' manager, Hall of Famer Rogers Hornsby, enjoyed a fine collection of pitchers, including ERA titlist Jim Davis (11–6, 2.44), victory leader Marv Grissom (20–11), and percentage leader Skinny Brown (16–6). Former major league star Joe Gordon, now player-manager at Sacramento, was the home run and RBI champ (.299, 43 HRs, 136 RBIs). Future major league star Dee Fondy (.376 in 70 games) clouted grand-slam home runs on consecutive days, September 3 and 4, while playing first base for LA against Hollywood. At the start of the season San Francisco established an unwanted record, losing the first 13 games of the year. The Seals finished last and drew fewer than 200,000.

Attendance across the league dropped by nearly one-third in 1951. Hollywood, which had been televising almost all home games, saw paid admissions fall to little more than half of the 1946 and 1947 totals, despite an excellent 1951 club. Televised baseball games probably proved less of a problem than network programming, as former fans chose to stay at home in front of a TV set. A major league Game of the Day began to be broadcast coast to coast over Mutual Radio in 1950, and the regular diet of big league ball made fans much more conscious that the PCL was a minor league. The rapid spread of Little League baseball, with two or three games per week and frequent practices, kept families away from professional ballparks in droves. And with the advent of home air conditioning an evening at the ballpark no longer was the best way to cool off on a warm summer night. By 1963 the number of minor leagues was reduced to just 18 and paid attendance was merely 9,963,174 (compared to 59 leagues and attendance of 41,872,762 in 1949).

Despite the plunge in attendance in 1951, the Coast League continued to press for an elevation in classification. In August 1951 the PCL announced that if it continued to be subject to the major league draft, the league would withdraw from Organized Baseball. The major leagues felt especially vulnerable because Congressional hearings were being held on baseball's exemption from anti-trust laws, and the situation involving the Pacific Coast League was receiving special focus. Major league owners decided to try to mollify the PCL by establishing an Open Classification, which would require a total population of 10,000,000 in league cities, with an aggregate ballpark seating capacity of 120,000 and average attendance over the previous five years of 2,250,000. All salary limitations were removed, players were not subject to the major league draft until they had five years experience, and the Open Classification league would have first call on drafted players who were sent back to the minors. The only circuit ever to attain Open Classification was the PCL, which retained this unique status until the landmark events of 1958.

Hoping that Open Classification would lead to major league status, the PCL expanded the 1952 schedule to 180 games.

Hollywood won the pennant, outdistancing their only serious challenger, defending champion Oakland. Fred Haney had a speedy offense and strong pitching. Left fielder Carlos Bernier (.301 with 65 steals) brought the first of five consecutive stolen base titles to Hollywood; after spending the next year with Pittsburgh, Hollywood's new affiliate, Bernier returned to record two more of the titles himself, in 1955 and 1956. The PCL's Most Valuable Player in 1952 was Johnny Lindell (24–9 with 190 Ks), who

*Left to right: George Kelly, a San Francisco native who was named to the Hall of Fame in 1973; Oakland manager Charlie Dressen; longtime National League star Cookie Lavagetto.*

— Courtesy Oakland Public Library

led the league in victories, winning percentage and strikeouts, and who frequently doubled up in the outfield.

LA's veteran lefthanded slugger, Max West, won his third PCL home run title (.262, 35 HRs, 91 RBIs). Joe Gordon, manager of last-place Portland, tied Lefty O'Doul's 1938 record when he walloped pinch hit homers in both games of a September 16 doubleheader against Los Angeles. On August 8 Portland righthander Fred Sanford gave up three home runs on consecutive pitches in the second inning of a game against the Oaks. Oakland reliever Mario Candini (9–6), despite not entering the PCL as a free agent until the season was more than a month old, established a new record by appearing in 69 games. On Thursday, April 4, Seals righthander Elmer Singleton pitched 12¹/₃ innings of no-hit, no-run ball against Sacramento; finally tiring, he gave up a run on three hits in the 13th and lost a heartbreaker, 1–0. While playing for Seattle in 1955, Singleton pitched — and won — a seven-inning no-hitter against San Diego.

In 1953 the Boston Braves moved to Milwaukee and set a National League attendance record by drawing 1,826,397 fans, a spec-

*A 1950 confrontation with an umpire.*
— Courtesy Oakland Public Library

tacular demonstration of the possibilities of transferring a major league franchise into a new area. Bill Veeck had been denied permission by the American League to move his St. Louis Browns to Milwaukee, and rumors erupted that the Browns would be in Los Angeles by 1954. In the face of declining attendance and revenue across the PCL, the loss of Los Angeles to the major leagues posed a crucial threat to the Coast League.

After leading the Hollywood Stars to the 1952 pennant, Fred Haney became manager of the Pittsburgh Pirates. Colorful, outgoing Bobby Bragan, a seven-year veteran of the National League, replaced Haney, then guided the Stars to a second consecutive championship. Johnny Lindell, Carlos Bernier, and other key players had been promoted to the Pirates, but Frank Kelleher (.329 in 1953), Jim Walsh (16–9), Red Lynn (10–4), stolen base champion Tom Saffell, and right fielder Ted Beard (.286 with 17 homers) were among several productive returnees. In an April 4 game against San Diego, Beard walloped four consecutive home runs, and later in the month he tied Mickey Heath's 1930 record by collecting 12 consecutive base hits. The best of Hollywood's newcomers were George O'Donnell (20–12), leader of the pitching staff,

---

**Invincible Tony Ponce**

Righthander Tony Ponce began 1953 with Ventura of the Class C California League. Ventura finished in last place, and Ponce (15–20 with 320 hits and 186 runs in 279 innings) set new league records for hits and runs yielded, while tying the old mark for losses. But San Francisco gambled and brought him up late in the season, whereupon Ponce suddenly came to life. In his first start on August 28 he beat Oakland, 15–2. The next week he won three decisions from Hollywood's championship club. During the closing week of the season he was even better, beating Los Angeles four times, including an iron-man stint on the last day. The September 13 season finale was the traditional Sunday doubleheader. Ponce won the opener, 4–2, then went on to blank the Angels, 1–0, in the nightcap. In 10 games he had posted six complete games in six starts, a 1.31 ERA and a perfect 8–0 record. The next year Ponce was 14–16 with the Seals, followed by a 10–12 mark in 1955. He faded from the PCL after that, but no Coast League pitcher ever had enjoyed a more spectacular debut.

---

and first baseman Dale Long (.272, 35 HRs, 116 RBIs), who won the home run and RBI titles and was named Most Valuable Player.

Sacramento outfielder Robert Dillinger (.366) was the 1953 batting champ, Oakland's Allen Gettel (24–14) posted the most victories in the league for a seventh-place club, and Los Angeles southpaw Joe Hatten (17–11) won the strikeout crown and pitched a no-hitter. One of the memorable brawls in Coast League history involved Hatten during an August 2 contest at Gilmore Field between the arch-rival Angels and Stars. Hatten, who had surrendered six straight hits to Frank Kelleher, nailed the veteran slugger with a fastball. Kelleher charged the mound, and after the resulting scuffle was broken up, Frank was ejected from the game. Ted Beard replaced Kelleher on the basepaths, and moments later slid hard into Murray Franklin, a former Star third baseman playing his first game for the Angels. Franklin and Beard started swinging, both benches emptied, and a general melée ensued as fans threatened to riot. When the dust finally settled, Franklin and Beard were ejected, and five players later were fined.

Bragan retained a number of key players in 1954, and Hollywood shook off numerous injuries in a valiant bid to become the third club in Coast League history to finish first three years in a row. Red Munger (17–8) and Mel Queen (16–8), dependable members of the previous two mound staffs, pitched excellent ball throughout the year. Center fielder Tom Saffell (.279 with 48 steals) repeated as stolen base champ, and he was flanked in left by Carlos Bernier (.313 with 38 steals), back with the Stars after a year in Pittsburgh. Jack Phillips (.300), third baseman for the 1952 and 1953 champs, was named MVP. Popular Frank Kelleher won five games as a pinch hitter, then retired after 10 years as a Hollywood Star. Welcome additions to the pitching staff were southpaw Roger Bowman (22–13) and Lino Dinoso (19–8), who was lost to the team for a month because of an appendectomy. Another serious loss came in August, when Carlos Bernier attacked an umpire over a strike call, and was suspended for the rest of the year. Hollywood hosted the first All-Star Game since 1950, losing to their All-Star opposition, 11–7, before a crowd of 5,964.

Hollywood led the league during much of the season, but San Diego finally took over first place. Managed by Lefty O'Doul, the Padres starred batting champ Harry Elliott (.350, 15 HRs, 110 RBIs), outfielder Earl Rapp (.337, 24 HRs, 111 RBIs), first baseman-outfielder Dick Sisler (.318, 19 HRs, 90 RBIs), and ERA titlist Bill Wight (17–5 with a 1.99 ERA).

By the end of the season the Stars and the Padres were deadlocked, with only the traditional Sunday doubleheader remaining on the schedule. The Padres split their doubleheader with the Angels, while Lino Dinoso lost a 1–0 heartbreaker to Portland. Roger Bowman had been knocked out of the Saturday game in the first inning, but Bobby Bragan brought him back to pitch the pressure-packed seven-inning nightcap. In one of the great clutch performances of Coast League history, Bowman, who had pitched a nine-inning no-hitter *against* Hollywood in 1952, twirled a perfect game to clinch a 10–0 triumph. A single-game playoff was scheduled for Monday in San Diego to determine the championship. Padres southpaw Bob Kerrigan (17–11) hurled a 7–2 victory to give San Diego its first regular season title.

Hollywood made another run at a pennant in 1955, behind the superb pitching of Red Munger (23–8 with a 1.85 ERA), who led the league in victories and ERA, and strikeout champ Bob Garber (20–16 with 199 Ks). Although the tobacco-chewing Munger was 36, he added a knuckleball and enjoyed his best season. But the

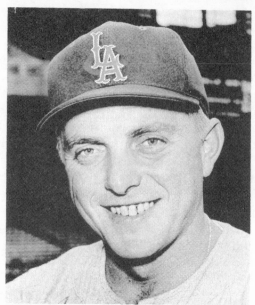

*Angels' first baseman Steve Bilko was named MVP three years in a row, 1955–57, for his prodigious slugging feats.*

— Author's collection

Stars had to settle for a third-place tie with Los Angeles, although Hollywood beat LA, three games to two, in a city championship postseason series held at Wrigley Field. San Diego's attempt to repeat as champions fell short by three games, as Seattle won the flag behind the pitching of Elmer Singleton (19–12) and Lou Kretlow (14–3).

One of the greatest PCL sluggers of all time made his debut in the circuit in 1955, although he was in his 11th year as a pro, including all or part of six seasons in the National League. Steve Bilko, a 6'1, 240-pound righthanded first baseman, won the first of three consecutive home run championships for the Angels (.328, 37 HRs, 124 RBIs). In 1956 he led Los Angeles to its 14th and final pennant by winning the Triple Crown (.360, 55 HRs, 164 RBIs) and also paced the league in hits and runs. The next year Bilko led the PCL in homers, RBIs and runs (.300, 56 HRs, 111 RBIs). In all three seasons he was voted Most Valuable Player. Bilko played for the Cincinnati Reds and Los Angeles *Dodgers* in 1958, then returned to the PCL the next season, winning an RBI title for Spokane (.305, 26 HRs, 92 RBIs). He spent 1960 with Detroit, played for the American League Los Angeles *Angels* in 1961 and 1962, then

---

**Softball Delivery**

Bob Fesler of Seattle was a magnificent softball pitcher, hurling over 150 no-hitters with the big ball. Fesler pitched an exhibition game against PCL competition and, working with a hardball from the softball distance of 46 feet, whiffed 11 batters. Manager Fred Hutchinson of the Rainiers was sufficiently impressed to sign Fesler to a contract in 1955. Unfortunately, when Fesler moved back to the regulation 60 feet 6 inches, he proved ineffective — in four games he was 0–2.

Ad Liska, whose 24-year career included 14 seasons with Portland (198 PCL victories), was a righthander whose submarine delivery resembled that of a softball pitcher. Certainly the rising trajectory of Liska's pitches was similar to softball offerings. Liska was 24–18 for Portland in 1937, he won 20 in 1939 and 1945, and if he had followed Bob Fesler to a softball diamond, he too might have recorded 150 no-hitters.

---

retired after one more year with Rochester in the International League. Bilko was extremely popular with LA fans, and he is the only player in Coast League history to hit 50 homers twice.

In 1956 the PCL showcased numerous future big league stars, including Rocky Colavito (.368 with 12 homers and 32 RBIs in 35 games for San Diego), Hollywood's Bill Mazeroski (.306), Albie Pearson (.297 in 31 games for the Seals), Vancouver fireballer Ryne Duren (11–11 with 183 strikeouts), and Hollywood southpaw Luis Arroyo (7–5 with a .359 batting average). Former big league and PCL star Larry Jansen seemed to regain his old form (11–2), but could not long resurrect his career. Seattle righthander Elmer Singleton (18–8 with a 2.55 ERA) won the ERA title, while Portland righty Rene Valdes (22–11) led the League in victories.

For the first time since 1938, the Coast League experienced a franchise move, when the Oaks were sold to Canadian interests and became the Vancouver Mounties. Vancouver was the PCL's first Canadian city, and visiting teams began to hear the strains of the Canadian National Anthem before each game. Vancouver finished last in 1956, 38¹/₂ games behind LA, but even second-place Seattle finished 12 games behind the last great Angels club. Los Angeles led the league in hitting (.297), home runs (202), and runs (1,000 — Portland was second with 798). Triple Crown winner Steve Bilko

*The PCL moved into Canada in 1956, when Oakland transferred to Vancouver. Vancouver's Capileno Stadium was just five years old, and eventually was renamed for longtime owner Nat Bailey.*

— Author's photo

was the unanimous choice for his second straight MVP award, but he had outstanding support from right fielder Joe Bolger (.326, 28 HRs, 147 RBIs), second baseman Gene Mauch (.348, 20 HRs, 84 RBIs), left fielder Bob Speake (.300, 20 HRs, 111 RBIs), and third sacker George Freese (.291, 22 HRs, 113 RBIs). The pitching staff was almost as good as the offense, featuring Dave Hillman (21–7), Gene Fodge (19–7), and reliever Bob Anderson (12–4 in 70 games). Throughout the season it was rumored that the Washington Senators would move to Los Angeles, and LA would indeed spend only one more season in the PCL, but the 1956 Angels were one of the finest teams in Coast League history.

Dodger owner Walter O'Malley, long dissatisfied with the seating and parking limitations of Ebbets Field, found it impossible to persuade Brooklyn officials to build a suitable stadium. In February 1957, he purchased Wrigley Field and the Angels franchise from the Cubs for $3,000,000 and the Dodgers' Texas League farm club in Fort Worth. Although O'Malley reassured PCL directors that the Angels would continue as a part of the Coast League, it was obvious that a Dodger move to the West Coast now could be readily accomplished, and Los Angeles city officials enthusiastically began to make plans to build a major league stadium. At the same time, Horace Stoneham of the New York Giants, dissatisfied with the Polo Grounds, had begun the maneuvers that would bring his National League club to San Francisco, where voters had approved a $5,000,000 stadium bond issue back in 1954. On May 28, 1957, the National League granted permission to both the Dodgers and the Giants to move from New York, and throughout the 1957 season there was excited speculation in Los Angeles and San Francisco that big league baseball might be on the way.

Meanwhile, back in the Coast League, Steve Bilko gave LA fans a third straight MVP performance, blasting 56 homers. Bilko had no supporting cast, however, and the Angels finished in sixth place, although pitcher Tom Lasorda (7–10) one day would return to lead Los Angeles to the World Championship. The 1957 Angels did enjoy one spectacular day. At Wrigley Field on June 22, the Angels unloaded nine home runs and defeated Sacramento 22–5. Right fielder Bert Hamric hit two homers and drove in seven runs. No one else, including Steve Bilko, hit more than one roundtripper. In the seventh inning the Angels scored 11 times while blasting a record five homers. Sacramento starter Roger Osenbaugh pitched into the seventh inning and was rocked for all 22 runs.

It was a different story in San Francisco. In what was to prove their final PCL season, the Seals were guided to the 1957 pennant by Joe Gordon. The offense was led by batting champ Ken Aspromonte (.334) and first baseman Frank Kellert (.308, 22 HRs, 107 RBIs), while the best pitchers were relievers Leo Kiely (21–6) and Bill Abernathie (13–2). All but one of Kiely's wins came in relief, including 14 in a row; he is the only PCL reliever to win 20 games, and his 14 consecutive relief victories also constitute a record.

Elsewhere around the league, the ERA champ was southpaw Morrie Martin (14–4, 1.90), and Hollywood utility infielder Dick Smith (.299) set a PCL record by collecting six consecutive pinch hits on July 20, 28 and 31, and August 25, 27 and 30. Seattle lefty Charles Rabe (16–10) pitched four consecutive shutouts in June and July, matching the 1905 record set by James Whalen of San Francisco and LA's William Tozer.

By the fall of 1957, it was certain that the Dodgers and Giants would be in Los Angeles and San Francisco in 1958. The impact on the Pacific Coast League would be profound. Los Angeles and San

*Outfielder Albie Pearson hit .297 for the Seals in 1957, then moved up to the big leagues.*

— Author's collection

Francisco always had been the key cities of the Coast League. Throughout much of the history of the PCL one or both of these cities had maintained two clubs, and the Angels and Seals had been flagship franchises of the circuit. Now a major regrouping would have to occur, and on December 2 PCL directors rearranged the league. The Dodgers would move the Angels franchise to Spokane and the Giants would place the Seals franchise in Phoenix. Longtime Hollywood President Bob Cobb bowed to the inevitable and reluctantly sold the Stars franchise to Salt Lake City interests.

Big league baseball at last came to the West Coast, and the PCL, with all hope of becoming a major league now lost, dropped back to AAA classification and reduced the schedule to a standard 154 games. PCL purists insist that the history of the "real" Coast League ended in 1957. But even though the schedule never again would extend to 180 or 200 games, there would be notable player exploits in the future, and although LA and Frisco and Hollywood were gone from the league, other vibrant and glamorous cities would become a part of the PCL. The Coast League had changed fundamentally, but minor league baseball was undergoing a basic

*Spokane entered the PCL in 1958, after 10,000-seat Multnomah Stadium was built in 90 days as the home of the Indians.*

— Author's photo

transformation, and a more flexible PCL would adapt successfully and remain a key part of the structure of Organized Baseball.

The revamped PCL of 1958 featured a number of future big league stars, including Willie McCovey (.319 for Phoenix), stolen base champ Vada Pinson (.343 with 37 steals for Seattle), Maury Wills (.253 for Spokane), Dick Stuart (.311 with 31 homers and 82 RBIs in just 80 games for Salt Lake City), Leon Wagner (.318 for Phoenix), and Claude Osteen (5–4 for Seattle). Vancouver right-hander George Bamberger, a 33-year-old PCL veteran, led the league in ERA (15–11, 2.45) and established a record in July and August by pitching 68$^2/_3$ innings without a walk (the old record of 64 innings was set in 1939 by Julio Bonetti of the Angels). The MVP was San Diego infielder-outfielder Earl Averill (.347), son of the Hall of Fame outfielder who had been a Seals star during the first three years of his career during the 1920s.

The Phoenix Giants successfully defended the Seals' 1957 championship. Phoenix led the league in hitting and home runs (205), walloping 43 roundtrippers over a record-setting 22 consecutive games. Shortstop Andre Rodgers (.354 with 31 homers) won

*When Salt Lake City rejoined the PCL in 1958, pro ball was played at Derks Field.*
— Author's photo

the batting title as Phoenix fans celebrated a pennant in their first PCL season.

There was no celebration the next year. Willie McCovey (.372, 29 HRs, 92 RBIs) led the league in homers and RBIs, despite being called up after playing just 95 games. Newcomer Jose Pagan (.312) also was impressive, and again Phoenix led the league in homers (196). Andre Rodgers slumped badly (.260 in 41 games after being sent down from San Francisco), and there was little pitching. The entire team stole merely 19 bases during the season (Sacramento totaled only 19 steals as well), and Phoenix plummeted to last place. Only 79,106 fans turned out, and the Giants moved their Coast League club to Tacoma in 1960.

The batting champ was Spokane's speedy outfielder, Tommy Davis (.345), while Steve Bilko (.305, 26 HRs, 92 RBIs) tied Willie McCovey for the RBI title. Strikeout leader Richard Stigman (9–17, but 181 Ks in 191 innings), a San Diego southpaw, pitched $10^2/_3$ innings of hitless ball against Salt Lake City on May 26. Finally he gave up a hit in the 11th inning of a scoreless duel. He yielded another hit in the 12th, was removed at the end of the inning, and San Diego finally won in the 15th, 1–0. Another San

*Willie McCovey broke into the PCL with Phoenix in 1958 (.319), then was promoted to the Giants after an explosive 95 games in 1959 (.372, 29 HRs, 92 RBIs).*

— Author's Photo

Diego lefthander, Jake Striker (12–8), tossed a 10-inning, one-hit, 1–0 victory over Phoenix. Striker walked a batter in the first, opened the second with a walk and the only hit he yielded, a clean single to right by Bob Speake, then retired the next 27 hitters in order — the equivalent of a perfect game. The best pitcher in the league was Salt Lake City righthander Dick Hall (18–5 with a 1.87 ERA), who was the circuit leader in victories, winning percentage

---

### Two RBIs on a Sacrifice

In Vancouver on August 4, 1958, Spokane loaded the bases with one out in the third. First baseman Jim Gentile lashed a line drive down the right field line. The right fielder made a good catch, but the runners on both third and second scored, as the throw went to second base (Tom Saffell did not tag up at second, but there was no appeal and his run counted). The throw to second doubled up the runner from first, but Gentile was awarded two RBIs on a double-play sacrifice fly.

and ERA. Hall led Salt Lake City to the 1959 championship, and was named Most Valuable Player.

League attendance in 1958 and 1959 was just 1,500,000. Five decades of baseball progress was short-circuited in the 1950s. The period began with declining attendance, and the downward trend continued despite various efforts to reverse this depressing situation. Years of franchise stability ended when first Oakland, then linchpins Los Angeles and San Francisco transferred their clubs. But the downward attendance spiral would continue into the 1960s, and the decade would bring revolutionary change to the PCL as well as all of minor league baseball.

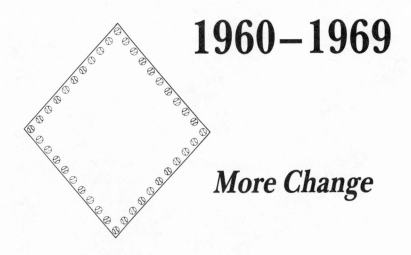

# 1960–1969

## *More Change*

The breakup of the Coast League in 1958 previewed an unsettling series of franchise changes which occurred during the 1960s. Tacoma, which had not played PCL ball since 1905, replaced Phoenix in 1960 (Phoenix would return six years later), and the next year exotic Honolulu acquired Sacramento's franchise. For the first time in league history, the PCL expanded to 10 teams in 1963, then to 12 the following season, before dropping back to eight clubs in 1969. During these years minor league baseball hit its lowest ebb; the worst season was 1963, when a paltry 18 circuits attracted a total paid attendance of just 9,963,174. The worst season for the PCL was 1962, when attendance dropped to 1,055,745. Paid attendance began to rise the next year, primarily because of the addition of extra franchises to the league. The American Association suspended play in 1963 for six years, leaving only two AAA leagues. When the American Association resumed play in 1969, the Coast League dropped from 12 to eight teams and attendance was reduced by 700,000 (a 40 percent drop) to 1,055,988. The All-Star Game was discontinued in 1964, not to be resumed for a decade. But when the Coast League split into two divisions in 1963, a postseason playoff series, absent from the Coast League schedule for a decade, was permanently restored. In addition to Honolulu, Coast

*When Tacoma returned to the PCL after a 55-game absence in 1960, 8,000-seat Che-*
*ney Stadium was built by the city and county for $900,000.*

— Courtesy Tacoma Public Library

League baseball was played during the 1960s in Indianapolis, Little Rock, Oklahoma City, Tulsa, Denver, Dallas, Fort Worth, Eugene, and Tucson. Aside from the breakup of the PCL's traditional
geography, other fundamental changes were wrought in the status
of the franchises and the quality of the players, particularly by de-
velopments which occurred in 1966. The 1960s would prove to be
an unsettled period of transition and adjustment.

    The Coast League opened the 1960s with only two California
cities, San Diego and Sacramento, along with Seattle, Tacoma,
Spokane, Portland, Salt Lake City, and Vancouver. Spokane dominated the PCL in 1960, winning the team batting, home run, and
stolen base titles, and taking the pennant by $11^1/_2$ games. Spokane
center fielder Willie Davis was named MVP after leading the
league in hitting (.346 with 30 steals and 26 triples), runs, hits and
stolen bases, and setting a new season record for triples (he played
in only 147 games, as opposed to as many as 200-plus by players in
earlier decades). Third baseman Ramon Conde (.325), shortstop
Charles Smith (.322, 20 HRs, 106 RBIs), outfielder Ron Fairly
(.303, 27 HRs, 100 RBIs), and massive Frank Howard (.371 in 26
games) swung big bats for the league's most explosive offense.

Leading the league at mid-season, Spokane hosted the All-Star Game and defeated the stars, 4–3, before a home crowd of more than 10,000.

Home run champ R. C. Stevens (.276, 37 HRs, 109 RBIs) and RBI leader Harry Bright (.313, 27 HRs, 119 RBIs) both took their cuts from the middle of the Salt Lake City lineup. Second-place Tacoma showcased such future stars as outfielder Matty Alou (.306), shortstop Jose Pagan (.295), and Juan Marichal (11–5). Sacramento infielder Jack Littrell (.274) tied Dick Smith's 1957 record by connecting for six consecutive pinch hits (May 30, 31, June 4, 6, 10, 11). From 1957 through 1960 pitchers William Kennedy (Seattle and Portland) and Chuck Churn (Hollywood, Seattle and Spokane) fielded their position flawlessly; Kennedy went 176 consecutive games (47 chances) without an error, while Churn played in 159 straight games (134 chances) with no muffs.

Although paid attendance dropped again in 1960 throughout the league, the move from Phoenix (79,106 in 1959) to Tacoma (1960 attendance leader with 270,024) greatly improved the overall picture. The next year the most innovative franchise transfer in PCL history took place when Sacramento moved to Honolulu. Like Hollywood had been and Las Vegas would be, Hawaii was an exotic and glamorous franchise. The vast distance to Hawaii caused scheduling adjustments, and the Hawaii franchise agreed to pay half of the visitors' flight fares. Players' wives usually do not go on road trips because of the expense, but just as wives often had made the trips to Hollywood to gaze at movie stars, player couples would save up for the series played in Hawaii.

Hawaii produced the 1961 batting champ, PCL veteran Carlos Bernier (.351), who had won three stolen base titles while playing for Hollywood during the 1950s. Salt Lake City lefthander Sam McDowell (13–10) led the league in strikeouts and pitched a 1–0, seven-inning no-hitter against Spokane. From August 5 through August 9, Vancouver third baseman Ed Charles spent an unprecedented five consecutive games without handling a single batted ball.

The Tacoma Giants won the 1961 pennant by a 10-game margin, despite finishing next-to-last in team batting. Gaylord Perry (16–10) and Ron Herbel (16–5) led the league in victories, and reliever Verle Tiefenthaler (13–6 in 56 appearances) had an outstanding season. Versatile infielder-outfielder Dick Phillips (.264

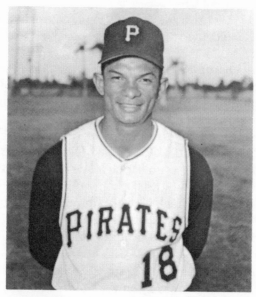

*Matty Alou hit .306 in 1960 for Tacoma, then went up to San Francisco. Matty was the younger brother of Felipe, who played for Tacoma two years earlier. The PCL's most famous brothers were Joe, Vince and Dom DiMaggio. Pete and Steve Coscarart played together for Portland's 1936 champions, while notable father-son combinations included Earl Averill, Sr. and Jr., Earl and Bud Sheely, and pitchers Herman and Duane Pillette. On April 7, 1918, Doc Crandall pitched no-hit ball for 8²/₃ innings. One out away from a no-hitter, Doc gave up a clean safety — to his brother Karl!*

*— Author's collection*

with 98 RBIs) was given the MVP award, while outfielder Manny Mota (.289) and second baseman Chuck Hiller (.324 in 73 games) also provided offensive support.

Although there were no franchise changes in 1962, attendance sagged by 300,000 to just over 1,000,000. It was San Diego's turn to run away with the pennant, outdistancing second-place Salt Lake City by 12 games. San Diego catcher Jesse Gonder (.342, 21 HRs, 116 RBIs) led the league in hitting and RBIs, and was voted Most Valuable Player. The Padres posted the best team batting average, behind Gonder, third baseman Tommy Harper (.333, 26 HRs, and a league-leading 120 runs), first baseman Rogelio Alvarez (.318), and stolen base champ Hiraldo Ruiz (.283 with 40 steals). The deep pitching staff featured John Flavin (12–2), John Tsitouris (13–8), and Sammy Ellis (12–6), who twirled a no-hitter against Tacoma. Tacoma's Gaylord Perry (10–7, 2.48 ERA) qualified for the ERA title, then went on to win the Cy Young award in the National League and in the American League (314–265 lifetime).

Vancouver, which finished next-to-last and drew only 88,075, withdrew from the Coast League at the close of 1962. At the same time the American Association found it necessary to suspend operations, leaving only the PCL and the International League in Class AAA. But there were 20 major league teams, each in need of a AAA affiliate, and both surviving AAA circuits expanded to 10 teams. In 1963 the PCL became a 10-club league for the first time in its history, adding Denver, Dallas-Fort Worth, and Oklahoma City from the American Association. The PCL now found it necessary to split into two divisions; this arrangement has continued until the present, sometimes with Northern and Southern Divisions, sometimes with Eastern and Western Divisions. With two divisions, it now became necessary to resume postseason playoffs, which had been discontinued after the 1951 season.

In 1963 Spokane ran away with the Northern Divisions outdistancing second-place Hawaii by 17 games. Danny Ozark managed the Indians to the best record in the league, while righthander Howard Reed (19–7) led the PCL in victories and winning percentage. Spokane hosted the All-Star Game, losing to the stars, 4–2. Attendance was 6,595, and the league decided to do away with the exhibition.

The Southern Division was a dogfight between Oklahoma City and San Diego. Padres infielder Hiraldo Ruiz (.298 with 50 steals) repeated as stolen base king, infielder-outfielder Deron Johnson (.277, 33 HRs, 91 RBIs) led the league in homers, and Sammy Ellis (12–10, 192 Ks in 192 innings, 2.62 ERA) was the ERA titlist. But Oklahoma City, skippered by Grady Hatton and led by outfielder Carroll Hardy (.316) and righthander Dave Giusti (13–11), edged the Padres for the division title by half a game. In the first playoffs in 12 years, a total of 38,000 fans saw Oklahoma City outlast Spokane, four games to three.

Denver finished last in the South, but led the league in team hitting and homers, and produced batting champ Chico Salmon (.325). Salt Lake City outfielder Billy Cowan (.315, 25 HRs, 120 RBIs) was the RBI champ and Most Valuable Player. The strikeout king was Bill Spanswick of Seattle.(14–8), a fireballing southpaw who fanned 209 batters in only 185 innings.

The PCL expanded again in 1964, adding Indianapolis and

*A major attraction in the minor leagues always occurs when the local ballpark hosts the big league affiliate in an exhibition. In 1963 Willie Mays posed with Tacoma Giants catcher Jacke Davis. Davis also played with Oklahoma City and Denver in 1964, as well as several big league clubs.*

— Courtesy Jacke Davis

Little Rock from the International League, which had found 10 teams unwieldy. Another change took place when Fort Worth separated from Dallas and rejoined the Texas League, leaving Dallas to carry on in the PCL. The "Coast League" now sprawled from Indiana to Hawaii, and reorganized into six-team Eastern and Western divisions.

Little Rock brought an exciting club into the PCL. The Arkansas Travelers, managed by Frank Lucchesi, had been stocked by the Philadelphia Phils (17 players eventually would play big league ball). Aided by a friendly right field fence at picturesque Ray Winder Field, the "Boom-Boom Travs" blasted 208 home runs. The lineup starred home run and RBI champ Costen Shockley (.281, 36 HRs, 112 RBIs) at first base, second baseman Norm Gigon (.274, 30 HRs, 76 RBIs) as the PCL's most powerful *leadoff* hitter, third sacker Wayne Graham (.305), catcher Pat Corrales (.304), center fielder Adolpho Phillips (.304, 29 HRs, 87 RBIs), and left fielder Alex Johnson (.316, 21 HRs, 71 RBIs in 90 games). Morrie Steevens (8–1) and Joel Gibson (10–7) each pitched no-hitters over

Dallas. The Boom-Boom Travs blasted their way to the Eastern Division title and the best record of 1964. But the Phils were in the thick of the National League pennant race, and by the time of the PCL playoffs, the heart of the Travs' lineup had been moved up to Philadelphia.

San Diego won a tight race in the West. Infielder Tony Perez (.309, 34 HRs, 107 RBIs) was the league's Most Valuable Player, while shortstop Tommy Helms (.309) and stolen base leader Cesar Tovar (.275 with 40 steals) were other key Padre players. In the playoffs an undermanned Arkansas squad fought valiantly, but San Diego manager Dave Bristol piloted his team to the championship, four games to three.

Future big league star Jose Cardenal (.289 with 40 steals) tied Tony Perez for the stolen base title while playing in Tacoma's outfield. The batting champ was Denver third sacker Lou Klimchock (.331, 19 HRs, 112 RBIs), who tied Costen Shockley for the RBI lead and recorded the best fielding percentage at his position. Luis Tiant (15–1 with 13 complete games in 15 starts, only 88 hits and 154 Ks in 137 innings, and a 2.04 ERA) was brilliant with Tacoma before going up to Cleveland (10–4 for a 25–5 season!). Indianapolis righthander Bruce Howard (15–8, 2.20 ERA) was the ERA leader, Tacoma fastballer Al Stanek (13–12 with 220 Ks in 223 innings) was the strikeout king, and Spokane reliever Ken Rowe (16–11 in 88 games) set a new record for most appearances and tied Robert Locker of Indianapolis (16–9) for most victories. Phil Niekro (11–5) tuned up for big league stardom with Denver, and Sudden Sam McDowell overwhelmed PCL hitters in nine games for Portland (8–0, 5 shutouts, 34 hits and 102 Ks in 76 innings, 1.18 ERA, and a no-hitter over Spokane). There were six no-hitters in 1964, an all-time PCL record.

Dallas finished last in 1964 (53–104), 42$^1$/$_2$ games behind Arkansas and with pitiful attendance (39,391). Dallas pulled out of the league, and Vancouver rejoined the PCL for 1965. Vancouver was in the thick of an unusually tight race in the Western Division; only 5$^1$/$_2$ games separated the top five clubs. Portland won the Western Division, sparked by righthander Tom Kelley (16–3 with 190 Ks in 185 innings), who pitched a no-hitter and led the league in winning percentage and strikeouts. Oklahoma City swept through the Eastern Division, then beat Portland, four games to one, in the playoffs. The 89ers boasted victory leader Chris Zach-

*Portland won the Western Division in 1965.*

— Courtesy Portland Beavers

ary (17–8), hard-hitting shortstop Roland Jackson (.330), and home run champ David Roberts (.318, 38 HRs, 114 RBIs), who was selected as Most Valuable Player.

For the third year in a row, Denver produced the batting champ, Ted Uhlaender (.340). Another Denver outfielder, Andy Kosco (.327, with 27 HRs and 116 RBIs in just 119 games) won the RBI title, and Hawaii switch hitter Fred Valentine (.324 with 25 homers and 58 steals) was the stolen base king. San Diego's Lee May (.321, 34 HRs, 103 RBIs) and Arkansas' Fergie Jenkins (8–6 with 112 Ks in 122 innings) had good seasons, then went on to big league stardom. Tacoma righthander Bill Hands (17–6, 2.19 ERA) tied Chris Zachary for the lead in victories and won the ERA championship. Tacoma lefty Richard Estelle pitched a no-hitter against Hawaii, to go with the one he twirled against Denver a year earlier.

Arkansas (77,570), Salt Lake City (98,951), and Tacoma (119,762) each experienced disappointing attendance in 1965. The next year Arkansas opted to return to Class AA as a member of the Texas League; Salt Lake City asked to withdraw temporarily from the PCL; and Tacoma's franchise was moved back to Phoenix (Phoenix had transferred to Tacoma in 1960). Tulsa replaced Ar-

---

**Hockey or Baseball?**

On May 11, 1966, a game in Vancouver erupted in a brawl which might have had a tragic ending. Vancouver outfielder Ricardo Joseph was hit by a pitch and charged the mound, precipitating a free-for-all. During the melee Vancouver first baseman Santiago Rosario seized a bat and walloped Seattle's catcher, Merritt Ranew, over the head. Ranew suffered a four-inch gash and a concussion so severe that he was shelved for the season. PCL President Dewey Soriano suspended Joseph for four days. Rosario was fined $250 and banned for the remainder of the season, a suspension that was extended to a calendar year by the National Association.

---

kansas, and the Chicago Cubs decided to place their Salt Lake City franchise in recently vacated Tacoma. Tacoma's attendance sagged still further in 1966 (104,719), but Phoenix (152,508) and Tulsa (158,595) compared well with Hawaii (191,367), the league's attendance leader.

Newcomer Tulsa, led by batting champ Walt Williams (.330, with a league-leading 107 runs and 54 doubles), won the Eastern Division over Phoenix. Seattle manager Bob Lemon, a future Hall of Famer who had pitched his final 12 games for San Diego in 1958, guided his club to the Western Division championship, then outlasted Tulsa, four games to three, in the playoffs. Seattle did not have a regular who hit .300, but led the PCL in team fielding and ERA.

Although Indianapolis finished third in the Eastern Division, catcher Duane Josephson (.324) was the league's MVP, Ron Clark (.294, 16 HRs, 94 RBIs) led all third basemen in fielding and tied for the RBI title, outfielder Edwin Stroud (.309 with 57 steals) was the stolen base king, righthander Bill Fischer (11–6, 2.35 ERA) won the ERA title, and another righty, Manly Johnston (18–7) fashioned the PCL's best winning percentage and was frequently used as a pinch hitter (.263 in 73 games). Denver southpaw Jimmy Ollom (20–8) became the PCL's first 20-game winner in a decade. A record-setting oddity occurred on July 23, when the first eight Hawaii batters went down by hitting the ball to Denver second baseman Frank Quilici.

By 1967 permanent and fundamental changes had been estab-

*Hall of Fame member Bob Lemon pitched the last 12 games of his career for San Diego in 1958. He returned to the PCL in 1964 as Hawaii's manager, then he skippered Seattle in 1965 and 1966, and Sacramento in 1974.*

— Author's collection

lished in the makeup of minor league rosters. Beginning in 1962, major league owners unanimously agreed to a program to reinforce minor league baseball. Class AAA would remain unchanged, but Class AA and A leagues were combined into a new Class AA, and the Class B, C and D circuits were brought together into the new Class A, while rookie leagues were created for freshman prospects. Each major league club would maintain one Class AAA and one AA affiliate, as well as three Class A and rookie league farm teams. Parent clubs would provide a manager for each affiliate, cover all spring training expenses, and reimburse the minor league teams for basic player salaries.

The Free-Agent Player Draft, a plan first employed in June 1965, would be conducted annually in January and June. At each session, clubs in Organized Baseball would systematically select players, thereby acquiring exclusive negotiating rights to each athlete. With National and American league franchises alternating, the major league teams would draft in reverse order of their standings the previous season. Major league teams would select just one player during each phase of each session, while Class AAA clubs would be permitted two selections apiece, Class AA teams four each, and each Class A team as many as desired. But since almost every minor league franchise has a major league affiliation (teams which tried to maintain their independence found it almost impossible to acquire players), in effect all selections are made by parent organizations. This movement toward major league control of the minors was solidified by the Player Development Contract, which went into effect in 1967.

With minor league emphasis now strictly on developing players for parent clubs, career minor leaguers became virtually extinct, and no more would experienced major leaguers finish out their careers with a few seasons in the high minors. The Pacific Coast League no longer would showcase veteran players with extensive big league backgrounds, and young players would not have the benefit of tutelage from old pros. For more than half a century, the Coast League had offered fans a balance between talented youngsters and experienced veterans, but teams no longer would be seasoned by career minor leaguers and ex-big leaguers.

Longtime minor leaguers had created a strong team identity with fans, which is one of the rich pleasures of regularly following a baseball club. Young players in the midst of outstanding seasons would be promoted to the parent team without regard to the needs of the minor league team, especially if the major league club were in the midst of a title race. There would be little roster continuity from season to season, and all too often a fine Coast League team would fade badly late in the year or during the playoffs, because the roster had been gutted by a parent club in need of young talent. Fans would reluctantly become accustomed to an annual parade of players as rosters were regularly juggled (sometimes more than 80 players would appear on a team's roster during a season). Players with marginal major league experience might go up and down to the parent club two, three or four times during a season, and few young athletes would spend more than three or four seasons — or *parts* of seasons — in the Coast League. Along with the absence of continuity and experience, the quality of play became less polished. The impressive records compiled through long PCL seasons and extended careers in the Coast League would never be threatened.

In 1967 Spokane beat out Portland and Vancouver in an airtight race for the Western Division title. San Diego won the Eastern Division with the season's best record, then defeated Spokane for the championship. Managed by Bob Skinner, the Padres had the tenth lowest batting average (.246) in the league, but led the PCL in home runs and staff ERA. The mound corps boasted righthanders John Tsitouris (17–7), Jeff James (13–5), and Gary Wagner (12–4), while third baseman Ricardo Joseph (.300) led the offense and was named MVP.

Joseph and batting champ Cesar Gutierrez of Phoenix (.322) were the only .300 hitters of the season. Hawaii outfielder Willie Kirkland (.241, 34 HRs, 97 RBIs) paced the PCL in homers and RBIs. Tom Hutton, Spokane's lefthanded first baseman, made only one error in 121 games for a record-setting .999 fielding percentage, and from April 21, 1967, through May 12, 1968, he went 141 consecutive games (1,272 chances) without an error. Spokane righthander Alan Foster (10–9) became the only pitcher in PCL history to hurl two no-hitters in a season. Both efforts were 1–0 victories over Seattle, a seven-inning nightcap on August 16 and, just two weeks later, a nine-inning triumph.

The 1968 PCL retained the same makeup for the third year in a row. Spokane easily won the Eastern Division behind a pitching staff which posted the league's best ERA. Leon Everitt (17–10) led the PCL in complete games, Joe Moeller (15–9) was the shutout leader (6), and Alan Foster (8–5) returned to put in a solid half season. But Tulsa led the league in team hitting and fielding, finished second in staff ERA, and posted the best record of 12 teams while winning the Eastern Division by 18 games over San Diego. Tulsa stars included batting champ and MVP Jim Hicks (.366), RBI leader Jose Laboy (.292, 15 HRs, 100 RBIs), first baseman Joe Hague (.293, 23 HRs, 99 RBIs), ERA and percentage leader Pete Mikkelson (16–4, 1.91 ERA), and Charles Taylor (18–7) and Sal Campisi (12–3), who respectively tied for the lead in victories and winning percentage. This talented club beat Spokane, four games to one, in the playoffs (but playoff attendance totaled a meager 8,871).

Tulsa's manager was pitching great Warren Spahn. Other 1968 skippers who had been noted major leaguers, and/or who would make their marks as major league managers, included Billy Martin (Denver), Whitey Lockman (Tacoma), Mickey Vernon (Vancouver), Don Zimmer (Indianapolis), Clyde King (Phoenix), Red Davis (Portland), Joe Adcock (Seattle), and Bob Skinner (San Diego).

*Tucson joined the PCL in 1969, with Hi Corbett Field (the spring training home of the Cleveland Indians) as the site of Coast League baseball.*

— Author's photo

Headed for distinguished big league playing careers from the PCL Class of '68 were Denver's Craig Nettles (.297) and Portland's Lou Piniella (.317, and .308 and .289 the previous two years). Phoenix righthander Richard Robertson (18–9, with 216 Ks) tied for the lead in victories, and was the strikeout king for the second year in a row. Bo Belinsky, a flamboyant southpaw who had attracted considerable attention with a few modest big league seasons, twirled a 1–0 no-hitter and whiffed 181 PCL batters in 176 innings, and the next year he was the league's percentage leader (12–5).

Major league expansion in 1969, along with the revival of the American Association, led to sweeping changes in the PCL. A National League franchise was placed in San Diego, while the American League moved into Seattle. In addition to the loss of these key cities, the reorganized American Association took Indianapolis, Denver, Oklahoma City and Tulsa, leaving only six clubs in the PCL. Tucson and Eugene placed teams in the Coast League, but even though there still were just eight franchises, PCL directors chose to maintain the divisional setup. Attendance inevitably dropped, reflecting the loss of one-third of the league and two mar-

*In 1969 Portland was managed by veteran Red Davis (standing at far right).*
— Courtesy Portland Beavers

kets of major league quality. Paid attendance in 1969 was just over one million, compared to nearly two million in 1967.

Newcomer Eugene, managed by Frank Lucchesi, surged to the Southern Division title by a 13-game margin. The Emeralds featured MVP second baseman Dennis Doyle (.310), shortstop Larry Bowa (.287 with 48 steals), who was the stolen base champ and fielding leader at his position, infielder-outfielder Jim Hutto (.306), and righthander Jeff James (13–10), the strikeout leader who finished in a five-way tie for the victory leadership.

But Whitey Lockman guided Tacoma to the Northern Division championship by a 14-game gap, then beat Eugene for the pennant, three games to two. Lockman's best players were infielder-outfielder Dick Bladt (.312), All-Star first baseman Roe Skidmore (.261), and ERA champ James Colburn (8–7, 2.28); Whitey justifiably was voted Manager of the Year.

The 1960s had been the most difficult decade in Pacific Coast League history. In previous decades the PCL had taken in stride the challenges posed by two world wars and the Great Depression, adapting to the worst problems — even to the loss of Los Angeles and San Francisco — within a few seasons. But the declining attendance of the 1950s worsened in the 1960s, and the PCL took on previously unimaginable geographic dimensions during the franchise instability of the decade. The primary cause of these difficulties was the most damaging change ever to strike minor league baseball, the transformation of minor league clubs into training stables for the parent organizations. Minor league rosters would undergo scores of changes during a season, as players were sent up and down for the benefit of distant major league teams. Minor league rosters lost all continuity, good players rarely spent more than half a season before being promoted, and key promotions often proved devastating to the pennant hopes of a minor league team. But the Coast League held on, made a major accommodation to preserve AAA ball, and faced an uncertain future with a gritty resolve derived from the traditions of baseball's greatest minor league.

# 1970–1979

## Prosperity Returns
to the PCL

During the first eight years of the 1970s, the PCL remained an eight-team circuit, expanding to ten clubs in 1978. There were five franchise transfers, one each in 1970, 1972, 1973, 1974 and 1977. Although total paid admissions remained around 1.3 million from 1970 through 1976, Hawaii enjoyed spectacular attendance during several seasons, and a few other franchises boasted one or two excellent years. Hawaii and Salt Lake City made the playoffs five times apiece, squaring off against each other in the finals three different times. Spokane won three championships in five years, and Albuquerque entered the league in 1972, appearing in the playoffs four times en route to becoming a dominant franchise. Despite several impressive pitching performances, playing emphasis remained on offense throughout the decade.

In 1970 Hawaii, under manager Chuck Tanner, won the Southern Division by 13 games and ran up the best record in the league before losing to Spokane in the finals. Outfielder Winston Llenas (.339, 20 HRs, 108 RBIs) led the league in RBIs and missed the batting title by one point, second baseman Doug Griffin (.326 with 35 steals) was the stolen base champ, southpaw Dennis Bennett (18–8) tied for the lead in victories for the second year in a row, and veteran lefthander Juan Pizarro (9–0) was invincible in

13 games. Attendance was an eye-popping 407,217 — nearly one-third of the PCL total — and the playoffs attracted another 40,056.

But Spokane, benefiting from the excellent Dodger farm system, totally dominated the Southern Division. The only team in the division to have a winning record, Spokane finished with a 26-game margin over second-place Portland, then won four straight from Hawaii in the playoffs. Tommy Lasorda was the manager, Steve Garvey (.319 with 87 RBIs in 95 games) played third and first before going up to the Dodgers, and Tom Hutton (.323) was named All-Star first baseman. The best members of a fine pitching staff were Jerry Stephenson (18–5, 2.82 ERA), who tied for most victories and was the ERA champ, Mike Strahler (15–5), southpaw Robert O'Brien (13–3), and knuckleballing reliever Charlie Hough (12–8 with a 1.95 ERA in 134 innings). The most spectacular performance came from shortstop Bobby Valentine (.340), who was voted MVP after leading the league in hitting, runs, games played (all 146), doubles, triples, total bases, sacrifice flies, and most times hit by pitch. Valentine played 10 seasons in the big leagues before becoming a manager, but the enormous potential he demonstrated as a player in 1970 was severely reduced by injuries.

Salt Lake City re-entered the PCL in 1970 as a replacement for Vancouver, but suffered through a last-place season, finishing 52½ games behind Hawaii. But Salt Lake City enjoyed a complete turnaround the next year. Manager Del Rice led the club to the Southern Division title after an extremely tight race (only 8½ games separated all four teams), then beat Tacoma in the playoffs. The hard-hitting championship roster included outfielders Tomas Silverio (.339), Tom Reynolds (.355 in 56 games) and John Rivers (.322 in 72 games), shortstop Bruce Christiansen (.309 in 82 games), first baseman Charles Vinson (.327 with 22 homers), second sacker William Parker (.306), third baseman Winston Llenas (.300 with 95 RBIs), and catcher Arthur Kusnyer (.316).

Tacoma boasted home run champ Adrian Garrett (.289, 43 HRs, 119 RBIs), third baseman Carmen Fanzone (.327, 28 HRs, 106 RBIs), stolen base leader Cleo James (.368 with 37 steals in just 71 games), righthander Roberto Rodriguez (15–8), and southpaw Larry Gura (11–8). Rookie Burt Hooten (7–4, 1.68 ERA, and 135 Ks with 73 hits in 102 innings) tied Charles Shields' 1905 single-game record on August 17 when he struck out 19 Eugene batters. Hawaii sagged to last place in team hitting and managed

*Bobby Valentine was voted MVP in 1970 after leading the PCL in hitting, runs, doubles, triples, total bases and several other categories.*

— Author's collection

only a .500 record, but still attracted an attendance of 375,957. Spokane again produced the MVP, batting champ Tom Hutton (.352, 19 HRs, 103 RBIs), while third baseman Ron Cey (.328, 32 HRs, 123 RBIs) led the league in RBIs. Eugene was the team leader in home runs, paced by first baseman Greg Luzinski (.312, 36 HRs, 114 RBIs) and outfielder Mike Anderson (.334, 36 HRs, 100 RBIs), but the massive Luzinski set a PCL record for most strikeouts in a season (167). Another new slugging mark was established by Portland third baseman Eric Soderholm (.275 with 22 homers), who hit four grand slams during the year. Portland righthander Richard Woodson (16–10 with 163 Ks) was the league leader in victories and strikeouts.

In 1972 the LA Dodgers transferred their AAA franchise from Spokane to Albuquerque, where the unique ballpark could accommodate more than 100 vehicles in a drive-in area which rimmed the outfield. Tommy Lasorda, still the manager, led the club to another championship. For the third year in a row, the team provided the league's Most Valuable Player, home run leader Tom Paciorek (.307, 27 HRs, 107 RBIs). Third baseman Ron Cey (.329, 23 HRs, 103 RBIs) had another outstanding year, outfielder Von Joshua

*Portland Beavers, 1971. General Manager Bill Cutler (standing at far right) would become PCL president in 1979. Steve Brye (standing fourth from left) hit .340, and Dick Woodson (standing, fifth from right) led the league in victories, strikeouts, starts and walks.*

— Courtesy Portland Beavers

(.337) won the batting title, second sacker Davey Lopes (.317 with 48 steals) was the stolen base champ, and outfielder Larry Hisle (.325, 23 HRs, 91 RBIs) helped the team post the league's highest batting average. Steve Luebber (13–13 with 199 Ks in 215 innings) was the strikeout king, while lefthander Doug Rau (14–3) registered the PCL's best winning percentage, and Charlie Hough again provided expert bullpen help (14–5 in 58 games).

Eugene fought off Hawaii to win the Western Division. The Emeralds blasted 201 home runs and were led by muscular Mike Schmidt (.291, 26 HRs, 91 RBIs), who played second, third and short. It was Schmidt's second year of pro ball, and he went up to Philadelphia at the end of the season. Shortstop Bill Robinson (.304) exploded for 20 homers and 66 RBIs in just 65 games, and southpaw Mike Wallace (16–7) led the league in victories.

Albuquerque defeated Eugene, three games to one, in a championship series which drew merely 8,006 in total attendance. Despite another .500 club in 1972, Hawaii pulled in 305,878 in paid admissions, and was selected as the site of the first — and only —

Kodak World Baseball Classic. Sponsored by the Eastman Kodak Company, the Classic was devised as a five-team, single elimination postseason tournament featuring the champions of the PCL, American Association (Evansville) and International League (Tidewater), along with an all-star team of Latin players from the Caribbean winter leagues, and a club from the host site (the Hawaii Islanders, of course). The opening contest pitted the Islanders against the Caribbean All-Stars — but attendance was just 1,877, and it worsened after the home team was defeated in the first game. The Albuquerque Dukes reached the finals, but lost to the Caribbean All-Stars, 6–2, before a "crowd" of just 992. The Kodak Classic was not repeated, and the Junior World Series, a decades-old seven-game playoff between the champions of the American Association and the International League, was resumed in 1973.

Spokane rejoined the PCL in 1973 when Portland, the last charter city of the Coast League, pulled out after an attendance of just 91,907 in 1972. Led by second baseman Bill Madlock (.338, 22 HRs, 90 RBIs), infielder-outfielder Don Castle (.325), and pitchers Mike Waits (14–7), Jim Shellenback (13–7), Jackie Brown (10–1), and Dick Henninger (12–5), the Indians overwhelmed the Western Division, then defeated Tucson in three straight for the championship.

Tucson won the team batting title and staff ERA; Manny Trillo (.312) led all second basemen in fielding, while righthander Glenn Abbott (18–8) was the PCL victory leader. Hawaii righty Dave Freisleben (16–8, 2.82 ERA, and 206 Ks in 195 innings) won the ERA and strikeout titles, and *lost* a seven-inning, 1–0 no-hitter to Albuquerque. Phoenix switch hitter Steve Ontiveros was the batting champ (.357), Salt Lake City outfielder John Rivera (.336 with 47 steals) won the theft title, and outfielder Eugene Martin, who played for Eugene and Hawaii, was the home run and RBI king (.288, 31 HRs, 106 RBIs). For the first time since 1963, an All-Star Game was played; attendance in Albuquerque was 3,197, as the West defeated the East, 9–6.

For five years Eugene had staunchly supported the Emeralds, but the city was too small to sustain AAA ball, and in 1974 the franchise was moved to Sacramento. But Sacramento's ballpark had been razed, and the only available facility was venerable Hughes Field, a horseshoe-shaped football stadium. After a diamond was laid out, the left field foul line loomed just 231 feet from

*The 1973 Tucson Toros posted the best record in the league and won the Western Division. The manager was former big league catcher Sherm Lollar (number 25). Future major leaguers included Phil Garner (3) and Manny Trillo (1). Glenn Abbott (17) led the PCL in victories.*

— Courtesy Arizona Historical Society Library, Tucson

home plate. Throughout 1974 an average of seven homers per game flew out of Hughes Field. Out of 491 home runs, Sacramento blasted a record 305 — but because Official Baseball Rule 1.04 requires a minumum outfield distance of 250 feet, all 1974 records set in Hughes Field are marked with a double asterisk in the PCL Record Book.

Nevertheless, Sacramento played crowd-pleasing offensive baseball, attracting a league-leading attendance of 295,831 for a team which finished last in the West. Third baseman Bill McNulty (.325, 55 HRs, 135 RBIs) led the league in homers, runs, total bases and RBIs, while outfielders Gorman Thomas (.297, 51 HRs, 122 RBIs) and Sixto Lezcano (.324 with 34 homers) made major contributions to the PCL's most explosive offense. Twice during the season, 14 home runs were hit in a single game, and twice there were five homers in a single inning. In one game there were four consecutive home runs, and in another there were three grand slams. The pitching staff, of course, finished dead last in team ERA (6.70).

*Safe at third! Albuquerque manager Stan Wasiak agrees with the call on the road in Portland on July 31, 1974.*

— Courtesy Tacoma Public Library

But the best staff ERA in the league was a generous 4.44, posted by Spokane. Again managed by Del Wilber, the Indians successfully defended their 1973 title by winning the Eastern Division with the season's best record, then downing Albuquerque in three straight postseason games (in 1973 and 1974 Spokane was 3–0 in the playoffs). Shortstop Pete Makanin (.291, 28 HRs, 103 RBIs) and stolen base champ David Moates (.300 with 42 thefts) were key offensive performers, while first baseman Tom Robson (.322, 41 HRs, 131 RBIs) was voted Most Valuable Player. There had been no MVP in 1973, and after Robson's selection the award was discontinued until 1980.

Albuquerque led the PCL in team hitting (.305) en route to another division title. Named to the All-Star team were second baseman Robert Randall (.338), shortstop Ivan DeJesus (.298), outfielder Charles Manuel (.329, 30 HRs, 102 RBIs), and right-hander Rex Hudson (16–4). The All-Star Game, held at Tacoma and won by the East, attracted an all-time low of just 1,871 in attendance.

Glenn Adams of Phoenix was the 1974 batting champ (.352), while Tacoma's Dan Walton (.263, 35 HRs, 109 RBIs) and Sacramento's Tommie Reynolds (.312, 35 HRs, 91 RBIs) were among the eight Coast League sluggers who walloped 30 or more home runs. The year's best pitching performance came on June 20, when Hawaii's Ralph Garcia (7–5 with 122 Ks in 116 innings) struck out 19 Spokane hitters, matching a record set by Charles Shields in 1905 and tied by Burt Hooten in 1971.

There were no franchise changes in 1975. Sacramento altered its left field fence by erecting a tall screen, but still led the league with 196 homers, and first baseman Robert Hansen (.279, 29 HRs, 102 RBIs) was the home run champ. Sacramento finished in the PCL cellar, but again was the attendance leader (252,201). Albuquerque infielder Jerry Royster (.333 with 33 steals) won the batting title and tied for most stolen bases before being promoted to the Dodgers. Tacoma righthander Steve Luebber, who was the 1972 strikeout king while pitching for Albuquerque, won the ERA crown (14–7, 2.39 ERA).

Hawaii won the first of three consecutive Western Division titles with the best record of 1975, then beat Salt Lake City in the playoffs, four games to two. The Islanders were led by outfielder John Turner (.329), righthander Clarence Metzger (15–7), and victory leader Gary Ross (16–8). On May 19 Ross became the fourth pitcher in PCL history to hurl a perfect game, but the contest lasted just five innings. In the first inning a record 20 Islander batters came up against Salt Lake City pitchers, and Ross coasted to a 19–0 victory.

Hawaii and Salt Lake City repeated as division winners in 1976. Salt Lake City infielder Paul Dade (.363) was the batting champ; although he appeared in just 91 games and fell far short of the required 389 at-bats, Official Baseball Rule 10.23 (a) gave him the crown under the provision that if 10 at-bats were added to his total of 320, he still would have the league's best average. Outfielder Carlos Lopez (.350) and strikeout leader Gary Wheelock (15–8, 138 Ks) also helped bring the Eastern Division title back to Salt Lake City. Hawaii again claimed the Western Division behind ERA leader Diego Segui (11–5, 3.18) and outfielders Eugene Richards (.331), John Scott (.315) and Rod Gaspar (.294). Hawaii won a good playoff series, three games to two, for the Islanders' second championship in a row. Although playoff attendance was miserable (3,936), Hawaii (306,236) and Salt Lake City (239,321) accounted for more than 40 percent of the paid attendance across the league.

*The grandstand at San Jose, which leased Sacramento's franchise in 1977.*

— Author's photo

Tacoma slugger Bob Gorinski (.285, 28 HRs, 110 RBIs) was the 1976 home run and RBI leader, and Phoenix outfielder-third baseman Jack Clark (.323) moved up to the Giants after a fine season. Sacramento led the PCL in team batting and home runs (.303 with 183 homers). The awesome hitting attack featured outfielders Lewis Beasley (.351 with 21 homers), Keith Smith (.325 with 23 homers), and Cirilio Cruz (.324), second sacker Bump Wills (.324, 26 HRs, 95 RBIs), and first baseman Doug Ault (.313 with 25 homers). But once more the pitching staff yielded an astronomical ERA (6.07) and gave up 206 home runs. Attendance dropped to 82,324, and it was decided to lease the franchise until a new stadium could be erected in Sacramento. But major league baseball now was being played in Oakland as well as San Francisco, rendering it impossible for nearby San Jose to generate acceptable attendance for two losing teams (88,265 in 1977 and just 67,037 the next year).

Attendance was excellent in Hawaii, however, as the 1977 Islanders won their third straight division crown and totaled almost 348,000 paid admissions. On July 4 Hawaii attracted the minor leagues' top crowd of the year, 33,904, after pulling in 25,189 on

April 26. Salt Lake City drew nearly 255,000 during the year, as fans enjoyed a club which averaged .305 and led the PCL with 150 homers. Despite a losing season and the nearby presence of major league ball in Seattle, Tacoma registered 207,538; the opening day crowd exceeded 10,000 — 300 more than the Seattle Mariners drew on the same date! Both the PCL and the International League tallied more than 1,500,000 for the first time since 1959.

Hawaii was led by switch hitter Richard Sweet (.323) and Julio Cruz (.366 in 75 games), outfielders Mike Dupree (.352 in 70 games) and Don Reynolds (.368 in 42 games), and Mark Wiley (16–7), who was the victory leader for the second year in a row. Phoenix won the Eastern Division behind first baseman Phil James (.308 with 97 RBIs), shortstop James Kennedy (.316), and pitchers Greg Minton 14–6) and Ed Plank (14–7). Phoenix thwarted Hawaii's bid for a third straight playoff championship by prevailing, four games to two.

Albuquerque won the team hitting title (.306) and dominated the individual offensive honors: first baseman Don Cardoza was the batting champ (.356), switch hitter Dan Walton led the league in runs, homers and RBIs (.289, 42 HRs, 122 RBIs), second baseman Rafael Landestoy was the stolen base king (.276 with 56 thefts), and outfielder Henry Cruz (.353) paced the league in base hits. First baseman Pedro Guerrero (.403 with 39 RBIs in 32 games) was off to a spectacular start before being disabled for the season, and outfielder Joe Simpson (.349 with 35 steals) also had a banner year. Third baseman Claude Westmoreland (.265 with 22 homers) set a PCL record by blasting home runs in seven consecutive games (June 27, 28, 29, 30, July 1, 2, 3). During this hitters' year, pitchers were regularly battered. There were zero no-hitters, Hawaii had the lowest staff ERA with a 4.47 mark, and Tacoma southpaw Eddie Bane (9–8, 4.14 ERA) won the title with an all-time high record for an ERA champ.

The Coast League expanded to 10 teams in 1978, adding two familiar cities, Portland and Vancouver. Portland promptly made the playoffs, leading the league in home runs (130) and hitting .306 as a team. The best Beavers of 1978 were outfielders Robert Ellis (.333, 21 HRs, 91 RBIs) and Dan Briggs (.330, 20 HRs, 109 RBIs), and victory leader Eric Wilkins (15–5).

With 10 clubs in the league, it was decided to return to a four-team playoff, pitting the top two clubs in each division against each other, after which the winners would square off. Tacoma boasted the PCL's finest mound corps, posting the best staff ERA (3.89), the most shutouts (11), and the season's only no-hitter (by Jim Beattie, who got off to a 3–0 start with a 1.57 ERA and immediately was promoted to the Yankees). Robert Kammeyer (12–2) was the percentage leader, Larry McCall (10–3, 2.93) was the ERA champ, and Roger Slagle (13–8) led the staff in wins.

In the East Albuquerque won the division title under manager Del Crandall. The Dukes hit .303 as a team and boasted batting champ Jeff Leonard (.365 with 93 RBIs), RBI titlist Pedro Guerrero (.337 with 116 RBIs), and stolen base leader Rudy Law (.312 with 79 steals), along with towering righthander Rich Sutcliffe (13–6). Spearheaded by home run leader Willie Aikens (.326, 29 HRs, 110 RBIs), Salt Lake City challenged Albuquerque, but lost three straight games to the Dukes in the opening round of playoffs. In the meantime, Tacoma and Portland deadlocked with two victories each when rain halted the series. Wet grounds and threatening forecasts, along with the need to promote players to expanded late-season big league rosters, prompted PCL President Roy Jackson to end postseason play. Jackson declared Hawaii and Tacoma, first-place finishers in their respective divisions, to be 1978 co-champions.

Jackson stepped down as president, and Bill Cutler, owner at Spokane and a longtime American League executive, was named the new PCL leader for 1979. After two years of fighting impossible odds, San Jose returned the Sacramento franchise to the league. Sacramento had not built a suitable ballpark, but the franchise was sold to baseball interests in Ogden, Utah. The PCL decided to try a new playoff scheme, splitting the season and letting the two Northern winners and the two Southern victors play each other for their respective division titles. Division winners then would square off for the championship; the opening playoff round would consist of two best-of-three series, while the finals would be decided by a best three-of-five set.

Albuquerque led the league in team hitting (.309) by a 21-point margin over second-place Ogden, and the powerful Dukes carved out the best record of 1979. The Dukes' lineup included five of the league's top eight batters: batting champ Mickey Hatcher (.374 with 93 RBIs in 103 games), catcher Mike Sciosia (.336), repeat RBI leader Pedro Guerrero (.333, 22 HRs, 103 RBIs), out-

*William S. Cutler, a former American League executive and PCL club owner and GM, was elected league president in 1979 and has provided stable leadership through the present.*

— Courtesy Pacific Coast League

fielder Robert Mitchell (.327), and second baseman John Perconte (.322). Salt Lake City also made the playoffs in the South. Shortstop Rance Mullinks (.343), first baseman John Harris (.325), outfielder Robert Clark (.304 with 97 RBIs), and stolen base leader Jose Mangual (.270 with 22 homers and 46 thefts) spearheaded an impressive attack. Salt Lake City had a losing record in the first half of 1979, but gathered momentum and edged Albuquerque by 1¹/₂ games in the second half. Two explosive offensive machines battled for the Southern Division title, with Salt Lake City advancing to the finals after winning the first two games.

In the North, Hawaii won the first half. The Islanders finished last in team hitting, but the pitching staff hurled 17 shutouts and a 3.49 ERA, heading the league in each category. Vancouver recorded the best fielding percentage in the PCL and the second lowest ERA, and squeezed out the second half title. Second baseman Lenn Sakata (.300) and outfielder Billy Severns (.318) paced the offense, and Severns set a PCL record by striking out only nine times in 442 plate appearances. The star of the team was righthander Mark Bomback (22–7 with a 2.56 ERA), who led the league in victories, ERA, shutouts (5), starts, complete games and innings pitched. Bomback was the first PCL 20-game winner since 1966, and the last to date. Another outstanding pitching performance was turned in by Tacoma strikeout leader Juan Berenguer, who overpowered 220 batters in just 166 innings.

Hawaii outlasted Vancouver, two games to one, for the Northern Division crown, and the finals would pit the league's most efficient pitching staff against the lethal hitting machine of manager Jimy Williams. This classic confrontation was decisively resolved by the Salt Lake City sluggers, who swept three consecutive games from the Islanders.

The 1979 split-season divisional playoff scheme proved so satisfactory that it has become a permanent fixture of the PCL. Attendance in 1979 was 1,761,487, highest of the decade. The PCL had grown back to 10 teams, and Albuquerque, Hawaii and Salt Lake City had become especially strong franchises, consistently successful on the field and at the gate. As a new decade approached, there seemed to be a slow but solid resurgence of interest in minor league baseball, and the Coast League was at the forefront of this encouraging trend.

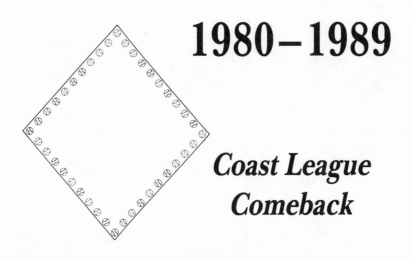

# 1980–1989

## *Coast League Comeback*

During the 1980s the PCL benefited fully from the resurgence of interest in minor league baseball. The makeup of teams constantly changed as rosters increasingly were juggled to provide fresh talent for the parent club, or to accumulate solid replacement players in case of injuries. But the frequent appearance of men with playing experience in the major leagues has proved attractive for fans in minor league cities. Indeed, there is little difference in the ability level of the lower third of major league rosters and the upper third of players on AAA teams. In a time when it is exorbitantly expensive to take the family to the movies or amusement parks, minor league baseball offers wholesome and affordable entertainment. Despite the lack of roster continuity during the season, fans regularly turn out to watch the stars of tomorrow or to see players with big league credentials or to enjoy an evening with the kids. Minor league franchises, which were serious financial liabilities during the 1950s and 1960s, currently are escalating in value — none more so than in the Pacific Coast League, where paid admissions annually have exceeded two million throughout the decade.

The PCL has maintained a lineup of ten teams during the 1980s, and there have been four franchise changes since 1981. The addition of Edmonton and Calgary has brought the number of Ca-

147

*Albuquerque won the first of three consecutive playoff titles in 1980. Manager Del Crandall stands at far left, and MVP Dennis Llewallyn stands fourth from left.*
— Courtesy Albuquerque Dukes

nadian cities to three; the Canadian National Anthem now is regularly heard throughout the Coast League. Although Hawaii was lost to the PCL in 1988, the addition of Las Vegas in 1983 has maintained an aura of glamour in the PCL. Hawaii earned four playoff berths during the 1980s, while Las Vegas made the playoffs four times and won two championships. Albuquerque has been the most dynastic club, however, appearing in the playoffs six times in nine years and winning four pennants.

Albuquerque began the 1980s with three consecutive playoff titles. Manager Del Crandall, who had guided the Dukes to playoff appearances in 1978 and 1979, skippered the team in each of the title years. Albuquerque led the league in team hitting in 1981 (.325) and 1982 (.313), and in each of these years the Dukes produced the batting champ and the league's best record.

The 1980 Dukes fielded three pitchers who tied with Salt Lake City's Paul Botting (15–8) for the lead in victories: Dave Stewart (15–10), lefty Gerald Hannahs (15–9), and reliever Dennis Lewallyn (15–2 in 55 appearances with a 2.13 ERA and 24 saves). After leading the PCL in victories, ERA, winning percentage and saves, Lewallyn was named Most Valuable Player. Tucson's playoff team was led by batting champ Danny Heep (.343) and RBI leader Alan Knicely (.318, 22 HRs, 105 RBIs). Portland outfielder Kim Allen (.294 with 84 steals) won the stolen base title and had a 35-game hitting streak, while Portland catcher Tony Pena (.327) would be in the big leagues by season's end. For the second year in a row, Hawaii defeated Vancouver in the opening rounds of playoffs. Tucson had the best record of 1980, but Albuquerque downed the Toros in two games, then beat Hawaii, three games to two, in the finals.

The Most Valuable Player of 1981 was Albuquerque first baseman Mike Marshall (.373, 34 HRs, 137 RBIs), who was the first Triple Crown winner since Steve Bilko in 1956. Second baseman John Perconte produced his third consecutive standout season for the Dukes (1979 — .322; 1980 — .326 with 44 steals; 1981 — .346 with 45 steals). Outfielders Rudy Law (.335 with 56 steals) and Candy Maldonado (.335, 21 HRs, 104 RBIs) helped the Dukes lead the PCL in team hitting by 22 points (.325). Dukes righthander Ted Power (18–3) paced the league in victories and winning percentage while Brian Holton (16–6) and Richard Wright (14–6) were almost as formidable.

Forty-year-old Luis Tiant, now pitching for Portland, topped a solid season (13–7) with a no-hitter over Spokane, and Portland's Robert Long (15–3) also was impressive. Hawaii charged back into the playoffs behind stolen base champ Alan Wiggins (.302 with 73 thefts), a switch-hitting All Star outfielder. Hawaii defeated Tacoma in the playoff opener, but the Islanders went down to the Dukes in three straight games in the finals. Albuquerque easily won both halves in the Southern Division en route to one of the best winning percentages (94–38, .712) in Coast League history.

In 1981 Edmonton joined the league, when local sports magnate Peter Pocklington brought the Ogden franchise to Canada. The Trappers inhabited Renfrew Park, a charming throwback to the irregular ballparks of an earlier era which would be a haven for sluggers. Indeed, the most spectacular hitting feat of the decade was provided in 1982 by Trapper outfielder Ron Kittle (.345, 50 HRs, 144 RBIs in 127 games). Kittle, a 6'4, 200-pound righthanded slugger, blasted 13 homers in April. The parent White Sox did not bring up Kittle until late in the season, and he continued to wallop roundtrippers as excited fans turned out to watch his num-

*The Edmonton Trappers first played in the PCL in 1981.*
— Courtesy Edmonton Trappers

bers mount. No PCL hitter had registered 50 home runs since Steve Bilko in 1956 and 1957, but on the last day of the season Kittle walloped number 50 out of Renfrew Park. Eight other Coast Leaguers had reached 50 home runs, but none in as few as 127 games. Such a sustained performance is highly unlikely in the contemporary minor league world, and Kittle was named the PCL's Most Valuable Player as well as Minor League Player of the Year by *The Sporting News*.

Kittle led the league in homers, RBIs and runs scored. Portland righthander Odell Jones (16–9 with 172 Ks in 190 innings) was the PCL leader in victories and strikeouts, while Tacoma's Chris Codiroli (10–3 in 16 games with a 1.90 ERA) qualified for the ERA title. The stolen base champ was switch hitter Gary Pettis (.288 with 53 steals), who was part of Spokane's impressive offensive unit. Third baseman Steve Lubratich (.338), first sacker Daryl Sconiers (.329), and catcher Jerry Narron (.311) spearheaded Spokane's drive to the Northern Division championship.

Winners of the other divisions, for the third year in a row, were the Albuquerque Dukes. Del Crandall's 1982 edition featured batting champ Mike Wilson (.378), shortstop Dave Anderson (.343),

*Albuquerque Dukes, 1981 champs. Mike Marshall (top row, fourth from left) was named MVP after winning the Triple Crown.*

— Courtesy Albuquerque Dukes

*Star of the 1982 Edmonton Trappers was MVP Ron Kittle (top row, third from left), who led the league in RBIs and hit 50 homers.*

— Courtesy Edmonton Trappers

### A Labor of Love

The philosophy of PCL owners and executives throughout the decades was clearly stated by Tacoma head man Stan Naccarato in 1982. "There's no 'killing' to be made anywhere in the minor leagues," said Naccarato, a former player who today is Tacoma's leading sports organizer. "Minor league baseball is a labor of love. If you don't love it, if you can't deal with the 10,000 problems you'll face over the course of a year, you're an absolute fool to get into it in the first place."

"You can talk all you want about pennant races and winning baseball," pointed out Portland General Manager Dave Hersh, "but it's no secret to anyone in baseball that when you talk about making a profit in the minor leagues, you're talking about being in the restaurant business. If you do everything else right, how many hot dogs and cokes you sell on a per-game basis will eventually determine whether your club makes it or comes out a loser."

By the 1980s PCL club executives efficiently marketed advertising on fences and game programs, baseball souvenirs, and concessions ranging from nachos to milk shakes (in Vancouver non-paying fans frequently gather on a hill overlooking right field, and concessionaires venture out to peddle drinks, hot dogs, etc.). Innovative general managers stage a promotion for every home game, and push season tickets across the community. Cold weather and rainouts may devastate a carefully planned season's campaign, because the cost of field maintenance, utilities for night games, baseballs (several thousand per year), and other non-variables must be paid. Arrangements for ballpark rental, concessions and parking profits are crucial. The financial arrangements for 1982 PCL franchises are listed below:

| Team | Percent of Concessions | Percent of Parking | Other Expenses (estimated)* |
|---|---|---|---|
| Albuquerque | 100 | None | $35,000 (rent, tax) |
| Edmonton | 96 of gross | None | $60,000 (rent, tax) |
| Hawaii | None | None | $75,000 (rent, maint.) |
| Phoenix | 100 | 100 | $35,000 (rent, tax) |
| Portland | 30 | None | $110,000 (rent, tax) |
| Salt Lake City | 100 | 100 | $40,000 (rent, tax) |
| Spokane | 100 | 100 | $60,000 (rent, maint.) |
| Tacoma | 100 | None | $65,000 (rent, tax) |
| Tucson | 25 | None | ? (no rent, tax only) |
| Vancouver | 100 | 100 | $35,000 (rent, tax) |

(continued)

> * Figures do not include personnel expenses, generally between $12–14,000 per month.
>
> Visiting teams add considerably to the local economy through dining, hotel and travel revenue. In addition to fulltime office and maintenance personnel, as many as 80 to 100 employees go to work at every home game. And despite the lack of continuity of player rosters, families turn out at the ballparks in increasing numbers. "People are looking for a bargain these days," explained Tucson General Manager Jack Donovan. "The times when they would pack up the family, go out to dinner, then take in a movie are gone. Nobody can afford it anymore, so they search for some form of entertainment that won't kill the family budget, and when they look around, they see us."

Mike Marshall (.388 in 66 games), and reliever Orel Hershiser (9–6 in 47 games). Albuquerque defeated Salt Lake City in two straight to take the playoff opener, then won a third consecutive flag by downing Spokane, four games to two, in the finals.

In 1983 Albuquerque made the playoffs for the sixth year in a row, and won another division title before finally falling in the playoffs. For the third consecutive year, the Dukes led the PCL in team hitting (.307) behind outfielder Lemmie Miller (.330), third baseman German Rivera (.328, 24 HRs, 103 RBIs), and first sacker Sid Bream (.307, 32 HRs, 118 RBIs), who led the league in RBIs and homers. Lefty Rich Rodas (16–4, 157 Ks) was the PCL leader in victories, winning percentage and strikeouts, while Orel Hershiser (10–8 with 10 starts and 16 saves) pitched well enough to earn a promotion to the Dodgers.

Phoenix switch hitter Chris Smith (.379, 21 HRs, 102 RBIs) was the 1983 batting champ, and Tucson outfielder Scott Loucks (.287 with 71 steals) was the stolen base king. Las Vegas outfielder Kevin McReynolds (.377 with 32 homers and 116 RBIs in 113 games) tied Bream for the home run title before going up to San Diego. In its first PCL season, Las Vegas earned a playoff berth and led the league in attendance (365,848 — paid admissions across the circuit exceeded 2.3 million).

Las Vegas was defeated in the playoff opener by Albuquerque. Also falling in the first playoff round was Edmonton. The Trappers hit .300 as a team, led the league in homers (179), and featured outfielders Mike Brown (.355, 22 HRs, 106 RBIs) and Gary Pettis

*Portland won the 1983 playoffs with a three-game sweep of defending champion Albuquerque.*

— Courtesy Portland Beavers

(.285 with 52 steals and a league-leading 138 runs in 132 games). Portland beat Edmonton for the Northern Division title, then won three straight from Hawaii to sweep the finals. Portland manager John Felske won the 1983 pennant behind a lineup bristling with such hitters as first baseman Len Matuszek (.330, 24 HRs, 92 RBIs), and outfielders Tim Corcoran (.311 with 93 RBIs) and Richard Davis (.328).

In 1984 the Las Vegas success story continued as the Stars again made the playoffs and led the league in attendance (320,157). RBI leader Rick Lancellotti (.287, 29 HRs, 131 RBIs in 133 games) and All Star shortstop Ozzie Guillen (.296) were the brightest Stars. Shortstop Danny Tartabull (.304), righthander James Lewis (15–9), and second baseman Harold Reynolds (.296) led Salt Lake City to a playoff berth. Although Hawaii finished last in team batting, the Islanders made the playoffs on the strength of the league's best pitching staff. By large margins the Islander staff led the PCL in ERA (3.16), complete games (43), shutouts (14) and strikeouts (813). Bob Walk (9–5, 2.26) was the ERA leader, Alfonso Pulido (18–6) was the league's best lefthander, and Mike Bielecki (19–3, 162 Ks) paced the PCL in victories and strikeouts. Hawaii won the

Southern Division with a three-game sweep of Las Vegas, but fell in the finals to Edmonton. The Trappers brought a PCL pennant to Canada for the first time behind first sacker Francisco Melendez (.312), third baseman Rick Schu (.301), and outfielder Jeff Stone (.307).

On the heels of its first pennant, Canada acquired a third team when the Salt Lake City club was moved to Calgary. The Calgary Cannons led the league in team hitting and produced the 1985 MVP, shortstop Danny Tartabull (.300, 43 HRs, 109 RBIs), who was the PCL's home run and RBI champ. Aided by the efforts of stolen base leader Mike Feider (.314 with 61 steals) and infielder Carlos Ponce (.320), Vancouver also reached the playoffs and made the Northern Division an all-Canadian shootout.

In the South Hawaii's pitching staff again led the PCL in ERA, shutouts, complete games and strikeouts. Bob Walk (12–5, 12 CG in 24 starts, and a 2.65 ERA) repeated as ERA champ and paced the league in victories and complete games. Hawaii ran up the PCL's best season record, but lost the Southern Division title to Phoenix. The Firebirds boasted righthander Roger Mason (12–1 in 24 starts), outfielder Mike Wilson (.318), switch hitter Ron Roenicke (.308 in 60 games), and second baseman Mike Woodard (.316). The Southern Division also provided the batting champ, Las Vegas outfielder John Kruk (.351), while Albuquerque first baseman Franklin Stubbs demonstrated excellent power and speed (.280 with 32 homers and 23 steals). Phoenix defeated Hawaii in a three-game sweep in the playoff opener as Vancouver swept Calgary in three straight. In the finals Vancouver won three in a row from Phoenix to bring a second consecutive pennant to Canada.

Vancouver returned to the finals in 1986 behind outfielder Glenn Braggs (.360), infielder-outfielder James Adduci (.339), shortstop Edgar Diaz (.315), and catcher B. J. Surhoff (.308). Vancouver won its second consecutive Northern Division crown with a three-game sweep over Tacoma. In the South, Tucson outfielder Ty Gainey (.351) won the hitting title, while Phoenix and Las Vegas battled for the division championship. The Firebirds starred home run champ Rich Lancellotti (.275, 31 HRs, 106 RBIs), third baseman Randy Johnson (.332), victory leader Mark Grant (14–7), and relievers Mike Jeffcoat (7–2 in 54 appearances) and Jon Perlman (7–3 in 45 games).

Las Vegas first baseman Tim Pyznarski (.326, 23 HRs, 119

*Calgary's 1985 opener was snowed out.*
— Courtesy Calgary Cannons

*Wally Joyner (top row, sixth from left) soon would vault to big league stardom.*
— Courtesy Edmonton Trappers

*Calgary shortstop Danny Tartabull was voted 1985 MVP after leading the PCL in homers and RBIs (.300, 43 HRs, 109 RBIs).*

— Courtesy Calgary Cannons

*Max Papkin, shown here at a 1986 Calgary appearance, has clowned his way through the PCL for decades.*

— Courtesy Calgary Cannons

*Jon Perlman was an ace reliever for Phoenix in 1986 (7–3) and 1987 (12–6, 18 saves — Fireman of the Year Award). He also pitched with Colorado Springs in 1988 (3–1), and has hurled for the Cubs, Giants and Indians.*

— Courtesy Jon Perlman

RBIs) led the PCL in RBIs and was voted Most Valuable Player. En route to the Stars' first pennant, Las Vegas recorded the most paid admissions in the league (291,060). Las Vegas battled Phoenix to the fifth game before winning the Southern Division, then outlasted defending champion Vancouver, three games to two, for the pennant.

Las Vegas fielded another playoff team in 1987, but the Stars were overwhelmed for the Southern Division title in three straight games by Albuquerque. Albuquerque's best pitcher was righthander Shawn Hillegas (13–5), while the Stars showcased righthanded reliever Todd Simmons (7–7 in 75 games with 22 saves and 57 games finished), who led the PCL in appearances, saves and finishes. The Northern Division produced batting champ James Eppard (.341 with 94 RBIs) of Edmonton, but Calgary won the team hitting title (.287) and ran up the best record of the year. Cannons first baseman Edgar Martinez (.329) had the league's second highest batting average, slugging outfielder Dave Hengel (.295, 23 HRs, 103 RBIs) was the home run and RBI king, and outfielder Donell Nixon (.323 with 46 steals) won the stolen base title — even though he played in only 82 games. Ace of the Cannons' staff was righthander Mike Campbell (15–2), who led the PCL in victories and winning percentage and won the MVP award. Mike Brown (10–2) also pitched well for Calgary, while other fine pitching performances were turned in by ERA champ Vicente Palacios (13–5, 2.58) of Vancouver, and Phoenix reliever Jon Perlman (12–6 with 18 saves).

Strikeout leader Tim Belcher (9–11, 133 Ks), Darrel Akerfelds (10–3), and southpaw Tim Birtsas (7–2) pitched Tacoma to a playoff berth, and the Tigers defeated Calgary for the Northern Division crown. Albuquerque, which had won the last of three consecutive playoff titles in 1982, swept Las Vegas to win the Southern Division, then beat Tacoma, three games to one, for the 1987 championship. Shawn Hillegas (13–5) anchored the Dukes' pitching staff, but manager Terry Collins had to juggle his batting order as players moved up and down — Jeff Hamilton (.360 in 65 games), Larry See (.304 in 66 games), Brad Wellman (.306 in 88 games), and George Hinshaw (.338 in 103 games). The championship quality of the Dukes was demonstrated in the third playoff game with Las Vegas. After two innings the Stars had jumped out to a 10–0 lead, but the Dukes battled back for an 18–11 triumph.

After the season the Hawaii franchise was moved to Colorado Springs. The PCL had been in Hawaii since 1961, but since the termite-ridden downtown park in Honolulu had been abandoned, with the loss to the team of all parking and concession revenue, the Islanders had lost large sums of money year after year. But the new ballpark in Colorado Springs was not ready by the start of the 1988 season. The Sky Sox's first "home" games were played in Yuma, then the team moved to a municipal park, Spurgeon Stadium, where high winds blew toward friendly outfield fences.

On May 7 Colorado Springs beat Phoenix, 33–12, sailing a total of 13 home runs out of the cozy confines of Spurgeon. In 1974, 14 homers had been hit during a game at Sacramento's Hughes Field, but left field was less than the regulation 250 feet. The official PCL record of 11 homers had been established in Salt Lake City in 1923, but after 65 years the Sky Sox hit eight roundtrippers and the Firebirds added five to set a new mark. Former major leaguer Ed Lynch had just reported to the Firebirds. He worked the first $3^2/_3$ innings, giving up 14 hits, five hom-

*Albuquerque returned to the PCL throne room in 1987.*
— Courtesy Albuquerque Dukes

*Mike Campbell (15–2) was named 1987 MVP.*
— Courtesy Calgary Cannons

*Calgary Cannons, 1987 Northern Division champs. Dave Hengel (second row from top, fourth from left) was the home run and RBI leader, and Donell Nixon (second row from top, third from right) was the stolen base king. The cannon is fired after every home run.*

— Courtesy Calgary Cannons

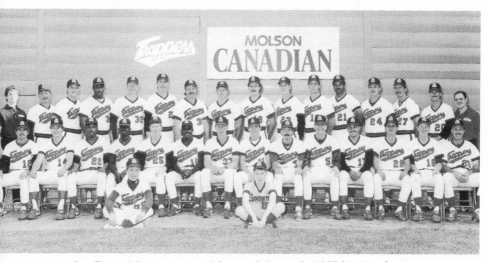

*Jim Eppard (top row, second from right) was the 1987 batting champ.*
— Courtesy Edmonton Trappers

ers and 15 runs for a 36.82 ERA — and he promptly retired. Eight days later the Sky Sox scored 12 runs in the first inning of a game against Las Vegas (Tacoma had tallied a record 14 runs in one inning in 1978). Sky Sox outfielder Luis Medina (.310 with 28 homers) hit six four-baggers in five games at Spurgeon, and he went on to win the home run title. DH Rod Allen (.324, 23 HRs, 100 RBIs) was the RBI leader, and outfielder Terry Francona (.323) was promoted to Cleveland after hitting in 21 straight games.

Another remarkable hitting feat was accomplished by Phoenix third baseman Matt Williams. On May 25 Williams struck out in his first at-bat, then homered his next four times up to lead an 11–8 victory over Albuquerque. Pete Schneider's record of five homers in a single game remained intact, but Williams tied Ted Beard's 1953 mark of home runs in four consecutive at-bats.

Las Vegas outfielder Shane Mack (.347) rode a 27-game hitting streak to a promotion to the Padres' roster, and Albuquerque infielder Tracy Woodson hit safely in 20 consecutive games. Calgary third baseman Edgar Martinez (.363) won the batting title over Phoenix first sacker Francisco Melendez (.361). Martinez broke his nose during spring training on a bad-hop grounder, then broke it again in a bench-clearing brawl against Albuquerque early in the season. Benches also were cleared in Phoenix when Vancouver manager Terry Bevington accused Firebirds pitching coach Marty DeMerritt of squatting outside the visitors' dugout to get a better look at opposing pitchers. There was a shouting match, then a brief melee, and the following night DeMerritt placed four orange traffic cones to mark off the disputed area.

The PCL had not conducted an All-Star Game since 1975, but in 1988 a Triple-A All-Star Game was organized. The best players from the PCL, American Association and International League were selected, aligning with opposing squads of American League and National League affiliates. Terry Collins of Albuquerque was named as manager of the National League team. PCL players included: *National League* — catcher Sandy Alomar, pitcher Greg Harris, shortstop Mike Brumley, second baseman Joey Cora (Las Vegas); first baseman Tracy Woodson, outfielders Mike Devereaux and Chris Gwynn (Albuquerque), infielder Tony Perezchica (Phoenix), outfielder Cameron Drew

*After playing their first seven "home" games of 1988 in Yuma, the Colorado Springs Sky Sox moved into temporary quarters at Spurgeon Stadium.*

— Author's photo

*Streamlined Sky Sox Stadium opened to enthusiastic crowds 46 games into the 1988 schedule.*

— Author's photo

(Tucson); *American League* — pitcher Donn Pall, outfielder Sap Randall (Vancouver), catcher Phil Ouelette, infielder Mario Diaz (Calgary), pitcher Urbano Lugo (Edmonton), pitcher Roy Smith (Portland), second baseman Lance Blankenship (Tacoma), and outfielder Luis Medina (Colorado Springs). The game was held on July 13 at Buffalo's new $56,400,000 Pilot Field. A capacity crowd of 19,500 watched the American League squeeze out a 2–1 victory in the ninth. The game was enthusiastically received, and was conducted in an American Association ballpark in 1989.

Some of the most talented All Stars — Mike Devereaux (.340), Chris Gwynn (.299) and Tracy Woodson (.319) — led Albuquerque to the league's best record, along with outfielder George Hinshaw (.340), second baseman Mike Sharperson (.319), Bill Brennan (14–8), Ken Howell (10–1), and lefthander Bill Krueger (15–5, 3.01), who was the PCL leader in victories, winning percentage and ERA.

Portland made the playoffs behind a hard-hitting lineup, outfielders Eric Bullock (.309), John Christensen (.304) and Alan Cockrell (.293), first baseman Kelvin Torve (.301), and catcher Brian Harper (.353). But Portland was swept in three games in the playoffs by Vancouver. The Canadians were led by second baseman Mike Woodard (.332), outfielder Lance Johnson (.307), and pitchers Roy Smith (12–9) and Balvino Galvez (11–7).

Las Vegas, which had missed the playoffs only one year (1985) since entering the PCL in 1983, won the Southern Division with a three-game sweep over Albuquerque. Sandy Alomar (.297) was considered the best catcher in the minor leagues. There were six switch hitters on the roster, including third baseman Bip Roberts (.353), outfielder Stan Jefferson (.317), Joey Cora (.296) and Mike Brumley (.315), while reliever Todd Simmons (12–5 in 54 appearances) recorded more victories than any starter. Las Vegas won the first game of the finals, but Vancouver evened the series in the second contest. But the Stars took the third game in the 10th inning, then shut out Vancouver to bring Las Vegas its second pennant in three years.

The makeup of the PCL remains unchanged in 1989, but in August 1988 Calgary and Edmonton played two league games in a football stadium in Winnipeg. Although Winnipeg had not

**The Lady Ump**

*Pam Postema*
— Courtesy Pacific Coast League

The plate umpire of the first Triple A All-Star Game was Pam Postema. Postema, 33, had umpired for 12 years, beginning at the Rookie League level and including six seasons in Class AAA. A former softball player who worked for UPS in Phoenix during the off-season, she was a PCL ump from 1983 through 1985. Three times Postema tossed Larry Bowa, manager of Las Vegas (Bowa was suspended after one clash). Bowa and other managers, as well as some players and fellow umpires, have expressed dislike or even contempt, but critics from earlier years conceded that Postema's work had improved noticeably. She was considered especially competent calling balls and strikes, and she hoped to become the first woman umpire in the big leagues. The only other female officials in professional baseball were Bernice Gera, who called one Class A game in 1972, and Christine Wren, who umpired from 1975 through 1977 in Rookie League and Class A ball. Postema shrugs off obscenities, "I've heard all the words, I know what they mean." She ignores dressing room inconveniences and keeps her eye on the future. "The major leagues are the goal of every umpire," said the PCL's only lady ump. "I've paid my dues like everybody else."

*The Albuquerque Dukes were led to the best record of 1988 by two of the PCL's brightest stars, Mike Devereaux (at the plate — .340 with 33 steals) and George Hinshaw (on deck — .340 with 94 RBIs).*

— Author's photo

fielded a professional baseball team in 16 years, over 24,000 fans turned out for the PCL games, encouraging a local businessman who hoped to attract a AAA franchise to the city. If the major leagues expand during the next few years, there would be a new AAA affiliate for each new big league franchise, and the PCL would readily add a couple of new clubs. Certainly the climate is favorable for minor league expansion. The 17 minor leagues totaled 18,383,413 in paid attendance, an increase over 1987.

Regarded throughout much of its history as baseball's premier minor league, the PCL resiliently has overcome difficulties imposed by two world wars, the Great Depression, and the destructive drop in attendance of the 1950s and 1960s. The Coast League has brought quality baseball to fans in 33 cities, showcasing a parade of enormously talented players since 1903. No league in Organized Baseball has a stronger identity than the PCL, and the circuit has vigorously displayed every trend and change of America's national pastime. The Coast League soon will march confidently into its tenth decade, continuing to offer a worthy version of the world's most graceful and gratifying game.

*PCL directors, 1988. Top row, left to right: Fred Whitacre (Colorado Springs president and GM), Michael Bucek (Phoenix GM), Joe Buzas (Portland owner and president), Paul Moskau (Tucson GM), Mel Kowalchuk (Edmonton president and GM), Pat McKernan (Albuquerque president and GM). Bottom row, left to right: Russ Parker (Calgary owner and president), Stan Naccarato (Tacoma president and GM), Bill Cutler (PCL president), Larry Koentopp (Las Vegas president and GM), Stu Kehoe (Vancouver vice-president and GM).*

— Courtesy Pacific Coast League

*A major answer for the excellent attendance of the 1980s.*

— Author's photo

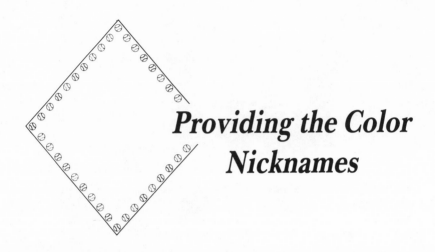

# *Providing the Color Nicknames*

Baseball players always have referred to each other by descriptive or picturesque or insulting nicknames, and they have been helped by newspaper reporters and radio announcers and countless leather-lunged fans. From "Rawmeat" Bill Rodgers to Charles "Sea Lion" Hall to "Kewpie Doll" Dick Barrett, Coast Leaguers have displayed a list of nicknames which compare in color and variety with the sobriquets shouted out in any other baseball circuit. Allen "Cowboy" Gettel — also called "Two-Gun" Gettel — acted in Western movies during the off-season. "Coffee Joe" Coscarart habitually sipped coffee, while Paul "Pills" Pettit consumed vitamin capsules. The PCL's first ERA champ, "Slim" Nelson, also was called "Six O'Clock" because he was so tall and slender that he resembled the hands of a clock at six.

Early in the century baseball veterans readily dubbed rookies and country boys "Babe" and "Rube" — as 1908 batting champ Babe Danzig and first baseman Babe Borton would confirm, along with pitchers Rube Evans and Rube Vickers. Lanky, drawling George O'Donnell was nicknamed "Ezra" by his teammates because of his hillbilly ways. Southpaw hurlers inevitably were tabbed "Lefty," and two of the finest were Lefty Williams and Lefty Gomez, while Lefty O'Doul would become a Coast League institution. An even more common nickname was "Red"; the appellation was assigned to generations of PCL carrot tops such as Red Adams, Red Davis, Red Lynn, Red Mann, Red Munger, Red Toner, Red Van Fleet and Red Witt. Earl "Whitey" Sheely and Henry "Cotton" Pippen were among many towheads in the PCL.

Appearance, physical characteristics and mannerisms produced many other sobriquets. Ernie "Schnoz" Lombardi and Cliff "Ears" Melton exhibited prominent features ("Mountain Music" Melton also enjoyed country-western melodies). Pitcher "Jittery" Joe Berry constantly fidgeted while on the mound. Mike "Old Baggy Pants" Hunt maintained a lower waistline than George "Highpockets" Kelly and "Highpockets" Bill Lawrence. "Stout" Steve Bilko was a massive slugger, "Bones" Sanders was a skinny first baseman, "Long Jim" Wiggs and Hector "Skinny" Brown also presented a lanky look, and "Minnie Mouse" Sheehan was a diminutive pitcher during the 1930s. The physiques of Dick "The Thin Man" Gyselman, Albert "Pudgy" Gould, "Wee Willie" Ludolph, "Hunky" Shaw, "Tiny" Bonham and "Tiny" Jim Chaplin also produced descriptive nicknames. But Clarence "Snake Eyes" Pickrel was not reptilian in appearance — rather he exhibited an affinity for dice.

The Coast League had such suitably nautical figures as "Barnacle Bill" Posedel, Ralph "Sailor" Stroud, and Fay "Scow" Thomas. "Frenchy" Uhalt, "Dutch" Ruether, "Irish" Meusel and "Irish" Harrist, Bobby "The Greek" Del Greco, "Turk" Lown, "Swede" Jensen, and Lou "The Mad Russian" Novikoff provided an international flavor to the PCL, while "Duke" Windsor added a note of royalty. "Doc" Cramer, "Doc" Newton and "Doc" White, along with Ed "Professor" Basinski, lent a professorial tone to certain Coast League games (perhaps they should have tutored "Dummy" Hoy). Reminiscent of the animal kingdom were "Moose" Krause, "Reindeer" Bill Killefer, "Buffalo" Bill Schuster, "Little Buffalo" Perry, "Mule" Haas, "Horse" Danning, "Bunny" Brief and "Bunny" High, "Kitty" Brashear, "Catfish" Metkovich, "Ox" Eckhardt, and "Spider" Baum.

On-field characteristics determined many appellations. "Bullet" Joe Bush, "Fireball" Hayes and "Sudden" Sam McDowell were fastball pitchers. Power hitters included "Dynamite" Dunn, "Rocky" Colavito, "Rip" Russell, and Dick "Socko" Stuart. But first baseman Stuart more commonly was called "Iron Glove," because of a dismaying tendency to drop thrown balls. Fred Hutchinson was known as "The Iceman" because he was cool under fire. Few hitters dug in on righthander "Wild Bill" Piercy, but Walter "Boom Boom" Beck often gave up gopher balls. Carl "Sub" Mays was a submariner, throwing with an underhanded motion. Carlos "The Comet" Bernier was a three-time PCL stolen base champ, while Forrest "Spook" Jacobs was a master at "spooking" the ball just beyond the reach of infielders for bloop hits. And pitcher Ralph "Pine Tar" Buxton was widely suspected of doctoring the ball with pine tar and other foreign substances.

Personality traits named "Happy" Finnern, "Sad" Sam Gibson, "Rowdy" Bartell, and "Gabby" Stewart — who rarely said a word. Thomas O. Davis was called "TOD" because of his initials, and K. C. Wise was known as "Casey." Casey Stengel, however, was from Kansas City (K. C.), while "Broadway Bill" Schuster suggested the Great White Way. "Tex" Westerzill was from the Lone Star State, but "Ozark Ike" Zernial hailed from Texas instead of Arkansas.

"Old Folks" Pillette played in the Coast League a record 23 years. "Jigger" Statz logged 18 seasons in the PCL, earning his famous nickname because when golfing he used an iron called a jigger. "Lucky" Jack Lohrke and Fred "Hard Luck" Gay were on opposite sides of Dame Fortune. There was also "Wahoo" Sam Crawford, "Ping" Bodie, "Ham" Schulte, "Rubber" Krapp, "Bugs" Werle, "Jeep" Trower and "Jeep" Handley, "Skeeter" Fanning, "Suitcase" Simpson, "Whimpy" Quinn, "Tookie" Gilbert, "Wheezer" Dell, "Old Scrapiron" Muller, "Hooks" Iott, "Chesty" Johnson, "Nippy" Jones, "Scooter" Smith, "Beauty" Bancroft, "Stump" Edington, "Mysterious" Tom Simmons, Ed "The Creeper" Stroud, and "Deadly" Dudley Lee. There were many more, of course, all adding to the color and enjoyment of Coast League baseball.

# *Coast League Ballparks*

Throughout its history, the PCL has boasted some of the finest and most unique parks in minor league baseball. When the Coast League opened play, San Francisco's Recreation Park was an impressive facility with a large covered grandstand, a bleacher section and plank outfield fences, features typical of most ballparks around the circuit. Recreation Park was relocated following the devastating earthquake of 1906, and a quarter of a century later Seals Stadium, a concrete and steel, 18,600-seat facility costing $600,000, became the home of professional baseball in San Francisco. Just as Recreation Park often had hosted the Oaks as well as the Seals, Seals Stadium also would be the home field of the Missions; three clubhouses were built — one for the Seals, one for the Missions, and one for the visitors. In 1958 and 1959, Seals Stadium was the home of the San Francisco Giants, and when Tacoma's Cheney Stadium was built in 1960, the Giants placed the seats and light standards in the new park, where they still serve baseball fans today.

In Los Angeles, PCL ball first was played in 15,000-seat Washington Park, which frequently served as home base not only of the Angels but also of the Vernon and Venice Tigers. More than one million dollars went into 22,000-seat Wrigley Field, a magnificent double-decked stadium which opened in 1927 and which also

171

*San Francisco's Recreation Park was built in 1896 and destroyed in the earthquake of
1906. Note the overflow crowd in the outfield.*

— Courtesy Oakland Public Library

*Fans crowding the bleachers of Tacoma's Athletic Park in 1924.*

— Courtesy Tacoma Public Library

*San Francisco's Seal Stadium was perpetuated when the seats and light standards were placed in Tacoma's Cheney Stadium in 1960.*

— Author's photos

would one day host major league ball. A longtime PCL landmark was the Wrigley Tower, which at one time housed the Coast League president, as well as club offices.

The Coast League's first night game was played at Sacramento's Edmonds Field on May 22, 1930. Edmonds Field had been replaced by a shopping center when Sacramento rejoined the PCL in 1974, and Coast League games were played in Hughes Field, a horseshoe-shaped football stadium where the left field fence loomed just 231 feet from home plate. After 491 home runs sailed out of Hughes Field in 1974, a left field barrier reminiscent of Fenway Park was erected. From time to time, other homer havens have raised outfield fences, most recently Cashen Field in Las Vegas, where the barrier was lifted from 10 feet to 20 feet — which also allowed the Stars to double advertising revenue on the fences.

The grand wooden ballparks of the early decades of the Coast League eventually would be replaced by modern stadiums. Oaks Ball Park, once considered a minor league showplace, eventually was dubbed the "Splendid Splinter Emporium," San Diego's Lane Field was razed because of termite damage, and Honolulu's downtown park became known as the "Termite Palace." Sick's Seattle Stadium, a 15,000-seat concrete and steel facility, replaced Dugdale Field, while Portland's Vaughn Street Park finally gave way to 24,500-seat Civic Stadium. The home of the Vancouver Canadians is Nat Bailey Stadium, patterned after Sick's Seattle Stadium — in fact, at each park a hill looming just beyond an outfield fence proved convenient for many non-paying spectators. But because of inclement weather, early-season games in Vancouver now are played beneath a dome, in 50,000-seat B. C. Place Stadium.

The playing surface of B. C. Place is astroturf, and so is the field at Portland Civic Stadium. Private sky boxes are all the rage in modern stadiums, and few minor league parks can boast more luxurious boxes than streamlined Cashman Field in Las Vegas and brand-new Sky Sox Stadium in Colorado Springs. Baseball, however, has more tradition than any other American game, and many diehard fans nostalgically prefer historic parks with eccentric features to modern conveniences. A fan can fall instantly in love with the zig-zag outfield angles at Edmonton's John Ducey Park, while Vancouver's Nat Bailey Stadium, Calgary's Foothills Stadium, and Tuscon's Hi Corbett Field offer an old-fashioned charm and intimacy that frequently is lacking in modern symmetrical stadiums which place fans up and away from the playing field.

*A unique feature of Albuquerque Sports Stadium is an outfield parking terrace 28 feet above the playing surface.*

— Author's photo

*The zig-zag outfield angles at Edmonton's charming John Ducey Park offer a nostalgic contrast to the symmetrical outlines of the majority of modern ballparks.*

— Author's photo

A special accommodation for fans is available at Albuquerque, where a parking terrace rims the outfield 28 feet above the playing surface. More than 100 vehicles can be fitted into this drive-in facility; fans stretch out on quilts and lawn chairs or enjoy the game from the rear section of a pickup truck. At parks around the PCL fans can watch the action from a beer garden or a picnic area. Like big league fans, PCL rooters stage tailgate parties before gametime, and during the game colorful mascots wander through the crowds and amuse children and adults alike.

Baseball remains a pastime, featuring a leisurely pace which contrasts appealingly with the fanatical violence of football and the frenetic pace of basketball. A special part of the charm of baseball is following the home team through a long season, becoming familiar with each player, enjoying the camaradarie of fellow fans — all at a familiar park which becomes a home away from home for several months each spring and summer. Baseball is the only game which stages its contests in facilities fittingly called "parks," and throughout the twentieth century Coast League fans have relaxed and cheered at a fascinating variety of historic, comfortable, and trend-setting ballparks.

*Cashen Field in Las Vegas originally featured a 10-foot outfield fence. The fence was double-tiered in 1985, which not only cut down home run totals but doubled fence advertising revenue.*

— Author's photo

*Vancouver, like all other PCL franchises, markets souvenirs at ballpark stands.*
— Author's photo

# Pacific Coast League Cities

There have been Pacific Coast League clubs in a total of thirty-three cities in thirteen states and two Canadian provinces. The geographic extent of the PCL has been greater than that of any other baseball league, stretching from Indianapolis on the east to Honolulu on the west, from Edmonton on the north to Tucson on the south. Just as there have been competing American League and National League franchises in Chicago, New York, Philadelphia, St. Louis and Boston, for years Los Angeles and San Francisco each supported two franchises from the same *league*. Seven PCL cities — Los Angeles, San Francisco, Oakland, San Diego, Seattle, and Dallas-Fort Worth — now hold major league franchises, and other PCL cities are pressing to enter the big leagues. As of 1989, Portland had participated in 81 of the 87 PCL seasons, and was the only charter member remaining in the league.

# *Albuquerque (Dukes)*

Albuquerque entered the PCL in 1972 following a long and successful progression through lower minor leagues. The Albuquerque Browns, a railroad team, barnstormed throughout New Mexico Territory in 1882 and never lost a game. The Browns played on a diamond near Traction Park in Albuquerque's Old Town. In the late 1920s, another Santa Fe railroad team prevailed upon local Santa Fe officials to donate lumber and ties for Albuquerque's first real stadium, Rio Grande Park, located on the site of an earlier diamond, Stover Field. Then in 1932 the city received a $10,900 grant from the Public Works Administration to erect adobe-based, 3,180-seat Tingley Field, and the Albuquerque Dons entered the Class C Arizona-Texas League.

The Dons trounced El Paso, 43–15, on opening day. But 1932 was the worst year of the Great Depression, and the circuit folded late in July. The Arizona-Texas League resumed play in 1937, and a year earlier the WPA had restructured Tingley Field with steel and expanded the seating capacity to 5,000. The Albuquerque Cardinals won the 1937 pennant and played through 1941.

The next season the Albuquerque Dukes entered the new Class D West Texas-New Mexico League. During a brawl, manager Dixie Howell was clobbered over the head with a chair by a combative fan, but a deadlier war was on and the league disbanded in July. After World War II the Dukes resumed play in the revived Class C West Texas-New Mexico League. Albuquerque stayed in the circuit through 1955, winning flags in 1948, 1949 and 1953. In 1956 Albuquerque moved up to the Class A Western League, but after three second-division finishes the debt-ridden team dropped out of Organized Baseball.

In 1958, however, wealthy oilman Tom Bolack absorbed the club's debts. Intending to advance Albuquerque to the high minors, Bolack placed his team in the Class D Sophomore League in 1960 and 1961, then bought a franchise in the Class AA Texas League. A year later Bolack affiliated with the Los Angeles Dodgers, and a parade of talented athletes began to play in Albuquerque. In nine Texas League seasons, Albuquerque won pennants in 1965 and 1967 and made the playoffs in four other years.

In 1969 Albuquerque Sports Stadium, the most unique ball-park in the minor leagues, opened alongside I-25. The streamlined facility was built to accommodate 10,610 fans — and 102 vehicles. An outfield parking terrace 28 feet above the playing surface permits drive-in baseball. At one dollar per adult, automobiles, vans, motorcycles, pickups and motor homes pulled in to watch ballgames, and were additionally serviced by a mobile chuckwagon and radio play-by-play. Over one-third of the grandstand seats were theater-style chairs, the Stadium Club offered a glass-enclosed restaurant and bar, the clubhouse, pressbox and women's restrooms were carpeted, and fans were ushered to their seats by lovely Dodgerettes. Despite a losing season in 1969, attendance increased 75 percent. Outfield dimensions — 360 feet down the left field line and 340 in right — would limit home run totals but encourage high batting averages.

After spending 1971 in the Class AA Dixie Association, the Albuquerque Dukes stepped up to the Pacific Coast League. The Dukes brought their Dodger affiliation, winning tradition, and splendid stadium with them. The PCL had not held an All-Star Game in a decade, but resurrected the showcase exhibition in 1973 — at Albuquerque Sports Stadium. The 1972 Dukes produced the best record in the league and won the playoffs. In 17 years in the PCL Albuquerque entered postseason play 10 times, including six years consecutively. Albuquerque won five PCL pennants, including three in a row, along with a co-championship, and the Dukes recorded the best regular season record six times.

The first PCL edition of the Dukes was managed by Tommy Lasorda. The Dukes won the team hitting title and featured four of the top eight batters in the league. Outfielder Von Joshua (.337) was the batting champion; third baseman Ron Cey (.329, 23 HRs, 103 RBIs) was on the verge of big league stardom; already a major league veteran, outfielder Larry Hisle (.325, 23 HRs, 91 RBIs) soon was back in the bigs; and second sacker Davey Lopes (.317 with 48 SBs) won the stolen base title. Lasorda's best pitchers were southpaws Doug Rau (14–3) and Geoff Zahn (10–1), and knuckle-balling reliever Charlie Hough (14–5). Most impressive of all was first baseman Tom Paciorek (.307, 27 HRs, 107 RBIs), who led the league in hits, runs, total bases, doubles and homers, and who was an easy choice for MVP. After sweeping Eugene for the PCL flag, the Dukes traveled to Hawaii for the first (and last) World Baseball

Classic. The Dukes beat the other AAA champions, Evansville and Tidewater, but lost the finals to a team of Caribbean All Stars.

The heart of this talented club was promoted to the Dodgers in 1973 as the Dukes dropped to last place. But Albuquerque bounced back into the playoffs in 1974, leading the league with a .305 team batting average. Sparking the explosive lineup was second baseman Bobby Randall (.338), first sacker Terry McDermott (.329), outfielders Charles Manuel (.329, 30 HRs, 102 RBIs) and Henry Cruz (.304), catcher Kevin Pasley (.314), and shortstop Ivan De-Jesus (.298). Righthander Rex Hudson (16–4) led the PCL in victories and winning percentage, and Eddie Solomon (11–4) stood out in merely part of a season.

For the next three years the Dukes uncharacteristically endured losing records. But in 1975 third baseman Jerry Royster (.333) won the batting and stolen base titles, and Charles Manuel (.325) was named to the All Star team as DH. The 1976 stolen base championship went to outfielder Glenn Burke (.300 with 63 SBs), while righthander Dennis Lewallyn (15–10) tied for the most victories. Although the 1977 Dukes finished last in the PCL, it was not because of a lack of hitting. The Dukes won the team hitting title (.306), first baseman Don Cardoza (.356) was the batting champ, and switch-hitting DH Dan Walton (.289, 42 HRs, 122 RBIs) led the PCL in RBIs and homers (the left field drive-in area became known as "Walton Country"). Veteran infielder Rafael Landestoy won the stolen base title (56), while outfielders Henry Cruz (.353) and Joe Simpson (.349) and shortstop Ron Washington (.323) pounded enemy pitching. Pedro Guerrero ripped opposing pitchers (.403 and 39 RBIs in 32 games) until he went on the disabled list with a broken ankle on May 19.

In 1978 the Dukes began a run of six consecutive playoff appearances. Outfielder Jeff Leonard (.365) was the PCL batting leader, infielder Pedro Guerrero (.333, 14 HRs, 116 RBIs) was the RBI champ, and outfielder Rudy Law (.312 with 79 SBs) became the fourth Duke in a row to win the stolen base title. Towering righthander Rick Sutcliffe (13–6) and starter-reliever Kevin Keefe (10–3) led the pitching staff. The Dukes won the Eastern Division, then defeated Salt Lake City in three straight games to take the opening round of playoffs. Tacoma, champs of the Western Division, had split four games with Portland when rain halted the series. With the parent clubs ready to call up numerous players, PCL

President Roy Jackson finally suspended the playoffs and declared Albuquerque and Tacoma co-champions.

The next year the Dukes raced to the best record in the PCL before being bumped off in postseason play. Albuquerque led the league in team hitting (.309) by 21 percentage points, and for the third consecutive season the batting champ, Mickey Hatcher (.371), wore a Dukes uniform. Now the Dukes' left fielder, Pedro Guerrero (.333, 22 HRs, 103 RBIs) again was the RBI leader, while catcher Mike Sciosia (.336), outfielder Bobby Mitchell (.326), and second baseman John Perconte (.322) were also among the league's top ten hitters.

In 1980 a veteran baseball executive, Pat McKernan, became Albuquerque's president and general manager, and the Dukes began a string of three consecutive championships. Dennis Llewallyn (15–2), Dave Stewart (15–10), and southpaw Gerald Hannahs (15–9) tied for the most victories (along with Salt Lake City's Ralph Botting, 15–8), while righthander Ted Power (13–7) also enjoyed a strong season. Llewallyn, a Dukes starter since 1975, was about to be demoted after the 1979 season when Albuquerque manager Del Crandall decided to try the tall righthander as a reliever. In 54 appearances (plus one start, a six-hit shutout!) he led the PCL in saves (24), ERA (2.13), and winning percentage (.882). His 15 victories were remarkable for a reliever, and Llewallyn was named Most Valuable Player. John Perconte (.326) and Bobby Mitchell (.320) returned to spark the offense. The Dukes put on a surge late in the season to make the playoffs and blank Tucson in the first round of playoffs, then came from behind to down Hawaii and claim the PCL crown.

The next year Crandall molded a talented band of Dukes into one of the finest clubs in PCL history. Within two weeks after the season opened Crandall had his team functioning as a dominant unit — indeed, at 94–38 (.712), the Dukes recorded the fewest season losses by a PCL club since the Angels of 1934. From June 12 through August 14, the Dukes rang up an incredible 50–12 (.807) record. This victorious run was doubly significant because it paralleled the major league strike. The Dukes were televised three times, and became known as the best team playing in Organized Baseball. The club batting average was an imposing .325, 22 points above second-place Phoenix. But when opposing pitchers tried to retaliate against an offensive onslaught, the aggressive

Dukes did not hesitate to engage in bench-clearing brawls. When the major league clubs finally prepared to resume play, Los Angeles flew in their AAA affiliate for a tune-up game — and the Dukes outdueled the Dodgers, 1–0, before a crowd of 40,000.

The most spectacular hitter was a big, 21-year-old first baseman, Mike Marshall (.370, 34 HRs, 137 RBIs) who won the Triple Crown and the PCL's Most Valuable Player award. John Perconte (.346) and Rudy Law (.335) once again were key members of the Dukes' lineup, while outfielder Candy Maldonado (.335, 21 HRs, 104 RBIs) added an explosive bat. During his first month as a Duke the 20-year-old Puerto Rican went 8-for-8 on April 30 and May 1. In these two games, he hit four home runs in four consecutive at-bats. Other hard-hitting outfielders were Ron Roenicke (.316), Tack Wilson (.315), Wayne Caughey (.314), and Bobby Mitchell (.311). Ted Power (18–3) led the PCL in victories and winning percentage. Other starters were Brian Holton (14–6), Dave Moore (12–5) and Bill Siwacki (11–5), while the best relievers were Alejandro Pena (1.61 ERA and a league-leading 22 saves) and Dave Patterson (7–1). This formidable team dominated the Southern Division in both halves of the season, then swept Tacoma in three straight to win the championship.

Crandall again led the Dukes to the PCL throne in 1982, as Albuquerque once more won the team batting title (.313). Candy Maldonado (.301, 24 HRs, 96 RBIs) returned for another fine year, and Mike Marshall (.388 in 66 games) again ripped into PCL pitching before being called up to the Dodgers. Shortstop Dave Anderson (.343) was outstanding in his second year of pro ball, and outfielder Mark Bradley (.317 with 101 RBIs) also was impressive. But most of the power was supplied by first baseman Greg Brock (.310, 44 HRs, 138 RBIs), while DH Tack Wilson (.378) was Albuquerque's seventh batting champ in 11 PCL seasons. Rich Rodas (14–8), Brian Holton (12–8), and future star Orel Hershiser (9–6 while used primarily in relief) led the pitching staff. By playoff time the Dukes had lost several key players to the Dodgers. But Crandall put together a patchwork lineup and beat Salt Lake City, then Spokane, and claimed a third straight PCL playoff title.

Promotions and trades rendered Albuquerque the youngest team in the PCL in 1983, and in June Del Crandall was named manager of the Seattle Mariners. But coach Terry Collins, a former Albuquerque player, took over the reins, and the Dukes made a

*In 1982 Albuquerque won a third straight championship. Tack Wilson (bottom row, third from right) was the batting champ, while Sid Fernandez (bottom, second from right) and Orel Hershiser (top, fourth from left) soon would pitch in the big leagues.*
— Courtesy Albuquerque Dukes

valiant effort to win a fourth consecutive PCL flag. Rich Rodas (16–4) led the league in victories, winning percentage, innings pitched and strikeouts. In a momentous decision for the future, Orel Hershiser (10–8), despite 16 saves by mid-season, was converted from a reliever to a starter.

As had become customary, Albuquerque won the PCL's team batting title with a hefty average (.307). Power was provided by first baseman Sid Bream (.307, 32 HRs, 118 RBIs), who led the league in RBIs and tied for the home run championship, and by third sacker German Rivera (.328, 24 HRs, 103 RBIs) and outfielder Tony Brewer (.315, 24 HRs, 96 RBIs). Catcher Dave Sax (.343 in 75 games) and hit leader Lemmie Miller (.330) added to the fireworks.

Albuquerque put together the season's best record and won the Northern Division crown from Las Vegas in a hard-fought five-game playoff opener, before finally dropping the championship series to Portland. For six consecutive years the Dukes had made the playoffs, finishing with the PCL's best season record four times and winning three straight pennants and a co-championship.

The Dukes dropped to last place in 1984, although once more claiming the team batting title (.298) and providing the PCL hitting titlist, outfielder Tony Brewer (.357). First baseman Sid Bream (.343) again was impressive at the plate, along with outfielders Ed Amelung (.351) and Lemmie Miller (.311). The team was so weakened by injuries that skipper Terry Collins and pitching coach Dave Wallace were placed on the active roster. But the Dukes continued to average 250,000 in attendance, and Pat McKernan was awarded the President's Trophy by the National Association.

Attendance remained high, even though the Dukes continued to lose in 1985 and 1986. Sid Bream (.370 in 85 games) and first baseman Franklin Stubbs (.280, 32 HRs, 93 RBIs) played well in 1985, while infielder Larry See (.289, 27 HRs, 106 RBIs) was the most consistent player on the last-place 1986 club.

In 1987 the Dukes bounced back to their familiar perch in the PCL throne room. Early in the season, Collins' crew came from a 10–0 deficit to beat Hawaii 15–14 in 11 innings, and the team began to make a specialty of late-inning surges. Second baseman Jack Perconte (.280) and shortstop Brad Wellman (.306) came back to provide stability and experience. First base was manned by George Hinshaw (.338), who was acquired in a trade at the start of the year, and infielder Jeff Hamilton (.360) was impressive in half a season. Shawn Hillegas (13–5) and reliever Tim Crews (7.2) were the most consistent pitchers. The Dukes downed Las Vegas in three straight games to advance to the playoff finals, where they won another pennant by defeating Vancouver.

The 1988 Dukes seemed likely to repeat as champions, reeling off the best record in the PCL. One of the league's premier stars was outfielder Mike Devereaux (.340 with 33 steals), and a year of maturity clearly had improved George Hinshaw (.340), who was moved to the outfield. Tracy Woodson (.319) was the new first sacker, Mike Sharperson (.319) was at second, and Juan Bell (.300) and Mariano Duncan (.286) split the season at shorstop. Bill Krueger (15–5 with a 3.01 ERA) led the PCL in victories, winning percentage and ERA. Ken Howell (10–1), a staff member in 1983 and 1984, returned to pitch superbly for the Dukes, and Bill Brennan (14–8) also was a mound mainstay. Terry Collins' team played well throughout the season, even though Albuquerque was blanked in the playoff opener.

| Year | Record | Pcg. | Finish |
|------|--------|------|--------|
| 1972 | 92-56 | .622 | First — won Eastern Division and playoff |
| 1973 | 62-82 | .431 | Eighth |
| 1974 | 76-66 | .535 | Second — won Eastern Division, lost playoff |
| 1975 | 71-73 | .493 | Fifth |
| 1976 | 66-78 | .458 | Sixth |
| 1977 | 60-78 | .435 | Eighth |
| 1978 | 78-62 | .557 | Second — won opener, declared co-champ |
| 1979 | 86-62 | .581 | First — lost opener |
| 1980 | 85-62 | .578 | Second — won opener and finals |
| 1981 | 94-38 | .712 | First — won finals |
| 1982 | 85-58 | .594 | First — won opener and finals |
| 1983 | 85-58 | .594 | First — won opener, lost finals |
| 1984 | 62-81 | .434 | Tenth |
| 1985 | 67-76 | .469 | Sixth |
| 1986 | 54-88 | .380 | Tenth |
| 1987 | 77-65 | .542 | Third — won opener and finals |
| 1988 | 86-56 | .606 | First — lost opener |

# Calgary
# (Cannons)

Calgary participated in the Western Canadian league in 1907, again from 1909 through 1914, and in 1920 and 1921. Calgary placed a Class A team in the Western International League in 1953 and 1954, and in later years was active in Canadian amateur baseball. Russ Parker, a local baseball enthusiast who had built the Calgary Copier Company, spent years arranging for another professional team, and in 1977 he headed a Calgary entry in the rookie Pioneer League. The old downtown ballpark had been razed, but Foothills Stadium went up in the west part of town. The Canadian Rockies rise 60 miles to the west, producing snow early in the season and frequent cool temperatures. After two years with the St. Louis Cardinals, Parker entered a successful affiliation with the Montreal Expos. But Parker was convinced that Calgary's population (650,000) would support a much larger franchise, and after the 1984 season, he purchased the Salt Lake City Gulls of the PCL. Parker sold his Pioneer League franchise to Edmonton, which established the Salt Lake City Trappers.

After eight years in the Pioneer League, Calgary now was the home of the Cannons, AAA farm club of the Seattle Mariners. Al-

*The Calgary Cannons' mascot.*

— Courtesy Calgary Cannons

though the first three games at Foothills Stadium were snowed out, the Cannons roared to the first half title of the Northern Division. The club slipped in the second half and was blanked by Vancouver in the opening round of playoffs. But the Cannons led the PCL in team hitting (.284) and home runs (159), and their exciting brand of ball produced a paid attendance of 272,322. Shortstop Danny Tartabull (.300, 43 HRs, 109 RBIs) was named MVP after leading the league in homers, total bases and RBIs. Outfielder John Moses (.321 with 35 stolen bases) led the PCL in doubles. Second baseman Harold Reynolds (.363 in 52 games), catcher Dave Valle (.344 in 42 games), third sacker Darnell Coles (.320 in 31 games), and outfielder Al Chambers (.308 in 100 games) ripped the ball throughout their stays in Calgary. The Cannon pitching staff was last in league ERA, but righthander Dave Tobik (12–6) put together a solid season despite a 5.18 ERA, and Frank Wills (4–3) twirled a 1–0 no-hitter against Tacoma.

Although Calgary sagged to last place in the Northern Division in 1986, the Cannons again led the PCL in home runs and attendance increased to 288,197. The Cannon lineup battered Firebird pitching for 30 hits in a 21–3 victory in Phoenix Municipal

Stadium on April 16. Outfielder Mickey Brantley (.318, 30 HRs, 92 RBIs) and second sacker Harold Reynolds (.314 in 29 games) had five hits each in this explosive contest. Other impressive hitters included first baseman-DH Randy Braun (.314, 21 HRs, 90 RBIs), first baseman-DH Pat Casey (.307), outfielders John Moses (.324 in 39 games) and Dave Hengel (.285, 27 HRs, 94 RBIs), and catcher Dave Valle (.312 with 21 HRs). The Cannons led the PCL in team fielding, but the pitching staff again ranked last in ERA — despite back-to-back shutouts at Foothills Stadium on May 7 and 8.

Manager Bill Plummer guided the Cannons to the PCL finals in 1987. Calgary again paced the league in team batting (.287) and home runs (120), along with numerous other offensive statistics. Dave Hengel (.295, 23 HRs, 103 RBIs) returned to lead the league in homers and RBIs, and even though outfielder Donell Nixon (.323 with 46 steals in just 82 games) played 46 games with Seattle, he was in Calgary long enough to win the stolen base title. Edgar Martinez (.329) manned the hot corner most of the year and was another of the usual stable of fine Cannon hitters.

But the pitching staff proved unusually strong. Mike Brown (10–2) and Terry Taylor (10–3) remained with the Cannons throughout the season, while reliever Paul Schneider (4–3) registered 14 straight appearances without surrendering an earned run. Righthander Mike Campbell (15–2 with a 2.66 ERA) was called up twice, but pitched so spectacularly that he was named MVP for 1987. On April 27 in Tucson, Campbell finished and won a suspended game, then went on to pitch five innings and gain the victory in the regularly scheduled contest. Campbell's two victories in one day helped him lead the PCL in victories and winning percentage (.882).

The Cannons recorded the best record in the league in 1987, then staged a dramatic comeback to win the Northern Division before dropping the playoff finals to Albuquerque. Paid admissions totaled more than 304,000, and Foothills Stadium was enlarged to a capacity of 7,500 after the season. During the renovation, the outfield wall was doubled in height, which would disappoint home run sluggers.

Despite a losing record in 1988, attendance jumped to 332,590. Even though home run totals were down — first baseman Dave Cochrane hit 15 to lead the team — third sacker Edgar Martinez (.363) became Calgary's first batting champ. Shortstop Mario

Diaz (.329) also was impressive at the plate, along with outfielders Greg Briley (.313), Bruce Fields (.321), John Rabb (.309), and Mike Kingery (.318).

Foothills Stadium is located near the impressive home of the 1988 Winter Olympics, and the site of the annual Calgary Stampede is across town. But under the leadership of Russ Parker and General Manager John Dittrich, the future of baseball in Calgary shines with promise.

| Year | Record | Pcg. | Finish |
|------|--------|------|--------|
| 1985 | 71-70 | .504 | Fourth — lost opener |
| 1986 | 66-77 | .462 | Eighth |
| 1987 | 84-57 | .596 | First — won opener, lost finals |
| 1988 | 68-74 | .479 | Fifth |

 *Colorado Springs (Sky Sox)*

The newest member of the PCL entered professional baseball in 1901. The Colorado Springs Millionaires played in the Western League from 1901 through 1904, and in 1916 the Wichita franchise was transferred in at mid-season. Colorado Springs rejoined the Western League in 1950 as the Sky Sox, Class A affiliates of the Chicago White Sox. This affilition continued for nine seasons, until the Western League disbanded in 1958. The Sky Sox finished first in 1953, 1955 and 1958.

Thirty years later the Sky Sox were resurrected when it was decided to move the PCL franchise out of distant Hawaii. Owner David Elmore decided upon Colorado Springs as the new home of his club, and a working agreement was obtained with the Cleveland Indians.

The old ballpark where the Sky Sox had entertained Western League opponents had been razed, replaced by Spurgeon Stadium, a community field with seating and outfield distances considered inadequate for AAA ball. Work commenced furiously in northeast Colorado Springs on 6,100-seat Sky Sox Stadium, but it became clear that the $3,400,000 facility would not be ready by the start of the season. The first seven "home" games were played at Desert Sun Stadium in Yuma. The Sky Sox also "hosted" a game at Van-

*Tailgate parties before a Saturday doubleheader at Sky Sox Stadium.*
— Author's photo

couver's Nat Bailey Stadium and another at Edmonton's John Ducey Park. Then the team moved into Spurgeon Stadium, where strong winds blowing toward the outfield rendered the 370-foot power alleys even more inviting. Indeed, left fielder Luis Medina walloped 13 homers in 22 games at Spurgeon. Not until their 46th game of the season did the Sky Sox finally play in their new stadium. There was an overflow crowd of 9,000, and despite gusty winds (which forced cancellation of a performance by The Chicken) Sky Sox officials hope soon to expand their streamlined new ballpark.

The Sky Sox finished last in the Southern Division, but Luis Medina (.310, 28 HRs, 81 RBIs) led the PCL in homers, while DH Rod Allen (.324, 23 HRs, 100 RBIs) was the RBI champ. Sky Sox fans enjoyed several other fine hitters: outfielders Terry Francona (.323), Dave Clark (.297) and Reggie Williams (.294); third sacker Eddie Williams (.301); and catchers Dan Firova (.309) and Ron Tingley (.285). Sky Sox fans enjoyed an exciting brand of baseball, and enthusiasm runs high for the future of Colorado Springs in the PCL.

| Year | Record | Pcg. | Finish |
|------|--------|------|--------|
| 1988 | 62-77  | .446 | Eighth |

# Dallas
# (Rangers)

The Dallas "Hams" won the first Texas League championship in 1888, and the Dallas Giants, Submarines, Steers, Rebels and Eagles played Texas League ball for seven decades. But when oilman Dick Burnett bought the franchise in 1948, acquiring a major league team became the primary goal of Dallas baseball interests. In 1959 Dallas moved up to the Class AAA American Association, along with Fort Worth and Houston. The next year Dallas combined resources with Texas League archrival Fort Worth for a joint American Association franchise. Although wheels were in motion to construct a ballpark between the two cities, Turnpike Stadium in Arlington would not open until 1965. Dallas and Fort Worth split the home schedule between their old Texas League parks, Burnett Field and LaGrave Field.

For three years the Dallas-Fort Worth Rangers played in the American Association. During this period hopes for a franchise in the proposed Continental League collapsed when American league expansion killed the new circuit before it came into existence. After the 1962 season, the American Association disbanded, and the PCL admitted Dallas-Fort Worth, Denver and Oklahoma City.

The 1963 Rangers were managed by Jack McKeon, who enjoyed good hitting from outfielders Pedro Oliva (.304), Joe Christian (.304), and Cesar Tovar (.297). Righthander Lee Strange went 7–1 in eight starts, then was promoted to Minnesota. There was not much pitching left, and the Spurs failed to break .500.

The next year the PCL expanded again, to 12 teams. Rangers owner Tommy Mercer, a Fort Worth businessman, decided to reinstate the Fort Worth Cats into the Texas League, while leaving the Dallas Rangers in the PCL. Jack McKeon would be Dallas' manager, but he had little to work with — the Rangers finished next to last in team batting and fielding, and tenth in ERA.

The best batter was pitcher Robert Colligan (.348), who hit better than he pitched (5–8 with a 5.23 ERA). Outfielder Ricardo Joseph (.278 with 17 homers) performed well, but first baseman Ken Harrelson (.232) was just one of many disappointments. Although Aurelio Monteagudo (10–5 with a 2.79 ERA) was effective from the mound, Lew Krausse (7–19), Bill Landis (4–17) and

other pitchers were pounded regularly. The Rangers finished dead
last (53–104), 42¹/₂ games off the pace.

Fort Worth also finished last in the Texas League in 1964, and
it was decided to reunite Dallas-Fort Worth as a Texas League
franchise in 1965. The team moved into 10,000-seat Turnpike Stadium (the facility would eventually be expanded to 41,284). Although there were only two winning years in six Texas League seasons, the club attracted large crowds, and the circuit's All-Star
Game was held at Turnpike Stadium in 1966, 1967 and 1968. The
team participated in the Class AA Dixie Association in 1971, and
after the close of the season the sale of the Washington Senators to
Dallas-Fort Worth was announced. In 1972 the Texas Rangers at
last brought major league baseball to the Dallas-Fort Worth metro-
plex.

| Year | Record | Pcg. | Finish |
|------|--------|------|--------|
| 1963 | 79-79  | .500 | Fifth  |
| 1964 | 53-104 | .338 | Twelfth |

# Denver
# (Bears)

Baseball in Denver can be traced with certainty to 1862, and
there was strong support for numerous amateur, semipro and
professional teams during the late nineteenth century. Denver
fielded a team from season to season in various versions of the
Western League, and was a charter member when the circuit joined
the National Association in 1902. Theodore Roosevelt was president of the United States, and Denver's nine was called the "Teddy
Bears," "Grizzlies" or "Cubs," eventually settling on the Denver
Bears.

Denver won three consecutive Western League pennants in
1910, 1911 and 1912, but thereafter a succession of poor teams
caused the Bears to suspend operations following the 1917 season.
Home of the Bears had been Broadway Park, but when Denver re-
entered the Class A Western League in 1922, Merchants Park was
constructed two miles to the south. Nicknamed the "brickyard" because of its hard playing surface, wooden Merchants Park seated

7,000 and featured deep outfield fences that encircled a vast grave-yard for home run hitters.

During the Depression poor attendance plagued the Bears, and other Western League clubs found the expense of travel to Denver oppressive. Denver gave up professional baseball after the 1932 season, fielded a Class D team in 1941, then rejoined the Class A Western league in 1947 when the circuit was reorganized after World War II. Ramshackle Merchants Park was replaced during the 1948 season by Bears Stadium, a beautiful half-bowl facility located at 20th and Federal Boulevard with a seating capacity of 18,523, largest in the league. In 1949 Denver set a Class A attendance record of 463,039, and in 1955 the city joined the Class AAA American Association. But the loss of traditional rivals and the frequent call-up of the team's best players by the parent club — for five years the New York Yankees, then the Detroit Tigers for three seasons — caused a disenchantment with AAA ball. Attendance in 1962 dipped below 185,000.

In 1963 the Bears affiliated with the Milwaukee Braves and joined the Pacific Coast League. The 1963 Denver Bears led the 10-team PCL in hitting and produced the batting champ in outfielder Chico Salmon (.325). For part of the season first baseman Tommy Aaron (.310 in 66 games) and third sacker Lou Klimchock (.352, 19 HRs, 68 RBIs in 81 games) hit impressively, and Bob Uecker (.283) performed well as a reserve catcher. But the pitching was weak — no hurler posted an ERA under 4.00 — and the Bears finished last in the Southern Division, attracting just 112,118 fans.

Lou Klimchock (.334, 19 HRs, 112 RBIs) was the 1964 titlist in average and RBIs, and Klimchock at third and Tommy Aaron (.277, 21 HRs, 86 RBIs) at first led the PCL in fielding. Phil Niekro (11–5) was the best pitcher, but the rest of the staff was unproductive and the Bears finished 16 games off the pace in the Eastern Division. The next year Denver again led the PCL in team hitting and produced a third consecutive batting champ, outfielder Ted Uhlaender (.340). Another outfielder, Andy Kosco (.327, 27 HRs, 116 RBIs) led the league in RBIs and doubles, but the mound staff finished 10th in a 12-team circuit in ERA.

The 1966 Bears again hit with authority, featuring Uhlaender (.341 in 43 games), first baseman Walt Bond (.316), third sacker Ron Clark (.294 with 94 RBIs, a tie for the PCL title), and outfielders Rich Reese (.327), Hilario Valdespino (.321 in 72 games), and

Frank Kostro (.300). Southpaw Jim Ollom (20–6) before being called up) paced the PCL in victories, and 44-year-old Art Fowler (8–2) was a reliable reliever. In 1967 Fowler (5–3) again pitched well in 39 relief appearances and performed double duty as a coach. But no starter could accumulate a winning record, and the Bears suffered through a dismal season.

By this time Bears Stadium was undergoing an expansion in several stages that would produce a seating capacity exceeding 75,000. The Bears long had been owned by Rocky Mountain Empire Sports, which also controlled the ballpark and the Denver Broncos. The Broncos, a major league franchise, were far more important inhabitants of Bear Stadium than a minor league baseball team. Rechristened Mile High Stadium (baseball diehards still referred to it as Bear Stadium), the facility could be converted from a baseball park to a football stadium within hours — but baseball "crowds" would be swallowed in the double-decked vastness that was filled for football games.

The 1968 Bears wobbled to a 7–22 start, and Billy Martin, serving as coach of the parent club Minnesota Twins, accepted appointment as manager, hoping to prove his qualifications to direct a big league team. Martin revived the Bears, turning the players into gambling baserunners and exhibiting the daring style of play that would exemplify his major league clubs. Outfielder Pat Kelly (.306) led the PCL in stolen bases (38), while third sacker Craig Nettles (.297, 22 HRs, 83 RBIs) and outfielder Bob Oliver (.297, 20 HRs, 93 RBIs) were on the threshold of minor league careers. Righthander Jerry Crider (18–10) tied for the most victories in the league, but the rest of the rotation was so weak that ancient Art Fowler (1–1 but an impressive 1.93 ERA in 28 games) even made two starts. The team finished one game above .500.

In six years in the PCL, Denver had recorded four winning seasons but had never made the playoffs. When the American Association reorganized in 1969, Denver rejoined the circuit. The next year Denver won the league championship (Art Fowler, now 48, went 9–5 with a 1.59 ERA), and in 1970 the Bears won a division title. From 1975 through 1977 the Bears took three consecutive division crowns and two successive American Association championships. Another victorious season in 1980 — featuring batting champ Tim Raines and homer-RBI leader Randy Bass — produced a total attendance of 565,214. The next year the Bears drew

555,806, and in 1982, 537,914 (with 65,666 on fireworks night to set an all-time minor league attendance record for one game). With its long tradition of minor league baseball and the spectacular attendance of recent years (along with the success of the Broncos), Denver clearly is a leading contender for an expansion or relocated big league franchise.

| Year | Record | Pcg. | Finish |
|------|--------|------|--------|
| 1963 | 71-87 | .449 | Ninth |
| 1964 | 80-78 | .508 | Eighth |
| 1965 | 83-62 | .572 | Second |
| 1966 | 80-68 | .541 | Fourth |
| 1967 | 69-76 | .476 | Ninth |
| 1968 | 73-72 | .503 | Sixth |

# Edmonton
# (Trappers)

Edmonton put a professional club in the Western Canada League in 1907, 1909 through 1914, and 1920 and 1921. In 1922 Edmonton participated in the Western International League, and three decades later rejoined the same circuit for the 1953 and 1954 seasons. Edmonton became famous in the sporting world for its championship Oiler hockey teams. Oiler superstar Wayne Gretzky would enjoy taking batting practice with the Trappers before his famous trade to Los Angeles. But Mel Kowalchuk persuaded Peter Pocklington, owner of the Oilers and of Edmonton's soccer club, to bring professional baseball to the city. At the end of the 1980 season, Pocklington purchased Ogden's PCL franchise and appointed Kowalchuk to run the new Edmonton Trappers. Kowalchuk and Pocklington strongly backed the Trappers through the 1980s, and even acquired a rookie league club. After the 1984 season, when Russ Parker bought Salt Lake City's PCL franchise for Calgary, Pocklington purchased Parker's Pioneer League franchise and created the Salt Lake City Trappers — this highly successful club continued to call itself the Trappers even after Pocklington sold it to local interests.

The city spent several hundred thousand dollars to upgrade Renfrew Park, a charming antique located beside the North Sas-

*John Ducey Park, home of the Edmonton Trappers.*
— Author's photo

katchewan River just below downtown Edmonton. Opened in 1933, Renfrew Park seats 5,200 and boasts the kind of idiosyncratic features that endear a ballpark to baseball fans. The double-decked outfield fence zigs and zags at angles which present an unwelcome defensive challenge. Until 1987 *both* bullpens were located in center field; today it is impossible to see home plate from the bullpens. Although Renfrew Park is the smallest ballpark in the PCL, it offers fans an old-fashioned intimacy unavailable in larger, streamlined stadiums.

Ogden had been the AAA farm club of Oakland, but the A's did not want to extend the affiliation to faraway Edmonton. Kowalchuk arranged a working agreement with the Chicago White Sox (since 1983 the Trappers have been affiliated with the LA Angels). Chicago's AAA affiliate in 1980 had been the Iowa Oaks, and 16 former Oaks donned Trapper uniforms in 1981. Edmonton played its first PCL game in Portland. Gary Holle blasted a grand-slam homer and the Trappers defeated crafty old Luis Tiant, 12–5. The next week the Trappers won their opening home game, 8–1.

The Trappers did not keep up the winning pace, but performed well offensively and attracted a total attendance of more than 187,000. The most productive hitter was 6'6 DH Gary Holle (.327, 26 HRs and 88 RBIs in just 108 games), and first baseman Chris Nyman (.297, 16 HRs, 90 RBIs). The steadiest pitchers were Rich Barnes (13–8) and Reggie Patterson (10–8).

In 1982 the Trappers again had a losing season but led the PCL in home runs (162). Nyman (.335, 14 HRs, 92 RBIs), Barnes (10–6) and Patterson (14–10) once more performed well, and outfielder Lorenzo Gray (.358) was impressive throughout the year.

Most impressive of all, however, was outfielder Ron Kittle (.345, 50 HRs, 144 RBIs in 127 games), who led the PCL in homers, runs scored and RBIs. Kittle, who had led the Eastern League in homers and RBIs in 1981 (.324, 40 HRs, 102 RBIs in just 109 games), blasted 13 roundtrippers in April 1982, and went on to wallop number 50 in the last game of the year. Edmonton fans became hooked on power baseball — season attendance would exceed 233,000. Kittle was named MVP and *The Sporting News'* Minor League Player of the Year. He went on to Rookie of the Year honors in 1983 as he hit 35 homers and knocked in 100 runs for the White Sox.

Under manager Moose Stubing, the 1983 Trappers produced the only winning record in Edmonton's first eight seasons in the PCL. As a team, the Trappers hit .300, again led the league in homers (179), and was the best fielding club in the PCL. Edmonton won the Northern Division in the first half of the season, but lost out to Portland in the playoff opener. Fans again enjoyed an explosive lineup, led by outfielders Mike Brown (.355, 22 HRs, 106 RBIs), Chris Clark (.315) and Juan Montaserio (.314), first baseman-catcher Jerry Narron (.301, 27 HRs, 102 RBIs), second sackers Tim Krauss (.325) and Steve Lubratich (.321), and catcher Mike O'Berry (.307).

In 1984 Stubing pulled off a spectacular managerial feat, overcoming a losing regular season record (69–73) to win the PCL pennant. Chris Clark (.335, 19 HRs, 104 RBIs) was back to lead another potent offense. Steve Lubratich (.305) and Tim Krauss (.290) also returned, and Mike Brown was on hand for 26 productive games (.343 with 24 RBIs). Catcher Darrell Miller (.326) and pitcher Rick Steirer (12–4) were also impressive. Edmonton won the Northern Division in the first half with a 35–35 record, then slumped in the second half to the seventh poorest mark over the regular schedule. But the Trappers outlasted Salt Lake City, three

games to two, in the opening round of playoffs, while Hawaii swept
Las Vegas. Then Edmonton defeated Hawaii in two straight games
to win the 1984 championship.

For the third year in a row, Chris Clark (.276) was in a Trapper uniform in 1985. Young Wally Joyner (.283) played through
the season for Edmonton, while third baseman Jack Howell was
spectacular (.373) before being called up to the Angels. The next
year, speedster Devon White (.291 with 42 steals) was the stolen
base champ, while outfielder-DH Mark Ryal (.340) was second in
hitting. Gus Polidor (.300) played well at shortstop, and Jack Howell (.359 in 44 games) again excited fans during part of the season.

In 1987 Edmonton produced its first batting champ, lefthanded first baseman James Eppard (.341). Mark Ryal was outstanding (.429) in 16 games, while switch-hitter Kevin King (.285,
20 HRs, 85 RBIs) led the PCL in slugging percentage. Outfielders
Tack Wilson (.314) and Dante Bichette (.300), and second baseman Bobby Coachman (.309) joined Eppard in the PCL's list of
top 10 hitters. In 1988 Eppard (.262), King (.263), Bichette (.267),
and Coachman (.265) all slumped, after failing to stick with the
Angels. But Mike Brown (.347) and Darrell Miller (.317) exhibited
great promise, while shortstop Gus Polidor (.364) and catcher
Edwin Marquez (.395) entertained fans during brief stints with the
Trappers. Edmonton was an excellent sports town, and fan support
for the Trappers remained solid throughout the 1980s.

| Year | Record | Pcg. | Finish |
|---|---|---|---|
| 1981 | 62-74 | .456 | Seventh |
| 1982 | 70-74 | .486 | Seventh |
| 1983 | 75-67 | .528 | Third — lost opener |
| 1984 | 69-73 | .486 | Seventh — won opener and finals |
| 1985 | 66-76 | .465 | Seventh |
| 1986 | 68-73 | .482 | Sixth |
| 1987 | 69-74 | .483 | Eighth |
| 1988 | 61-80 | .433 | Ninth |

# Eugene
# (Emeralds)

During the AAA realignment of 1969, Eugene and Tucson entered the Pacific Coast League. Eugene had fielded a team in the
Class D Far West League in 1950 and 1951, then participated as

*Picturesque Civic Stadium was built in 1939.*

— Author's photo

charter members of the Northwest League from 1955 through 1968. Although the Northwest League was advanced to Class A status in 1963, Eugene's move to the Class AAA PCL was a big jump for a small city of 100,000.

But manager Frank Lucchesi guided Eugene, a Philadelphia affiliate, to the best record in the 1969 PCL. Although Eugene lost the championship playoff to Tacoma, the club attracted the league's second highest attendance (152,256) en route to the Southern Division title. Picturesque old Civic Stadium, built in 1939 in the south part of town, often was filled to its 6,300-seat capacity. Switch hitter Larry Bowa (.287 with 48 stolen bases) was the PCL theft leader and the best fielding shortstop in the league. First basemen Calvin Emery (.400 in 101 games) and Jim Hutto (.306) provided offensive punch, while second sacker Dennis Doyle (.310) led the league in hits and total bases. The best pitcher was righthander Jeff James (13–10), the strikeout leader who tied for the most victories.

Eugene sagged to a losing record in 1970, although outfielder Joe Lis (.324, 36 HRs, 107 RBIs) was the home run champ. Southpaw Ken Reynolds (13–10) pitched well, but Jeff James (6–14) was ineffective. The next year Eugene recorded the poorest record in the league, despite the hitting of muscular first baseman Greg Luzinski (.312, 36 HRs, 114 RBIs), outfielder Mike Anderson (.334, 36 HRs, 100 RBIs), and outfielder-first baseman Pete Koegel (.309).

In 1972 the Phils stocked Eugene with rising young stars who copped the Western Division title. Twenty-two-year-old infielder Mike Schmidt (.291, 26 HRs, 91 RBIs) and catcher Bob Boone (.308) would end the year in Philadelphia, while outfielders Joe Lis (.338 with 26 HRs and 58 RBIs in just 65 games) and Bill Robinson (.304 with 20 HRs and 66 RBIs in 65 games) would spend half the season with the Phils. Southpaw Mike Wallace (16–7) led the PCL in victories, and the loss to Albuquerque in the championship playoffs was the only disappointment of the year.

Although outfielders Richard Wissel (.319) and Clarence Vaughns (.306) hit well in 1973, the Emeralds pitching staff was last in team ERA (5.27) and the standouts of 1972 had all been promoted. Eugene finished last in the west, and after the season the franchise was moved to Sacramento.

Eugene immediately rejoined the Northwest League. By 1980 the Class A circuit played a short season, but in 1982 Eugene became the first team in the league to employ a year-round general manager. The GM of the Emeralds was knowledgeable, aggressive Bob Beban, a former PCL umpire, and Eugene drew as many fans in half a season in 1989 as it did in a full year in the Pacific Coast League.

| Year | Record | Pcg. | Finish |
|------|--------|------|--------|
| 1969 | 88-58  | .603 | First — won opener, lost finals |
| 1970 | 66-80  | .452 | Sixth |
| 1971 | 66-79  | .455 | Eighth |
| 1972 | 79-69  | .534 | Fourth — won opener, lost finals |
| 1973 | 61-79  | .448 | Seventh |

# Fort Worth
# (Rangers)

In 1988 Fort Worth became a charter member of the Texas League, competing for seven decades in the historic circuit and establishing one of the greatest dynasties in baseball history — six consecutive pennants from 1920 through 1925. Following a first-place finish in 1958, Fort Worth, along with Dallas and Houston, withdrew from the Class AA Texas League to move up to the American Association. But after one year, the AAA circuit cut back from ten to eight teams, and Dallas and Fort Worth formed a joint franchise. After three years in the American Association, Dallas-Fort Worth moved to the PCL when the AA disbanded. Although plans had been made to construct a baseball facility between Dallas and Fort Worth, Turnpike Stadium in Arlington would not open for play until 1965. Dallas and Fort Worth split the home schedule between their old Texas League parks.

Fort Worth's 13,000-seat LaGrave Field hosted its only PCL action in 1963. Jack McKeon managed the Rangers to a break-even record, but fans enjoyed several fine hitters: outfielders Pedro Oliva (.304, 23 HRs), Joe Christian (.304), Ceaser Tovar (.297) and Joe Nossek (.293); third baseman George Banks (.280, 25 HRs); and first sacker Ray Jablonski (.267, 26 HRs). The best pitchers were Ted Sadowski (15–13), reliever D. R. Williams (8–5 with a 2.65 ERA), and Lee Strange (7–1) with a 2.05 ERA in his first nine games), who promptly was called up to Minnesota.

Fort Worth businessman Tommy Mercer bought the DFW franchise, leaving Dallas in the PCL and returning the Fort Worth Cats to the Texas League. After the Cats finished last, however, Dallas and Fort Worth reunited at Turnpike Stadium to play for six more years in the Texas League. Attendance was excellent, Turnpike Stadium was expanded (in 1989 it seated 41,284), and in 1972 the Texas Rangers entered the American League.

| Year | Record | Pcg. | Finish |
|------|--------|------|--------|
| 1963 | 79-79  | .500 | Sixth  |

# Fresno
# (Fresnos)

Baseball received strong support in Fresno throughout the late 1800s. Frank Chance, a native of Fresno, learned the game in his home town, became known as the Peerless Leader of the Chicago Cubs, and a Fresno athletic park was named for him. Fresno teams, usually known as the Fresnos, were fielded in all manner of amateur leagues and tournaments. Tacoma and Portland played their 1904 season opener in Fresno, and even though only 600 fans attended, the two teams soon returned to the California city.

During the 1905 season Tacoma's club was forced to finish the year in Sacramento, and the franchise was located in Fresno for 1906. Manager Mique Fisher was given a floral horseshoe for good luck in the opening game, but the talisman did not work, as Portland outdueled the Fresnos 1–0 before a good crowd of 2,500. A week into the season, the disastrous San Francisco earthquake wrecked the Seals' and Oaks' ballparks, and Oakland played some of their "home" games in Fresno while new grounds were being prepared.

Support for the local team soon eroded, however, as the Fresnos proved to be futile at the plate. Four regulars hit below .200; catcher Hap Hogan, for example, batted only .175, while first baseman Ed Cartwright hit just .216. Only one regular hit above .260, and no one on the team batted higher than .285. The team lost 117 games and finished dead last.

Fresno dropped out of the PCL, along with Seattle, and for the next two years the circuit had just four clubs. A California State League franchise operated in Fresno during the 1910, 1913 and 1914 seasons, then professional baseball was absent from the city for more than a quarter of a century. In 1941 Fresno joined the California League and remained a mainstay of the circuit. For three decades Fresno was a Giants farm club, but in 1988 the franchise became independent, with hopes of reaching AAA status with the PCL.

The Fresno Suns obtained nine players from the Giants, six from the Orioles, and four from Japan's Hanshin Tigers. On April 15, 1988, Suns southpaws Rob Rowen and Atushi Tagi established a California League record by pitching 11 innings of no-hit ball. But John Euless Park was condemned and the grandstands torn down; efforts to build a new park were unsuccessful, and a return to the PCL seemed years away.

| Year | Record | Pcg. | Finish |
|------|--------|------|--------|
| 1906 | 64-117 | .353 | Sixth  |

# Hollywood
# (Stars, Sheiks, Twinks)

The Hollywood Stars (often labeled "Sheiks" or "Twinks" by journalists) provided for PCL fans color and glamour unique in minor league baseball. From 1909 through 1925, Los Angeles supported two PCL teams, the Angels and the Tigers of suburbs Vernon (1909–12 and 1915–25) or Venice (1913–14). But after the 1925 season, Vernon owners sold the franchise to San Francisco interests, and Bill Lane determined to move his Salt Lake City Bees to the Los Angeles area. The Bees had been unprofitable, league members disliked the travel expenses necessary for long trips to Salt Lake City, and Lane readily secured approval from the owners to relocate to Hollywood, LA's most spectacular suburb.

Hollywood city fathers were delighted to have a baseball team, even though there was not a suitable ballpark available in the movie capital. Bill Lane would rent Wrigley Field, a splendid minor league facility which had been opened late in the 1925 season as the home of the Angels. Although 273,000 fans would pay to see the sixth-place Stars during their initial season, Wrigley Field was a considerable distance from Hollywood proper, and as long as the team stayed at Wrigley Field they would be unable to acquire a strong following or identity.

Bill Lane wanted to continue to call his club the Bees, but Hollywood "Stars" was a universal sobriquet, and soon the uniforms were changed as a concession to popular opinion. Oscar Vitt, who had spent ten years as an American League infielder, would manage the Stars through the 1934 season. His first two clubs finished sixth, but the Stars climbed into a tie for second place in 1928, then charged into the playoffs the next three years. In July 1928, the Stars became the first professional baseball team to fly. When it was determined that the Stars could not make train connections after a Sunday doubleheader in Seattle in time to open a home stand in Los Angeles on Tuesday, several members of the team left on Saturday with the equipment trunks. Lane persuaded a sufficient number of players to stay behind and play the doubleheader, then board a rickety plane (all planes were rickety in 1928) to Portland, where they made the necessary rail connection.

By 1928 spitballer Frank Shellenback had become the finest

pitcher in the PCL, averaging almost 24 victories per year over the next six seasons. Shellenback pitched for the Stars all ten seasons of the PCL's first tenure in Hollywood, heading the mound staff of what became a potent offensive machine.

During this period, the Coast League employed a split-season format, with winners engaging in a best-of-seven playoff. In 1929 and 1930 the Stars won the second half, and with late season momentum defeated the Missions of San Francisco in seven games for the 1929 playoff title, then won four out of five from the arch-rival Angels in 1930. Shellenback was 26–12 in 1929, leading the PCL in victories and winning percentage, and in 1930 Jim Turner was 21–9. Mickey Heath, Stars first sacker from 1927 through 1930, led the playoff champions in power hitting (1929 — .349, 38 HRs, 156 RBIs; 1930 — .324, 37 HRs, 136 RBIs, and a record 12 consecutive base hits).

The 1929 Stars hit .311 as a club, bolstered by 37-year-old right fielder Bill Rumler (.386, 26 HRs, 120 RBIs), left fielder Elias Funk (.384, 13 HRs, 125 RBIs — Lane sold Funk to Detroit for $40,000 and two players), and Russ Rollings (.324). Catcher Hank Severeid, a 15-year major league veteran, came to Hollywood in time to play 79 games, and his bat would be a major factor for three seasons (1929 — .415; 1930 — .367; 1931 — .347). Center fielder Cleo Carlyle also was an offensive force for years (1929 — .347, 20 HRs, 136 RBIs; 1930 — .326; 1931 — .320; 1932 — .346, 106 RBIs; 1933 — .320). Rumler again hit well in 1930 (.353), and so did catcher Johnny Bassler (.365), newcomer Jess Hill (.356), and second baseman Otis Brannon (.307, 18 HRs, 130 RBIs).

In 1931, with two consecutive playoff titles under their belts, the Stars won the first half. Shellenback was in top form (27–7), while Dave Barbee (.332, 47 HRs, 166 RBIs) was the home run champ. But the Stars faltered in the second half, then lost the playoff series to the Seals in four games.

The Stars came back strong with a second-place finish in 1932, but there was no playoff that year. Shellenback, 26–10, with 35 complete games in 36 starts, again led the PCL in victories, and former Yankee star Bob Meusel, .329 in 64 games as a Star, saw part-time duty. The 1933 club won 107 games, good for third place, and boasted nine .300 hitters. Vince DiMaggio made an impressive debut as a Star (.348 in 74 games), and would be the regular left fielder in 1934 and 1935. The 1933 pitching staff boasted four 20-

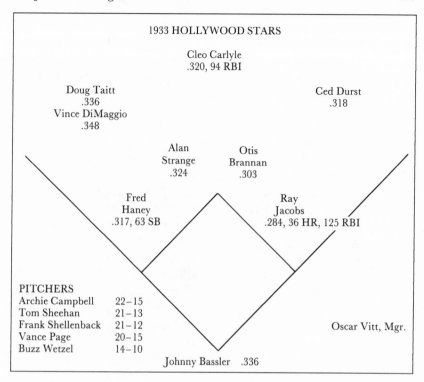

1933 HOLLYWOOD STARS

Cleo Carlyle
.320, 94 RBI

Doug Taitt
.336
Vince DiMaggio
.348

Ced Durst
.318

Alan
Strange
.324

Otis
Brannan
.303

Fred
Haney
.317, 63 SB

Ray
Jacobs
.284, 36 HR, 125 RBI

PITCHERS
Archie Campbell    22–15
Tom Sheehan        21–13
Frank Shellenback  21–12
Vance Page         20–15
Buzz Wetzel        14–10

Oscar Vitt, Mgr.

Johnny Bassler   .336

game winners: Shellenback (21–12), Archie Campbell (22–15), Tom Sheehan (21–13), and Vance Page (20–15).

Third baseman Fred Haney led the league in stolen bases in 1934 (63) and 1935 (71), while southpaw Joe Sullivan (25–11) was impressive in 1934, his only season with Hollywood. Right field was inhabited by the legendary slugger Smead Jolley in 1934 (.360, 23 HRs, 133 RBIs) and 1935 (.372, 29 HRs, 128 RBIs).

In 1935 Bill Lane asked Oscar Vitt to resign so that the club could save money by utilizing Frank Shellenback as a player-manager. Although he still was the best pitcher on the team, Shellenback (14–9) was past his prime, and so were the Stars. Hollywood finished last in the second half, the team drew merely 90,000, and in the face of already severe financial losses, Lane was informed that the rent on Wrigley Field would be doubled to $10,000. He investigated locations in the San Francisco Bay area and Phoenix, then decided to relocate his franchise to San Diego.

There was no professional baseball in Hollywood during the 1936 and 1937 seasons. But the 1937 Mission club was a failure on the field and at the box office, and after the season it was decided to place the franchise in Hollywood. The Angels, with vivid recollections of a long series of disagreements with Bill Lane, would agree to rent Wrigley Field for just one season. Gilmore Field was erected just east of Gilmore Stadium, which was an oval park used for auto racing and football and which had been used by the Hollywood Stars as a spring training base during the 1920s. Pan Pacific Auditorium was located nearby, and so was the popular Farmers Market. Gilmore Field was a comfortable wooden park with nearly 13,000 seats. Beneath the grandstand, a replica of a playing field was hung where a picture of each starter was attached to his position before each game. A large foul screen stretched from dugout to dugout, and instead of the usual chalked foul lines in the outfield, pieces of wood were buried and painted white (on at least one occasion a batted ball caromed off the wood past an approaching outfielder, leading to an inside-the-park home run). At the suggestion of manager Fred Haney, Hollywood began the custom of dragging the infield after the fifth inning, thereby enticing fans to the concession stands during this break in the action. In 1939 a local station televised a Hollywood game, and by the late 1940s every home game was being carried on TV, although declining attendance during ensuing seasons caused a reduction of television coverage.

Lefthanded center fielder Frenchy Uhalt hit .332 in 1938 and led the PCL in stolen bases, but the supporting cast was weak, and the Stars finished seventh. Indeed, during the next decade Hollywood was usually in the second division and made the playoffs only in 1941, when the fourth-place Stars were knocked off in the first round. In 1943 player-manager Charlie Root, a 17-year National League veteran, went 15–5 at the age of 44. That same year left fielder Johnny Dickshot hit .352 and started the season with a 33-game batting streak that excited wartime fans.

Babe Herman, a lifetime .324 hitter in the big leagues (he had hit .316 with 131 RBIs for Seattle in 1925), played for the Stars from 1939 through 1944, batting .317, .307, .346, .322, .354, and (at the age of 41) .346. In 1946 Eddie Erautt twirled eight shutouts in a 20–14 season and led the PCL with 234 strikeouts. The next season first baseman Tony Lupien (.341, 21 HRs, 110 RBIs, 40 SBs) was named MVP for a sixth-place club. Left fielder Gus Zernial was impressive in 1948 (.322, 40 HRs, and a league-leading 156 RBIs), and the big Texan went to the American League the following season.

Stockholders during these years included such movie luminaries as Cecil B. DeMille, Gary Cooper, Bing Crosby, Gene Autry, Barbara Stanwyck, George Burns and Gracie Allen, Robert Taylor, William Powell and George Raft. In 1955 Jayne Mansfield was named Miss Hollywood Stars. Ads touted "the Hollywood Stars baseball team, owned by the Hollywood stars," and many local fans and visiting players' wives attended the games primarily to spot movie stars in the crowd. Board meetings sometimes were held at the Brown Derby (Stars president Bob Cobb owned the famous restaurant) or aboard a yacht. For Sunday and holiday games, a Dixieland band added to the showbiz atmosphere.

The Stars experimented with pinstripe shorts and long socks in 1950, on the theory that players would run faster, according to manager Fred Haney. Doubtless this sporty attire was speedier than the baggy flannel uniforms of the day, but shorts-clad players were painfully self-conscious even in Hollywood, and the abbreviated togs were discarded after a few seasons. The Stars also were one of the earliest teams to wear batting helmets, at the direction of their longtime parent club, the Pittsburgh Pirates.

Further color was added by such characters as Bobby Bragan, a player-manager who sometimes smoked a long, black cigar through his catcher's mask. Thrown out of a game, Bragan once lit a cigar and stretched out across home plate. On another occasion, Bragan was at the helm when the Stars dropped hopelessly behind the hated Angels. Bragan sent nine pinch-hitters (mostly pitchers) in for one batter, running in a new hitter after each pitch (Bobby was suspended for a few days after this antic, even though he pointed out that his tactic was legal).

Fred Haney guided the Stars to a first-place finish and victory in the playoffs in 1949. Pinky Woods (23–12) and Willard Ramsdell (18–12, with a league-leading 2.60 ERA) led the mound staff, while third sacker Jim Baxes (24 HRs and 108 RBIs) and longtime outfield star Frank Kelleher (29 HRs and 90 RBIs) added power hitting. Center fielder Irv Noren (.330, 29 HRs, 130 RBIs) was named MVP, then went to the American League.

The Stars slipped to third place in 1950, although Kelleher led the PCL with 40 HRs and Jack Salveson (15–4 with a 2.84 ERA) was the ERA champ. Right fielder George Schmees (.328, 26 HRs, 100 RBIs) and righthander Ben Wade (16–6) paced the Stars to a second-place finish in 1951, but Haney's club lost in the playoff finals. Although there were no playoffs in 1952 and 1953, the Stars captured first place both years.

Haney led the Stars to the 1952 flag, and Johnny Lindell was voted MVP. Lindell had been a New York Yankee outfielder for a decade. Early in his career he had been a fine minor league pitcher, and when his big league days seemed over, he employed a knuckle-ball and took the mound for the Stars. At 24–9, Lindell led the PCL in victories, winning percentage and strikeouts (190), and he also hit eight home runs in 74 games as an outfielder and pinch hitter. Left fielder Carlos Bernier (.301 with 65 SBs) paced the offense, and won the first of five consecutive stolen base titles for the Stars. Bernier repeated as stolen base king in 1955 and 1956, while center fielder Tom Saffell was the best in the league in 1953 and 1954.

After five years at the helm of the Stars, Fred Haney became manager of the Pittsburgh Pirates. The colorful Bobby Bragan succeeded Haney and led the Stars to a second straight pennant. First baseman Dale Long (.272 with a league-leading 35 HRs and 116 RBIs) was named MVP. Right fielder Ted Beard exploded in April, hitting four home runs in a game against San Diego and tying a 1930 PCL record (set by Mickey Heath of the Stars) by banging out 12 consecutive hits. George O'Donnell (20–12) and veteran reliever Red Lynn (10–4) led the pitching corps.

Bragan almost delivered a third consecutive flag in 1954, despite numerous injuries, which hampered Dale Long and other key offensive performers. Carlos Bernier (.313 in 119 games) was the leading hitter, but when he angrily slapped umpire Jack Valenti after a strike call, he was suspended for the rest of the season. But Bragan commanded a deep mound staff which included Roger Bowman (22–13), Lino Dinoso (19–8), Red Munger (17–8) and Mel Queen (16–8), and which led the PCL with a 2.29 cumulative ERA. On the last day of the season, Bowman twirled a seven-inning perfect game to put the Stars in a tie for first place with San Diego. The Padres won a playoff game, 7–2, the next day, and Hollywood lost the opening round of the postseason series. Frank Kelleher, perhaps the most popular player ever to wear a Stars uniform, retired at the end of the season, having hit 226 homers for Hollywood.

In 1955 the Stars were young and did not have as much offensive power as in the past. There were two 20-game winners: Red

Munger (23–8 with 25 complete games in 35 starts and 1.85 ERA) led the PCL in victories and ERA, and Bob Garber (20–16 with 199 Ks and 10 relief appearances), the league leader in losses and strikeouts. Although the club finished third, no playoffs were scheduled, so the Stars and Angels staged a best-of-five series at Wrigley Field to determine the city champs of Los Angeles. Hollywood ended 1955 on a successful note, downing the Angels three games to two.

Although Pittsburgh shuffled players to and from Hollywood during 1956 and 1957, the Stars managed to post winning records, placing fourth and third. Attendance declined rapidly, but remaining fans saw such future Pirate stars as Bill Mazeroski, Gene Freese, Dick Stuart and Bob Purkey. In 1957 they also saw Dick Smith rap out six consecutive pinch hits to establish a PCL record, and they witnessed lefthanded first sacker Tony Bartimore play third base during several games when the Stars were shorthanded.

CBS had purchased the property where Gilmore Field and Gilmore Stadium were located, and the company announced plans to raze these facilities in 1958 to build a vast television headquarters. The Stars considered renting Wrigley Field for the 1958 season, but the Dodgers and Giants decided to move to the West Coast, and the PCL found it necessary to transfer the franchises from Los Angeles, San Francisco and Hollywood. Bob Cobb, longtime president of the Stars, reluctantly sold his club, and the operation moved to Salt Lake City — the city which had relocated its franchise to Hollywood in 1926.

| Year | Record | Pcg. | Finish |
|------|--------|------|--------|
| 1926 | 94-107 | .468 | Sixth |
| 1927 | 92-104 | .469 | Sixth |
| 1928 | 112-79 | .586 | Second (tie) |
| 1929 | 113-89 | .559 | Third — won playoffs |
| 1930 | 119-81 | .595 | First — won playoffs |
| 1931 | 104-83 | .556 | Second — lost playoffs |
| 1932 | 106-83 | .561 | Second |
| 1933 | 107-80 | .572 | Third |
| 1934 | 97-88 | .524 | Third |
| 1935 | 73-99 | .483 | Sixth |
| 1938 | 79-99 | .444 | Seventh |
| 1939 | 82-94 | .466 | Sixth |
| 1940 | 84-94 | .472 | Sixth |
| 1941 | 85-91 | .483 | Fourth — lost playoff opener |
| 1942 | 75-103 | .421 | Seventh |
| 1943 | 73-82 | .471 | Fifth |

| 1944 | 83-86 | .491 | Sixth |
| 1945 | 73-110 | .399 | Eighth |
| 1946 | 95-88 | .519 | Third — lost playoff opener |
| 1947 | 88-98 | .473 | Sixth |
| 1948 | 84-104 | .447 | Sixth |
| 1949 | 109-79 | .583 | First — won playoff opener and finals |
| 1950 | 104-96 | .520 | Third |
| 1951 | 93-74 | .557 | Second — won playoff opener, lost finals |
| 1952 | 109-71 | .606 | First |
| 1953 | 106-74 | .589 | First |
| 1954 | 101-68 | .598 | Second — lost playoff opener |
| 1955 | 91-81 | .529 | Third |
| 1956 | 85-83 | .506 | Fourth |
| 1957 | 94-74 | .560 | Third |

# Honolulu
# (Islanders)

In 1961 the Coast League added the coasts of Hawaii, as regular jet travel made it possible to move the Spokane franchise to Honolulu. After the 1960 season, Salt Lake City businessman Nick Morgan, Jr., purchased the Spokane club and obtained league permission to move it to Hawaii. PCL teams flew out for one long series each year — the trip was a favorite of players' wives — and Hawaii was required to pay half of the round trip fare. When Hawaii traveled east, players had to endure 21 days on the road. The home of Hawaii Islanders was downtown Honolulu Stadium, a rambling, old, wooden facility which seated nearly 25,000. But through the years, games would be played at a total of nine different ballparks on three of the Hawaiian Islands, including 50,000-seat Aloha Stadium, home of the Hula Bowl. Originally the configurations of Aloha Stadium could be changed to fit the event but mechanisms eventually rusted. Islander performances would include spring training and postseason series against teams from Japan. Occasionally there was a morning game, and Islander fans once were treated to a classic old minor league show, a wedding on the pitcher's mound between games of a doubleheader — followed by an unscheduled but even more classic baseball happening, a bench-clearing brawl during the nightcap.

It would take 10 years for the Islanders to make the PCL playoffs, but Hawaii fans enthusiastically harassed visiting players and cheered such heroes as outfielder Carlos Bernier. In the Islanders' first season, Bernier won the batting title (.351), and fellow out-fielder George Prescott (.301 with 32 homers) helped the team wal-lop more roundtrippers (163) than any other club in the PCL.

Although Bernier would prove to be Hawaii's only batting champ in 27 years of PCL ball, the next year he again hit well (.313), while outfielder Stan Palys (.332 with 33 homers) won the home run title, and southpaw Richard Egan (17–11 with 201 strikeouts) led the league in victories and strikeouts. In 1963 Is-lander fans again were able to root for Bernier (.300) and Palys (.305), as well as second-year player-manager Irv Noren, a former Yankee and PCL star. Bernier was back for one more solid season (.294 with 27 homers) in 1964, while outfielder Fred Valentine, a major league veteran, was the 1965 stolen base champion (.324 with 25 homers and 58 thefts). In 1967 outfielder Willie Kirkland led the PCL in home runs (34) and RBIs (97). Chuck Tanner be-came manager in 1969, and Hawaii led the league in home runs (107). Third baseman John Werhas (.298, 15 HRs, 90 RBIs) and outfielder Tomas Silverio (.313) were named to the All-Star team, while lefty Dennis Bennett (13–11) tied for the lead in victories. Another southpaw, the colorful Bo Belinski (12–5), enjoyed a strong second season with Hawaii (in 1968 Bo twirled a 1–0 no-hit-ter over Tacoma).

Tanner guided the 1970 Islanders to the best record in the PCL. Bennett (18–8) again tied for the most victories, and right-hander Tom Bradley was spectacular (11–1) before being called up to the Angels. Outfielder Winston Llenas (.339, 20 HRs, 108 RBIs) missed the batting title by one point, second sacker Doug Griffin (.326 with 35 SBs) was the stolen base champ, and John Werhas (.283) and Charles Vinson (.268, 22 HRs, 91 RBIs) re-turned to man third and first. The Islanders won the Southern Di-vision by 13 games, but dropped four straight to Spokane (victors in the North by 26 games!) in the championship playoff. Hawaii led all minor league teams with a spectacular paid attendance of 467,217, and repeated as attendance leaders the next year when support for a losing club totaled 375,957.

Hawaii changed affiliations in 1971, and did not rise above .500 until 1975. But Jerry Crider (9–4, 3.29 ERA) was the 1971 ERA champ, and righthanded fireballer Dave Freisleben (16–8 with 206 Ks in 195 innings and a 2.82 ERA) was the 1973 ERA and strikeout leader. Slugging outfielder Gene Martin, obtained from Eugene during the 1973 season, was the home run and RBI king (.288, 31 HRs, 106 RBIs).

From 1975 through 1977, the Islanders won three consecutive Western Division titles and two PCL pennants. The 1975 Islanders posted the best team ERA in the league, Gary Ross (16–8) won the most games, Butch Metzger (15–7) was right behind, and Jerry Johnson (10–3) logged an excellent half season. The offense was sparked by lefthanded outfielder John Turner (.329) and catcher Robert Davis (.329). Skipper Robert Hartsfield guided the Islanders to the best record in the league, then beat Salt Lake City in the playoffs to bring Hawaii its first PCL flag.

Hartsfield won a second straight championship in 1976. Diego Segui (11–5, 3.19 ERA) was the ERA leader, and reliever Charles Hartenstein (11–5, 3.19 ERA) posted similar numbers. The lineup bristled with dangerous hitters: outfielders Gene Richards (.331), John Scott (.315), and Rod Gaspar (.294); first baseman-DH Bobby Valentine (.304); and returnees James Fairey (.299) and shortstop William Almon (.291), who had tied for the stolen base title in 1975.

In 1977 Hartsfield and most of his players were gone, but James Fairey was back (.319) to lead the run for a third consecutive pennant. Switch-hitting catcher Richard Sweet (.323) was named to the All-Star team, and veteran infielder Chris Arnold (.302) provided stability throughout the season. Outstanding performances for half of the season were turned in by second baseman Julio Cruz (.366) and outfielders Don Reynolds (.368) and Mike Dupree (.352). Hawaii was the best fielding team in the league, the pitching staff recorded the lowest ERA, and righthander Mark Wiley (16–7) posted the most victories. Attendance soared to 347,931 as the Islanders won the Western Division for the third year in a row, then finally fell to Phoenix in six games during the playoff finals. On April 26 the Islanders drew 25,189, a minor league attendance record for the year exceeded only by — the Hawaii Islanders on July 4, 33,904!

After a dropoff in 1978, the Islanders rebounded for back-to-back division titles. Dick Phillips, who had managed the 1977 champs, guided the Islanders to the top of the Northern Division in the first half of 1979, then beat Vancouver for the division crown before losing to Salt Lake City in the finals. Although the Islanders finished dead last in team hitting, the club was second in fielding, first in double plays, and led the PCL in staff ERA.

Doug Rader was the new manager in 1980. Again the Islanders were last in hitting, while finishing second in fielding and first in staff ERA. And again the Islanders took the first half in the North, won the division title in the playoff opener, then went to the last game of the finals before losing to Albuquerque. Righthander Tom Tellman (13–5) was Rader's best pitcher, while the offense was led by first baseman Brod Perkins (.312), DH Craig Kusick (.305), and DH Tim Flannery (.346 in 47 games).

In 1981 Rader once more took the first half in the North, but this time the Islanders were knocked off in the opening round of playoffs. Speedy outfielder-second baseman Alan Wiggins (.302 with 73 SBs) won the stolen base title, and infielders Jose Moreno (.305) and Craig Stimes (.303) added offensive punch. Tony Gwynn (.328) flashed his skills in 93 games in 1982 before going up for the rest of the season with San Diego, and big Andy Hawkins (9–7 with a 2.18 ERA) also was promoted to the Padres. But the Islanders again ranked last in team hitting, and the club failed to make the playoffs in 1982.

In 1983 Hawaii switched affiliations from the Padres to the Pirates, but again missed the playoffs. The pitching staff, however, once more led the PCL in ERA, and righthander Jose DeLeon (11–4, 3.04 ERA) qualified for the ERA title before going on to finish the year with the Pirates (7–3, 2.83 ERA). The 1984 Islanders followed what had become a typical pattern — last in team batting and first in staff ERA. Righthander Mike Bielecki (19–3) led the PCL in victories and strikeouts; southpaw Alfonso Pulido (18–6) was the leader in winning percentage, innings pitched, complete games (16) and shutouts (4); and big Bob Walk (9–5, 2.26 ERA) qualified as ERA champ before going up to the Pirates (where he spent most of the rest of the year on the disabled list). Outfielder Trench Davis won the stolen base title (53), and Tommy Sandt was voted manager of the year. Sandt led the Islanders to the best record of 1984, then won the Northern Division in the playoffs before being defeated in the finals.

The next year Sandt once again guided his team to the PCL's best record, as the Islanders typically recorded the worst batting average and best ERA. Bob Walk was back (16–5), this time leading the league in victories and complete games, while major league veteran Rick Reuschel quickly worked his way onto the Pirates' roster (6–2 in 8 games), and Lee Tunnell (4–1 in 7 games) and lefthanded reliever Dave Tomlin (8–2, 2.09 ERA) also made strong contributions from the mound. Mike Diaz (.312 with 22 homers) was the best catcher in the circuit, and Trench Davis (.270 with 33 SBs) returned for another solid year.

The 1985 Islanders were swept in three straight in the opening round of the playoffs, but of deeper concern was a serious decline in attendance. Despite two first-place finishes, Hawaii attendance was disappointing, and after a losing record in 1986, the total dropped below 85,000. The dilapidated downtown ballpark (Honolulu Stadium had become known as "Termite Palace") had been razed, and when the Islanders moved fulltime to Aloha Stadium, the team was not allowed any revenue from concessions, parking or fence ads. Therefore there was no incentive for management to increase crowds through promotions, and as attendance nosedived the financial status of the franchise became shaky.

In 1986 the Islanders finished — where else? — last in team batting, but first in ERA. For the fourth consecutive year, the mound staff provided the ERA champ, righthander Dave Johnson, while southpaw Bob Patterson was the strikeout king. Outfielder Barry Bonds (.311) played 44 games for the Islanders, then logged 113 games in a Pirate uniform, and Trench Davis (.311) produced another good season. But the Islanders recorded the next-to-worst record in the PCL in 1986 and again in 1987. After the 1987 season, owner Dave Elmore and GM Fred Whitacre explored relocation sites, eventually settling on Colorado Springs. But for nearly one-third of the current lifespan of the PCL, the Hawaii Islanders had provided an exotic glamour that will remain a nostalgic part of the circuit's history.

| Year | Record | Pcg. | Finish |
|------|--------|------|--------|
| 1961 | 68-86 | .442 | Sixth |
| 1962 | 77-76 | .503 | Fifth |
| 1963 | 81-77 | .513 | Fourth |
| 1964 | 60-98 | .380 | Tenth |
| 1965 | 75-72 | .510 | Sixth |
| 1966 | 63-84 | .429 | Tenth |
| 1967 | 60-87 | .408 | Twelfth |
| 1968 | 78-69 | .531 | Third |
| 1969 | 74-72 | .507 | Fourth |
| 1970 | 98-48 | .671 | First — won Western Division and pennant |

| | | | |
|---|---|---|---|
| 1971 | 73-73 | .500 | Sixth |
| 1972 | 74-74 | .500 | Fifth |
| 1973 | 70-74 | .486 | Fifth |
| 1974 | 67-77 | .465 | Sixth |
| 1975 | 88-56 | .611 | First — won Western Division and pennant |
| 1976 | 77-68 | .531 | Second — won Western Division and pennant |
| 1977 | 79-67 | .541 | Second — won Western Division, lost playoff |
| 1978 | 56-82 | .406 | Ninth |
| 1979 | 72-76 | .486 | Eighth — won opener, lost finals |
| 1980 | 79-60 | .568 | Third — won opener, lost finals |
| 1981 | 72-65 | .526 | Third — lost opener |
| 1982 | 73-71 | .507 | Fifth |
| 1983 | 72-71 | .503 | Fifth |
| 1984 | 87-53 | .621 | First — won opener, lost finals |
| 1985 | 84-59 | .587 | First — lost opener |
| 1986 | 65-79 | .451 | Ninth |
| 1987 | 65-75 | .464 | Ninth |

# *Indianapolis*
# *(Indians)*

Indianapolis fans enjoyed American Association baseball from 1902 through 1962. But the AA suspended play after the 1962 season, and Indianapolis joined the International League for 1963. In 1964 the PCL expanded from 10 to 12 teams, and when Indianapolis moved to the Coast League the Indians became the easternmost club in the history of the Pacific Coast League.

During five seasons in the PCL, Indianapolis fielded three clubs with winning records, but the Indians never made the playoffs. Managers were George Noga (1964), Les Moss (1965–66), Don Gutteridge (1967), and Don Zimmer (1968). The best attendance (183,602) was recorded in 1966.

Shortstop Lee Elia supplied most of the power during the first PCL season, belting 29 homers with 101 RBIs, and a .261 average. Tommie Agee roamed the outfield, but hit only .226. Dave De-Busschere (15–12) was the best pitcher on a losing team.

Marv Stachie was a mainstay during the three winning seasons, playing second base and hitting .301 (1965), .297 (1966), and .273 (1967). In 1965 shortstop Dal Maxvill hit .285 and outfielder James Hicks added a .288 average to the offense. Also in the 1965 outfield was the old White Sox great, Minnie Minoso, who hit .264

in 52 games. Bruce Howard (15–8) led the league in ERA (2.20). Bob Locker (16–9), Dave DeBusschere (15–8), and Ed Hobaugh (10–4) rounded out a mound corps which posted the lowest ERA of 1965.

In 1966 Bill Fisher (11–6) led the PCL in ERA (2.35), while Manly Johnston led the club in victories (18–7). Indianapolis had the best fielding percentage of 12 PCL clubs in 1966, while catcher Duane Josephson (.324), first baseman Ray Conde (.311), and outfielder Ed Stroud blistered the ball (.345) for 27 games, then was promoted to the White Sox. Outfielder Charles Nash supplied good power (.274, 28 HRs, 79 RBIs), while Bill Fisher (12–4, 2.36 ERA) led the pitching staff.

Conde again hit well (.282) in 1968. Hal McRae (.295) manned second base, Cal Emery (.289) was at first, and Pat Corrales (.273) was behind the plate. The leading pitcher was Don Secrist (11–2). These men headed the final entry in the PCL, because the American Association reorganized for 1969, and Indianapolis moved back to the AA.

| Year | Record | Pcg. | Finish |
|------|--------|------|--------|
| 1964 | 70-78  | .473 | Ninth  |
| 1965 | 89-79  | .563 | Fourth |
| 1966 | 80-68  | .541 | Fourth |
| 1967 | 76-71  | .517 | Fifth  |
| 1968 | 66-78  | .458 | Ninth  |

# Las Vegas (Stars)

Since 1983, the Las Vegas Stars have brought PCL baseball to the "Entertainment Capital of the World." Las Vegas first participated in professional baseball during the postwar boom, fielding teams in the Sunset League (1947–50), Southwest International League (1951–52), the Arizona-Mexico League (1957), and the California League (1958). All of these were Class C circuits, and games were played in a wooden ballpark on North Las Vegas Boulevard, across town from the luxurious hotels and casinos. But Class C baseball did not catch on in Las Vegas, nor did indoor-outdoor soccer or Continental League basketball. The only professional sport that worked was PCL baseball.

*The sky boxes and grandstand at luxurious Cashman Field.*
— Author's photo

Stars president-GM Larry Koentopp brought the Spokane franchise to Las Vegas for the 1983 season. The old, wooden park was razed and replaced by magnificent Cashman Field, where fans could sip martinis along with more traditional concession fare. The scoreboard was one of the most entertaining in professional baseball — Koentopp maintained that there must be a strong element of show-biz in order to compete for the entertainment dollar in Las Vegas. Tourists came to Las Vegs to visit casinos, not the ballpark, but Koentopp built a strong following for the Stars among local residents. Annual attendance regularly soared over 300,000, one of the highest figures in minor league ball.

A major reason for fan support is the fine quality of baseball played by the AAA Padres athletes. In six seasons the Stars missed the PCL playoffs just once, and won two pennants in the last three years. The first edition of the Stars finished with the PCL's second-best record, but lost to Albuquerque in the opening round of the 1983 playoffs. The Stars continued their winning ways the next year, before being blanked in the first round of playoffs by Hawaii.

The 1983 Stars were led by the PCL's Most Valuable Player, Kevin McReynolds (.377, 32 HRs and 116 RBIs in just 113 games). His fellow outfielders, Rogers Brown (.331) and Gerald Davis (.298, 23 HRs, 100 RBIs), also were impressive, and Tony Gwynn (.342) earned a promotion to the Padres after just 17 games. Steve Fireovid (14–10) and reliever Floyd Chiffer (10–4) skillfully handled the difficult job of pitching at Cashen Field. Power alleys were only 364 feet and the fence was just 10 feet high. The desert air not only helped batted balls to carry but often stopped curves from breaking. Fans, of course, enjoyed the resulting offensive shows, and first-year attendance at Cashen Field was a league-leading 365,848.

During their first two seasons, the Stars demonstrated an amazing ability to come from behind at home, winning 67 percent of their games when they trailed by two or more runs after the seventh inning. In 1984 the Stars were paced by RBI champ Rick Lancellotti (.287, 29 HRs, 131 RBIs), All-Star shortstop Ozzie Guillen (.296), and lefthanded outfielder John Kruk. The next year the outfield fence was raised to 20 feet, which decreased home run totals while increasing revenues. But the Stars still boasted the top three hitters in the PCL: batting champ Kruk (.351), and outfielders Kerry Tillman (.337) and Ray Smith (.325).

Fiery Larry Bowa was named manager in 1986, and as usual the Padres had stocked the roster with hitters. The Stars led the PCL in batting, and first baseman Tim Pyznarski (.326, 23 HRs, 119 RBIs) won the RBI title and was named MVP. Catcher Benito Santiago (.286) was a bellweather of the team, and righthander Mark Williamson (10–3 in 65 appearances) was deadly out of the bullpen. Offensive production was added by infielder Mark Wasinger (.307), second baseman Edwin Rodriguez (.301), and outfielders Greg Smith (.309) and James Steels (.307). This explosive team charged into the playoffs, beat Phoenix three games to two, then defeated Vancouver in five games to bring Las Vegas its first PCL flag.

Despite a losing record in 1987, manager Jack Krol won the Southern Division in the second half of the season, although the Stars were blanked by Albuquerque in the opening round of playoffs. Righthanded reliever Todd Simmons led the league with 57 games finished and 22 saves in 75 games, while infielder Steve Garcia (.312), switch hitter Bip Roberts (.306) and outfielder Shawn Abner (.300) were among the top ten hitters in the PCL.

Steve Smith, who managed the Wichita Pilots to the 1987

Texas League flag, led Las Vegas to another pennant in 1988. Infielder Bip Roberts was back to pace the offense (.353), and Todd Simmons (12–5 in 54 appearances) again was the ace of the Stars' bullpen. Sandy Alomar (.297) was considered the best catching prospect in the minor leagues. Other hot bats were wielded by outfielders Shane Mack (.347), Stan Jefferson (.317) and Jerald Clark (.301), shortstop Mike Brumley (.315), and third baseman Tom Brassil (.310). This hard-hitting Stars team downed Albuquerque in three straight in the playoff opener. The Stars split the first two games of the finals with Vancouver, defeated the Canadians in extra innings in the third contest, then took the pennant with a three-hit shutout by righthander Joe Bitker, who also had pitched for the 1986 champions. After the victory, Larry Koentopp and his staff began working to bring yet another PCL flag to Las Vegas.

| Year | Record | Pcg. | Finish |
|------|--------|------|--------|
| 1983 | 83-60 | .580 | Second — lost opener |
| 1984 | 71-65 | .522 | Third — lost opener |
| 1985 | 65-79 | .451 | Tenth |
| 1986 | 80-62 | .563 | Third — won opener and finals |
| 1987 | 69-73 | .486 | Seventh — lost opener |
| 1988 | 74-66 | .529 | |

# Little Rock
# (Arkansas Travelers)

Little Rock was a charter member of the Southern Association, participating in that historic circuit from 1901 through 1958, except for an interlude from 1910–14 and a few months in 1956, when the club finished the season in Montgomery. Ray Winder, owner and president and heart of pro baseball in Little Rock, brought his team back home for the 1957 and 1958 seasons, but poor attendance forced him to sell the club. After a year without baseball in 1959, a public stock drive allowed the Travs to participate in the last two seasons of the Southern Association in 1960 and 1961, then another year without baseball followed in 1962.

With Ray Winder again in charge, Little Rock moved up to AAA in 1963, playing a season in the International League. The Philadelphia Phillies supplied the players and manager Frank Lucchesi, and Little Rock enjoyed a winning season. Little Rock shifted over to the expanded PCL in 1964, with Frank Lucchesi still at the helm. The Phillies stocked the roster with sluggers, and the "Boom-Boom Travs" proved to be one of the most remarkable clubs in the long history of Little Rock baseball.

The Boom-Boom Travs led the league in team hitting and pounded out 208 home runs, establishing a PCL record and almost doubling the old club record (111 in 1960). First baseman Costen Shockley (.281, 36 HRs, 112 RBIs) blasted more homers than any other lefthanded hitter in Trav history. Norm Gigon (.274, 30 HRs, 76 RBIs) was a slugging second baseman and leadoff batter, Pat Corrales (.304) was behind the plate, Alex Johnson (.316, 21 HRs, 71 RBIs in 90 games) was one of a trio of hard-hitting outfielders, Wayne Graham (.305) manned the hot corner, and Lee Elia was the shortstop. A total of 17 men from the 1964 squad would play in the big leagues.

On July 3 righthander Joel Gibson (10–7) no-hit Dallas, 3–0. Two months later, on September 9, southpaw Morris Steevens took the mound on Traveler Appreciation Night as 3,516 fans turned out to honor Ray Winder for his 50th year in baseball. The 23-year-old Steevens was perfect for nine innings, retiring every man in the Ranger lineup except Jim Hughes, who reached on a ground ball error in the sixth. For the second time in 1964 a Trav pitcher hurled a 3–0 no-hitter against Dallas, and fans collected $390 for Steevens after the game.

The Boom-Boom Travs walloped 105 homers at Ray Winder Field and 103 on the road, but the team was nearly invincible at home (54–19). The team drew only 132,170, however, and late in the season most of the standout players were called up to the Phillies. The Travs easily won the Eastern Division, but fell to San Diego, champs of the Western Division, in seven games in the finals.

Frank Lucchesi was back in 1965, and so was a slumping Norm Gigon (.254 with a mere five homers), along with outfielder Bill Sorrell (.274 with 15 homers, down from 22 in 1965). Morris Steevens (7–5) and future big league star Ferguson Jenkins (8–6) were the best pitchers, but the anemic offense was last in the PCL (.227, the worst average of 12 teams, and just 99 home runs). Only two teams endured worse records, and attendance sagged to 77,570.

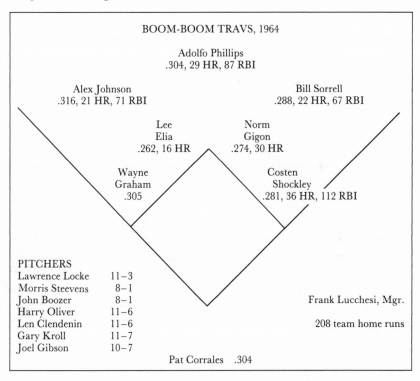

BOOM-BOOM TRAVS, 1964

Adolfo Phillips
.304, 29 HR, 87 RBI

Alex Johnson                                          Bill Sorrell
.316, 21 HR, 71 RBI                                   .288, 22 HR, 67 RBI

Lee             Norm
Elia            Gigon
.262, 16 HR     .274, 30 HR

Wayne                    Costen
Graham                   Shockley
.305                     .281, 36 HR, 112 RBI

PITCHERS
Lawrence Locke      11–3
Morris Steevens      8–1
John Boozer          8–1
Harry Oliver        11–6                        Frank Lucchesi, Mgr.
Len Clendenin       11–6
Gary Kroll          11–7                        208 team home runs
Joel Gibson         10–7

Pat Corrales   .304

The Travs, wanting to return to AA ball, pulled out of the
PCL. The Phillies shifted their AAA franchise to San Diego, Tulsa
moved to the PCL from the Texas League, and the Travs assumed
Tulsa's Texas League affiliation with the St. Louis Cardinals. For
more than two decades the Arkansas Travelers have been a mainstay of the Texas League, with frequent playoff appearances and
one of the most nostalgic ballparks in professional baseball.

| Year | Record | Pcg. | Finish |
|------|--------|------|--------|
| 1964 | 95-61 | .609 | First — won Western Division, lost playoff |
| 1965 | 67-79 | .459 | Tenth |

# Los Angeles
# (Angels)

For more than half a century, Los Angeles was a cornerstone city of the PCL. Like San Francisco, the Los Angeles area long supported two teams: in addition to the LA Angels (1903–57), the Vernon Tigers (1909–12 and 1915–25), the Venice Tigers (1913–14), and the Hollywood Stars (1926–35 and 1938–57). Los Angeles for many years had fielded a team in the California League. In 1893 Athletic Park was rigged with lights — 20 kerosene lamps and a swiveled search light to follow the ball from atop the grandstand — and with future evangelist Billy Sunday in center field, Los Angeles defeated Stockton in a *night* game on July 2 before 9,000 kranks, as nineteenth-century fans were called.

When the Pacific Coast League opened play in 1903, the Angels were at home in Washington Park. A wooden facility which seated 15,000, the ball yard was located at Eighth and Hill Streets, and it also was known as Chutes Park because it was near an amusement park with "chute the chutes" rides. In 1913 and 1914 the Venice Tigers played most of their games at Washington Park, as did the Vernon Tigers during the 1920s. From 1926 through 1935 and in 1938, the Hollywood Stars shared Wrigley Field, new home of the Angels. Los Angeles baseball fans enjoyed constant home games throughout the long PCL seasons, and important series between the Angels and their cross-town rivals drew particularly well. The Tigers and Stars always had a hardcore following, but the Angels usually attracted far greater attendance each season.

The Angels captured the hearts of LA fans immediately, winning the first 15 PCL games they played and the first Coast League pennant, barely losing the next year, then repeating as champions in 1905, 1907 and 1908. Four of the first six Coast League flags belonged to Los Angeles. Stars of the early Angel teams included first baseman Pop Dillon (.360 and 43 stolen bases in 1903, and player-manager of the 1905, 1907 and 1908 champions), and the legendary Hal Chase, an unusually gifted fielder who was suspected of throwing both major and minor league games to gamblers. Shortstop Kitty Brashear was the PCL batting champ (.303) in 1905.

Pitching always would be a hallmark of the Angels, and the early championship teams set the standard. Doc Newton (35–12 in

1903 and 39–17 in 1904), Warren Hall (32–18 in 1903), Dolly Gray (30–16 in 1905, 32–14 in 1907, and 26–11 in 1908) were the most spectacular winners of a superb stable of hurlers.

Although seven seasons would pass before the Angels won another championship, William Tozer enjoyed a magnificent year in 1909 (31–12), and outfielder Harry Heitmuller won the batting title in 1912 (.335). Outfielder Harry Wolter won back-to-back hitting championships in 1914 (.328) and 1915 (.359). During those same two seasons, southpaw Slim Love won the first two PCL ERA titles (1.56 and 1.95 in 1915, a year in which he went 23–15 in 59 games and 359 innings).

Pitching was the key to the pennant-winning Angels of 1916, as John Ryan (29–10) and Pete Standridge (20–10) headed another fine mound staff. The Angels finished second the next three years, and won a postseason series with first-place Vernon in 1918 which gave them a sixth PCL flag. The 1917 Angels featured Brad Hogg (27–13), Doc Crandall (26–15), and future National League star Emil "Irish" Meusel (.311 with a league-leading 69 stolen bases). Starring on the 1919 club was right fielder Sam Crawford (.360), first sacker Jack Fournier (.328), manager-center fielder Wade Killefer (.320), and pitcher Doc Crandall (28–10) and Curly Brown (25–8, and the PCL ERA champ at 2.03).

Killefer led the Angels to a seventh pennant in 1921, as Crandall (24–13), ERA champ Vic Aldridge (20–10 with a 2.16 ERA), and percentage leader Art Reinhart (15–5) formed the nucleus of another championship mound corps. Fans enjoyed the hurling of former Chicago Cubs star Charlie Root in 1924 (21–16) and 1925 (25–13), while Crandall again won big in 1925 (20–7) and 1926 (20–8). Doc Crandall, who won 101 major league games, played for LA from 1916 through 1926, winning 20 games five times.

Playing manager Marty Krug (.390) brought another flag to LA in 1926, with a fine stable of pitchers — Crandall, Earl Hamilton (24–8), Elmer Jacobs (20–12 with a league-leading 2.20 ERA) and Wayne Wright (19–7), and a hard-hitting outfield — Art Jahn (.337 with 118 RBIs) in left, Art Weis (.317) in right, and Jigger Statz (.354, leading the PCL with 291 hits and 18 triples) in center.

Statz wore an Angel uniform in 1920 and 1921, and in 1925 and 1926, while putting in eight seasons (.285 in 683 games) with four big league clubs. He returned to the Angels for good in 1929, playing through the 1942 season when he was 44. In his 18 seasons with the Angels, Statz averaged .315, playing in 2,790 games and coming to bat 10,657 times. He hit over .300 in 12 seasons, and led the PCL in runs scored four times (1931, 1932, 1936 and 1938, when he turned 41 before year's end). The speedy center fielder was the stolen base champ three times (1931–45, 1935–53, 1936–43) and swiped a personal high of 61 for the sensational 1934 club. Statz was the recipient of the PCL's first MVP award in 1932 when he batted .347 and led the league in runs for a fifth-place team. He hit .311 in 1939 at the age of 41, and was player-manager from 1940 through 1942. A superb outfielder, Statz cut a hole in the palm of his glove to have a better feel for the ball, and for years after he retired critical fans would shout "Jigger would have had it" when a ball would get past Angel center fielders.

In 1921 the Angels were purchased for $150,000 by William K. Wrigley, Jr., of the Wrigley Gum Company and the Chicago Cubs. After LA city officials refused Wrigley's request to build underground parking facilities at Washington Park, the gum magnate decided to erect a new stadium at 42nd and Avalon. Wrigley Field, built at a cost of well over one million dollars, opened on September 27, 1927, with the dedication speech delivered by Baseball Commissioner Judge Kenesaw Mountain Landis. The Angels defeated the Seals; Doc Crandall was the winning pitcher, and Jigger Statz hit for the cycle. The new park was double-decked from left to right field, and bleachers in right field brought the seating capacity to 22,000. Although center field was 412 feet and the foul lines a respectable 340 feet and 338 feet in left and right, the power alleys were just 345 feet from home plate, and Wrigley Field would become a haven for PCL sluggers.

Following the 1926 championship, the Angels plunged to last place in 1927. In 1929 Marty Krug, in his seventh season as Angels manager, was fired and replaced with 43-year-old Jack Lelivelt, who had averaged .301 in seven years as an American League outfielder and who had managed ten seasons in the Western League and American Association. In 1930 Lelivelt won the first half, but lost the second half and playoff series to the Hollywood Stars. Ed Baecht (26–12) was the best pitcher, left fielder Wes Schulmerich (.380, 28 HRs, 130 RBIs) the best hitter, third sacker Fred Haney (.312 with 52 SBs) the PCL theft champ for the second year in a row, and Jigger Statz (.360) filled in admirably at third while Haney was out with an injury. The installation of lights at mid-

season, along with the race with the Stars, produced an attendance exceeding 400,000.

By 1933 Lelivelt and Angels management had put together a
powerhouse team that would win two consecutive titles and produce one of the all-time great minor league clubs. Colorful, eccentric Buck Newsom (30–11, the PCL titlist in victories and strikeouts with 212), who would pitch in the major leagues until he was
46, was the leader of the 1933 Angels, posting 15 consecutive victories during one stretch and being named MVP. Other fine pitchers
were Dick Ward (25–9) and big Fay Thomas (20–14), a former
USC tackle. The explosive offense was led by right fielder Tuck
Stainback (.335, 19 HRs, 148 RBIs), left fielder Marv Gudat (.333,
113 RBIs), first sacker Jim Oglesby (.313, 20 HRs, 137 RBIs), and
third baseman Gene Lillard (.307, 43 HRs, 149 RBIs), at 19 the
youngest home run champ in PCL history.

Newsom and Stainback went up to the big leagues for 1934,
and other moves left Fay Thomas the only returning regular on the
mound staff. But Thomas (28–4 with 204 Ks) won his first 15
games (setting a PCL record with 22 consecutive victories in 1933
and 1934) and led the league in victories, winning percentage and
strikeouts. Lou Garland (21–9) won 12 in a row, while Dick Ward
(13–4, with part of the season spent in a Cubs uniform), Roy Henshaw (16–4), and Emmitt Nelson (14–5) were other members of a
deep pitching corps. Gene Lillard (.289, 27 HRs, 119 RBIs) and
Marv Gudat (.319, 125 RBIs) again supplied power, but the leading hitter was Frank Demaree, who had played in the Cubs' outfield in 1932 and 1933. Demaree ripped into PCL pitching (.383, 45
HRs, 173 RBIs, also leading the PCL in runs, hits and total bases),
winning the Triple Crown and the MVP award. The 1934 Angels
won 23 of 26 weekly series (including 29 straight in 1933 and 1934)
and established a new PCL record for victories and winning percentage (137–50, .733), eclipsing the original Coast League Angels
(133–78 in 1903).

Frank Demaree went back to the Cubs, where he would spend
the next decade, and Fay Thomas was sold to the St. Louis Browns.
Most of the rest of the roster remained intact, and the Angels won
the first half of the 1935 season. But LA dropped to fourth in the
second half, then lost the playoff. Jim Oglesby, however, enjoyed
another fine season (.350, 24 HRs, 132 RBIs), and Gene Lillard
was spectacular (.361, 56 HRs, 147 RBIs), leading the PCL in
homers and setting an Angels record.

Big Truck Hannah, who caught for the Angels from 1926 through 1937, replaced Lelivelt as manager in 1937. Hannah brought the Angels to a pennant in 1938, with third baseman Charles English (.303, 19 HRs, 143 RBIs) his best hitter and Fay Thomas (18–8) and Gene Lillard (16–10) his leading pitchers. Scow Thomas had returned to the Angels after one year with the Browns, enjoying a 23–11 record with the 1937 Angels, while Lillard turned to the mound after riding the bench with the Cubs in 1936 (.206 in 19 games).

Rip Collins, a star of the Cardinals Gas House Gang, tried to resurrect his big league career in 1939 as the Angels' first baseman, leading the PCL in homers and RBIs (.334, 26 HRs, 128 RBIs). Julio Bonetti (20–5) led the pitching staff, and the Angels won 19 straight games, finally finishing third. But the PCL had adopted the Shaughnessy playoff plan, and the Angels would not fare well under this system. In eight of the next ten seasons, the Angels would make the playoffs, losing the opening series three times, and in an eleventh playoff appearance, the 1951 Angels again dropped the first round of postseason play. On four occasions, the Angels won the playoff opener only to lose in the finals.

The sole playoff championship for the Angels occurred in 1947, following a first-place finish. The 1943 and 1944 Angels also had finished first but were beaten in the playoffs. Bill Kelly, who had managed in the lower minors for the Cubs organization, took the club all the way behind the pitching of Cliff Chambers (24–9, the PCL leader in wins and strikeouts), and the hitting of left fielder Clarence Maddern (.332) and third baseman John Ostrowski (.292, 24 HRs, 110 RBIs).

More than 622,000 fans trooped through the turnstiles in 1947, and despite numerous playoff disappointments, LA fans enjoyed many individual performances through the years. Lou Novikoff won the Triple Crown in 1940 (.363, 41 HRS, 171 RBIs), and also led the PCL in runs scored and base hits. Andy Pafko was named MVP in 1943 after winning the hitting and RBI titles (.356, 18 HRs, 118 RBIs), and this fine Angels club set a single-season record by reeling off 21 consecutive victories. Southpaw Ray Prim was with the Angels for nine seasons during the 1930s and 1940s, winning 150 games, including four 20-victory years. Center fielder Frank Baumholtz won the 1950 batting title (.379), and big first baseman Chuck Connors was the most popular Angel of 1951 (.321

with 22 homers — he would later become famous as *The Rifleman,* among other TV and movie roles). Slugging outfielder Max West pounded 35 roundtrippers in 1951 and again in 1952, winning the home run title (his third in the PCL) in the latter year.

In 1955 the man who would become the most popular player in franchise history was assigned to the Angels. A journeyman first baseman who would spend all or part of 10 seasons in the major leagues, big Steve Bilko would turn in a remarkable hitting performance during his three years as an Angel: 1955 — .328, 37 HRs, 124 RBIs; 1956 — .360, 55 HRs, 164 RBIs; 1957 — .300, 56 HRs, 140 RBIs. In each of these three seasons Bilko led the PCL in home runs and RBIs, in 1956 he became the third Angel to win the Triple Crown, and was named Most Valuable Player for an unprecedented three consecutive years.

Bilko led the 1956 Angels to LA's final PCL flag and to one of the best records (107–61, .637, and a 16-game margin over second-place Seattle) in league history. Six Angel sluggers hit 20 or more home runs and the team led the Coast League in most offensive categories (202 homers fell two short of the record set by Salt Lake City in 32 more games in 1923, while the cumulative average of .297 was the highest mark in the PCL since 1935). Bob Scheffing was the manager, and the most spectacular players, besides Bilko, were right fielder Jim Bolger (.326, 28 HRs, 147 RBIs), second baseman Gene Mauch (.348, 20 HRs, 84 RBIs), and reliever Bob Anderson (12–4 in 70 appearances).

After the season, the Cubs sold the Angels and Wrigley Field to Walter O'Malley, owner of the Brooklyn Dodgers. Dissatisfied with obsolete Ebbets Field and weak attendance in Brooklyn, O'Malley was strongly considering relocating the Dodgers, and the purchase of the Angels would give him territorial rights to an area long considered a promising major league site. The St. Louis Browns had almost transferred to LA in 1942, for years there had been rumors of a major league move to the West Coast, and Los Angeles city officials lost little time in offering an attractive proposal to O'Malley. With far-reaching consequences to the PCL as well as to major league baseball, the Dodgers moved to LA for the 1958 season, playing in the Los Angeles Coliseum instead of Wrigley Field.

For three years the historic PCL ballpark was unused. But when the American League expanded to Los Angeles in 1961, as a

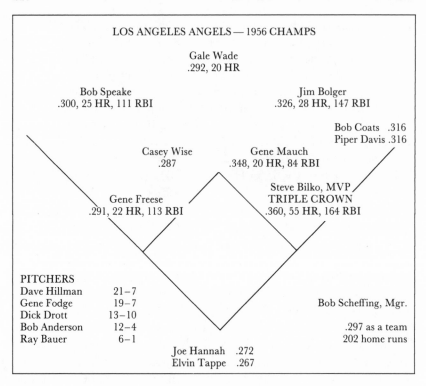

LOS ANGELES ANGELS — 1956 CHAMPS

Gale Wade
.292, 20 HR

Bob Speake
.300, 25 HR, 111 RBI

Jim Bolger
.326, 28 HR, 147 RBI

Bob Coats  .316
Piper Davis .316

Casey Wise
.287

Gene Mauch
.348, 20 HR, 84 RBI

Steve Bilko, MVP
TRIPLE CROWN
.360, 55 HR, 164 RBI

Gene Freese
.291, 22 HR, 113 RBI

PITCHERS
Dave Hillman    21–7
Gene Fodge      19–7
Dick Drott      13–10
Bob Anderson    12–4
Ray Bauer        6–1

Bob Scheffing, Mgr.

.297 as a team
202 home runs

Joe Hannah   .272
Elvin Tappe  .267

part of the territorial agreement O'Malley was permitted to dictate the playing site for the appropriately-named Angels. Steve Bilko, now wearing a major league Angel uniform, hit 20 home runs as big leaguers sent 248 homers sailing out of the cozy park. After one year, the Angels moved with the Dodgers to newly-opened Dodger Stadium in Chavez Ravine. Wrigley Field was razed, and today a community center stands where crowds once cheered the heroes of the Coast League.

| Year | Record | Pcg. | Finish |
|------|--------|------|--------|
| 1903 | 133-78 | .630 | First |
| 1904 | 119-97 | .551 | Second — lost playoff |
| 1905 | 120-94 | .561 | First — won playoff |
| 1906 | 95-87  | .522 | Third |
| 1907 | 115-74 | .608 | First |
| 1908 | 110-78 | .585 | First |
| 1909 | 118-97 | .549 | Third |
| 1910 | 101-121| .455 | Fifth |
| 1911 | 82-127 | .392 | Sixth |
| 1912 | 110-93 | .542 | Third |
| 1913 | 100-98 | .484 | Fifth |

| 1914 | 116-94 | .552 | Second |
| 1915 | 110-98 | .529 | Third |
| 1916 | 119-79 | .601 | First |
| 1917 | 116-94 | .552 | Second |
| 1918 | 57-47 | .548 | Second — won playoff |
| 1919 | 108-72 | .600 | Second |
| 1920 | 102-95 | .517 | Third |
| 1921 | 108-80 | .574 | First |
| 1922 | 111-88 | .558 | Third |
| 1923 | 93-109 | .460 | Sixth |
| 1924 | 107-92 | .538 | Second |
| 1925 | 105-93 | .530 | Fourth |
| 1926 | 121-81 | .599 | First |
| 1927 | 80-116 | .408 | Eighth |
| 1928 | 87-104 | .455 | Sixth |
| 1929 | 104-98 | .510 | Fifth |
| 1930 | 113-84 | .574 | Second — lost playoff |
| 1931 | 98-89 | .524 | Fourth |
| 1932 | 96-93 | .508 | Fifth |
| 1933 | 114-73 | .609 | First |
| 1934 | 137-50 | .733 | First |
| 1935 | 98-76 | .563 | Second — lost playoff |
| 1936 | 88-88 | .500 | Fifth |
| 1937 | 90-88 | .506 | Fifth |
| 1938 | 105-73 | .590 | First |
| 1939 | 97-79 | .551 | Third — won opener, lost finals |
| 1940 | 102-75 | .576 | Second — won opener, lost finals |
| 1941 | 72-98 | .424 | Seventh |
| 1942 | 104-74 | .584 | Second — won opener, lost finals |
| 1943 | 110-45 | .710 | First — lost opener |
| 1944 | 99-70 | .586 | First — won opener, lost finals |
| 1945 | 76-107 | .415 | Seventh |
| 1946 | 94-89 | .514 | Fourth — lost opener |
| 1947 | 106-81 | .567 | First — won opener and finals |
| 1948 | 102-86 | .543 | Third — lost opener |
| 1949 | 74-113 | .395 | Eighth |
| 1950 | 86-114 | .430 | Seventh |
| 1951 | 86-81 | .515 | Third — lost opener |
| 1952 | 87-93 | .483 | Sixth |
| 1953 | 93-87 | .517 | Third |
| 1954 | 73-92 | .442 | Sixth |
| 1955 | 91-81 | .529 | Fourth |
| 1956 | 107-61 | .637 | First |
| 1957 | 80-88 | .476 | Sixth |

# Mission — San Francisco
# (Missions, Monks,
# Bells, Bears, Reds)

On September 7, 1914, the bankrupt Sacramento franchise was transferred by the league to San Francisco, where the Seals played to enthusiastic crowds. It was hoped that the new club, called the Missions, would draw fans into new Ewing Field while the Seals were on the road. The Missions staggered into next-to-last place and after the season the league sold the franchise to Bill Lane of Salt Lake City, but the idea of a second San Francisco team would not be forgotten.

In November 1925, the last-place Vernon Tigers were sold to a group of San Francisco baseball enthusiasts who resurrected the Missions name and concept. Games would be played in Recreation Park, home of the Seals; each San Francisco club would inhabit the field while the other home team was out of town. Occasionally called "Monks," "Bells," "Bears" and "Reds," the team was generally known as the "Missions." For the first five years the Missions played at 15,000-seat Recreation Park, home of the Seals since 1907, except for the 1914 season, when the Seals and Missions learned that Ewing Park was too susceptible to fog. In 1931 the San Francisco teams moved into the new concrete and steel Seals Stadium, which boasted numerous amenities, including *three* clubhouses — one for the Seals, one for the visitors, and one for the Missions.

Led by the legendary minor league hitter Ike Boone (.380, 32 HRs, 137 RBIs) the Missions paced the PCL in team hitting during their first season. Bert Cole (29–12) and Herman Pillette (21–16) headed a mound staff that brought the Missions into third place. "Old Folks" Pillette toiled regularly for the Missions from 1926 until 1933, when he was traded during the season to Seattle.

Boone went to the Chicago White Sox in 1927, and the Missions plunged to seventh place. Boone returned during the 1928 season, hitting .354 as the team batting average went to .301. The other outfielders, Irvin Hufft (.371) and Ewar Swanson (.346 with 49 stolen bases) also blistered the ball, as did first baseman O. C.

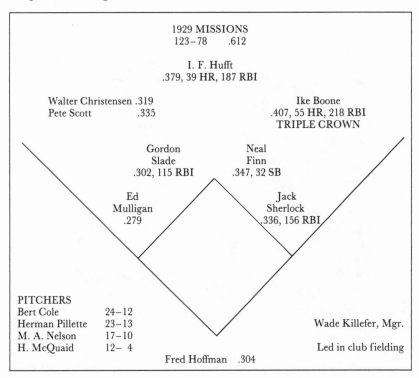

1929 MISSIONS
123–78    .612

I. F. Hufft
.379, 39 HR, 187 RBI

Walter Christensen .319
Pete Scott    .335

Ike Boone
.407, 55 HR, 218 RBI
TRIPLE CROWN

Gordon
Slade
.302, 115 RBI

Neal
Finn
.347, 32 SB

Ed
Mulligan
.279

Jack
Sherlock
.336, 156 RBI

PITCHERS
Bert Cole       24–12
Herman Pillette  23–13
M. A. Nelson    17–10
H. McQuaid      12– 4

Wade Killefer, Mgr.

Led in club fielding

Fred Hoffman    .304

McDaniel (.327, 27 HRs, 102 RBIs) and shortstop Gordon Slade (.306).

The next season, Boone and Hufft led the team to the best record in franchise history. The Missions posted a torrid .319 team average to lead the league. All but one regular hit .300, including Hufft (.379, 39 HRs, 187 RBIs), first sacker Jack Sherlock (.336 with 156 RBIs), second baseman Neal Finn (.347 with 32 stolen bases) and shortstop Gordon Slade (.302 with 115 RBIs). Ike Boone won the Triple Crown with colossal numbers (.407, 55 HRs, 218 RBIs, along with 323 hits). The best pitchers were Bert Cole (24–12 with a .326 batting average) and Old Folks Pillette (23–13). The Missions bolted from the starting gate and ripped the Coast League apart, causing the owners to declare a split-season in hopes of maintaining fan interest throughout the 202-game schedule. The Hollywood Stars edged the Missions by a single game on the last day of the season to win the second half. Although the Missions boasted by far the best season record, the Stars won the playoff, four games to three.

*In 1929 Bert Cole (left) was 24–12 and Herman Pillette was 23–13 for the first-place Missions.*

— Author's collection

In 1930 Boone exploded for a .448 average in the first 83 games, but he was sold to the Brooklyn Dodgers before mid-season. Hufft (.356), outfielder Henry Rosenberg (.368), first baseman George Burns (.349, 22 HRs, 131 RBIs), and second baseman J. A. Monroe (.350, 28 HRs, 106 RBIs) took up the slack as the team hit .306. But the pitching was weak and the Missions slid to seventh place.

Throughout the history of the Missions the fans would enjoy ferocious hitting, but poor pitching would doom the club to just four winning seasons in twelve years. In 1931 Ike Boone's place in the outfield was taken by Ox Eckhardt, a big Texan who swung a fearsome bat. After leading the PCL with a .369 average in 1931, he started the next season with the Boston Braves. But soon he was sent back to the Missions, and again he won the batting crown by hitting .371. In 1933 he set an all-time PCL record with a phenomenal .414 mark. The next year he hit .378, then won his fourth batting title in five seasons as a Mission by hitting .399 in 1935. In 1936 he went back to Brooklyn, then finished his career in other minor circuits, establishing a .367 average as a minor leaguer.

Eckhardt's incredible exploits overshadowed a number of

other fine hitting performances during the 1930s. Outfielder Louis Almada was outstanding in 1933 (.357) and 1934 (.332). In 1932 shortstop Mark Koenig hit .335 before being sold to the Chicago Cubs at mid-season. San Francisco native Babe Dahlgren hit well in 1933 (.315) and 1934 (.302 with 136 RBIs) before beginning a long major league career. Catcher William Outen powdered the ball in 1935 (.367), 1936 (.334), and 1937 (.316), while outfielders Harry Rosenberg and Max West hit productively in 1936 (.334 and .307, respectively) and 1937 (.330 each).

Despite the parade of hitters, the Missions were eclipsed in San Francisco by the far more consistent Seals. A last-place finish in 1937 predictably resulted in poor attendance. Club owner Herbert Fleischaker, a brewery magnate, was losing money because of the Depression and needed to sell the team, but no buyers could be found in San Francisco. The league arranged to move the franchise to Hollywood; Fleischaker had to operate the Hollywood Stars during the 1938 season, then managed to sell out to a group of Los Angeles baseball fans.

| Year | Record | Pcg. | Finish |
|------|--------|------|--------|
| 1926 | 106-94 | .530 | Third |
| 1927 | 86-110 | .439 | Seventh |
| 1928 | 99-92 | .518 | Fourth |
| 1929 | 123-78 | .612 | First — lost playoff |
| 1930 | 91-110 | .453 | Seventh |
| 1931 | 84-103 | .449 | Seventh |
| 1932 | 71-117 | .378 | Eighth |
| 1933 | 79-108 | .422 | Seventh |
| 1934 | 101-85 | .543 | Second |
| 1935 | 87-87 | .500 | Fifth |
| 1936 | 88-88 | .500 | Sixth |
| 1937 | 73-105 | .410 | Eighth |

# Oakland
# (Oaks)

Baseball in the Bay Area can be traced to the 1860s, and there was a strong baseball tradition in Oakland by the time the PCL was organized. Oakland became a charter member of the Coast League, finishing last in the inaugural season. Indeed, Oakland inhabited the cellar six times in the first 19 years of PCL history, but

*Oaks' Park, built in 1912 with a seating capacity of 11,000.*
— Courtesy Oakland Public Library

the enthusiasm of the city's highly knowledgeable fans was un-dimmed.

In 1904 Oakland hurler James Buchanan went 33–20 and right fielder Robert Ganley led the league in stolen bases (72). Oakland's first batting champ was shorstop Truck Eagan in 1905 (.335). Other Oakland hitting titlists were Duke Kennedy in 1916 (.314), Hack Miller in 1921 (.347), Les Scarsella in 1944 (.328), and George Metkovich, center fielder for the final Oaks team in 1955 (.355).

The 1910 pitching staff boasted two big winners in John Lively (31–15) and Walter Moser (31–20). Second sacker George Cut-shaw led the league in stolen bases in 1911 (90), while the following season brought Oakland its first PCL flag. Hard throwing south-paw Harry Ables was the PCL leader in victories and strikeouts (25–18 with 303 Ks) for the champs. The 1912 pitching staff also featured Bill Malarkey (20–11), Jack Killilay (15–4), and several other strong hurlers. The offense was paced by stolen base leader (80) Bill Leard, the second baseman, and by outfielder Bert Coy, who led the PCL in home runs in 1912 and 1913 (19 and 18, re-spectable home run numbers during the dead ball era).

The 1912 pennant prompted owners to build a new park. The old grounds, known as Freeman's Park (earlier called Bareilles Park and Eureka Park) was a wooden structure seating several thousand fans. Built in 1889, it was located at 5901 San Pablo, but Oakland played there only one afternoon a week and on Saturdays and Sundays — other "home" games were played in San Francisco. J. Cal Ewing controlled both the San Francisco and Oakland clubs, and when San Francisco's ballpark was destroyed in the earth-quake of 1906, the Seals played out their home schedule in Oak-land.

Oaks Ball Park was constructed on a seven-acre plot at Park Avenue and San Pablo with a seating capacity of 11,000. Decades later it would derisively be called the Splendid Splinter Emporium, but when it was built there were claims that it was the finest ballpark west of Chicago. Vendors were nattily attired in white uniforms; one longtime peanut vendor, who had just one arm, was noted for accurately firing bags of peanuts to fans seated at formidable distances. Bleacher seats cost fifty cents, and the right field stands became known as a location for fans who would bet loudly on virtually every pitch. The usual knot-hole gang avidly peered through the fence at game action, but late in the game a gate adjacent to left field was opened for the convenience of exiting fans, and the kids would slip inside for the last few innings. Emeryville, the suburb where Oaks Ball Park was located, was a beehive of activity at night, and nearby restaurants such as Angelo's and Lindy's enjoyed brisk business after games. For years visiting teams stayed at the California Hotel on 36th and San Pablo.

Oaks Ball Park would not host a pennant-winner until 1927. But fans responded to the play of athletes such as Buzz Arlett, an Oakland native who joined the club as a 19-year-old rookie in 1918. Arlett wore an Oaks uniform for 13 consecutive seasons, first as a standout pitcher, then as a slugging outfielder (he also played second and first in a pinch). In 1919 the big righthander — Arlett stood 6'3 and weighed 225 — went 22–17, and the next year he led the PCL in victories and innings pitched (29–17 with 427 innings). After a 25–19 season in 1925, the powerful switch hitter was moved to the outfield. During eight seasons as an Oakland outfielder, Arlett twice led the PCL in doubles, and once was the triples leader. Five times he hit 30 or more home runs and drove in 140 or more runs. His batting averages were .330, .328, .344, .382, .351, .365, .374 and .361. Perhaps his best season was 1929, when he hit .374 with 39 homers, 70 doubles, 189 RBIs and 22 stolen bases. Arlett hit .313 in 121 games with the Phillies in 1931, his only major league season. With Baltimore in 1932, he twice hit four home runs in a single game, finishing with a total of 54 for the year. His lifetime batting average as a minor leaguer was .341.

Speedy outfielder Bill Lane was with Oakland from 1916 through 1920, twice leading the PCL in stolen bases (he would win the theft title two more times while playing with Seattle). Frenchy Uhalt roamed the outfield at Oaks Ball Park from 1928 through

1936, hitting .350 in 1933. During the 1920s, when he was at the end of his career, righthander George Boehler pitched five seasons for the Oaks, three times winning the strikeout championship while posting 22 or more victories. Another righthander, Harry Krause, was a three-time 20-game winner (28–26 in 1917) while hurling for the Oaks from 1917 through 1928 (he won 300 games as a minor leaguer).

At the age of 40, Krause was 15–6 during the championship year of 1912, Boehler was 22–12, and Buzz Arlett (.351, 30 HRs, 123 RBIs) led the Oaks to the 1927 team batting title (.307). There would not be another pennant in Oakland for more than two decades, although the 1936 club finished a close second and went to the playoff finals. Wee Willie Ludolph (21–6) led the pitching staff, Leroy Anton (.317) was the 1936 stolen base king, while outfielder Harlan Pool (.394 in 62 games) and rookie Joe Gordon (.300) contributed to a productive offense.

In 1943 Brick Laws, a knowledgeable baseball operator, bought control of the Oaks, and the next year the team was in the playoffs for the first time since 1936. Laws spent $250,000 in major renovations of Oaks Ball Park, and in 1946 he hired Casey Stengel, an eccentric but gifted former big league manager, to direct the club. Casey led the Oaks to a second-place finish in 1946, then beat Los Angeles in the opening series of the playoffs before losing to the Seals in the finals. First baseman Les Scarsella (.332), who had won the 1944 batting title, was Oakland's best hitter in 1946, while big Frank Shea (15–5) and southpaw Gene Bearden (15–4) were Casey's most reliable pitchers. In 1947 Casey again guided Oakland to the playoff finals. Outfielders Hershel Martin (.361), a six-year veteran of the big leagues, and Brooks Holder (.311), along with second sacker Dario Lodigiani (.311) and Bearden (16–7), led another solid ball club.

Casey had become noted throughout the league for juggling his lineup incessantly, a tactic he would use to perfection while winning 10 pennants with the New York Yankees. He most effectively utilized his 25-man Oaks roster in 1948, when he mixed aging major league veterans — the "nine old men" — and promising newcomers into a team which won first place and the playoffs. Forty-year-old Ernie Lombardi, a future Hall of Famer, handled his share of the catching, and Oakland native Cookie Lavagetto, a 10-year National Leaguer, hit .304 in 86 games. First baseman

Nick Etten, the American League home run king of 1944, was the team's best power hitter (.313, 43 HRs, 155 RBIs), while center fielder George "Catfish" Metkovich (.336) had played five years in the American League. Brooks Holder (.297), Les Scarsella (.271) and Dario Lodigiani (.303) continued to play key roles, and fiery newcomer Billy Martin (.277) pleased Stengel with his drive. The Oaks' most spectacular victory was the second game of a double-header sweep over Los Angeles; the Angels led, 9–2, but Oakland stormed back to win, 23–15.

After the season, Stengel was named manager of the New York Yankees, and Brick Laws hired Charlie Dressen to take his place. Dressen brought the club in second, losing the playoff opener in seven games. The Oaks won the team batting title and shortstop Artie Wilson (.348) took the hitting crown. Outfielders Earl Rapp (.344) and Catfish Metkovich (.337) added explosive bats, and infielder Billy Martin (.286 with 92 RBIs) would rejoin Stengel the next year as a Yankee.

In 1950 Dressen brought another pennant to Oakland with a first-place finish (no playoffs were held). Again the Oaks led the PCL in team batting, featuring outfielders Earl Rapp (.347, 24 HRs, 145 RBIs), Catfish Metkovich (.315, 24 HRs, 141 RBIs) and Loyd Christopher (.303), catchers Don Padgett (.348) and Ray Noble (.316), and shortstop Artie Wilson (.312). Forty-one-year-old Billy Herman, a future Hall of Famer, came out of retirement for a final season (.307 in 71 games) as an Oaks infielder. The pitching staff was headed by Allen Gettel (23–7, with 24 starts, 27 relief appearances, and a .348 batting average), Earl "Irish" Harrist (18–8, with 23 starts and 29 relief appearances). Gettel pursued a part-time acting career, appearing in Western movies and TV shows. Baseballers called him "Two-Gun" Gettel, and Brick Laws encouraged his star pitcher because of the favorable publicity.

Dressen went to Brooklyn as manager in 1951 and Mel Ott was hired by the Oaks. The team finished fifth but once more led the league in hitting, behind third baseman Bert Haus (.331), Earl Rapp (.322), Loyd Christopher (.309) and Don Padgett (.303). Ott produced a second-place finish the next year, but there were no playoffs.

After spending a year with the New York Giants, righthander Allen Gettel returned to Oakland in 1952 (17–14), then led the

PCL in victories in 1953, 24–14. Charlie Dressen returned as manager in 1954, brought the Oaks up from seventh place to third, then beat San Diego and San Francisco to cop the playoff title without a defeat. First baseman Jim Marshall (.285, 31 HRs, 123 RBIs) led the league in homers and RBIs, while the pitching staff was anchored by Allen Gettel (17–15), Don Ferrarese (18–15, with a .290 batting average that included 12 pinch-hitting appearances), and Art Schallock (12–4).

Brick Laws hired Lefty O'Doul to manage the 1955 Oaks, but the club sagged to seventh place. Veteran outfielder Catfish Metkovich gave the fans something to cheer about, however, pounding his way to the batting crown (.355). By now the Splendid Splinter was in such disrepair — line drives sometimes would knock a plank off the outfield fence — that renovation costs were prohibitive, and attendance was the lowest in the league (141,397). Reluctantly Laws accepted a favorable stadium offer, and after 57 seasons the charter franchise moved to Canada as the Vancouver Mounties. Oaks Ball Park was torn down in 1957 and replaced by a Pepsi-Cola bottling plant, and Oakland fans had to travel to San Francisco to enjoy professional baseball. But in 1968 Charles O. Finley moved his Kansas City A's to Oakland, and soon the Coliseum would host championship major league play.

| Year | Record | Pcg. | Finish |
|------|--------|------|--------|
| 1903 | 89-126 | .414 | Sixth |
| 1904 | 116-109 | .516 | Fourth |
| 1905 | 103-119 | .464 | Fourth |
| 1906 | 77-110 | .411 | Fifth |
| 1907 | 97-101 | .489 | Third |
| 1908 | 83-116 | .417 | Fourth |
| 1909 | 88-125 | .413 | Fifth |
| 1910 | 112-98 | .555 | Second |
| 1911 | 111-99 | .528 | Third |
| 1912 | 120-83 | .591 | First |
| 1913 | 90-120 | .429 | Sixth |
| 1914 | 79-133 | .372 | Sixth |
| 1915 | 93-113 | .451 | Fifth |
| 1916 | 72-136 | .346 | Sixth |
| 1917 | 103-108 | .488 | Fifth |
| 1918 | 40-63 | .388 | Sixth |
| 1919 | 86-96 | .473 | Fifth |
| 1920 | 95-103 | .508 | Fifth |
| 1921 | 101-85 | .543 | Fifth |
| 1922 | 88-112 | .446 | Sixth |
| 1923 | 91-111 | .450 | Seventh |

| | | | |
|------|---------|------|---|
| 1924 | 103-99  | .510 | Fourth |
| 1925 | 88-112  | .442 | Sixth |
| 1926 | 111-92  | .547 | Second |
| 1927 | 120-75  | .615 | First |
| 1928 | 91-100  | .476 | Fifth |
| 1929 | 111-91  | .549 | Fourth |
| 1930 | 97-103  | .485 | Fifth |
| 1931 | 86-101  | .460 | Fifth |
| 1932 | 80-107  | .428 | Seventh |
| 1933 | 93-92   | .502 | Fifth |
| 1934 | 80-98   | .449 | Fifth |
| 1935 | 91-83   | .523 | Third |
| 1936 | 95-81   | .540 | Second — won opener, lost finals |
| 1937 | 79-98   | .446 | Seventh |
| 1938 | 65-113  | .365 | Eighth |
| 1939 | 78-98   | .443 | Seventh |
| 1940 | 94-84   | .528 | Third |
| 1941 | 81-95   | .460 | Sixth |
| 1942 | 85-92   | .480 | Sixth |
| 1943 | 73-82   | .471 | Sixth |
| 1944 | 86-83   | .509 | Fourth — lost opener |
| 1945 | 90-93   | .492 | Fifth |
| 1946 | 111-72  | .607 | Second — won opener, lost finals |
| 1947 | 96-90   | .516 | Fourth — won opener, lost finals |
| 1948 | 114-74  | .606 | First — won opener and finals |
| 1949 | 104-83  | .556 | Second — lost opener |
| 1950 | 118-82  | .590 | First |
| 1951 | 80-88   | .476 | Fifth |
| 1952 | 104-76  | .578 | Second |
| 1953 | 77-103  | .428 | Seventh |
| 1954 | 85-82   | .509 | Third |
| 1955 | 77-95   | .448 | Seventh |

# Ogden
# (A's)

Ogden's first venture into professional baseball was a three-year experience with the Class D Union Association (1912–14), followed by another three seasons with the Class C Utah-Idaho League (1926–28). Half a century later Ogden boldly installed a Class AAA Pacific Coast League franchise in John Affleck Park on South Wall Street.

This unstable franchise had originated in Eugene (1969–73)

during the major AAA realignment of 1969, then was moved to Sacramento (1974–76), leased to San Jose (1977–78), before being returned to the league and sold to Ogden (and after two years in Ogden the franchise would be transferred to Edmonton). Ogden was an affiliate of the Oakland A's, and the manager was former big leaguer Jose Pagan. Pagan was unable to produce a winner in two seasons, but the light Utah air promoted exciting hitting — Ogden was second in team batting both years. Of course, staff ERAs ballooned — Ogden's mound corps was last in team ERA in 1979 (5.20) and next to last in 1980 (5.42).

The most impressive batter in 1979 was first baseman Danny Goodwin (.349, 20 HRs, 94 RBIs in just 100 games). Like Goodwin, most of the best hitters only spent part of the season with Ogden — outfielders Rickey Henderson (.309), Mike Patterson (.324) and Robert Grandas (.294); catchers Tim Holsey (.302) and Pat Dempsey (.282); and outfielder-first baseman Mark Budaska (.290). Outfielder Ray Casey (.314) and second sacker Jeff Cox (.285) played a full season in Ogden. Righthander Brian Kingman (7–2) was called up after a fast start, but Jeff Jones (13–7) and reliever Richard Lysander (10–3) were solid throughout the year.

Although Rickey Henderson was in the big leagues to stay, Ogden fans enjoyed a number of hard-hitting returnees in 1980: Dempsey (.318), Budaska (.306), Holsey (.301), Casey (.296), Cox (.288), and Grandas (.277). The best newcomers were outfielder Derek Bryant (.342) and first baseman Kelvin Moore (.282, 25 HRs, 100 RBIs).

But all of the offensive fireworks could only attract about 77,000 fans per year, lowest attendance in the PCL. Ogden was too small to support AAA baseball, and the franchise was moved to Edmonton. John Affleck Park was demolished and today the site is occupied by a shopping mall.

| Year | Record | Pcg. | Finish |
|------|--------|------|--------|
| 1979 | 72-75  | .486 | Seventh |
| 1980 | 59-83  | .415 | Ninth  |

# *Oklahoma City*
# *(89ers)*

The Oklahoma City 89ers joined the Pacific Coast League in 1963, when the PCL expanded to 10 teams. The original '89ers founded the Oklahoma City team in 1889 and promptly nailed together a grandstand of planks and beer kegs. During the late 1800s local kranks enjoyed the play of Oklahoma City nines such as the Dudes, Pirates, Statehoods and Browns. Early in the twentieth century, Oklahoma City fielded its first professional club in the Class C Western Association. After four seasons, Oklahoma City moved up to the Texas League in 1909, but three years later the franchise was moved to Beaumont. In 1914 the Oklahoma City "Indians" rejoined the Western Association, then switched to the Class A Western League in 1918. The Indians were readmitted to the Texas League in 1933, playing in the historic circuit through the 1957 season.

Three consecutive weak teams and the problems confronting all minor league clubs in the 1950s caused attendance to plunge to 51,128 in 1957 (down from more than 333,000 for a losing season in 1951). Oklahoma City withdrew from professional play after 1957, but would find a new baseball future in Class AAA. In 1962 the Oklahoma City 89ers, American Association affiliate of the Houston Colt 45s expansion team, moved into beautiful, new All Sports Stadium. Attendance was merely 44,000, and the American Association disbanded.

But the 89ers moved into the expanded Pacific Coast League, then proceeded to win the 1963 pennant. Pilot Grady Hatton led the team to the Southern Division title and downed Spokane in seven games for the championship. Outfielder Johnny Weekly (.363) blistered the ball before being called up to Houston at midseason. Another outfielder, Carroll Hardy (.316), hit well all year, while Gerald Nelson (14–8) and Dave Giusti (13–11) were the best pitchers. In 1964 Nelson (13–12), Giusti (10–6) and Hardy (.321 in half a season) were back, along with a slumping Weekly (.258). Hatton also returned to guide the 89ers to another winning record, but the team failed to make the playoffs.

In 1965, however, Hatton led the 89ers back to the PCL throne room. Outfielder Dave Roberts (.318, 38 HRs, 114 RBIs) was the home run champ, while first baseman Charles Harrison

*All Sports Stadium has been the home of the Oklahoma City 89ers since 1962.*
— Author's photo

(.270, 34 HRs, 105 RBIs) and catcher John Bateman (.297, 21 HRs, 66 RBIs in just 76 games) helped the 89ers lead the PCL in homers (166). Shortstop Roland Jackson (.330 with 52 stolen bases) led the league in runs scored, and righthander Chris Zachary (17–8) tied for the most victories. The 89ers posted the best record in the 12-club circuit, captured the Eastern Division crown, then defeated Portland, four games to one, to bring Oklahoma City its second PCL flag in three seasons.

Hatton moved up to manage Houston, and Mel McGaha took over in Oklahoma City. Chris Zachary (10–7) again performed well, and outfielder-first baseman Tom Murray (.248, 26 HRs, 73 RBIs) won the home run title. But the pitching staff ranked last in ERA, team hitting was next-to-last, and the 89ers stumbled to the worst record in the league. Attendance, a league high in 1965 (218,129), plummeted to the lowest (97,761) among the 12 clubs in 1966. McGaha pulled the 89ers up to the break-even level the next year, with a strong performance from righthander Howard Reed (19–8), who led the PCL in victories.

But in 1968 the 89ers wobbled into last place in the Eastern Division, 32$^1$/$_2$ games off the pace. Oklahoma City placed last in the

PCL in staff ERA and team fielding. When major league expansion triggered a resurrection of the American Association, Oklahoma City was one of four PCL clubs which withdrew to join the Association.

| Year | Record | Pcg. | Finish |
|------|--------|------|--------|
| 1963 | 84-74 | .532 | Second — won Southern Division and playoff |
| 1964 | 88-70 | .557 | Fifth |
| 1965 | 91-54 | .628 | First — won Eastern Division and playoff |
| 1966 | 59-89 | .399 | Twelfth |
| 1967 | 74-74 | .500 | Seventh |
| 1968 | 61-84 | .421 | Eleventh |

# Phoenix
# *(Giants, Firebirds)*

Arizona's capitol city first promoted professional baseball in the Class D Arizona State League (1928–30) and the Arizona-Texas League (1931–32). The Great Depression interrupted pro ball in Phoenix, but the Muni — old Phoenix Municipal Stadium at Central Avenue and Mohave — began to host Senators games after World War II. Phoenix played in three Class C circuits, Arizona-Texas League (1947–50, 1952–54), Southwest International League (1951), and the Arizona-Mexico League (1955–57). The following year, New York's National League franchise moved to San Francisco, and Frisco's PCL franchise was placed in Phoenix as the AAA affiliate of the Giants.

Phoenix fans were treated to a pennant in their first PCL season. Fiery Red Davis, who recently had managed fine clubs in Dallas, the Giants' Texas League farm team, skippered the Phoenix Giants to first place in a non-playoff year. Phoenix walloped a spectacular 205 home runs while winning the team hitting title, and shortstop Andre Rodgers (.354 with 31 HRs) was the batting champ. Veteran big leaguer Dusty Rhodes (.269, 25 HRs, 100 RBIs) tied for the RBI title, while outfielder Felipe Alou (.319 in 55 games), outfielder-third baseman George Prescott (.309, 24 HRs, 96 RBIs), and impressive first sacker Willie McCovey (.319) provided other explosive bats.

McCovey was even more impressive in 1959 (.372, 29 HRs, 92

*Phoenix Municipal Stadium, home of the Firebirds.*
— Author's photo

RBIs); he played only 95 games before being called up to San Francisco, and he did not qualify for the batting title, but he won the home run championship and tied for the RBI lead. George Prescott (.306) again performed well, and shortstop Jose Pagan (.312) soon would be a San Francisco regular. But even though the Giants again led the PCL in homers (196), Red Davis' team dropped to last in the standings. Only 79,106 fans — lowest total in the league — came out to the Muni, and the Giants were moved to Tacoma.

But San Francisco began conducting spring training in Phoenix in 1961 — each spring the Giants would place a trolley car in front of the concrete Muni. In 1964 a new, 10,000-seat Phoenix Municipal Stadium was opened in the east end of town. Supervised by genial Tommy Gonzales, who regularly produced a superb playing surface, the new Muni continued to host San Francisco, as well as the fine baseball teams from nearby Arizona State University. And in 1966 the Tacoma franchise was moved back to Phoenix.

Phoenix again fielded a hard-hitting team, featuring slick-fielding shortstop Robert Schroder (.317), infielder Marv Breeding (.313), and outfielder Frank Johnson (.308). On the pitching staff was Don Larsen (8–5), who had hurled a perfect game in the 1956

World Series. The Giants finished with the third-best record in the PCL, but failed to make the playoffs. Indeed, despite nine winning seasons in their first 11 years back in the PCL, the Giants did not make a playoff appearance until 1977.

But there were many fine playing performances through the years. The 1967 Giants won the team hitting title and third baseman Cesar Gutierrez (.322) was the batting champ. Righthander Richard Robertson was the strikeout king in 1967 and 1968, and in the latter year tied for most victories (18–9). Outfielder George Foster (.308) showed signs of big league stardom in 1970, and the next year Dave Kingman (.278, 26 HRs and 99 RBIs in just 105 games) demonstrated his slugging ability. Bob Garibaldi, a big righthander who had been a stalwart of the Phoenix pitching staff for five years, had his best season in 1970 (15–10), and second baseman Chris Arnold, in the first of five seasons with Phoenix, got off to a notable start in 1970 (10–2 in 55 games), while Jack Clark stepped into the big leagues to stay after spending 1976 (.323) with Phoenix. In 1973 switch-hitting outfielder Steve Ontiveros (.357) won the hitting title, and the next year's batting champ was another Phoenix outfielder, lefthanded Glenn Adams (.352).

Finally, after 12 years in the PCL, Phoenix broke the playoff barrier en route to the 1977 championship. The manager was Rocky Bridges, Chris Arnold provided experience and a good bat (.302), and first baseman Phil James (.308) and shortstop Junior Kennedy (.316) made the All-Star team. The pitching staff was led by Ed Plank (14–7, after a 15–10 record in 1976), Greg Minton (14–6), southpaw strikeout leader Frank Ricelli, and reliever Tom Toms (10–3 in 53 appearances). The Giants won the Eastern Division with the best record in the league, then defeated Hawaii, four games to two, in the title playoff.

From 1979 through 1983, Phoenix finished last four times, and there were no further playoff appearances until 1985. But Phoenix fans watched future big league standouts Bob Brenly in 1980 and 1981, Jeff Leonard in 1981 (.401 in 47 games) and 1982 (.356 in 17 games), Dan Gladden in 1982 (.308), 1983 (.303), and 1984 (.397 in 59 games), and Rob Deer in 1984 (home run champ with 31). Switch hitter Chris Smith won the batting title in 1983 (.379, 21 HRs, 102 RBIs), and the next season, outfielder Alejandro Sanchez became the only Phoenix MVP to date (.318, 28 HRs, 108 RBIs, 34 SBs).

In 1985 and 1986, manager Jim Lefebvre led the Giants to consecutive playoff appearances. Fleet outfielder Tack Wilson (.319 with 56 SBs) and All-Star second baseman Mike Woodard (.316 with 33 SBs) provided solid offense in 1985, while righthander Roger Mason (12–1) proved almost unbeatable in 24 starts. The Giants swept Hawaii in three games to claim the Southern Division title, then battled to the last game of the championship series before losing to Vancouver.

Sporting a new nickname, the Phoenix Firebirds charged back into the playoffs in 1986. Tack Wilson slumped (.253), but Mike Woodward (.319 in 62 games) put in a solid half-season. Randy Johnson (.332) was an outstanding third baseman, and lefthanded first baseman-outfielder Rick Lancellotti (.275, 31 HRs, 106 RBIs) was the home run champ. Righthander Mark Grant (14–7) led the PCL in victories, while the best relievers were southpaw Mike Jeffcoat (7–2) and tall righthander Jon Perlman (7–3). Despite the second best record in the league, the Firebirds were knocked off in the playoff opener, but Lefebvre received his second straight Manager of the Year award.

Wendell Kim, who had played at Phoenix in 1977 (.284) and 1979 (.313), was named manager in 1987. The Firebirds enjoyed another winning season as the offense was sparked by lefthanded first baseman Francisco Melendez (.327). Despite four tours of duty during the season with San Francisco, reliever Jon Perlman (12–6) led the team in victories and saves (18) and was voted Rolaids Relief Man Award for the PCL. Veteran slugger Dave Kingman, who had stepped into the majors after a fine 1971 season with Phoenix, played 20 games (.210 with only two homers), but failed to resurrect his career. Melendez missed the 1988 batting title by just two points (.361), and second baseman Tony Perezchica (.306) and outfielder Charlie Hayes (.307) offered Kim solid bats in the lineup. But struggling San Francisco made an astronomical number of roster changes, which doomed the Firebirds to a losing season.

In 1990 Firebirds owner Marvin Stone hoped to bring major league baseball to Phoenix. Although he wanted a new ballpark of suitable size, in 1988 he withdrew from an agreement to share a proposed $160 million domed stadium with the NFL's Phoenix Cardinals. Nearby suburbs — Tempe, Mesa and Chandler — hoped to attract the Firebirds by constructing a ballpark Stone would like, while Phoenix interests were concerned that the city might lose professional baseball.

| Year | Record | Pcg. | Finish |
|------|--------|------|--------|
| 1958 | 89-65 | .578 | First |
| 1959 | 64-90 | .416 | Eighth |
| 1966 | 81-67 | .547 | Third |
| 1967 | 75-72 | .510 | Sixth |
| 1968 | 76-71 | .517 | Fifth |
| 1969 | 75-71 | .514 | Third |
| 1970 | 85-61 | .582 | Third |
| 1971 | 74-70 | .514 | Third |
| 1972 | 81-67 | .547 | Second |
| 1973 | 70-73 | .490 | Fourth |
| 1974 | 75-69 | .521 | Fourth |
| 1975 | 66-77 | .462 | Sixth |
| 1976 | 75-67 | .528 | Third |
| 1977 | 81-59 | .579 | First — won Eastern Division and playoff |
| 1978 | 72-68 | .514 | Sixth |
| 1979 | 59-88 | .401 | Tenth |
| 1980 | 53-95 | .358 | Tenth |
| 1981 | 69-63 | .523 | Fifth |
| 1982 | 58-86 | .403 | Tenth |
| 1983 | 61-82 | .427 | Tenth |
| 1984 | 69-74 | .483 | Eighth |
| 1985 | 80-62 | .563 | Second — won opener, lost finals |
| 1986 | 81-61 | .570 | Second — lost opener |
| 1987 | 77-67 | .535 | Fourth |
| 1988 | 67-76 | .446 | Eighth |

POBTLAND
BEAVERS

# Portland
# (Browns, Giants,
# Ducks, Beavers)

Portland was the only charter city remaining in the PCL in 1990, and a Portland club played in 80 of the 86 seasons that the Coast League operated. By the late 1800s, there were several good amateur teams in the city and the best players formed the nucleus of Portland's first professional club. In 1901 the Portland "Webfooters" won the first championship of the four-team Pacific Northwest League, but when the Pacific Coast League was organized in 1903, Portland switched circuits. Portland's team first was called "Browns" and "Giants" — and one year "Ducks" — before settling upon "Beavers."

*Civic Stadium seats 24,500 and is located in downtown Portland. Alice Spackman, a PCL superfan since 1944, is seated in her front-row box behind the home dugout.*

— Author's photo

A diamond and a small grandstand went up on Vaughn Street and Northwest 24th Avenue in 1901. The grandstand was rebuilt in 1905 in conjunction with the track and field events of the Lewis and Clark Exposition. Seven years later, the park was expanded to a seating capacity of 12,000 with bleachers along the entire outfield, and a large covered grandstand that extended all the way down the right field line. For three decades, Rocky Benevento was the groundskeeper, and in later years he would hustle up and down the grandstand with a bucket of water to douse fires that would begin to smolder from discarded cigarettes (Tacoma's fire chief threatened to condemn the old park as a fire hazard). At first labeled "Recreation Park," then "Lucky Beaver Stadium," the comfortable old Stadium was known to generations of Portland fans only as "Vaughn Street Park." Today the Beavers play on artifical turf at 24,500-seat Portland Civic Stadium, but Vaughn Street Park was lamented long after it was razed in 1955.

The first three Portland teams lost well over 100 PCL games each year, but in 1906 the club dominated the league behind batting champ Mike Mitchell (.351) and player-manager Walter McCredie (.301). A fine outfielder, McCredie signed on in 1904 (his uncle, Judge W. W. McCredie, owned the club), and would lead Portland to five PCL pennants. McCredie was the only .300 hitter in 1907, as Portland dropped to last place. The next year, first baseman Babe Danzig won the batting crown with a dead-ball average (.298), and Robert Groom led the league in victories (29–15).

In 1910 Portland began a string of championships that would include four pennants in five years. The 1910 team hit an anemic .218, lowest composite average in Portland history, but the pitching staff was superb: strikeout king Vean Gregg (32–18 with 376 Ks and an incredible 14 shutouts), Gene "Rubber" Krapp (29–16), Bill Steen (23–17), and Tom Seaton (17–17). Gregg and Krapp (and catcher Gus Suhr) were purchased by Cleveland for 1911, but Steen (30–15) and Seaton (24–16) took up the slack, along with Elmer Koestner (25–15) and Ed Henderson (21–12). Center fielder Bud Ryan (.333 with 23 homers and 39 steals) led the league in batting average and home runs.

Ryan and shortstop Roger Peckinpaugh went up to Cleveland, and Portland lost 100 games in 1912. But the ballpark was rebuilt and expanded, and so was the team, again registering consecutive championships in 1913 and 1914. Bus Fisher (.292) was back behind the plate in 1913, and his best pitchers were strikeout champ Bill James (24–16 with 215 Ks) and Irv Higginbotham (21–12). In 1914 Fisher had a superb season (.355), and second baseman W. K. Rodgers (.292 with 71 steals) was the stolen base champ. Higginbotham (31–20) led the league in victories, while Hal Krause (22–18) also pitched well. Following a long illness, Walter McCredie returned to Portland as manager in 1934. But he was seriously ill, and he died at the age of 57 on July 29, the eve of a pregame ceremony scheduled in his honor at Vaughn Street Park.

There would be only one winning record in the 15 seasons following the championship dynasty, and there would not be another pennant until 1932. But fans were entertained by individual exploits. Allen Sothoron (30–17) led the PCL in victories in 1916, while outfielder Kenneth Williams (.313 with 24 homers and 61 steals) was the 1917 home run champ. In 1918 Portland dropped out of the PCL because of the difficulties of wartime travel, but participated in the Class B Pacific Coast International League. The PCL expanded to eight teams in 1919, and Portland was readmitted after an absence of just one year.

Hard-hitting James Poole played first base for four years: 1921

(.330, 20 HRs, 107 RBIs); 1922 (.299, 22 HRs, 109 RBIs); 1923 (.339, 27 HRs, 136 RBIs); and 1924 (.353, a league-leading 38 HRs, and 159 RBIs). During the same period infielder Frank Brazill put in three good seasons — 1922 (.318); 1923 (.316); and 1924 (.351, 36 HRs, 148 RBIs). Portland fans enjoyed the play of the legendary Jim Thorpe in 1922 (.308 in 35 games), and of outfielder Paul Strand in 1926 (.326) and 1927 (.355). In 1924 catcher Mickey Cochrane hit well enough (.333) in his second year of pro ball to move up to the American League and a Hall of Fame career. Outfielder-first baseman Bill Bagwell (.391) was the 1926 batting champ, while outfielder Elmer Smith won back-to-back home run titles in 1926 (.336, 46 HRs, 133 RBIs) and 1927 (.368, 40 HRs, 141 RBIs).

Following the 1927 season, shortstop Bill Cissell (.323) was sold to the Chicago White Sox for $123,000, considerably brightening the financial picture of a second-division year for Portland. First baseman James Keesey was purchased by Connie Mack's Philadelphia Athletics after hitting impressively in 1928 (.326 with 104 RBIs) and 1929 (.349 with 124 RBIs). Following the 1931 season outfielder Ed Coleman (.358, 37 HRs, 183 RBIs) moved up to the Athletics after winning the RBI title.

In 1932 the Beavers returned to the PCL throne room behind an offense that led the league in hitting: shortstop Pinkey Higgins (.326, 33 HRs, 132 RBIs), soon to become a standout American League third baseman; outfielders Lou Finney (.351), James Moore (.335 in 46 games), and Fred Berger (.305 with 105 RBIs); second baseman J. A. Monroe (.328); first sacker James Keesey (.309 with 123 RBIs); and catcher John Fitzpatrick (.306). The best pitchers were Bill Shores (19–11) and starter-reliever Lou Koupal (16–6), while reliever Art Jacobs (11–7) had the team's second-highest batting average (.347).

The next year the Beavers finished second with a hitting attack that featured Monroe (.323), Berger (.313), first baseman Earl Sheely (.359), and outfielders George Blackerby (.340) and Henry Oana (.332, 29 HRs, 163 RBIs). The pitching staff was led by Joe Bowman (23–11), Lou Koupal (16–9), Art Jacobs (17–7), and Rudy Kallio (17–7).

In 1936, specializing in late-inning comeback victories, Portland came in first after an exciting pennant race. The Beavers verified their championship credentials in the playoffs, sweeping Seattle in four straight in the opener, then beating Oakland four out of five in the finals. The manager was Bill Sweeney, who had played shortstop for Portland three decades earlier. Outfielder-first baseman John Frederick (.352) led the offense, along with catcher Earle Brucker (.339), third sacker Fred Bedore (.337), and veteran outfielder Moose Clabaugh (.317, 20 HRs, 112 RBIs). Pitching leaders were George Caster (25–13 with a .304 batting average), Bill Posedel (20–10), and Ad Liska (15–12).

Frederick played four more years for the Beavers (.301, .319, .326, and .306) before retiring in 1940 with a lifetime average of .323, as well as a .308 mark in 805 games with the Brooklyn Dodgers. Ad Liska pitched for Portland from 1936 through 1949, when he retired at the age of 43 with 248 minor league victories, including 198 for the Beavers. His best seasons for Portland were 1937 (24–18), 1939 (20–16), 1943 (17–11 with a 1.98 ERA), and 1945 (20–12). Outfielder Ted Norbert was outstanding in his two years with Portland, winning the home run title in 1941 (.278 with 20 homers), then repeating the next year and winning the batting championship (.378 with 28 homers).

From 1939 through 1942, the Beavers suffered through four consecutive last-place finishes, before reaching the playoffs in four of the next five seasons. First baseman Larry Barton was a key figure during this period (1942–46), enjoying his best seasons in 1942 (.305) and 1945 (.318). John Wesley Gill also was a regular throughout these years, posting his best records in 1940 (.323), 1942 (.302), and 1943 (.323). There was a fine pitching staff in 1944, built around Marino Pieretti (26–13), who led the league in victories, southpaw Roy Heiser (20–16), and Ad Liska (18–9).

Although none of the playoff clubs (1943, 1944, 1945 and 1947) made it past the opening round, the 1945 Beavers finished first by 8½ games and brought another PCL pennant to Portland. There were three 20-game winners, Liska (20–12), Heiser (20–14), and Burt Pulford (20–11), and solid hitting from shortstop John O'Neill (.315), third Baseman Marvin Owen (.311), and outfielders Frank Shone (.304 with 39 steals) and Frank Demaree (.304).

Third baseman Harvey Storey was the 1946 batting champion (.326), and he also was productive for the 1947 playoff team (.305 with 119 RBIs). Former Detroit Tiger star Tommy Bridges (7–3 and a 1.64 ERA in 13 games) was the 1947 ERA champ, and Vic Raschi (8–2 in 12 games) soon would be a standout with the New

York Yankees. More than 421,000 fans — the all-time Portland attendance record — trooped into Vaughn Street Park in 1947. In 1948 the 40-year-old Bridges (15–11, 2.86 ERA) posted the best ERA on the Beavers staff, and the next year righthander Harold Saltzman (23–13) tied for the most victories in the PCL.

During the 1950s and 1960s, the Beavers won no championships and made just one playoff appearance per decade, but there were numerous impressive performances through the years. Stolen base champs included Luis Marquez in 1950, switch-hitting outfielder Solly Drake in 1957, and second baseman Dave Nelson in 1967. Red Adams (15–16, 2.17 ERA) was the 1952 ERA champ, southpaw Royce Lint (22–10) led the PCL in winning percentage the next year, and in 1956 Rene Valdes (22–11) won the most games in the league.

On April 17, 1956, Portland opened the season with a crowd of 34,450, still the record for a PCL day-night doubleheader. The 1956 All-Star Game was held in Portland before an impressive throng of 10,437, and in 1962 the exhibition returned to Portland and drew 12,198. Noel Mickelsen was the 1960 strikeout king, in 1965 Tom Kelley (16–3 with six shutouts and 190 Ks in 185 innings) led the PCL in strikeouts, winning percentage and shutouts, and in 1971 Richard Woodson (16–10 with 163 Ks) was the league leader in victories and strikeouts. Luis Tiant was brilliant in the first half of 1964 (15–1 in 17 games, 13 complete games in 15 starts, 154 Ks in 137 innings, 2.04 ERA), and he was almost as good (10–4) with the Cleveland Indians in the second half. First baseman Eugene Oliver (.302, 36 HRs, 100 RBIs) was the 1961 home run champ, while outfielder Russ Nagelson (23 homers) won the title in 1969. Lou Piniella roamed the Portland outfield in 1966 (.289), 1967 (.308), and 1968 (.317), then went on to stardom in the American League.

By 1972, with no pennant since 1945 and just two brief playoff appearances in the past quarter century, the seventh-place Beavers drew fewer than 92,000 fans. After the season, the franchise was transferred to Spokane, but Portland immediately joined the Class A Northwest League, and in 1978, when the PCL expanded to 10 teams, Portland rejoined the circuit. Eric Wilkins (15–5) led the league in victories, and outfielders Robert Ellis (.333) and Dan Briggs (.330, 20 HRs, 109 RBIs) hit well in ushering the Beavers back into the Coast League.

In 1980 catcher Tony Pena (.327) vaulted to major league stardom on the heels of a fine season with the Beavers, while left-hander Mickey Mahler (14–8) won the strikeout title. Odell Jones (12–6) was the 1981 strikeout king, and the next year he repeated the feat while leading the league in victories (16–9).

The 1983 Beavers finally brought the PCL pennant back to Portland. Most of the best players were on the roster only part of the season, and skipper John Felske did a masterful job of juggling an ever-changing lineup. First baseman Len Matuszek (.330, 24 HRs, 92 RBIs) and outfielder Tim Corcoran (.311 with 93 RBIs) were mainstays all year, but third baseman Alfonso Garcia (.345 in 35 games), second sacker Juan Samuel (.330 with 33 steals in 65 games), outfielder Richard Davis (.328 in 87 games), and shortstop Luis Aguayo (.284 in 71 games) performed well in sports. In the playoffs, the Beavers defeated Edmonton to take the Northern Division title, then won the championship with a three-game sweep over Albuquerque.

Four losing seasons followed, but in 1988 the Beavers, now affiliated with the Minnesota Twins, earned a playoff berth with the third-best record in the league. The outfield featured stolen base champ Eric Bullock (.309 with 51 steals), John Christensen (.304), and Allen Cockrell (.293). Catcher Brian Harper (.353) and first baseman Kelvin Torve (.301) also were offensive leaders, while the most dependable pitchers were righthanders Roy Smith (12–9), Balvino Galvez (11–7), and Fred Toliver (7–2 in 13 games). Under the able leadership of team president Joe Buzas, a former Yankee shortstop who has operated 66 minor league clubs in 33 years as an owner, in 1990 Portland was poised to carry on the Coast League traditions it commenced in 1903.

| Year | Record | Pcg. | Finish |
|------|--------|------|--------|
| 1903 | 95-105 | .468 | Fifth |
| 1904 | 79-136 | .368 | Sixth |
| 1905 | 94-110 | .461 | Fifth |
| 1906 | 115-60 | .657 | First |
| 1907 | 72-114 | .388 | Fourth |
| 1908 | 95-90 | .514 | Second |
| 1909 | 112-87 | .563 | Second |
| 1910 | 114-87 | .567 | First |
| 1911 | 113-79 | .589 | First |
| 1912 | 85-100 | .459 | Fourth |
| 1913 | 109-86 | .571 | First |
| 1914 | 113-84 | .573 | First |

| 1915 | 78-116  | .402 | Sixth |
|------|---------|------|-------|
| 1916 | 93-98   | .487 | Fifth |
| 1917 | 98-102  | .490 | Fourth |
| 1919 | 78-96   | .448 | Seventh |
| 1920 | 81-103  | .440 | Eighth |
| 1921 | 51-134  | .276 | Eighth |
| 1922 | 87-112  | .437 | Seventh |
| 1923 | 107-89  | .546 | Third |
| 1924 | 88-110  | .444 | Seventh |
| 1925 | 92-104  | .470 | Fifth |
| 1926 | 100-101 | .498 | Fourth |
| 1927 | 95-95   | .500 | Fifth |
| 1928 | 79-112  | .414 | Seventh |
| 1929 | 90-112  | .446 | Sixth |
| 1930 | 81-117  | .409 | Eighth |
| 1931 | 100-87  | .535 | Third |
| 1932 | 111-78  | .587 | First |
| 1933 | 105-77  | .577 | Second |
| 1934 | 66-117  | .361 | Eighth |
| 1935 | 87-86   | .503 | Fourth |
| 1936 | 96-79   | .549 | First |
| 1937 | 90-86   | .511 | Fourth |
| 1938 | 79-96   | .451 | Sixth |
| 1939 | 75-98   | .434 | Eighth |
| 1940 | 56-122  | .315 | Eighth |
| 1941 | 71-97   | .423 | Eighth |
| 1942 | 67-110  | .379 | Eighth |
| 1943 | 79-76   | .510 | Fourth — lost opener |
| 1944 | 87-82   | .515 | Second — lost opener |
| 1945 | 112-68  | .622 | First — lost opener |
| 1946 | 74-109  | .404 | Eighth |
| 1947 | 97-89   | .522 | Third — lost opener |
| 1948 | 89-99   | .473 | Fifth |
| 1949 | 85-102  | .454 | Sixth |
| 1950 | 101-99  | .505 | Fourth |
| 1951 | 83-85   | .494 | Fourth — lost opener |
| 1952 | 92-88   | .511 | Fourth |
| 1953 | 92-88   | .511 | Fourth |
| 1954 | 71-94   | .430 | Eighth |
| 1955 | 86-86   | .500 | Fifth |
| 1956 | 86-82   | .512 | Third |
| 1957 | 60-108  | .357 | Eighth |
| 1958 | 78-76   | .506 | Fourth |
| 1959 | 75-77   | .493 | Sixth |
| 1960 | 64-90   | .416 | Eighth |
| 1961 | 71-83   | .461 | Fifth |
| 1962 | 74-80   | .481 | Sixth |
| 1963 | 73-84   | .465 | Seventh |
| 1964 | 90-68   | .570 | Third |

| | | | |
|---|---|---|---|
| 1965 | 81-67 | .547 | Third — won opener, lost finals |
| 1966 | 69-79 | .466 | Ninth |
| 1967 | 79-69 | .534 | Third |
| 1968 | 72-72 | .500 | Seventh |
| 1969 | 57-89 | .390 | Eighth |
| 1970 | 68-78 | .466 | Fifth |
| 1971 | 71-71 | .500 | Fourth |
| 1972 | 61-87 | .412 | Seventh |
| 1978 | 76-62 | .551 | Third |
| 1979 | 73-74 | .497 | Sixth |
| 1980 | 69-76 | .476 | Seventh |
| 1981 | 72-65 | .526 | Fourth |
| 1982 | 65-79 | .451 | Eighth |
| 1983 | 75-67 | .528 | Fourth — won opener and finals |
| 1984 | 62-78 | .443 | Ninth |
| 1985 | 68-74 | .479 | Fifth |
| 1986 | 68-73 | .482 | Sixth |
| 1987 | 45-96 | .319 | Tenth |
| 1988 | 76-66 | .535 | Third — lost opener |

# Sacramento
# (Sacts, Senators, Solons)

The Sacramento Gilt Edges won three consecutive pennants, 1897–99, in the California League, and when the PCL was organized California's capitol city eagerly became a charter member. The Sacramento Sacts hosted Oakland in the season opener, winning 7–4 and marching on to a second place finish. Tom Thomas was the leading pitcher (27–15), and swung a strong bat in the bargain (.283). Under the direction of manager Mique Fisher, the Sacts hit well, if not spectacularly, and ran the bases like racehorses. The shortstop was Truck Eagan (.326 with 56 stolen bases), Pearl Casey (.290 with 65 steals) was the second baseman, at first was Townsend (.296), and catching chores were handled by Charles Graham (.271). In left field was George Hildebrand (.296 with 47 steals), in center Charles Doyle (.246 with 55 steals), and in right McLaughlin (.284 with 75 steals).

Despite a strong performance on the field, it was decided to move the club to Tacoma for the 1904 season. Fisher took most of his players with him, and the team won the pennant. In 1905, with most of the roster still intact, Tacoma won the first half of a split schedule. But the team plummeted to last place during the second half, and the franchise was moved back to California's capitol city late in the season. Almost the entire lineup was familiar to Sacramento fans, and although batting averages were down, Fisher still had his team tearing up the basepaths — outfielders McLaughlin (53 steals) and Doyle (43 steals), and first sacker Lou Nordyke (48 steals). This hard-running team played Los Angeles, winners of the second half, in a best-of-nine postseason playoff, but Sacramento lost five games of the first six.

Sacramento went back into the outlaw California League for the next few seasons, but returned to Organized Baseball in 1909, when the PCL added two teams. Charles Doyle (.231) still roamed center field, and Fred Brown (16–23) again took the pitcher's mound, but the 1909 Sacts could do no better than fourth place. For several years Sacramento fielded weak clubs, except for 1913, when the Sacts finished second behind the pitching of Ralph "Sailor" Stroud (25–15) and John Williams (17–7). When the 1914 Sacts staggered through another lackluster performance, attendance became so poor that the franchise was surrendered to the league on September 5, finishing the season as the San Francisco Missions.

Four years later, when Portland dropped out of the league because of travel problems exacerbated by World War I restrictions, Sacramento was readmitted, and this time the city would remain in the Coast League through 1960. For nearly two decades, the Solons, as the team now was called, usually wound up in the second division, and there were four eighth-place finishes. But the hard-running tradition of Sacramento baseball was carried on by stolen base champs Patsy McGaffigan (55 steals in 1921) and Merlin Capp (80 steals in 1923). The weak-hitting 1921 team finished a close second behind the pitching of southpaw Paul Fittery (25–14) and righthander Bill Prough (20–12). Fittery (15–14) and Prough (20–11), along with "Chief" Moses Yellowhorse (22–13) and catchers Pip Koehler (.356) and Robert Schang (.348), led the Solons to another second-place finish in 1923.

In 1928 Sacramento won the second half of the season by defeating San Francisco in a playoff, but lost the ensuing playoff series to the Seals. The offense was sparked by first sacker Earl Sheely (.381, 21 HRs, 128 RBIs), a veteran big leaguer, while the best pitchers were Ray Keating (27–10) and Louri Vinci (23–11). The

*An early group of Solons.*
— Courtesy California State Library, Sacramento

shortstop was Ray French (.287), who played more games at his position (2,736) than any other minor leaguer. He also came to bat more times (12,174) than any other minor league player, twice leading the PCL (1928 — 814, and 1930 — 848) while with Sacramento. French held down shortstop for Sacramento for 10 seasons, 1925–34.

Another longtime Sacramento player, pitching ace Tony Freitas, led Sacramento in 1937 to the initial first-place finish in the team's history. A lefthander, Freitas won more games (342–238) than any other minor league hurler, along with 25 major league victories. Freitas pitched for Sacramento from 1929 until 1932, when he went to the Philadelphia A's. He returned to Sacramento in 1937, winning 20 or more games until he entered the military service in 1943. During these six seasons Freitas was a model of consistency — 23–12, 24–11, 21–18, 20–19, 21–15, and 24–13. After the war, he returned to Sacramento, but he was 34 and no longer could dominate PCL hitters. In 1950 Freitas went down to Modesto in the California League and finished 20–6. The next season he went 25–9, and he concluded his career at the age of 45 in 1953 by leading the California League in victories (22–9) with Stockton.

Along with Freitas, third baseman Art Garibaldi (.313 and the PCL's MVP) was a key to the first-place finish in 1937. The 1937 Solons were eliminated in postseason play, but the team bounced back to win the playoffs the next two years. In addition to Freitas, who was the club's best player, four regulars wore Solon uniforms in each of these three seasons — pitcher Bill Schmidt (15–11, 16–19 and 15–13), outfielder Earl Adams (.299, .293 and .280), and the double-play combination, shortstop Joe Orengo and second sacker Dibrell Williams.

The Solons were back in the playoffs in 1941, behind Freitas (21–15), Bill Schmidt (13–9), Al Hollingsworth (21–9), infielder Gene Handley (.313), and stolen base leader Don Gutteridge (.309). The Solons also produced stolen base champs in 1943 (Oral Burnett), 1944 (Bill Ramsey), and 1945 (Gene Handley). The 1941 Solons finished second after leading the league throughout most of the season, blanked San Diego in four straight in the opening round of playoffs, then went to the seventh game in the championship series before losing to Seattle.

With Freitas in top form (24–13) before going into the military, the Solons copped the 1942 flag with a dramatic finish. First-place Los Angeles came to Sacramento for the last week of the season, needing to win just three of seven games from manager Pepper Martin's second-place Solons to wrap up the pennant. The Angels won the first two games, and only one more victory in the remaining five games would clinch the title. But after trailing 4–1 in the eighth, outfielder Buster Adams and catcher Ray Mueller (the PCL's MVP of 1942) pounded back-to-back home runs and the Solons won in the last inning, 5–4.

Freitas hurled the Solons to victory in the Friday contest, and Saturday's game went to extra innings. The Angels scored a run in the top of the eleventh, but PCL veteran Gene Lillard, acquired by Sacramento late in the season (.340 in 29 games), pinch hit a two-run homer to win the game.

The season ended with a Sunday doubleheader. The Angels squandered a five-run lead, falling behind, 7–5, as Buster Adams and Ray Mueller *again* belted back-to-back home runs. Freitas came on in the ninth to sew up the victory with a flawless inning of relief. Then Freitas returned to the mound to twirl a four-hitter in the nightcap, winning his 24th game and bringing Sacramento its first — and only — PCL pennant. The postseason playoff was anticlimactic, as the spent Solons dropped the opener to Seattle.

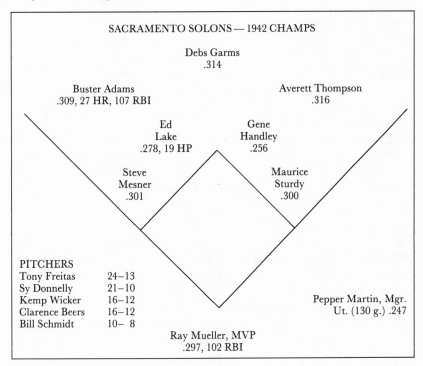

SACRAMENTO SOLONS — 1942 CHAMPS

Debs Garms
.314

Buster Adams
.309, 27 HR, 107 RBI

Averett Thompson
.316

Ed
Lake
.278, 19 HP

Gene
Handley
.256

Steve
Mesner
.301

Maurice
Sturdy
.300

PITCHERS
Tony Freitas    24–13
Sy Donnelly     21–10
Kemp Wicker     16–12
Clarence Beers  16–12
Bill Schmidt    10– 8

Pepper Martin, Mgr.
Ut. (130 g.) .247

Ray Mueller, MVP
.297, 102 RBI

Freitas and others departed for the service after the season, and Sacramento plunged to last place in 1943, despite the heroics of Alpha Brazle (11–8 with a 1.69 ERA), who won the ERA title before finishing the year with the St. Louis Cardinals (8–2). Sacramento was little better in 1944, although Clem Dreisewerd (20–9, 1.61 ERA) produced another ERA title for the Solon pitching staff. Batting champ Jo Jo White (.355 with 40 stolen bases) led the 1945 Solons to a playoff berth. Third-place Sacramento featured outfielder George Mandish (.333), second baseman Gene Handley (.307 with 56 stolen bases), righthander Guy Fletcher (24–14), and southpaw B. L. Beasley (12–4). But the Solons did not get past the first round of playoffs, and for the next 15 seasons Sacramento rarely emerged from the second division, finishing last five times from 1948 through 1955. In 1948 Edmonds Field burned at midseason, forcing the Solons to play on the road while their park was rebuilt.

During these dismal years, Sacramento fans managed to enjoy a few outstanding individual performances. Former American League star Joe Gordon became player-manager in 1951, leading the PCL in homers and RBIs (.299, 43 HRs, 136 RBIs) while alternating between second base and shortstop. In 1953 outfielder Robert Dillinger, a six-year veteran of the big time, won the batting championship (.366), and he hit well (.301) the following season. Southpaw Marshall Bridges (16–11, 205 Ks) was the 1958 strikeout leader while tying for most victories.

But such high points proved to be too few and far apart, especially after the Giants moved to San Francisco in 1958. Attendance in 1960 was merely 117,506, and the franchise was sold to Hawaii. For 14 years there was no professional baseball in Sacramento. But after the 1973 season, it was decided that the population of Eugene was too small to support AAA baseball, and the team was moved to Sacramento.

Edmonds Field had been replaced by a shopping center, and the only available playing facility was old Hughes Field, a horseshoe-shaped football stadium with a seating capacity of 23,500. But when lined off for baseball, the left field barrier was merely 231 feet from home plate. During the 1974 season there was an average of seven home runs per game. On August 6 Sacramento and Tacoma blasted seven homers *each*, breaking a 50-year-old PCL record for total home runs in a game. On June 4 another record was set when four consecutive Tacoma players hit homers; during the season Sacramento walloped 305 roundtrippers, and a total of 491 homers sailed out of Hughes Field in 1974. (All of these records are marked with a double asterisk in the PCL *Record Book*, since Official Baseball Rule 1.04 prescribes a minimum outfield distance of 250 feet.)

In 1974 Sacramento was managed by Cleveland Indian Hall of Fame pitcher Bob Lemon. Lemon's pitching staff produced merely one shutout all season and yielded an astronomical team ERA of 6.70. But the inviting left field fence sparked an exciting offense headed by outfielders Gorman Thomas (.297, 51 HRs, 122 RBIs) and Sixto Lezcano (.325, 34 HRs, 99 RBIs), and third sacker Bill McNulty (.329, 55 HRs, 135 RBIs), who led the PCL in runs scored, homers, total bases and RBIs. Sacramento finished last in the Western Division, but almost 300,000 fans — tops in the PCL — trooped through the turnstiles to watch the offensive fireworks.

Although the left field fence was altered for 1975 with a tall screen, Sacramento still led the league in homers (196) and attendance (252,201), while the pitching staff again was last in ERA (5.71). First baseman-DH Robert Hansen (.279, 29 HRs, 102

RBIs) paced the PCL in home runs and RBIs, but the Solons again brought up the Western Division cellar. The 1976 Solons led the league in team hitting (.303) and home runs (183), as outfielders Lewis Beasley (.351, 21 HRs, 86 RBIs), Cirilo Cruz (.324, 13 HRs, 83 RBIs) and Keith Smith (.325, 23 HRs, 73 RBIs), second baseman Bump Wills (.324, 26 HRs, 95 RBIs), and first sacker Doug Ault (.313, 25 HRs, 83 RBIs) formed another impressive offense. But again the pitching was weak (last with a 6.07 ERA), and a third consecutive losing record plummeted attendance (82,324) to last in the league, while other clubs recorded dramatic increases.

The Sacramento franchise was leased to San Jose, with the hope that a new stadium soon would be built. But the Sacramento stadium did not materialize, and after two years of going head-to-head with the nearby San Francisco Giants and Oakland A's, San Jose management surrendered the franchise to the league, which sold it to Ogden. In 1989 it was announced that the Atlantic Richfield Company planned to donate $25 to $35 million to construct a 40,000-seat baseball stadium in Sacramento (Arco already was building a new arena for the Sacramento Kings of the NBA). City officials hoped that the facility would be ready by 1990, and that Sacramento could acquire a major league franchise.

| Year | Record | Pcg. | Finish |
| --- | --- | --- | --- |
| 1903 | 105-105 | .500 | Second |
| 1905 | 106-107 | .498 | Second |
| 1909 | 97-107 | .475 | Fourth |
| 1910 | 83-128 | .393 | Sixth |
| 1911 | 95-109 | .466 | Fourth |
| 1912 | 73-121 | .376 | Sixth |
| 1913 | 103-94 | .523 | Second |
| 1914 | 90-121 | .426 | Fifth |
| 1918 | 48-48 | .500 | Fourth |
| 1919 | 85-83 | .506 | Fourth |
| 1920 | 89-109 | .449 | Seventh |
| 1921 | 105-80 | .568 | Second |
| 1922 | 76-124 | .380 | Eighth |
| 1923 | 112-87 | .563 | Second |
| 1924 | 88-112 | .440 | Eighth |
| 1925 | 82-119 | .408 | Seventh |
| 1926 | 99-102 | .493 | Fifth |
| 1927 | 100-95 | .513 | Fourth |
| 1928 | 112-79 | .586 | Third — won opener, lost finals |
| 1929 | 85-117 | .421 | Seventh |
| 1930 | 102-96 | .515 | Third |
| 1931 | 86-101 | .460 | Sixth |

| 1932 | 101-88 | .534 | Third |
| 1933 | 96-85 | .530 | Fourth |
| 1934 | 79-109 | .420 | Seventh |
| 1935 | 75-100 | .429 | Eighth |
| 1936 | 65-111 | .369 | Eighth |
| 1937 | 102-76 | .573 | First — lost opener |
| 1938 | 95-82 | .537 | Third — won opener and finals |
| 1939 | 88-88 | .500 | Fourth — won opener and finals |
| 1940 | 90-88 | .506 | Fifth |
| 1941 | 102-75 | .576 | Second — won opener, lost finals |
| 1942 | 105-73 | .590 | First — lost opener |
| 1943 | 41-114 | .265 | Eighth |
| 1944 | 76-93 | .450 | Seventh |
| 1945 | 95-85 | .528 | Third — lost opener |
| 1946 | 94-92 | .505 | Fifth |
| 1947 | 83-103 | .446 | Seventh |
| 1948 | 75-113 | .399 | Eighth |
| 1949 | 102-85 | .545 | Third |
| 1950 | 81-119 | .405 | Eighth |
| 1951 | 75-92 | .449 | Seventh |
| 1952 | 66-114 | .367 | Eighth |
| 1953 | 75-105 | .417 | Eighth |
| 1954 | 73-94 | .437 | Seventh |
| 1955 | 76-96 | .442 | Eighth |
| 1956 | 84-84 | .500 | Fifth |
| 1957 | 63-105 | .375 | Seventh |
| 1958 | 71-83 | .461 | Sixth |
| 1959 | 78-76 | .506 | Fourth |
| 1960 | 73-81 | .474 | Sixth |
| 1974 | 66-78 | .458 | Seventh |
| 1975 | 59-85 | .410 | Eighth |
| 1976 | 71-72 | .497 | Fifth |

# Salt Lake City
# (Bees, Angels, Gulls)

On March 31, 1915, 10,000 fans crowded into compact Bonneville Park to cheer the Salt Lake City Bees to a 9–3 victory over the Vernon Tigers. It was the first Pacific Coast League game held in Salt Lake City, but the community had a strong background in Organized Baseball. Salt Lake City fielded a team in the Pacific National League in 1903 and 1904, and in the Union Association from 1911 through 1914. Owner of the Union Association club was Bill

Lane, who had fought Indians in the last years of the western fron-
tier, mined for gold in Alaska and the Yukon, and participated in
Utah politics. When a franchise became available in the PCL, Lane
purchased the San Francisco Missions, the first of three Coast
League teams to play in Salt Lake City (there would be PCL franchises in 1915–25, 1958–65 and 1970–84).

The 1915–25 teams would prove unable to bring a PCL pennant to Salt Lake City, but the light air and cozy dimensions of
Bonneville Park provided explosive offense for 11 seasons. The Bees
led the PCL in team hitting in 1915, 1916, 1917, 1919, 1920, 1923
(.327, establishing the all-time record), 1924 (.327 again) and 1925
(.321). The most prolific slugfest took place on May 11, 1923, when
Vernon hit nine home runs (five by Pete Schneider, who registered
14 RBIs) and beat the Bees (who had two homers) 35–11. The
1923 Bees blasted 204 home runs, which remained a PCL record
for 35 seasons.

In 1916 first baseman Bunny Brief (.314, 33 HRs, 133 RBIs,
with 149 runs) led the PCL in homers and runs scored, after hitting
.363 in 82 games the previous year. Switch hitter Morrie Rath won
the batting title in 1917 (.314), outfielder Bill Rumler took the
crown in 1919 (.362), and Earl Sheely and Paul Strand accounted
for three more hitting championships in the next few years. First
sacker Sheely was the batting and home run champ in 1920 (.371,
33 HRs), he also hit the most homers in 1919 (.305, 28 HRs), and
he tied for the home run title in the war-shortened season of 1918
(.300, 12 HRs). Player-manager Duffy Lewis played spectacularly
in 102 games in 1921 (.403), and was almost as good as a regular
outfielder in 1924 (.392). Lefty O'Doul was sensational as an outfielder in 1924, (.392, 101 RBIs) and 1925 (.375, 191 RBIs), a season in which he led the PCL in triples (17) and hits (309). Veteran
outfielder Joe Wilhoit played his final three seasons, 1921–23
(.339, .317 and .360) for the Bees, and outfielder Vess Maggart also
finished his career in Salt Lake City, leading the league in runs
(127) in 1919 and batting .370 in 1920. Lefthanded outfielder John
Frederick, a lifetime .323 minor league performer, who also averaged .308 in six years as a National Leaguer, recorded three fine
seasons with Salt Lake City: 1923 (.328), 1924 (.353) and 1925
(.309).

Paul Strand, another lefthanded outfielder who pounded out a
.334 lifetime batting average as a minor leaguer, enjoyed three not-

able seasons as a Bee. He warmed up to Bonneville Park in 1921 (.314), then, incredibly, won the Triple Crown the next two seasons (.384, 28 HRs, 138 RBIs in 1922, and .394, 43 HRs, 187 RBIs in 1923). In 1923 he also paced the PCL in hits (325) and runs, and he chipped in 66 doubles, 13 triples and 22 stolen bases. Tony Lazzeri was almost as spectacular. He hit .354 in 39 games during his rookie season of 1923; the next year he was farmed out, but did manage a .283 average with 16 homers in 85 games with the Bees. In 1925 he became the regular shortstop and performed superbly, batting .355 and setting all-time PCL records with 60 home runs and 222 RBIs.

Such hitting feats overshadowed the pitchers, who often were battered mercilessly in Bonneville Park. But in 1915 Lefty Williams (33–12 in 64 games and 294 strikeouts in 419 innings) led the league in victories, games and innings pitched, and strikeouts. Another southpaw, Paul Fittery, also enjoyed a fine season in 1915 (22–17 in 58 games), and the next year (29–19 in 65 games and 203 strikeouts in 448 innings) led the PCL in games, innings pitched, and strikeouts. There was a trio of 22-game winners in 1917 — longtime big leaguer Jean Dubuc (22–16), southpaw Tiny Leverenz, a three-season veteran of the St. Louis Browns (22–18), and righthander Bill Evans (22–19). Tiny Leverenz led the PCL in victories (16–5) and winning percentage in the abbreviated 1918 season, while righthander Ralph Stroud (26–13) was the percentage leader in 1920.

Despite the offensive fireworks and the sale of his stars to major league clubs (Connie Mack of the Philadelphia Athletics bought Paul Strand for $40,000), the relatively small size of Salt Lake City restricted profit potential. PCL owners also resented the travel costs necessary for trips to Utah, and in January 1926 the league approved the transfer of Lane's franchise to Hollywood.

For the next three years Salt Lake City fielded a team in the Class C Utah-Idaho League. But after the circuit folded following the 1928 season, the city would not enjoy professional baseball until 1939, when the Class C Pioneer League was organized. Aside from a three-year recess during World War II, Salt Lake City participated in the Pioneer League through the 1957 season, when the PCL again beckoned.

Salt Lake City rejoined the PCL in the realignment following the major league move to the West Coast. The Bees now played in a fine facility several blocks south of the downtown area. First known as Community Park, it was rechristened Derks Field in memory of John C. Derks, editor of the *Salt Lake Tribune*. The 1958 Bees were much like the early PCL Salt Lake City clubs, second-division teams with little pitching but explosive offense. Outfielder Jim McDaniel (.293, 37 HRs, 100 RBIs) led the PCL in homers and RBIs, while first sacker Dick Stuart (.311 with 31 HRs and 82 RBIs in just 80 games), second baseman Ken Toothman (.307), and outfielders Carlos Bernier (.332) and Joe Christopher (.327) battered opposing pitchers throughout the league.

The 1959 Bees brought Salt Lake City its first PCL pennant. Righthander Dick Hall (18–5 with 1.87 ERA) led the league in victories, winning percentage and ERA, and he was voted Most Valuable Player. The offense was headed by outfielders Sammy Miley (.333), Charles Harmon (.310) and Carlos Bernier (.281). The Bees finished first, 1¹/₂ games ahead of Vancouver, and there were no playoffs.

In 1960 the Bees slumped to third, despite the efforts of outfielders Miley (.318) and Harmon (.287), RBI champ Harry Bright (.313, 27 HRs, 119 RBIs), and home run leader R. C. Stevens (.276, 37 HRs, 109 RBIs). Outfielder Walt Bond (.320) and third sacker Max Alvis (.319) led the Bees to second place in 1962, but the most unusual victory of the year was produced by southpaw Bob Allen (5–2). Allen entered a tie game with Tacoma with two out in the top of the ninth, recording the third out with one pitch. In the bottom of the ninth, Allen singled, then scored the winning run, securing a win with a single pitch.

Despite a losing season in 1963, the Bees turned out the MVP and RBI champ in outfielder Billy Cowan (.315, 25 HRs, 120 RBIs). But the 1964 and 1965 teams suffered dismal years, with attendance dropping to 89,000 and 98,000, and Salt Lake City surrendered its franchise. After a year without professional baseball, Salt Lake City rejoined the Pioneer League in 1967 for three solid seasons, and in 1970 the Vancouver franchise was moved to Utah's capitol city.

The 1970 club suffered through a last-place season (44–99), but the next year Salt Lake City rebounded to a pennant. Several players performed so well that they were moved up to the parent Angels during the season, but Tom Reynolds (.355), Tom Silverio (.339), Charles Vinson (.327), Mickey Rivers (.322), Art Kusnyer

(.316), Bruce Christensen (.309), and second baseman Bill Parker (.306, 27 HRs, 115 RBIs) helped the SLC Angels win the PCL team batting title (.295). Salt Lake City won the Southern Division, then defeated Tacoma for the flag.

Speedy outfielder Mickey Rivers was back for 59 games in 1972 (.336), and he hit just as well in a full season in 1973 (.336 with a league-high 47 stolen bases) before going on to stardom in the American League. Salt Lake City won the Eastern Division in 1975 and 1976, but lost the pennant in the playoffs both years to Hawaii of the Western Division. Third baseman Paul Dade won the 1976 batting title (.363), outfielder Carlos Lopez (.350) also bolstered the lineup, and the pitching staff was led by strikeout champ Gary Wheelock (15–8), who also tied for the lead in victories.

The Angels again earned back-to-back playoff appearances in 1978 and 1979. In 1978 the Angels were blanked by Albuquerque in the opening round of playoffs, but first sacker Willie Aikens (.326, 29 HRs, 110 RBIs) was the PCL home run champ, and outfielder Robert Jones (.307, 14 HRs, 102 RBIs) also provided a powerful bat. Managed by Jimy Williams, the 1979 Angels recorded the best record in the league, then swept Albuquerque and Hawaii in the playoffs to bring a third PCL pennant to Salt Lake City. The home run titlist was DH Isaac Hampton (.289, 30 HRs, 97 RBIs in just 106 games), and outfielder Jose Mangual (.270, 22 HRs, 48 SBs) was the stolen base champ. Shortstop Rance Mullinks (.343) and third sacker Floyd Rayford (.294) were the best fielders at their positions, while first baseman John Harris (.325) and outfielders Robert Clark (.304) and Gil Kubski (.295) were other tough outs. The best pitchers were righthander Robert Ferris (14–7), southpaw David Schuler (10–4), and relievers Mike Overy (11–6) and Daniel Boone (9–2).

Harris (.333), Kubski (.307) and Ferris (14–8) produced well again in 1980, but most of the other players had departed and Salt Lake City failed to make the playoffs. It was the same story the next year, despite impressive hitting by first baseman Daryl Sconiers (.354), catcher Brian Harper (.350, 28 HRs, 122 RBIs), and outfielder Tom Brunansky (.332, 22 HRs, 81 RBIs in just 96 games).

In 1982 Salt Lake City became a farm club of the Seattle Mariners and earned a postseason appearance, but a number of the best players had been brought up to Seattle, and the team was blanked

*Sunday afternoon at sun-drenched Derks Field. The ball always carries well in Salt Lake City.*
— Author's photo

by Albuquerque in the playoff opener. A losing season followed in 1983, although attendance soared past 280,000. In 1984, led by third baseman Darnell Coles (.318), shortstop Danny Tartabull (.304), outfielder Ivan Calderon (.365), and infielder Jim Presley (.317), Salt Lake City again made the playoffs. But by season's end, most of the stars had been pulled up to Seattle, and once more the team lost out in the opening round of playoffs. Attendance dropped to fewer than 168,000, a 40 percent plunge, and the franchise was moved to Calgary.

But the most spectacular feat in the baseball history of Salt Lake City lay in the future. Calgary's Russ Parker, who had bought the Salt Lake City franchise, sold his Pioneer League club to the Edmonton Trappers. Thus the Salt Lake City Trappers rejoined the Pioneer League — now a Class A rookie league which plays a short season — and won pennants in 1985 and 1986. In 1987, with a team composed of players rejected by numerous scouts and big league organizations, the Trapper misfits tore the league apart. En route to their third consecutive championship, the Trappers went on a winning streak which threatened the all-time Organized Baseball record of 27 victories in a row, established by the Corsicana

Oilers of 1902 and matched by the Baltimore Orioles of 1921. "The Streak," as it became known, finally reached 29, and a crowd of nearly 10,000 watched the Trappers break the 85-year-old record. Averaging 5,000 fans per game, Salt Lake City drew more than 170,000 — a new record for a Class A short season team, and the fifth highest total of all 162 minor league clubs. Perhaps the future will bring a fourth PCL tenure for the baseball fans of Salt Lake City.

| Year | Record | Pcg. | Finish |
|------|--------|------|--------|
| 1915 | 108-89 | .548 | Second |
| 1916 | 99-96 | .507 | Third |
| 1917 | 102-97 | .513 | Third |
| 1918 | 48-49 | .495 | Fifth |
| 1919 | 88-83 | .515 | Third |
| 1920 | 95-92 | .508 | Fifth |
| 1921 | 73-110 | .399 | Seventh |
| 1922 | 95-106 | .473 | Fourth |
| 1923 | 94-105 | .472 | Fifth |
| 1924 | 101-100 | .502 | Fifth |
| 1925 | 116-84 | .580 | Second |
| 1958 | 77-77 | .500 | Fifth |
| 1959 | 85-69 | .552 | First |
| 1960 | 80-73 | .523 | Third |
| 1961 | 67-87 | .435 | Eighth |
| 1962 | 81-73 | .526 | Second |
| 1963 | 73-85 | .462 | Eighth |
| 1964 | 58-98 | .372 | Eleventh |
| 1965 | 56-91 | .381 | Twelfth |
| 1970 | 44-99 | .308 | Eighth |
| 1971 | 78-68 | .534 | Second — won Southern Division and Playoff |
| 1972 | 80-68 | .541 | Third |
| 1973 | 79-65 | .549 | Third |
| 1974 | 69-73 | .486 | Fifth |
| 1975 | 80-64 | .556 | Second — won Eastern Division, lost playoff |
| 1976 | 90-54 | .625 | First — won Eastern Division, lost playoff |
| 1977 | 74-65 | .532 | Second |
| 1978 | 72-65 | .526 | Fifth — lost opener |
| 1979 | 80-68 | .541 | Second — won opener and finals |
| 1980 | 77-65 | .542 | Fourth |
| 1981 | 63-71 | .470 | Sixth |
| 1982 | 73-70 | .510 | Fourth — lost opener |
| 1983 | 67-75 | .472 | Seventh |
| 1984 | 74-66 | .529 | Second — lost opener |

# San Diego
# (Padres)

San Diego's first professional baseball club played in the four-team, short-lived Southern California Trolley League in 1910. When the circuit attempted a revival in 1913, San Diego did not field an entry, and there was no further professional ball until 1929, when the city spent the season in the California State League. In 1936, despite the fact that San Diego had a population of just 200,000 and no history of success in Organized Baseball, Hollywood owner Bill Lane decided to relocate his franchise to the border city. Lane had moved his team from Salt Lake City to Hollywood in 1926, but the club had to share Wrigley Field with the Los Angeles Angels. The Angels attempted to double the rent for 1926, following a season in which Hollywood had drawn fewer than 90,000 paid admissions, and Lane determined to install his team into a new ballpark promised by San Diego officials.

These officials enlisted the efforts of the Works Progress Administration, and a wooden stadium was rapidly erected on the waterfront and christened "Lane Field." The grandstand roof had not been built when the season started, and since there was no screen behind the plate, fans suffered an assortment of welts and broken noses until the roof and foul screen went up. Years later, it was discovered that the distance from home plate to first base was only 87 feet and that the right field foul line was just 325 feel long, instead of 335 feet as the fence sign always had proclaimed.

Second baseman Bobby Doerr starred for the new San Diego Padres, batting .342 and leading the PCL in hits and assists (in one game Doerr rapped out six hits). Third baseman Ernie Holman hit .314 with 108 RBIs and outfielder Vince DiMaggio hit .293 with 102 RBIs as the Padres tied for the 1936 PCL batting lead with a .292 team average. Fans enthusiastically supported this explosive club, and attendance exceeded 203,000 for the year. During the season, Bill Lane signed a pitcher-slugger out of San Diego's Herbert Hoover High School. Lanky Ted Williams struck out in his first time at bat, but he hit .271 and showed enormous promise.

Young Williams was a mainstay of the pennant-winning Padres of 1937. The first Padre club tied for second place but dropped the first round of playoffs. The 1937 Padres lagged in the final weeks of the season because of injuries, but powerful hitting kept them in the playoff picture. Catcher George Detore (.334) led the PCL in batting, first basemen George McDonald (.312 with 102 RBIs) and James Reese (.314) led a hard-hitting infield, while the outfield featured Williams (.291 with 23 homers and 98 RBIs), Harold Patchett (.306), Rupert Thompson (.326) and Cedric Durst (.293). Jim Chaplin (23–15) and Manuel Salvo (19–13) led the pitching staff. The Padres swept first-place Sacramento in four straight games to open the playoffs, then repeated the feat against Portland to bring San Diego its first pennant.

Outfielder Dominic Dellessandro (.368) won the 1939 batting title, while George Detore (.356) and third baseman Mike Haslin (.345) provided spectacular hitting for a second-division club. The Padres qualified for the playoffs three consecutive years, 1940–42, but lost in the first round each season. During these three seasons, the best hitting performances were turned in by shortstop Steve Mesner (1940 — .341), infielder Mike Haslin (1940 — .321), outfielder Ed Stewart (1940 — .320), and George Detore (1940 — .321, and 1941 — .320). Righthander Dick Newsome (23–11 in 1940) and southpaw Preacher Hebert (22–10 in 1941 and 22–15 in 1942) produced seasons which took them to the big leagues. One of the most notable pitching efforts in PCL history occurred in 1941, when righthander Yank Terry won the Triple Crown. Terry led the league in victories (26–8), strikeouts (172) and ERA (2.31), and was named Most Valuable Player.

For the next six seasons, San Diego was mired in the second division, but postwar crowds enjoyed several explosive Padre hitters. Outfielder Max West, a lefthanded slugger who had played six seasons in the National League, took aim at the inviting right field fence at Lane Field. In 1947 West hit .306 and led the PCL with 43 homers and 124 RBIs. West spent 1948 with Pittsburgh, hit .178 and rejoined the Padres to again win the home run and RBI titles in 1949. He hit .291, blasted 48 homers and 166 RBIs, and drew an all-time PCL record 201 walks.

In 1948 another lefthanded power hitter, outfielder-first baseman Jack Graham, hit .298 with 136 RBIs in 138 games and a league-leading 48 home runs. Graham was voted MVP — for a seventh-place club! In 1948 34-year-old Luke Easter broke into Organized Baseball with San Diego (he had played throughout his prime in the Negro leagues). A lefthanded-hitting first baseman who stood 6'4½ and weighted 240 pounds, Easter batted .363, ripped PCL pitching for 25 homers and 92 RBIs in just 80 games, and was promoted to the Cleveland Indians (Easter would twice lead the International League in home runs and RBIs when he was in his 40s).

Paced by Easter, West, third baseman Al Rosen (.319) and outfielder Minnie Minoso (.297 with 22 homers), the 1949 Padres reversed the losing trend by going to the playoff finals. The next year San Diego won 114 games and finished second, led by future big league star Minoso (.339, 20 HRs, 115 RBIs and 30 stolen bases), lefthanded slugger Harry Simpson (.323, 33 HRs, and a league-leading 156 RBIs), and Jack Graham (.293, 33 HRs, 136 RBIs). After playing in the major leagues, Simpson returned to San Diego to repeat as RBI champ in 1961 (.303, 24 HRs, 105 RBIs).

In 1954, managed by the legendary Lefty O'Doul, San Diego battled to the initial first-place finish in franchise history. Southpaw Bill Wight (17–5, 1.93 ERA) led the PCL in winning percentage and ERA, but the strength of the club was hitting. The Padres led the league in team batting (.276) and runs scored, and outfielder Harry Elliott (.350 with 110 RBIs) won the hitting title. Other offensive threats included outfielder Earl Rapp (.337, 24 HRs, 111 RBIs), first sacker Dick Sisler (.318, 19 HRs, 90 RBIs), second baseman Al Federoff (.278 with a league-leading 108 walks and 110 runs), shortstop Carl Peterson (.289 with 39 steals), and outfielder-third baseman Milton Smith (.294). The Padres finished the season in a deadlock with Hollywood, beat the Stars 7–2 (Elliott hit two homers) to win the pennant, but were defeated by Oakland in the opening round of the Governor's Cup playoffs.

San Diego's old wooden ballpark was the site of the 1955 All-Star Game, which was lost by the defending champs to the PCL stars, 7–4. After the 1957 season, C. Arnholt Smith, owner of the Westgate-California Tuna Packing Corporation, purchased the Padres and immediately decided to abandon termite-ridden Lane Field. Westgate Park, a handsomely-landscaped stadium which seated 8,200 (plus large overflow crowds on grassy hills beyond the outfield fences) was constructed on Smith property in Mission Valley. The 1959 All-Star Game, pitting North vs. South squads, was held in Westgate Park.

In 1959 Richard Stigman became the latest in a long line of Padre power pitchers to lead the PCL in strikeouts (despite a record of only 9–17). Manuel Salvo was the strikeout king in consecutive seasons (1937 and 1938), and so was Frank Dasso (1943 and 1944, when he whiffed 253 batters in a 20–19 year). Yank Terry won the pitcher's Triple Crown in 1941, and Vallie Eaves was the strikeout leader in 1945. Sad Sam Jones overpowered 246 hitters in 1951, while Mudcat Grant won the crown in 1957 (he was 18–7, and went up to Cleveland the next year).

San Diego's next first-place club also led the PCL in team batting (.280) and runs scored. The 1962 Padres charged to the pennant (there were no playoffs at season's end), finishing 12 games ahead of second-place Salt Lake City. The batting champion and MVP was catcher Jesse Gonder (.342, 21 HRs, 116 RBIs). Third baseman Tommy Harper (.333, 26 HRs, 84 RBIs) finished second in the hitting race, while outfielder Ken Walters (.300, 22 HRs, 96 RBIs) and first sacker Roselio Alvarez (.318) led the offense, while Sam Ellis (12–6 with a no-hitter), John Tsitouris (13–8), John Flavin (12–2) and George McWilliams (12–7) formed the nucleus of a deep pitching staff.

Two years later San Diego took another title. The 1964 Padres, paced by infielder Tommy Holms (.309) and Atanasio Perez (.309, 34 HRs, 107 RBIs), won the Western Division, then defeated explosive Arkansas (208 team homers) for the pennant. The final PCL championship came in 1967, when the Padres won the Eastern Division with the league's best record and downed the Western Division champs, Spokane, for another flag. Manager Bob Skinner stayed on to direct the last edition of the PCL Padres; the 1968 club had the fourth best record in the league and played in 50,000-seat San Diego Stadium (now called Jack Murphy Stadium), where the Chargers already had put in a season of football.

The streamlined new facility was completed in 1967 in Mission Valley, five miles from Westgate Stadium, which was razed to make room for a multi-million-dollar shopping center. A National League expansion team was organized for 1969, and the Padres became a major league baseball operation.

| Year | Record | Pcg. | Finish |
|------|--------|------|--------|
| 1936 | 95-81 | .540 | Second (tie) — lost opener |
| 1937 | 97-81 | .545 | Third — won opener and finals |
| 1938 | 92-85 | .520 | Fifth |
| 1939 | 83-93 | .472 | Fifth |
| 1940 | 92-85 | .520 | Fourth — lost opener |
| 1941 | 101-76 | .571 | Third — lost opener |

*San Diego contributed The Chicken to baseball.*

— Author's collection

| 1942 | 91-87 | .511 | Fourth — lost opener |
| 1943 | 70-85 | .455 | Seventh |
| 1944 | 75-94 | .444 | Eighth |
| 1945 | 82-101 | .448 | Sixth |
| 1946 | 78-108 | .419 | Sixth |
| 1947 | 79-107 | .425 | Eighth |
| 1948 | 83-105 | .441 | Seventh |
| 1949 | 96-92 | .510 | Fourth — won opener, lost finals |
| 1950 | 114-86 | .570 | Second |
| 1951 | 79-88 | .473 | Sixth |
| 1952 | 88-92 | .489 | Fifth |
| 1953 | 88-92 | .489 | Sixth |
| 1954 | 102-67 | .604 | First — won first-place playoff, lost opener |
| 1955 | 92-80 | .535 | Second |
| 1956 | 72-96 | .429 | Seventh |
| 1957 | 89-79 | .530 | Fourth |
| 1958 | 84-69 | .549 | Second |
| 1959 | 78-75 | .510 | Third |
| 1960 | 77-75 | .507 | Fourth (tie) |
| 1961 | 72-82 | .468 | Fourth |
| 1962 | 93-61 | .604 | First |
| 1963 | 83-74 | .529 | Third |
| 1964 | 91-67 | .576 | Second — won Western Division and playoff |
| 1965 | 70-78 | .473 | Eighth |

| 1966 | 72-75 | .490 | Eighth |
| 1967 | 85-63 | .574 | First — won Eastern Division and playoff |
| 1968 | 76-70 | .521 | Fourth |

# San Francisco
# (Seals)

Baseball was played in San Francisco as early as 1860, when the Red Rovers and the Eagles fought to a 33–33 tie. In 1868 California's first enclosed baseball park was opened in San Francisco at 25th and Folsom Streets as the Eagles beat the Wide Awakes, 37–23. In 1887 the first championship of the California League was declared a tie between two San Francisco clubs, the Haverlys and the Stars.

When the Pacific Coast League was organized in 1903, San Francisco became the largest charter member and long would be a cornerstone city of the circuit. Indeed, like Los Angeles, San Francisco for several years would support two PCL franchises, and across the bay Oakland also fielded a PCL team. Another San Francisco club operated for a few seasons as part of the outlaw California State League.

During 55 years in the PCL, San Francisco's Seals finished first 12 times and won seven playoff titles. Appropriately, San Francisco was the victor in its first PCL game in 1903 over Portland, 7–3, before 5,500 fans at Recreation Park, the best weekday crowd ever enjoyed in Frisco to this point. Recreation Park had been built in 1896 at Eighth and Harrison Streets, and for years a baseball barker called Foghorn Murphy rode a horse up and down Market Street announcing home games and batteries through a megaphone. The ballpark was destroyed in the earthquake of 1906, forcing San Francisco to finish the season playing "home" games in Oakland. A new Recreation Park went up at 14th and Valencia Streets (it also was called the Valencia Street Grounds). The 1907 season opened with a morning game won by San Francisco over Portland, 4–3, while Portland won the afternoon contest. An overflow crowd of 10,000 witnessed the doubleheader, although Recreation Park was expanded in 1917 to seat 15,000. The season of 1914 was played at Ewing Field, a $100,000 park in the Richmond District. But the inaugural game was shortened by fog and cold (fans regularly brought blankets), and the Seals decided to return to Recreation Park the next year because of schedule interruptions due to fog.

San Francisco fans did not savor a PCL championship until 1909, but there were several outstanding individual performances during the early seasons. James Whalen was the bellweather of the first three pitching staffs (28–21 in 1903, 32–23 in 1904, 32–25 in 1905), and there were stolen base titles in 1903 (Dan Shay with 83 thefts), 1907 (George Hildebrand, a native of San Francisco who later was a fine PCL and American League umpire, with 59 SBs), and 1908 (Rollie Zeider with 93 SBs). The 1909 pennant-winners (132–80) featured Frank Browning (32–16), Cack Henley (31–10), who led the league in victories and winning percentage, and batting titlist Henry Melchior (.298). The next year San Francisco infielder Hunky Shaw won the dead-ball era batting crown with the lowest championship average (.281) in PCL history. But outfielder Ping Bodie walloped 30 home runs in 1910, the highest total so far amassed in the Coast League, while workhorse Cack Henley (34–19) paced the circuit in wins. In 1911 Harry Sutor (22–22 in 55 games and 365 innings) led the league in strikeouts (339), in 1913 Skeeter Fanning (28–15) won more games than any other PCL hurler, and that same year outfielder Jimmy Johnston (.304 with 124 stolen bases) set an all-time record for base stealers.

Fanning (25–15 in 58 games), Spider Baum (30–15 in 55 games), Ping Bodie (.325) and first baseman Harry Heilmann (.364 — the native San Franciscan would average .342 in his Hall of Fame career) led San Francisco to its second pennant in 1915. Another pennant followed in 1917, as righthander Eric Erickson posted a remarkable record (31–15 in 62 games, 307 strikeouts in 444 innings, and a 1.93 ERA) to win the pitcher's Triple Crown, overshadowing another stellar performance by Spider Baum (24–17).

San Francisco boasted an extremely stable roster during the 1920s, with a number of Seals regulars — many with several years' experience in the big leagues — returning to their positions season after season. A nucleus of fine players produced flags in 1922, 1923 and 1925. In 1922 center fielder Jimmy O'Connell (.335) and third baseman Willie Kamm (.342, 20 HRs, 124 RBIs) brought great profit to Seals' management. O'Connell was sold to the New York

Giants for $75,000 and Kamm went to the Chicago White Sox for $100,000. Slugging first baseman Bert Ellison (.358 with 129 RBIs in 1923, and .325 with 160 RBIs in 1925) provided power in all three championship seasons (as well as a .381 year with 35 homers in 1924), and he served as manager of the 1923 and 1925 pennant winners. Catcher Sam Agnew did not bat under .312 in the title seasons, and outfielder Gene Valla hit no less than .333 during these years (along with a .367 average in 1924). Shortstop Hal Rhyne and second sacker Pete Kilduff provided a hard-hitting double-play combination in all of the flag seasons. Rookie outfielder Paul Waner broke in spectacularly in 1923 (.369), led the PCL in 1925 (.401), then moved up to a Hall of Fame career in the big leagues.

The championship pitching staffs were formidable, as Robert "Speed" Geary was a 20-game winner in each title year. In 1922 the big winners were Geary (20–9), Jim "Death Valley" Scott (25–9), and Willis Mitchell (24–7). The next season, Geary (21–11), John Shea (21–10), Doug "Buzz" McWeeney (20–9), and Henry Courtney (19–6) paced the staff. In 1925 there were four 20-game winners: McWeeney (20–5), Geary (20–12), Guy Williams (21–10), and Mitchell (20–8), who hit .308 and who had his best year in 1924 (28–15).

The Seals plunged to last place in 1926, but outfielders Earl Averill (.348) and Smead Jolley (.346) were thunderous additions to San Francisco baseball. Jolley won the PCL batting and RBI titles the next year (.397, 33 HRs, 163 RBIs), then followed with a Triple Crown in 1928 (.404, 45 HRs, 188 RBIs) as the Seals stormed to another pennant. Other stars of this championship team were Averill (.354, 36 HRs, 174 RBIs), outfielder Roy Johnson (.360), first baseman Hollis Thurston (.347), native San Franciscan Gus Suhr (.314, 22 HRs, 133 RBIs), shortstop Hal Rhyne (.312, 106 RBIs), ERA and strikeout champ Elmer Jacobs (22–8), and Dutch Ruether (29–7), who led the PCL in victories and winning percentage and who frequently was used as a pinch hitter (.316 in 72 games).

Although San Francisco finished second the next year, Jolley (.387, 35 HRs, 159 RBIs) and second sacker Suhr (.381, 51 HRs, 177 RBIs) led another explosive team. In 1930 an eight-year big league veteran, first baseman Earl Sheely, led the PCL in hitting and RBIs (.403, 29 HRs, 180 RBIs). The Seals won another flag in

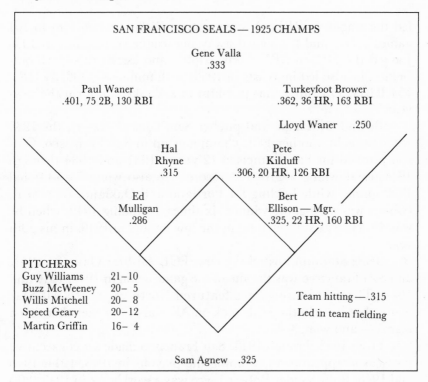

SAN FRANCISCO SEALS — 1925 CHAMPS

Gene Valla
.333

Paul Waner
.401, 75 2B, 130 RBI

Turkeyfoot Brower
.362, 36 HR, 163 RBI

Lloyd Waner    .250

Hal
Rhyne
.315

Pete
Kilduff
.306, 20 HR, 126 RBI

Ed
Mulligan
.286

Bert
Ellison — Mgr.
.325, 22 HR, 160 RBI

PITCHERS
Guy Williams      21–10
Buzz McWeeney     20– 5
Willis Mitchell   20– 8
Speed Geary       20–12
Martin Griffin    16– 4

Team hitting — .315
Led in team fielding

Sam Agnew    .325

1931, led by righthander Sam Gibson (28–12), who won the pitcher's Triple Crown. The team hit .314 to lead the league, as first baseman James Keesey (.358 with 113 RBIs), outfielder Henry Oana (.345 with 161 RBIs), and shortstop Frank Crosetti (.343 with 143 RBIs) paced a devastating linuep.

The 1931 champs played in a new park, Seals Stadium, a concrete and steel facility located at 16th and Bryant Streets. Built at a cost of $600,000, Seals Stadium seated 18,600 and boasted three clubhouses — one for the Seals, one for the visitors, and one for the Missions. The outfield wall was 30 feet high, there was no roof over the grandstand, and the lighting system was so good that it later was moved to Cheney Stadium in Tacoma.

In 1932 outfielder Vince DiMaggio (.270 in 59 games) arranged a tryout for his 17-year-old brother, Joe, who played in three games at the end of the season. The next year Joe hit safely in 61 consecutive games, setting an all-time PCL record and presaging his major league record of 56 straight games for the New York Yankees in 1941. In his rookie season (.340, 28 HRs, 169 RBIs) he led the league in RBIs. A knee injury in 1934 limited him to 101 games (.341) and frightened away big league scouts. But in 1935 Joe led the PCL in RBIs, runs, triples, and assists (a superb outfielder, he also led in assists in 1933) with numbers (.398, 34 HRs, 154 RBIs, 173 runs) that put him in a Yankee uniform the next year.

Behind DiMaggio and pitcher Sam Gibson (22–4), the 1935 Seals brought another PCL championship to San Francisco. Gibson pitched for San Francisco 12 years, 1931 and 1934 through 1944, establishing a 210–123 record. He also won 17 additional PCL games while hurling for Portland and Oakland. As a Seal, Gibson was a 20-game winner six times, including 1942, when he was 43. He was still pitching in the low minors in 1949, in his 50th year.

Seals Stadium hosted the first PCL All-Star Game in 1941, and San Francisco was the site of the game again in 1944, 1946 and 1948. Three of these games featured North vs. South All-Star teams, but in 1946 the Seals took on All-Stars from the other seven teams — and won, 3–0.

From 1943 through 1948, San Francisco made six consecutive postseason appearances, winning the playoffs in 1943, 1944, 1945 and 1946. Righthander Robert Joyce was a workhorse in 1943 (20–12), 1944 (21–20), and 1945 (31–11), when he led the PCL in victories, winning percentage, innings pitched, complete games (35), and ERA (2.17). Southpaw Tom Seats posted an exceptional record in 1944 (25–13), and Larry Jansen became the PCL's last 30-game winner for the 1946 titlists (30–6, with a league-leading 1.57 ERA). The 1946 RBI leader was Ferris Fain (.301 with 112 RBIs) — a slick-fielding first baseman who claimed he was paid $200 per month under the table while he starred for East Oakland High School in 1939. Robert Chesnes (22–8 with a 2.32 ERA) was the percentage and ERA leader in 1947, and he hit .311 in 50 games. The 1948 playoff club was led by batting titlist Gene Woodling (.385, 22 HRs, 107 RBIs) and ERA champ Con Dempsey, who also paced the PCL in strikeouts in 1948 and 1949.

In 1945 Paul I. Fagan, whose fortune was based on banking, steamship and Hawaiian pineapple interests, bought into the Seals with the intention of bringing major league baseball to the West Coast by 1950. Fagan upgraded Seals Stadium and removed all advertising from the outfield walls (at an annual sacrifice of $20,000 in revenue). He spent $10,000 to install baseball's first glass back-stop, established a deluxe pressbox, and built a tower to pinpoint drunks or troublesome rowdies. The tower also helped prevent a miscarriage and save a heart attack victim. Fagan installed the first female usherettes in Organized Baseball, outfitting the pretty, young ladies in expensive, tailor-made uniforms. Ladies' restrooms were so sumptuous that some women spent most of their time there, listening to the game amidst luxurious surroundings. Fagan brought in an expert from a Scottish golf course to install rare turf, and groundskeeper Harvey Spargo soon was maintaining the finest field in baseball.

The Seals' clubhouse was equipped with a barber chair, a shoe shine stand, a soda fountain and draft beer. Individual cubicles were provided with personalized comb and brush sets and with electric razors. On the road, the Seals stayed at the best hotels, ate the finest food, and became the first minor league team to travel regularly by plane. Fagan took the Seals to Hawaii for spring training in 1946, and later he financed a tour of Japan. The lowest-paid Seal would earn $5,000 per season, equivalent to the major league minimum salary, while Fagan's stars were handsomely remunerated. When Ferris Fain went to the Philadelphia Athletics after the 1946 season, and when Bill Werle went to Pittsburgh two years later, each player initially balked because their salaries were better with San Francisco. Fagan paid Lefty O'Doul, the Seals' colorful and highly capable manager, a salary in the $45,000–$50,000 range so that he would not be lured away to the majors.

O'Doul was a native San Franciscan who played for his home team in 1918, his second year as a professional. A southpaw hurler, he went 12–8 and was purchased by the New York Yankees. After riding the bench in New York for two years, O'Doul returned to San Francisco in 1921 to post a 25–9 record with a 2.39 ERA. Two more unproductive years in the American League followed, then he came back to the PCL as an outfielder with Salt Lake City. He hit .392, and after two more spectacular seasons as an outfielder, again donned a Seals uniform. He hit .378 with 40 stolen bases, led the PCL in hits and runs, and was named Most Valuable Player of 1927. O'Doul bounced back to the majors at the age of 31, twice winning the National League batting title (.398 in 1929 and .368 in 1932). In 1935 O'Doul, now 37, returned to the Seals as manager, winning a pennant in his first season. Although his best days as a player were over, for years he occasionally inserted himself in the lineup as a pinch hitter, outfielder or pitcher. Hugely popular with fans, O'Doul played up his Irish background by wearing green suits and sport coats. A large brewery was located across the street from Seals Stadium and often suds would be expelled into the atmosphere. O'Doul, stationed in the third base coach's box, would "catch" a capful of suds and pretend to drink brew from his cap before a delighted audience. To incite a rally, O'Doul would pull a handkerchief from his hip pocket and begin waving it at the opposing pitcher, and throughout Seals Stadium, the "Handkerchief Brigade" would enthusiastically follow suit. O'Doul managed the Seals from 1935 through 1951, and was named vice president of the club in 1948.

But by 1949 the Seals had entered the longest championship slump in the history of the franchise. Fagan's lavish expenditures had been part of his effort to transform the PCL into a major league, and he urged other clubs not to deal their best players to American and National league teams. But other club owners, unlike Fagan, made their living from baseball, and could not afford to stick with the long-range plan to make the PCL a major league. Increasingly the Seals became cut off from major league assistance, and when a disappointed Fagan pulled out, the franchise eventually became owned by fans who purchased stock in a community backed team.

The Seals finally affiliated with the Boston Red Sox, and even as talk swirled that major league franchises soon would be moved to the West Coast, the Seals put together one final championship club. In 1957 Joe Gordon, formerly a standout American League second baseman, directed his team to the flag during San Francisco's last season in the PCL. The Seals' offense was triggered by batting champ Ken Aspromonte (.334) and first baseman Frank Kellert (.308, 22 HRs, 107 RBIs). The pitching staff was led by a pair of relievers who enjoyed remarkable seasons, William Abernathie (13–2) and Leo Kiley (21–6), who led the PCL in *victories*.

On the last day of the season, with the pennant clinched and the announcement made public that the New York Giants would move to San Francisco in 1958, a festive crowd of nearly 16,000 turned out to the Seals' final appearance. Governor Goodwin Knight and Mayor George Christopher were on hand to preside over the farewell rites, and the Municipal Band played "Take Me

Out to the Ball Game." Sacramento won the first game with a ninth-inning home run, and the second game was played strictly for fun. Outfielder Albie Pearson (.297 during the season) played five positions and was charged with the loss after pitching for an inning. Manager Joe Gordon pitched and played shortstop, going 1 for 3 and reaching base twice. Late in the game, which the Seals lost, 14–7, Sacramento Manager Tommy Heath inserted himself as a pinch runner — for Gordon! At the close of the day the fans sang "Auld Lang Syne," then repaired across the street to the Double Play and Flukie's Third Base to talk baseball.

The San Francisco Giants played the 1958 and 1959 seasons in Seals Stadium, and despite the limited seating capacity, almost 2,700,000 fans turned out to watch the big leaguers. Major league baseball had arrived at last in San Francisco, but after Candlestick Park opened, historic Seals Stadium fell to the wrecking ball. As the author discovered in the summer of 1988, however, longtime baseball enthusiasts in San Francisco still harbor fond memories of Lefty O'Doul and the Seals.

| Year | Record | Pcg. | Finish |
|------|--------|------|--------|
| 1903 | 107-110 | .493 | Fourth |
| 1904 | 101-114 | .469 | Fifth |
| 1905 | 125-100 | .556 | Second |
| 1906 | 91-84 | .520 | Fourth |
| 1907 | 104-99 | .515 | Second |
| 1908 | 100-104 | .490 | Third |
| 1909 | 132-80 | .622 | First |
| 1910 | 114-106 | .518 | Third |
| 1911 | 95-112 | .459 | Fifth |
| 1912 | 89-115 | .436 | Fifth |
| 1913 | 104-103 | .502 | Fourth |
| 1914 | 115-96 | .545 | Third |
| 1915 | 118-89 | .570 | First |
| 1916 | 104-102 | .504 | Fourth |
| 1917 | 119-93 | .561 | First |
| 1918 | 51-51 | .500 | Third |
| 1919 | 84-94 | .472 | Sixth |
| 1920 | 103-96 | .517 | Fourth |
| 1921 | 106-82 | .564 | Third |
| 1922 | 127-72 | .638 | First |
| 1923 | 124-77 | .617 | First |
| 1924 | 108-93 | .537 | Third |
| 1925 | 138-71 | .641 | First |
| 1926 | 84-116 | .420 | Eighth |
| 1927 | 106-90 | .541 | Second |
| 1928 | 120-71 | .628 | First — won playoff |

| 1929 | 114-87  | .567 | Second |
| 1930 | 101-98  | .508 | Fourth |
| 1931 | 107-80  | .572 | First — won playoff |
| 1932 | 96-90   | .516 | Fourth |
| 1933 | 81-106  | .433 | Sixth |
| 1934 | 93-95   | .495 | Fourth |
| 1935 | 103-70  | .595 | First — won playoff |
| 1936 | 83-93   | .472 | Seventh |
| 1937 | 98-80   | .551 | Second — lost opener |
| 1938 | 93-85   | .522 | Fourth — won opener, lost finals |
| 1939 | 97-78   | .554 | Second — lost opener |
| 1940 | 81-97   | .455 | Seventh |
| 1941 | 81-95   | .460 | Fifth |
| 1942 | 88-90   | .494 | Fifth |
| 1943 | 89-66   | .574 | Second — won opener and finals |
| 1944 | 86-83   | .509 | Third — won opener and finals |
| 1945 | 96-87   | .525 | Fourth — won opener and finals |
| 1946 | 115-68  | .628 | First — won opener and finals |
| 1947 | 105-82  | .561 | First (tie) — lost tiebreaker and opener |
| 1948 | 112-76  | .596 | Second — lost opener |
| 1949 | 84-103  | .449 | Seventh |
| 1950 | 100-100 | .500 | Fifth |
| 1951 | 74-93   | .443 | Eighth |
| 1952 | 78-102  | .433 | Seventh |
| 1953 | 91-89   | .506 | Fifth |
| 1954 | 84-84   | .500 | Fourth — won opener, lost finals |
| 1955 | 80-92   | .465 | Sixth |
| 1956 | 77-88   | .467 | Sixth |
| 1957 | 101-67  | .601 | First |

# San Jose
# (Missions)

Located just 45 miles southeast of San Francisco, San Jose first fielded professional baseball clubs in the California State League in 1910 and 1913–15. In 1942 San Jose entered the California League, then resumed play in the circuit from 1947 through 1958, when the nearby major league presence of the San Francisco Giants provided a magnet for area baseball fans.

Twenty years later, San Jose tried again when Sacramento leased out its PCL franchise in order to construct a new stadium. The neighboring Oakland A's assumed the role of parent club, appointing Rene Lachemann as manager. But the San Jose Missions

*San Jose was the home of PCL ball in 1977 and 1978.*
— Author's photo

would finish last in team hitting during both years in the PCL. Although first baseman Jerry Tabb hit .344 and catcher Tim Hosley batted .321 in 1977, both men spent much of the season with the A's. Outfielder Derek Bryant hit .302, catcher Dennis Haines batted .276, and outfielder Mark Williams hit .277, but the rest of the lineup provided little offense. San Jose brought up the cellar of the Western Division in 1977.

The Seattle Mariners backed the San Jose club in 1978, retaining Lachemann, but in just their second year of existence, proving unable to adequately stock their top minor league club. First baseman Charles Beamon hit .328 in 90 games and second sacker Manuel Estrada batted .280, but no other regular hit higher than .261. T. F. Jones had the best ERA on the team (3.87), but his won-lost mark was just 7–8, and the top reliever, Tom Brown, posted the same record.

The lackluster performance of the Missions, combined with the proximity of the San Francisco Giants and Oakland A's, produced a 1978 attendance of merely 67,000, by far the worst in the PCL. The franchise was returned to the PCL and sold to Ogden, but local baseball fans still can enjoy the San Jose Giants of the Class A California League.

| Year | Record | Pcg. | Finish |
|------|--------|------|--------|
| 1977 | 64-80  | .440 | Seventh |
| 1978 | 53-87  | .378 | Tenth |

# Seattle
# (Indians, Rainiers, Angels)

By the time the Pacific Coast League was organized, baseball had an enthusiastic following in Seattle. For years local fans had crowded into the YMCA Park at 12th and Jefferson Streets, and there was a Seattle club in the Class C Pacific Northwest League. The Seattle Indians of the fledgling PCL moved into a new park at Fifth Avenue and Republican Street. Although the 1903 and 1904 Seattle entries in the PCL could only finish third, the Indians produced the first two batting champs — center fielder Harry Lumley, .387 in 1903; and left fielder Emil Frisk, .337 in 808 at-bats. Lumley was sold to Brooklyn in 1904, while Frisk, a former major league pitcher, went to the St. Louis Browns' outfield in 1905.

James Hughes was 34–15 in 1903 and 26–19 the next year, and Sea Lion Hall was 28–19 in 1904. Rube Vickers, a big right-hander, posted a herculean season in 1906. He pitched in 64 games, worked 517 innings (an all-time record for Organized Baseball), allowed just 395 hits and 139 walks, and set a PCL record of 409 strikeouts. His record was 39–20, and he led the PCL in games pitched, innings, strikeouts and victories.

Although Seattle finished second in 1906, the PCL reduced itself to four teams, and the Indians competed in the Class B Northwestern League from 1907 through 1917. Seattle re-entered the PCL in 1919 when the circuit expanded to eight teams. The Indians wound up eighth in the 1919 standings, and there were last-place finishes in 1928, 1929, 1931 and 1933, as well as several sixth- and seventh-place finishes. But in 1924, managed by former big leaguer Wade Killefer and paced by stolen base leader Bill Lane (.336 with 45 thefts), slugger Ray Rohwer (.325 with 33 HRs), hard-hitting outfielders Brick Eldred (.351) and Jim Welsh (.342), and righthander Vean Gregg (25–11), the Indians brought Seattle its first Coast League pennant. Seattle did not begin its championship drive until late in the 202-game season, and clinched the flag on the last day of the schedule.

Brick Eldred played 13 of his 15 professional seasons in the PCL, roaming the outfield for the Indians from 1920 through 1928. He hit .332 in his rookie season (1916) for Seattle of the Northwestern League. A lifetime .327 hitter, he posted averages of .339 (1920), .354 (1922), .353 (1923), .351 (1924) and .340 (1926), while ripping out an average of 64 doubles per year from 1920 through 1925.

Fans cheered Eldred and the 1924 champs at Dugdale Field, a wooden park which seated 15,000. Dugdale Field was built in 1913 at Rainier and McClellan Streets, and named after Dan Dugdale, who caught in the National League in 1886 and 1894 and who came to Seattle in 1898 as player-manager of the local Northwest League team. On July 4, 1932, apparently ignited by holiday fireworks, Dugdale Field burned to the ground. The Indians, on the road at the time of the fire, shifted operations to Civic Stadium. Originally built for high school sports, Civic Stadium had a hardpan dirt playing surface and served as the "temporary" home of the Indians for six years.

Sluggers rarely flourished in the heavy air of Seattle, but the windblown, cozy confines of Civic Stadium permitted fans to enjoy strong hitting performances for a few years. In 1932 second baseman Freddy Muller became the first Indian to lead the PCL in homers with 38. Muller and Indian left fielder Art Hunt shared the home run title in 1936 with 30 apiece. The next year Hunt led the PCL with 39 roundtrippers, while Indian outfielder Harlan Pool won the batting crown with a .334 average.

The PCL heyday of Seattle baseball commenced prior to the 1938 season, when beer baron Emil Sick bought the club for a reported $200,000. Sick was not a baseball expert, but he realized that owning a club could be "a lot of fun" if he could produce a consistent winner. He authorized the expenditure of $25,000 for new players, hired Jack Lelivelt, who had steered LA's Angels through their magnificent 1934 season, as field manager, and renamed his team the "Rainiers," in deference to 14,000-foot Mount Rainier, which loomed west of the city. Sick began construction of a new ballpark on the site of old Dugdale Field. Sick's Seattle Stadium was a minor league showplace. The grandstand was constructed of steel and concrete, and wooden benches produced a total of 15,000 seats.

Other fans often watched from "tightwad hill" beyond the left

*Emil Sick built his 15,000-seat stadium on the site of the old Dugdale Field.*
— Courtesy Mariana York

field fence. For years a fixture in his box seat behind the home team's third base dugout was florist Charles Sullivan, who handed out ten-dollar bills to Seattle players who would stroke a home run or pitch a shutout. Sick's Seattle Stadium hosted the PCL All-Star Game in 1949 and 1961.

Beginning in 1938, the Rainiers made the playoffs for six consecutive seasons, finishing first in 1939, 1940 and 1942. The 1938 club featured 18-year-old phenom Fred Hutchinson, a recent star at Seattle's Franklin High School. In an amazing performance, the teenager led the PCL in victories, winning percentage and ERA (25–7, .781, 2.48), and was named Most Valuable Player. Sold to Detroit after the season for $35,000 and four players, Hutchinson enjoyed a long major league career as a pitcher and manager, sandwiching in a triumphal return to Seattle in 1955 by managing the club to a PCL championship.

Heroes were numerous during the dynasty years. Seven-year Detroit veteran Jo Jo White came to Seattle in the Hutchinson deal, holding down center field for the next four seasons, hitting well and leading the PCL in stolen bases (47) in 1939. Dick Gyselman, another solid hitter, was a fixture at third base for a decade (1935 through 1944, and part of 1947); Gyselman played more games (2,520) at third than any other minor leaguer. First baseman George Archie hit .330 in 1939 and .324 the next year, was voted MVP in 1940, and went up to the American League. Righthander Hal Turpin pitched for Seattle from 1937 through 1945, annually keeping his ERA under 3.00 and winning 20 games four years in a row: 1939 (23–10), 1940 (23–11), 1941 (20–6), and 1942 (23–9).

Even more consistent from the mound was a wild southpaw (he yielded a record 2,096 walks in the minors), "Kewpie Doll" Dick Barrett, who hurled for Seattle from 1935 through 1942 and from 1947–49, when he was past his prime. Starting in 1935, he was a 20-game winner in seven of the next eight seasons, twice leading the league in victories, strikeouts, and innings pitched, once in ERA — and three times in walks. His best years were 1940 (24–5) and 1942 (27–13, with 178 strikeouts and a 1.72 ERA — the pitcher's Triple Crown, most victories, strikeouts, and lowest ERA).

After being a dominant power in the circuit for several years, the club suffered an inevitable decline, but Seattle enjoyed occasional highlights during its last quarter century in the PCL. In 1947 infielder Tony Layne, a three-year American League veteran, hit .367 to win the PCL batting championship. Outfielder Jim Rivera, named Most Valuable Player, hit .352 to cop the batting title in 1951 and led Seattle to a first-place finish. Hall of Famer Rogers Hornsby was the manager, the best pitchers were Marv Grissom (20–11) and Hector "Skinny" Brown (16–6). The team won both playoff rounds to claim the flag.

Fred Hutchinson managed Seattle to another pennant in 1955. The final Coast League championship came in 1966, with future Hall of Famer Bob Lemon at the helm. By now a Los Angeles affiliate, the Seattle Angels won the Western Division title, then took the championship series in seven games from Tulsa.

After two more years of PCL play, Seattle was awarded an expansion franchise by the American league for 1969. Emil Sick had sold his club in 1960, and Seattle Stadium was now owned by the city. The seating capacity was enlarged to 25,000, but the Seattle Pilots never played to a full house. Following a troubled, last-place season, the bankrupt franchise was sold to Milwaukee.

The Pacific Coast League pursued legal action, seeking one million dollars in damages for the loss of a valuable franchise. The PCL eventually was awarded $300,000, but for two years after the

Pilots folded, Seattle was out of professional baseball. Then Seattle obtained a franchise in the Northwest League, playing for five seasons in the Class A circuit. In 1977, following construction of the Kingdome, the Seattle Mariners re-entered the American League for good.

| Year | Record | Pcg. | Finish |
|------|--------|------|--------|
| 1903 | 98-100 | .495 | Third |
| 1904 | 114-106 | .518 | Third |
| 1905 | 93-111 | .456 | Sixth |
| 1906 | 99-83 | .544 | Second |
| 1919 | 62-108 | .365 | Eighth |
| 1920 | 102-91 | .528 | Second |
| 1921 | 103-82 | .557 | Fourth |
| 1922 | 90-102 | .457 | Fifth |
| 1923 | 99-97 | .505 | Fourth |
| 1924 | 109-91 | .545 | First |
| 1925 | 103-91 | .531 | Third |
| 1926 | 89-111 | .445 | Seventh |
| 1927 | 98-92 | .516 | Third |
| 1928 | 64-127 | .335 | Eighth |
| 1929 | 67-135 | .332 | Eighth |
| 1930 | 92-107 | .462 | Sixth |
| 1931 | 83-104 | .444 | Eighth |
| 1932 | 90-95 | .462 | Sixth |
| 1933 | 65-119 | .353 | Eighth |
| 1934 | 81-102 | .443 | Sixth |
| 1935 | 80-93 | .462 | Seventh |
| 1936 | 93-82 | .531 | Fourth — lost opener |
| 1937 | 81-96 | .458 | Sixth |
| 1938 | 100-75 | .571 | Second — lost opener |
| 1939 | 101-73 | .580 | First — lost opener |
| 1940 | 112-66 | .629 | First — won opener and finals |
| 1941 | 104-70 | .598 | First — won opener and finals |
| 1942 | 96-82 | .539 | Third — won opener and finals |
| 1943 | 85-70 | .548 | Third — won opener, lost finals |
| 1944 | 84-85 | .497 | Fifth |
| 1945 | 105-78 | .574 | Second — won opener, lost finals |
| 1946 | 74-109 | .404 | Eighth |
| 1947 | 91-95 | .489 | Fifth |
| 1948 | 93-95 | .495 | Fourth — won opener, lost finals |
| 1949 | 95-93 | .508 | Fifth |
| 1950 | 96-104 | .480 | Sixth |
| 1951 | 99-68 | .593 | First — won opener and finals |
| 1952 | 96-84 | .533 | Third |
| 1953 | 98-82 | .544 | Second |
| 1954 | 77-85 | .475 | Fifth |
| 1955 | 95-77 | .552 | First |
| 1956 | 91-77 | .542 | Second |

| | | | |
|------|-------|------|-----------------------------------------------|
| 1957 | 87-80 | .521 | Fifth |
| 1958 | 68-86 | .442 | Eighth |
| 1959 | 74-80 | .481 | Seventh |
| 1960 | 77-75 | .507 | Fifth |
| 1961 | 86-68 | .558 | Third |
| 1962 | 76-74 | .507 | Fourth |
| 1963 | 69-90 | .430 | Tenth |
| 1964 | 81-75 | .519 | Seventh |
| 1965 | 79-69 | .534 | Fourth |
| 1966 | 83-65 | .561 | Second — won Western Division and playoff |
| 1967 | 69-79 | .466 | Tenth |
| 1968 | 71-76 | .483 | Eighth |

# Spokane
# (Indians)

When Walter O'Malley brought the Dodgers to Los Angeles for the 1958 season, LA's Coast League franchise was moved to Spokane as a Dodgers AAA affiliate. Montreal had been relatively convenient to Brooklyn, but the LA Dodgers would need a closer city — Spokane — to juggle players from AAA to the parent club. In January 1958, construction started on Multnomah Stadium in the west end of town, and 90 days later the 10,000-seat home of the Spokane Indians was ready for PCL play.

The Dodgers had a model organization, and Spokane would enjoy the parade of future stars, as well as numerous playoff appearances, division titles and league championships. In 1959 the batting champ was fleet outfielder Tommy Davis (.345), while PCL legend Steve Bilko (.305, 26 HRs, 92 RBIs) tied for the RBI title. The next year, Willie Davis (.346 with 30 steals) won the batting crown and the stolen base title, and was named MVP. Spokane registered the highest team batting average in the league, helped by third baseman Ramon Conde (.325) and shortstop Charles Smith (.322, 20 HRs, 106 RBIs). The pitching staff was led by southpaw Mel Nelson (13–7), righthander Ed Rakow (12–6), and reliever Clarence Churn (13–7 in 57 games). Under the guidance of manager Preston Gomez, the Indians raced to the pennant, finishing 11¹/₂ games ahead of second-place Tacoma in a non-playoff year. In first place at mid-season, the Indians hosted the All-

Star Game, defeating the Stars 4–3 before a crowd of more than 10,000 at Multnomah Stadium.

Two losing seasons followed, but in 1963 Danny Ozark skippered the Indians once more to the league's best record. Spokane again hosted the All-Star Game, losing this time 4–2. But the Indians won the Northern Division with a massive 17-game gap over second-place Hawaii, before losing in the seventh game of the championship series. Righthander Howard Reed (19–7) led the PCL in victories and winning percentage, and solid seasons were contributed by Joe Moeller (16–11), outfielder Al Ferrara (.321 with 19 homers), third sacker Johnny Werhas (.295 with 96 RBIs), the best fielder at his position, and righthanded reliever Ken Rowe (10–4 with a 1.70 ERA in 38 games).

The next year Rowe turned in a superb performance in his third season with the Indians (he was 9–9 in 70 games in 1962). In 1964 he established an all-time PCL record with 88 relief appearances, finishing a record 74 games. Rowe was 16–11 with a brilliant 1.77 ERA, and — strictly in relief — he tied for most victories. In 1966 righthander Bill Singer (13–11), in his third season with the Indians, suddenly found a strikeout pitch (217 Ks in 233 innings). In the same year, Johnny Werhas played his fifth season with the Indians, fielding smoothly at third and hitting well year after year. "Peaches" could never stick with the Dodgers and was traded to the Angels in 1967.

Manager Roy Hartsfield piloted the Indians to back-to-back Western Division titles in 1967 and 1968. Stars of the 1967 club included switch-hitting third baseman Roy White (.343 in 84 games), outfielder James Fairey (.303), and versatile infielder-outfielder Cleo James (.297). James returned the next year (.268), along with first baseman Tom Hutton (.276), who led the league in fielding in 1967 and 1968, and another fielding leader, shortstop Tommy Dean. The 1968 offense was unspectacular but solid, built around third baseman-outfielder John Miller (.287), second sacker Bart Shirley (.280), outfielder Willie Crawford (.295 in 87 games), and third baseman Gustavo Sposito (.296 in 78 games). The pitching staff led the league in ERA (2.95), and featured veteran righthander Joe Moeller (15–9, 2.21 ERA) and Leon Everitt (17–10, 2.93 ERA).

Cleo James (.327) had a fine season in 1969, and southpaws Fred Norman (13–6) and Larry Staab (13–11) were among five pitchers who tied for most victories. Tommy Lasorda managed the 1970 Indians to a Northern Division title, then beat Hawaii in four straight games in the championship playoff. This superb club starred shortstop Bobby Valentine (.340, 14 HRs, 80 RBIs), who was named MVP after leading the league in most offensive categories, including batting average, total bases, runs, hits (211), doubles (39), and triples (16). Valentine also stole 29 bases and walloped two grand-slam homers for good measure. Outfielder Tom Paciorek (.326, 17 HRs, 101 RBIs), first baseman Tom Hutton (.323 in 90 games), and first baseman-outfielder Bill Buckner (.335) were key contributors to an offense that led the league in team hitting (.299). Jerry Stephenson (18–5, 2.82 ERA) was the ERA champ and tied for most victories, southpaw Robert O'Brien (13–3) had the league's best winning percentage, while Mike Strahler (15–5) and reliever Charlie Hough (12–8 with a 1.95 ERA in 49 games) were other members of a formidable mound corps.

Lasorda was back in 1971, and so were Hough (10–8), Strahler (11–7), and Stephenson (9–13, 5.18 ERA). Paciorek also returned (.305, 15 HRs, 101 RBIs), and Valentine played in seven games (.333). The most spectacular returnee, however, was first sacker Tom Hutton (.352, 19 HRs, 103 RBIs), who led the PCL in batting average, runs, hits and doubles, and who brought the MVP award to Spokane for the second year in a row. Third baseman Ron Cey (.328, 32 HRs, 123 RBIs) was the RBI champ and demonstrated the talent of a future big league star.

But somehow these talented players did not jell and a losing season ensued. Far more disappointing, however, was the Dodgers' decision to move their PCL club to Albuquerque, which was closer than Spokane and which boasted an innovative new stadium. But Spokane fielded a team in the Class A Northwest League, then returned to the PCL in 1973 as a replacement for Portland.

Now the AAA affiliate of the Texas Rangers, Spokane promptly recorded back-to-back pennants under manager Del Wilber. The 1973 Indians won the Western Division, then swept Tucson in three straight to claim the PCL crown. Infielder Bill Madlock (.338, 22 HRs, 90 RBIs) led the offense, along with infielder-outfielder Don Castle (.325), outfielder David Moates (.302), and All-Star catcher Bill Fahey (.278). The pitching staff featured Richard Henninger (12–5), lefties Mike Waits (14–7) and Jim Shellenback (13–7), and starter-reliever Jackie Brown (10–1 in 19 games).

The next year the Indians repeated as Western Division champs with the best record in the league before clinching another pennant with a three-game sweep of Albuquerque. The mound corps led the league in ERA as Mike Waits (12–6) had another good season. David Moates (.300 with 42 SBs) was the stolen base champ, and second baseman Mike Cubbage (.316), slugging shortstop Pete Mackanin (.291, 28 HRs, 103 RBIs), and outfielder Robert Jones (.300, 16 HRs, 91 RBIs) added to the league's highest-scoring offense. Don Castle, Bill Fahey, and first sacker Steve Greenberg returned to solidify the defense. Also returning was outfielder-first baseman-DH Tom Robson (.322, 41 HRs, 131 RBIs), who performed sensationally and was voted MVP.

During the next seven years, Spokane enjoyed only one winning season. Tom Robson (.320 in 87 games), Mike Cubbage (.313 in 56 games), and David Moates (.275 in 90 games) played well during part of 1975. The Indians affiliated with the Milwaukee Brewers in 1976, and Spokane fans enjoyed the play of infielder Kurt Bevacqua (.337), while outfielder Richard Davis (.335) missed the 1977 batting championship by half a percentage point. In 1979 Spokane became the AAA affiliate of the Seattle Mariners. The next year, infielder-outfielder Kim Allen (.294 with 84 steals in just 118 games) became the stolen base champ while hitting safely in 35 games in a row, and in 1981 performed almost as well (.286 with 50 steals in 109 games).

In 1982 skipper Moose Stubing led Spokane's final PCL team into the playoffs. The Indians boasted heavy hitters such as third sacker Steve Lubratich (.338), first baseman Daryl Sconiers (.329), catcher Jerry Narron (.311), and infielder Ricky Adams (.310). The team defeated Tacoma to win the Northern Division before losing to Albuquerque in the finals. Although attendance exceeded 221,000, the franchise was transferred to glamorous Las Vegas. But Spokane returned to the Northwest League, and in 1989 the Indians continued to play to strong crowds in Multnomah Stadium.

| Year | Record | Pcg. | Finish |
|------|--------|------|--------|
| 1958 | 68-85 | .444 | Seventh |
| 1959 | 77-77 | .500 | Fifth |
| 1960 | 92-61 | .601 | First |
| 1961 | 68-86 | .442 | Seventh |
| 1962 | 58-96 | .377 | Eighth |

| 1963 | 98-60 | .620 | First — won Northern Division, lost playoff |
| 1964 | 85-73 | .538 | Sixth |
| 1965 | 57-90 | .388 | Eleventh |
| 1966 | 75-73 | .507 | Seventh |
| 1967 | 80-68 | .541 | Second — won Western Division, lost playoff |
| 1968 | 85-60 | .586 | Second — won Western Division, lost playoff |
| 1969 | 71-73 | .493 | Fifth |
| 1970 | 94-52 | .644 | Second — won Northern Division and playoff |
| 1971 | 69-76 | .476 | Sixth |
| 1973 | 81-63 | .563 | Second — won Western Division and playoff |
| 1974 | 78-64 | .549 | First — won Western Division and playoff |
| 1975 | 64-78 | .451 | Seventh |
| 1976 | 65-78 | .455 | Seventh |
| 1977 | 75-69 | .521 | Fourth |
| 1978 | 64-75 | .460 | Eighth |
| 1979 | 68-79 | .463 | Ninth |
| 1980 | 60-80 | .429 | Eighth |
| 1981 | 56-84 | .400 | Tenth |
| 1982 | 78-65 | .545 | Third — won opener, lost finals |

# Tacoma
# (Tigers, Giants, Cubs, Yankees, Twins, Tigers)

In 1874 the Tacoma Invincibles became the city's first baseball team, and their first (and last) game was a 29–28 loss. Numerous other amateur aggregations were organized, but Tacoma's first professional club commenced play in 1890 as charter members of the Pacific Northwest League. Playing at a park located at South 11th and L Streets, the Tacoma Tigers participated in the circuit through 1903, the inaugural season of the Pacific Coast League. Then Sacramento's franchise was shifted to Tacoma for the 1904 season.

Six thousand fans crowded into the wooden grandstand and bleachers and watched Tacoma's mayor throw out the first ball for PCL play. Most of the Sacramento players had made the move to the north, and the team was a crack outfit. Manager Mique Fisher's best pitchers were Bobby Keefe (34–15) and Bill Thomas (27–24, the second year in a row he won 27 games). Second baseman Perle Casey (.295 with 65 stolen bases), shortstop Truck Eagan

(.320 with 56 steals), and third sacker Bill Sheehand returned to the infield. Charlie Graham again was the catcher, while Charles Doyle (.246 with 55 steals) and George McLaughlin (.284 with 75 thefts) continued to patrol the outfield.

Tacoma finished first in both halves of the season, but second-place Los Angeles claimed that if Tacoma played off and lost a game that had been tied earlier in the season, then LA would be in front. Mique Fisher and Jim Morley of Los Angeles arranged a best-of-nine playoff series. Tacoma won five, LA took four games, and there was one tie. PCL President Eugene Bert awarded the pennant to Tacoma.

Virtually the entire championship roster returned for 1905, again under the leadership of Mique Fisher. Keefe (30–22) and Thomas (20–16) were bolstered by Brown (22–21). Batting averages were light, but again stolen base totals were high as the club took the first half of the schedule. In the second half, however, Tacoma sagged to last place while Los Angeles surged to the top. Late in the season, the club was shifted back to Sacramento, and another playoff series was arranged with Los Angeles, which LA won, five games to one.

From 1906 through 1917, Tacoma fielded an entry in the Northwestern League. In 1907 Athletic Park was built at South 14th and Sprague Streets, but in 1910 the old park was reoccupied when a second Tacoma team played in the Washington State League. In 1918, 1920 and 1921, Tacoma participated in the Pacific Coast International League before joining the Western International League for the 1922 season. Fifteen years passed without professional ball in Tacoma, but the city then resumed its association with the Western International League, playing from 1937 through 1951, except for three seasons when the circuit suspended operations during World War II. After the war, a new park was constructed at 38th and Lawrence Streets, but soon conditions which ravaged the minor leagues during the 1950s left Tacoma without professional baseball for eight years.

But Tacoma baseball enthusiasts long had hoped to re-enter the Coast League, and there had been sporadic efforts to acquire the Sacramento franchise. In 1920 a Tacoma buyout was averted at the last minute when Sacramento merchants raised $38,000 to keep their team. In 1944 the parent St. Louis Cardinals put the Sacramento club up for sale, and Tacoma backers immediately raised

$50,000 toward the purchase price of $175,000. But a door-to-door "Save-Our-Solons" campaign again kept Sacramento in the PCL. Another attempted Tacoma purchase was thwarted by a Sacramento Chamber of Commerce committee which raised enough cash and pledges to satisfy the PCL. The Sacramento franchise finally moved in 1961, but to Hawaii — Tacoma had acquired the Phoenix club in 1960.

For years Tacoma would take on the name of the parent club, and in 1960 the T-Giants opened at new Cheney Stadium. When Phoenix officials, following the 1959 season, called with an offer to move their franchise to Tacoma, they stipulated that a new stadium must be ready by opening day. Lumber magnate Ben Cheney, long a key supporter of every level of baseball in Tacoma, spearheaded the stadium drive. While a swampy area at South 25th and Bantz Boulevard was being leveled, prefabricated concrete sections were fashioned. Construction began January 2, 1960, and three and a half months later 8,010-seat Cheney Stadium was completed. A splendid ballpark, the facility would perpetuate PCL history — seats and light standards from Seals Stadium in San Francisco were installed at Cheney. Ed Honeywell, sportswriter for the Tacoma *News Tribune*, became a fixture at Cheney Stadium. Honeywell already had put in 12 years as Tacoma's official scorer in the Western International League, and he logged 20 more seasons in the same capacity, missing only one PCL game at Cheney Stadium in two decades.

Rain plagued the T-Giants' debut, but gasoline was burned on the skinned part of the infield and helicopters were used to make the field playable, while Ben Cheney helped mop out the dressing rooms so that "his" stadium could open on schedule. The 1960 T-Giants were good enough for second place, behind a fine pitching staff — Eddie Fisher (17–12), Juan Marichal (11–5 in 18 games), and reliever Sherman Jones (a spectacular 10–0 in 47 appearances). Young Willie McCovey (.286 in 17 games) also was on hand for a time, catcher Tom Haller hit three homers in one game, and Tacoma led the PCL in attendance (270,021).

In 1961 Tacoma again was the attendance leader as second-year manager Red Davis led the T-Giants to their best PCL season ever. In a non-playoff year, the T-Giants roared to the pennant, 10 games ahead of second-place Vancouver. Once again the heart of the team was a solid pitching staff, including starters Ron Herbel

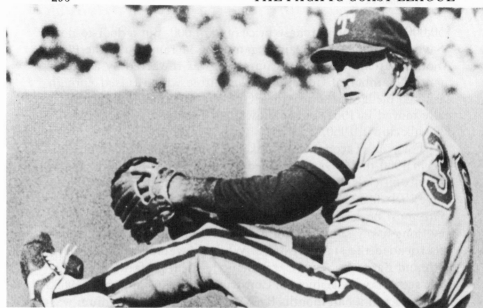

*Gaylord Perry led the PCL in victories while pitching for Tacoma in 1961, then won promotion to the big leagues during the next season.*

— Author's collection

(16–5) and Gaylord Perry (16–10), who led the league in victories, and Georges Maranda (10–4); and relievers Verle Tiefenthaler (13–6 in 56 appearances) and Ray Daviault (10–9 in 58 appearances). Second baseman Chuck Hiller (.324 in 73 games), first sacker Bob Farley (.307), shortstop Denis Menke (.293), and outfielders Rafael Alomar (.313) and Manny Mota (.289).

The next year Red Davis brought the T-Giants to a third-place finish. Gaylord Perry (10–7, 2.48 ERA) logged enough innings before being promoted to San Francisco to qualify for the PCL ERA title. In 1964 outfielder Jesus Alou (.324) missed the batting championship by one point, while older brother Matty (.313 in 25 games) worked himself back into shape after a poor season with San Francisco. Although the T-Giants were last in batting in 1964, outfielder Jose Cardenal (.289 with 40 steals) was the stolen base champ, and lefthander Al Stanek (13–12 with 220 Ks in 223 innings) was the strikeout king. The next year, righthander Bill Hands, in his third season as a T-Giant pitcher, led the league in victories and ERA (17–6, 2.19). Southpaw Dick Estelle pitched a no-hitter in 1964 and another in 1965.

Whitey Lockman became manager at Tacoma — now the T-

Cubs — in 1967, but the roster boasted little talent and there were two losing seasons. In 1969, however, Lockman led the T-Cubs to a Northern Division title, then beat Eugene, three games to two, to claim Tacoma's second PCL championship. The T-Cub pitching staff posted the league's best ERA (3.01) and righthander James Colburn (8–7, 2.28) was the ERA champ, while Archie Reynolds (10–10, 2.32 ERA) was just behind. Infielder-outfielder Dick Bladt (.312) led the offense, and Rod Skidmore was named All-Star first baseman.

In 1970, despite the efforts of outfielder Bryshear Davis (.332), the T-Cubs dropped to last in team hitting and next-to-last in the standings. But the next year, new skipper Jim Marshall guided the club to the league's best record and another Northern Division title before losing to Salt Lake City in the finals. Once more the T-Cubs posted the best staff ERA, and pitchers Roberto Rodriguez (15–8), Larry Gura (11–8), James Colburn (9–8 as a starter-reliever), and fastballer Juan Pizarro (9–6 in 17 games) provided reliable mound work. There was an explosive offense, featuring home run champ Adrian Garrett (.289, 43 HRs, 119 RBIs), third baseman Carmen Fanzone (.327, 28 HRs, 106 RBIs) and first sacker Ozzie Blanco (.305). Bryshear Davis (.345) blistered the ball for 22 games, outfielder Jose Ortiz (.327 in 64 games) also was outstanding in part of a season, and outfielder Cleo James (.368 and 37 steals in 71 games) won the stolen base title in just half a season of play.

Two losing years followed, and Tacoma became the T-Twins. The 1974 All-Star Game was held at Cheney Stadium, and that season righthander Juan Veintidos (12–4, 3.67 ERA) was the ERA titlist. The next season's ERA champ was another Tacoma righthander, Steve Luebber (14–7, 2.39). In 1976 righthander Mark Wiley (15–15) tied for most victories, while lefty Mike Pazik (14–5) led in winning percentage, and DH Bob Gorinski (.285, 28 HRs, 110 RBIs) led the league in homers and RBIs. The next year Wiley again topped the PCL in victories (16–7) and southpaw Ed Bane was the ERA champ (4.14 — it was a hitters' year!).

Tacoma affiliated with the New York Yankees in 1978 and immediately recorded another PCL championship. Offensive leaders were first baseman Dennis Werth (.333, and the best fielder at his position), and outfielders Garry Smith (.325), Darryl Jones (.322), Cirilo Cruz (.319) and Rogers Brown (.310 and 24 steals in 66 games). A trio of righthanders, ERA champ Larry McCall (10–4 and 2.93 in 18 games), Bob Kammeyer (12–2, which produced the PCL's best winning percentage), and Roger Slagle (13–8), made up the heart of a pitching staff which led the PCL in ERA. Another righthander, Jim Baettie (3–0 and 1.57 in four games) twirled a no-hitter against Spokane. The T-Yankees won the Western Division with the league's best season record, but when rain left the playoffs tied with more unplayable weather predicted, PCL President Roy Jackson declared Tacoma and Albuquerque co-champs.

In 1979 righthander Juan Berenguer struck out batters at a ferocious pace, including 18 in one game, and was the league's strikeout king (220 Ks in just 166 innings). That year Tacoma affiliated with the Cleveland Indians and adopted "Tugs" as a nickname. The "Tacoma Tugs" proved to be universally unpopular, and in 1980 the club made a permanent switch to the original PCL nickname, "Tigers."

The 1981 Tigers, now the AAA affiliate of the Oakland A's, brought another division title to Tacoma. Slugging first baseman Kelvin Moore (.327, 31 HRs, 109 RBIs), fleet shortstop Jimmy Sexton (.319 with 56 steals), outfielder Mike Davis (.287), and catcher Bob Kearney were named to the All-Star team. Manager Ed Nottle led the Tigers to a Northern Division championship before losing in the finals to an outstanding Albuquerque team. Nottle guided the Tigers back into the playoffs in 1982, although the club fell in the opening round. Tacoma's pitchers took the ERA title, Chris Codiroli (10–3 with a sparkling 1.90 ERA in 16 games) was the ERA champ, and Steve Baker (13–5, 2.48 ERA) was the All-Star righthander. Mike Davis (.316 with 40 steals) repeated as an All-Star, Jimmy Sexton (.310 in 24 games) also made a brief return, and Kelvin Moore (.264, 21 HRs, 84 RBIs) was back at first. Outfielders Richard Bosetti (.322) and Danny Goodwin (.301), infielder Keith Drumright (.329), and catcher Darryl Cias (.316 in 47 games) also contributed to another fine team.

Three straight losing seasons followed, although righthander Jose Rijo mowed down 179 batters in 149 innings to claim the 1985 strikeout title. In 1986 and 1987, the Tigers made it to the first round of playoffs. Putting in outstanding half-seasons for the 1986 Tigers were third sacker Mark McGwire (.318) and outfielders Roy Johnson (.343) and Stan Javier (.327). Darrell Akerfelds (10–3) and southpaw Tim Birtsas (7–2 in 10 games) were the best pitchers, and outfielder Brian Harper (.310) worked a strong relief stint when the bullpen was bare. In 1988 the Tigers posted a losing season, but switch-hitting outfielders Luis Polonia (.335) and Felix Jose (.317), and shortstop Ed Jurak (.295) showed great promise for the future.

Tacoma began its 30th season in 1989, the longest continual tenure of any current PCL member. Energetic Stan Naccarato, general manager since 1972, saved PCL baseball in Tacoma by gaining sponsorship from 21 local businessmen in a marathon 16-hour telephone session. Naccarato cheerfully battled for fan support within the shadow of the nearby Seattle Mariners. On opening day in 1977, Tacoma had a standing-room-only crowd of more than 10,000 (300 more than the Mariners drew on the same date!), and in 1987 season attendance reached a record-high 306,000.

| Year | Record | Pcg. | Finish |
|------|--------|------|--------|
| 1904 | 130-94 | .580 | First — won playoff |
| 1905 | 106-107 | .498 | Third — lost playoff |
| 1960 | 81-73 | .526 | Second |
| 1961 | 97-57 | .630 | First |
| 1962 | 81-73 | .526 | Third |
| 1963 | 79-79 | .500 | Fifth |
| 1964 | 73-82 | .471 | Ninth |
| 1965 | 75-72 | .510 | Sixth |
| 1966 | 63-85 | .426 | Eleventh |
| 1967 | 73-75 | .493 | Eighth |
| 1968 | 65-83 | .439 | Tenth |
| 1969 | 86-60 | .589 | Second — won Northern Division and playoff |
| 1970 | 45-98 | .315 | Seventh |
| 1971 | 78-65 | .545 | First — won Northern Division, lost playoff |
| 1972 | 65-83 | .439 | Sixth |
| 1973 | 65-79 | .451 | Sixth |
| 1974 | 75-66 | .532 | Third |
| 1975 | 73-69 | .514 | Third |
| 1976 | 76-69 | .524 | Fourth |
| 1977 | 68-75 | .476 | Fifth |
| 1978 | 80-57 | .584 | First — won Western Division, tied playoff |
| 1979 | 74-73 | .503 | Fourth |
| 1980 | 74-74 | .500 | Sixth |
| 1981 | 78-61 | .561 | Second — won Northern Division |
| 1982 | 84-59 | .587 | Second — lost opener |
| 1983 | 65-77 | .458 | Eighth |
| 1984 | 69-71 | .493 | Sixth |
| 1985 | 66-76 | .465 | Seventh |
| 1986 | 72-72 | .500 | Fourth — lost opener |
| 1987 | 78-65 | .545 | Second — lost opener |
| 1988 | 62-82 | .431 | Tenth |

# Tucson
# (Toros)

Tucson entered the Pacific Coast League in 1969 during the massive AAA realignment occasioned by the revival of the American Association. The last professional team, the Tucson Cowboys of the Class C Arizona-Mexico League, had folded more than a decade earlier, but Tucson's baseball history dated back to the Indian-fighting era. The soldiers at Fort Lowell brought the game to Tucson, and in 1885 a town team was organized to play the boys in blue. Soon the Old Pueblo club was traveling by mule train and stagecoach to contest the Tombstone Miners, and trips also were made to play nines from Phoenix, Bisbee, Florence, Benson and other towns. When the team heard about newfangled catcher's masks, a collection was taken and a rush order was placed with the Spalding Company. But no mention was made of what kind of mask, and when a fencer's mask arrived the players could not figure out how to see the baseball. The upper part of the face screen was cut out, but when the players finally saw a real catcher's mask, a new order was hurriedly placed.

Because of the favorable climate, baseball could be played most of the year in Tucson, and the Excelsiors, True Blues and Groves were some of the local nines which played Sunday afternoon games at the diamond on the Military Plaza near the current site of the Santa Rita Hotel. The Drachman family had been the heart of Tucson baseball since the earliest games, and in 1903 Manny Drachman acquired the 13 acres of Carillo Gardens, located between the east bank of the Santa Cruz River and Main Street. Carillo Gardens featured swimming ponds and a grove of shady cottonwoods. Drachman renamed the property Elysian Grove, built an outdoor theater, a saloon — and a baseball park. His Elysian Grove team was the most active club to date, and by this time professionals frequently barnstormed in the area after the close of the regular season back east.

In 1928 Tucson fielded its first professional club in the Class D Arizona State League, and after three seasons switched to the Arizona-Texas League. After the Arizona-Texas League disbanded in July 1932, Tucson did not resume professional play until 1947, when the Cowboys rejoined the circuit, now elevated to Class C

*Tucson baseball team, 1893. For decades major leaguers would play winter ball in Tucson and other western locales after the close of the season back East.*
— Courtesy Arizona Historical Library, Tucson

status. Tucson played in the Arizona-Texas League from 1947 through 1954, except for a season in the Class C Southwest International League in 1951. The Cowboys became charter members of the Class C Arizona-Mexico League in 1955, but after the circuit ceased play in 1958, there was no more professional baseball in Tucson until the Pacific Coast League beckoned.

The Tucson Toros were the top farm club of the Chicago White Sox from 1969–72. Other affiliations have been with the Oakland A's, 1973–76; the Texas Rangers, 1977–79; and the Houston Astros, 1980–88. Home of the Toros was 9,500-seat Hi Corbett Field, a concrete structure built in the 1920s and named after Hiram Corbett, longtime president of the Old Pueblo Baseball Club. In 20 PCL seasons, the Toros enjoyed just five winning records and two playoff appearances, but Tucson's support of baseball remained surprisingly strong.

In the Toros' first season Tucson fans cheered a batting champ, lefthanded outfielder Angel Bravo (.342), who also led the league in triples with 16, the all-time Tucson record. In 1970 right-hander Darrell Brandon (15–10) was the strikeout champ, out-fielder Jose Ortiz (.308) was the Toros' best hitter, and Chuck

Brinkman led all catchers with 75 assists while cutting down 38 runners attempting to steal. The next year Steve Huntz (.299) was named shortstop on the All-Star team, while third sacker Mickey McGuire (.349) missed the batting championship by just three percentage points.

The 1972 Toros were last in team hitting and ERA, and brought up the bottom of the standings. Dissatisfied with the quality of players assigned to Tucson, the Toros affiliated with Oakland, and the move immediately paid off. Managed by former big league catcher Sherm Lollar, the Toros won the Eastern Division title with the best record of 1973, before losing to Spokane in the championship playoff. Tucson jumped from last to first place in team hitting, paced by All-Star second-baseman Manny Trillo (.312), All-Star catcher Larry Haney (.287), third sacker Phil Garner (.289), and Jose Morales (.355 in 76 games), big league veteran Jay Johnstone (.347 in 62 games), and John Summers (.333 in 94 games).

The pitching staff also improved from last to first place in ERA, while lanky righthander Glenn Abbott (18–8) led the PCL in victories. Gary Waslewski (8–3 and a 2.20 ERA in 44 appearances) was the team's best reliever. Attendance exceeded 233,000, the best in Tucson history, and in one game an overflow crowd of more than 10,000 saw the Toros record a 3–0 victory.

Lollar returned in 1974, and so did the popular Phil Garner (.330 in 96 games). Other returnees — Manny Trillo (.253) and John Summers (.263) — were off form, and the Toros dropped back to last place in team hitting. Glenn Abbott was around for just 11 games (6–2), and with little pitching, Tucson nosedived to the poorest record in the league. Fortunes improved in 1975, but the next year — for the second time in three seasons — the Toros finished last, despite the efforts of All-Star shortstop Wayne Gross (.324) and slugging outfielder Rich McKinney (.317, 22 HRs, 95 RBIs), who logged a record sixth season in a Toros uniform.

Again dissatisfied with the player pool, Tucson affiliated with the Rangers. Although the team did not jell, there were numerous exciting players in 1977. They included third baseman Kurt Bevaqua (.352); outfielder-first baseman Pat Putnam (.301 with 102 RBIs); shortstop LaRue Washington (.300 with 43 stolen bases); and outfielders Lewis Beasley (.328) and Richard Sweet (.323). The next year Tucson led the PCL in team hitting (.308), as Washington (.324 with 50 steals) and Putnam (.309, 21 HRs, 96 RBIs) again had good seasons. Even better were outfielders Mike Bucci (.331) and Billy Sample (.352, 18 HRs, 99 RBIs), who led the PCL in runs (141) and walks (109), and who was named AAA Minor League Player of the Year. Switch hitter Mike Hart (.303 with 122 walks) led the 1979 offense, but the team was another disappointment.

Again the Toros switched affiliations, and association with the Astros produced an immediate playoff team. Managed by Tucson native Jimmy Johnson, the 1980 Toros led the PCL in team hitting. Outfielder Danny Heep (.343) was the batting champ, and catcher Alan Knicely (.318, 22 HRs, 105 RBIs) was the RBI leader. Outfielder Gary Rajsich (.321, 21 HRs, 99 RBIs) and Gary Woods (.313 with 36 steals), along with third baseman Brod Perkins (.312) and second sacker Jimmy Sexton (.296 with 55 steals) contributed to a potent offense. The mound corps had unusual depth, including righthanders Billy Smith (12–4), Richard Williams (14–11), Gary Wilson (12–9) and Gordon Pladson (10–5 in 17 games), and southpaw Brent Strom (11–6). This solid club won the first half in the South, came close in the second half, but lost to Albuquerque in the division playoff.

Attendance was more than 207,000 in 1980, but even though six straight losing seasons ensued, fan support remained strong (an overflow crowd of 12,863 turned out for a 1981 victory over Salt Lake City). Stars of 1981 included second baseman Johnny Ray (.349 with a league-leading 50 doubles) and third sacker Greg Cypret (.307 with a league-leading 13 triples). The next year, fans again enjoyed Cypret (.288), as well as outfielders Bob Pate (.347), Jim Tracy (.318 with 100 RBIs), Tim Tolman (.302) and Larry Ray (.294), and switch-hitting second baseman Billy Doran (.302). In 1983 Larry Ray (.307) and Greg Cypret (.297) once more played well, along with stolen base champ Scott Loucks (.287 with 71 thefts) and righthander Jeff Heathcock (10–3 in 15 games).

Future big league star Glenn Davis played 15 games in Tucson at the end of 1983, and in 1984 the lefthanded slugger became a fixture at first base for the Toros (.297 with 94 RBIs). Davis finished the year with Houston (.213), but started 1985 with the Toros (.305 in 60 games) before moving up to the Astros for good. Other fine players in 1985 were outfielders Chris Jones (.338), who also was called up at mid-season, and Eric Bullock (.319 with 48 steals).

In 1984 Canadian businessman Bill Yuill bought the Toros, and two years later sought league permission to move the team to Winnipeg. The three Canadian cities supported the move, but the six American franchises voted down the proposal. On the playing field, former big leaguers Dan Driessen, Dale Berra and Matt Keough wore Toros uniforms during part of 1986. Lefthanded outfielder Ty Gainey (.351) became Tucson's third batting champ, and Jeff Heathcock (10–8) returned to play part of his fourth consecutive season in Tucson. In 1987 Heathcock (11–6) was the club's leading pitcher as the Toros somehow recorded a winning season, even though 22 players were juggled between Tucson and Houston.

Heathcock (3–5) played part of a sixth season for Tucson in 1988, although Anthony Kelley (13–6) was more effective. Outfielder Cameron Drew (.356), catcher Craig Boggio (.320), and second baseman Craig Smajstria (.310) were the best offensive performers. After the season ended, Yuill sold the Toros to Richard M. Holtzman, owner of four other minor league franchises.

| Year | Record | Pcg. | Finish |
|------|--------|------|--------|
| 1969 | 60-86 | .411 | Seventh |
| 1970 | 81-65 | .555 | Fourth |
| 1971 | 69-76 | .476 | Seventh |
| 1972 | 60-88 | .405 | Eighth |
| 1973 | 84-60 | .583 | First — won Eastern Division, lost playoff |
| 1974 | 65-78 | .455 | Eighth |
| 1975 | 72-71 | .503 | Fourth |
| 1976 | 54-88 | .380 | Eighth |
| 1977 | 65-73 | .471 | Sixth |
| 1978 | 69-71 | .493 | Seventh |
| 1979 | 74-74 | .500 | Fifth |
| 1980 | 87-59 | .596 | First — lost opener |
| 1981 | 57-82 | .410 | Ninth |
| 1982 | 59-83 | .415 | Ninth |
| 1983 | 68-74 | .479 | Sixth |
| 1984 | 69-71 | .493 | Sixth |
| 1985 | 65-75 | .464 | Ninth |
| 1986 | 71-72 | .497 | Fifth |
| 1987 | 75-67 | .528 | Fifth |
| 1988 | 68-75 | .476 | Sixth |

# Tulsa
# (Oilers)

In 1905 Tulsa, a booming oil town, obtained its first professional franchise in the Missouri Valley League. The Tulsa Oilers moved to the Oklahoma-Arkansas-Kansas League in 1907 and the Oklahoma-Kansas League the following year. The Oilers played in the Western Association in 1910 and 1911, tried the Oklahoma State League in 1912, then returned to the Western Association from 1914 through 1917. The Oilers joined the Western League in 1919, won five pennants, then became a part of the Texas League from 1933 through 1965, reeling off 21 playoff appearances during the previous 28 seasons.

Through the years, the Oilers played in a number of ballparks, beginning with Athletic Park on West Archer. After a few seasons, the ballpark was moved to East Archer near First Street, then a few years later to South Main. When the Oilers joined the Western League in 1919, McNulty Park was built in 22 days at 10th and Elgin. A decade later, McNulty Park was sold to commercial interests and demolished, which forced the Oilers to drop out of baseball in 1930. Playing on a diamond in front of the old fairgrounds race track grandstand, the Oilers rejoined the Western League in 1931 and 1932. In 1934, after a year in the Texas League, the Oilers moved from their makeshift grandstand diamond to a new wooden park just to the north. First called Tulsa County Stadium, the facility later was known as Texas League Park, then Oiler Park.

By the 1960s the metropolitan area had grown to more than 500,000, and Tulsa's continued success in the Texas League fostered attendance exceeding 200,000 for three years in a row, 1963 through 1965. Owner-president A. Ray Smith thus was encouraged to try AAA ball. The Arkansas Travelers were happy to assume the St. Louis Cardinals' AA franchise in the Texas League, which allowed Smith's Oilers to replace the Travs in the PCL.

Tulsa roared into the PCL in 1966, racking up the best record in the 12-team league, winning the Western Division, and taking the team batting title (.289) by 14 points. Muscular outfielder Walt Williams (.330) was the hitting champ, but offensive fireworks were added by outfielders Alex Johnson (.355 in 80 games), Ted Savage (.317) and John Kindl (.314), second baseman Jose Laboy

(.308), catcher David Ricketts (.327), infielder Bobby Tolan (.333 in 44 games), and third baseman Ed Spiezio (.301). Like many of the hitters, southpaw Steve Carlton (9–5) spent much of the season with the Cardinals, and Tulsa lost to the Seattle Angels, Eastern Division titlists, in seven games in the championship playoffs.

Jose Laboy (.298) was one of the few returnees in 1967, while catcher Pat Corrales (.274) was one of the few solid newcomers. Although fans suffered through a losing season, 46-year-old manager and future Hall of Famer Warren Spahn treated Tulsans to three pitching performances.

The next year Spahn led the Oilers to the PCL pennant. For the second time in three years the Oilers won the team hitting title and produced the batting champ, outfielder Jim Hicks (.366 with 23 HRs and 85 RBIs in just 117 games). Jose Laboy (.292, 15 HRs, 100 RBIs) led the PCL in RBIs and doubles, while first baseman Joe Hague (.293, 23 HRs, 99 RBIs) and catcher Danny Breeden (.273) were the best in the league at their positions. Righthander Pete Mikkelsen (16–4 with a 1.91 ERA) was the ERA champ, Mikkelsen and starter-reliever Sal Campisi (12–3) led the league in winning percentage, Charles Taylor (18–7) tied for most victories, and southpaw Dick LeMay (16–10) rounded off a fine pitching staff. The Oilers reeled off the best record in the PCL, raced away with the Eastern Division title by a margin of 18 games, then defeated Spokane, four games to one, for the pennant.

The Oilers ended their successful three-year PCL tenure in the AAA realignment following the 1968 season. Tulsa was one of four PCL teams which joined the newly reorganized American Association. After eight years Smith, frustrated by the city's persistent refusal to build a new stadium, moved his franchise to New Orleans. But construction executive Bill Rollings, a boyhood fan of the Oilers, and country music star Roy Clark bought the AA Lafayette franchise and installed the Texas League "Drillers" into Tulsa's decaying ballpark. In 1981 the Drillers moved into a new 7,300-seat facility located just east of old Texas League Park. Tulsa County Stadium has featured strong fan support for the Drillers, and another venture into an AAA league could be readily accomplished.

| Year | Record | Pcg. | Finish |
|------|--------|------|--------|
| 1966 | 85-62 | .578 | First — won Eastern Division, lost playoff |
| 1967 | 65-79 | .451 | Eleventh |
| 1968 | 95-53 | .642 | First — won Eastern Division and playoff |

# Vancouver
# *(Mounties, Canadians)*

Although Vancouver did not enter the PCL until 1956, Coast League baseball was nothing new to fans of the British Columbia city. Hardcore baseball enthusiasts from Vancouver long had listened to regular radio broadcasts of Seattle games, and frequent trips were made down to Sick's Seattle Stadium to root for what Vancouverites considered "their" team. Professional ball in Vancouver dated back to 1905 and a season in the Northwestern League. Vancouver then played in the Class B circuit from 1907 through 1917, followed by a year in the Class B Pacific Coast International League. There were two more seasons, 1920 and 1921, in the Pacific Coast International League, then Vancouver became a charter member of the Class B Western International League. This circuit folded at mid-season and Vancouver was without pro ball until the league was revived 15 years later. The Vancouver Capilanos participated from 1937 through 1942 and from 1946 through 1954, when the Western International League disbanded for good.

A year later Vancouver became the first Canadian city to hold a PCL franchise. Until 1951 the home of professional baseball in Vancouver was Athletic Park, a diminutive facility located on Fifth Avenue. Capilano Stadium, patterned on Sick's Seattle Stadium, was built at Ontario and Thirty-third, adjacent to magnificent Queen Elizabeth Park. In recent years, when a sufficient number of non-paying onlookers seat themselves on the hill beyond the right field fence, concessionaires are sent out to hawk food and drinks. Capilano Stadium was only five years old when Oakland owners moved the franchise to Vancouver, and 8,149 eager fans turned out to watch the first home game of the Mounties. Lefty O'Doul, a PCL institution and the manager, was especially helpful to fireballer Ryne Duren. But the rest of the pitching staff was weak, and the Mounties finished last in team hitting and fielding — and in the standings.

After the season restaurateur Nat Bailey and several other Vancouver businessmen bought the franchise for $150,000. With local leadership and a contending team, attendance more than doubled in 1957 to a league-leading 306,145. Lefthander Morrie Martin (14–4 with a sparkling 1.90 ERA) posted the PCL's best ERA and winning percentage. Other fine pitchers were righthander Ervin Palica (15–12) and southpaw Don Ferrarese (11–5). The best hitters were outfielder Lenny Green (.311), shortstop Carl Peterson (.298), and slugging first baseman Jim Marshall (.284, 30 HRs, 102 RBIs). The Mounties battled San Francisco for the pennant all year before settling for second place.

Vancouver dropped to third in 1958, primarily because of another last-place finish in team batting. The pitching staff again was strong, led by ERA champ George Bamberger (15–11, 2.45 ERA) and returnee Ervin Palica (15–13). Vancouver made a successful bid for the All-Star Game, and 8,349 fans swarmed into Capilano Stadium for mid-season exhibition.

In 1959 future superstar Brooks Robinson (.331 in 42 games) flashed his extraordinary skills before being brought up to Baltimore, and second baseman Marv Breeding was the stolen base champ. Chuck Estrada (14–6) led another good mound corps, along with Mountie veterans Ervin Palica (13–10) and George Bamberger (11–7). Again the Mounties were contenders all year before finishing second, just 1½ games from the pennant. The Mounties dropped to next-to-last in 1960, although southpaw Chester Nichols (18–6) led the league in victories and winning percentage.

Vancouver rebounded to another second-place finish in 1961. The Mounties led the PCL in team hitting behind first baseman Frank Torre (.307) and third sacker Edwin Charles (.305). Ron Piche (14-7 with a 2.26 ERA) won the ERA title, and George Bamberger (12–6 after going 12–12 in 1960) logged another good season. The next year Bamberger again was reliable (12–12), but the Mounties plunged to the bottom of the league in team hitting and finished next-to-last in the standings. Attendance dropped to just 88,075, and Vancouver withdrew from the PCL.

Two years later the Mounties were back, replacing the Dallas franchise. This time Nat Bailey kept his team in the league from 1965 through 1969, enjoying winning seasons the first three years. During a game with Seattle at Capilano Stadium on May 11, 1966, a free-for-all erupted when Mounties outfielder Ricardo Joseph charged the mound after being hit with a pitch. First baseman Santiago Rosario walloped Seattle catcher Merritt Ranew on the head with a bat, inflicting a concussion and a four-inch gash. Ranew was out for the season — and so was Rosario, suspended for a year by PCL President Dewey Soriano.

*Vancouver fans lined up at Nat Bailey Stadium to obtain player autographs.*
— Author's photo

In 1968 the Mounties were hapless, dropping to last place in a 12-team league. Another losing season followed, lowering 1969 attendance to merely 62,666. Financially it was no longer feasible for Nat Bailey to maintain the team, and after the 1969 season Vancouver again dropped out of the league, to be replaced by Salt Lake City. This time Vancouver was out of baseball for eight seasons, but when new ownership brought the city back into the PCL in 1978, the name of the refurbished ballpark was fittingly changed to Nat Bailey Stadium.

The new manager was Jim Marshall, the hard-hitting first baseman for the 1957 Mounties. The team now was called the Canadians, and the parent Oakland A's stocked the roster with solid ball players. First baseman Jerry Tabb (.357), catcher Bruce Robinson (.299) and outfielder Derek Bryant (.297) led the 1978 Canadians to a winning record. The next year there was another strong club, featuring All-Star second baseman Lenn Sakata (.300) and outfielder Billy Severns (.318). The star of 1979 was righthander Mark Bomback (22–7, 2.56 ERA), who led the league in victories, shutouts (5), ERA, innings pitched, winning percentage and complete games, and who became the first (and last) 20-game winner in the PCL since 1966.

In 1980 the Canadians made the PCL playoffs for the first time in Vancouver history, but were defeated in the opening round. The lineup bristled with good hitters, including outfielders Bobby Smith (.316) and Marshall Edwards (.291 with 68 steals), switch-hitting second baseman Mike Henderson (.305), infielder Tim Flannery (.346 in 47 games), and catcher Ned Yost (.309 in 80 games), who was called up to finish the season with the parent Milwaukee Braves.

Vancouver did not enjoy another winning season until 1985. In 1983 outfielder Dion James (.336) and third baseman Randy Ready (.329) were impressive. Ready returned at the end of the next season (.325 in 43 games), then started 1985 (.326 in 52 games) and was converted to the outfield before going back to the Brewers.

In 1985 Ready contributed to Vancouver's first PCL championship. Manager Tom Trebelhorn led the Canadians to first place in the Northern Division during the second half of the season, and with momentum the Canadians swept Calgary in three straight to claim the division title, then took three from Phoenix to win the pennant. Switch-hitting outfielder Mike Felder (.314 with 61 steals) was the stolen base champ. DH Carlos Ponce (.320) and righthander Rick Waits (10–5 in 17 games) were other key members of the championship team, along with popular outfielder Doug Loman (.294), who had spent five seasons with Vancouver (his best year was 1984, when he hit .324 with 102 RBIs and led the PCL in hits).

The Canadians, managed in 1986 by Terry Bevington, roared to the best record in the league. Named to the All-Star team were outfielder Glenn Braggs (.360 in 90 games), catcher B. J. Surhoff (.308), and righthanded reliever Chris Bosio (7–3, 2.28 ERA). Strong contributions also were made by righthanders Mike Birkbeck (12–6) and Bob Gibson (10–4 in 16 games), shortstop Edgar Diaz (.315), and infielder-outfielder Jim Paciorek (.309). This talented club beat Tacoma in the playoff opener to repeat as Northern Division titlists, and went to the last game of the finals before falling to Las Vegas.

After failing to make the playoffs in 1987, Vancouver changed affiliations to the Chicago White Sox. Terry Bevington, who had skippered the 1986 champs (and who had caught briefly with the Canadians in 1980), was rehired after a one-year absence. Once again he led Vancouver into the playoffs, winning another Northern Division championship with a three-game sweep of Portland, before losing to Las Vegas in the finals. Adam Peterson (14–7), Jeff Bittiger (4–1 in 5 games with a 1.08 ERA), starter-reliever Joel Davis (7–1) and Jack Hardy (9–5), and relievers Donn Pall (5–2, 2.23 ERA) and southpaw Ken Patterson (6–5, 3.23 ERA) led a deep mound corps. Second baseman Mike Woodard (.332) and outfielders Dave Gallagher (.336) and Lance Johnson (.307 with 49 stolen bases) sparked the offense.

When Vancouver resumed PCL play in 1978, an announced long-range objective was the construction of a domed stadium with the hope of attracting a major league franchise. B. C. Place Stadium opened in 1982, and five years later General Manager Stu Kehoe played the first eight games of the season under the dome. Even after opening the season in a Southern Division city, the Canadians customarily played early home games before tiny groups of fans shivering beneath blankets. Domeball has permitted Kehoe to save money by avoiding rainouts and extreme cold, and the 1988 schedule arranged the first 11 games for B. C. Place. Minor league "crowds" rattle around in the 50,000-seat facility, and the balance of the schedule is played in beautiful, intimate Nat Bailey Stadium, but the Canadians have brought domeball to the Coast League.

| Year | Record | Pcg. | Finish |
|------|--------|------|--------|
| 1956 | 67-98 | .406 | Eighth |
| 1957 | 97-70 | .581 | Second |
| 1958 | 79-73 | .520 | Third |
| 1959 | 82-69 | .543 | Second |
| 1960 | 68-84 | .447 | Seventh |
| 1961 | 87-67 | .565 | Second |
| 1962 | 72-79 | .477 | Seventh |
| 1965 | 77-69 | .527 | Fifth |
| 1966 | 77-71 | .520 | Sixth |
| 1967 | 77-69 | .527 | Fourth |
| 1968 | 58-88 | .397 | Twelfth |
| 1969 | 71-73 | .493 | Fifth |
| 1978 | 74-65 | .532 | Fourth |
| 1979 | 79-68 | .537 | Third |
| 1980 | 79-60 | .568 | Fifth — lost opener |
| 1981 | 56-76 | .424 | Ninth |
| 1982 | 72-72 | .500 | Sixth |
| 1983 | 60-80 | .429 | Ninth |

| 1984 | 71-71 | .500 | Fourth |
|------|-------|------|--------|
| 1985 | 79-64 | .552 | Third — won opener and finals |
| 1986 | 85-53 | .616 | First — won opener, lost finals |
| 1987 | 72-72 | .500 | Sixth |
| 1988 | 85-57 | .599 | Second — won opener, lost finals |

# Venice
# (Tigers)

For four seasons, 1909–12, Peter Maier operated his PCL club in Vernon, a tiny suburb north of Los Angeles. In 1913 the franchise was shifted 14 miles to the west, to the beach-front community of Venice. It was hoped that significant attendance could be generated from Los Angeles baseball fans. Most "home" games for the Venice Tigers were scheduled to be held in Washington Park, headquarters of the Angels, while the Los Angeles team was on the road. Only Sunday morning and a few holiday games were staged in Venice.

Managed by fiery Hap Hogan, the first Venice team went 107–102, good for a third-place finish. There were three 20-game winners on the pitching staff — Spider Baum (23–19), Bruce Hitt (22–15), and Bob Koestner (24–26), who led the league by working 411 innings. Specs Harkness (16–12) and John Raleigh (12–10) rounded out a fine mound corps.

Although the 1914 record was better, 113–98, Venice dropped to fifth in the standings. On March 14 manager Hap Hogan — whose real name was Wallace Bray — died suddenly at the age of 37. Hitt returned to lead the pitchers (25–18 with a 2.05 ERA in 364 innings, his fifth consecutive 20-win season as a Tiger), while Big Ed Klepfer, only 4–7 in 1913, became one of the best hurlers in the PCL (23–15, with a league-leading 212 strikeouts in 378 innings). Doc White had a good season (17–13), after 13 years in the big leagues, and ended his career after one more year in a Tiger uniform.

Tiger fans enjoyed a hard-hitting outfield in both seasons: Dick Bayless (.324 in 1913 to lead the PCL, .296 in 1914), Paul Meloan (.275 and .304), and Sugar Kane (.280 and .288). The catcher was Rowdy Elliott (.273 and .309). In 1914 the club was bolstered by outfielder Joe Wilhoit (.349) and first baseman Babe Borton

*Venice Tigers, 1913. Batting champ Henry Bayless is on the ground, third from right, and pitching great Spider Baum (325 minor league victories, 261 in the PCL) is standing second from right.*

— Courtesy Ted Leach

(.307). Borton was the best fielding first sacker in the PCL, Bayless and Meloan led all outfielders, and Venice led all clubs in team fielding.

Bayless returned in 1915, but had a poor season. Most of the other key players were gone, and attendance was weak. On July 6 the franchise was moved back to Vernon, marking the end of Venice's two-and-a-half seasons in professional baseball.

| Year | Record | Pcg. | Finish |
|------|--------|------|--------|
| 1913 | 107-102 | .512 | Third |
| 1914 | 113-98 | .535 | Fourth |

# Vernon
# (Tigers)

After two years as a four-team circuit, in 1909 the PCL again went to six clubs by readmitting a Sacramento franchise and by placing a team in Vernon, a small town just north of Los Angeles.

It was hoped that Los Angeles fans would provide primary support while the Angels were out of town. Angels owner Henry Berry consented to infringement of his territorial rights so that a sixth team could be established, and the four existing clubs made players available to Vernon. The Vernon Tigers were owned by Peter Maier, who had prospered in the meat packing business and who built Maier Park for his new team.

The first Vernon Tigers were weak offensively and finished last. The club's best hitter was a pitcher appropriately named Hitt, who batted .298 while going 15–29 from the mound. The top hurler was Schaefer, who somehow fashioned a 20–16 record. In 1910 the leading batter again was a pitcher, Willett, who hit .276. Although Hitt dropped to .183 at the plate, he was one of the league's best pitchers at 26–18. Willett was 20–19, Brackenridge was 20–22, and Carson was 19–16. Because of the fine pitching staff, the Tigers stayed in the pennant race until late in the season, and the club acquired a reputation as scrappy and colorful.

In 1911 Vernon enjoyed an offensive turnaround, leading the PCL in hitting and finishing a close second to Portland. Outfielders Stinson (.317) and McDonnell (.292) hit well, along with second baseman Brashear (.297) and first sacker Patterson (.285). Again there was a fine pitching staff: Hitt (21–15, with a .314 batting average), Castleton (22–13), Raleigh (20–18), Stewart (19–12, and a .293 batting average), and Carson (13–7).

The Tigers were even better in 1912, but lost the pennant on the last day of the race. Dick Bayless, who would become a fixture in the Tiger outfield, hit .318 in his first season. Brashear (.314) again hit well, and outfielders Kane (.310) and Carlisle (.283) also were offensive leaders. Once more Hitt (21–12), Stewart (18–12), and Castleton (13–8) led a strong pitching staff.

In 1913 Maier moved his Tigers to Venice, another Los Angeles suburb 14 miles due west on the coast. The team continued to win, but Venice was too small to provide adequate fan support, and most of the games were played at the Angels' Washington Park. On July 6, 1915, Maier brought the Tigers back to Vernon. In 1916 and 1917, Vernon was dead last in team hitting, and in 1916 the leading batter again was a pitcher, Hess (.323 and 13–11). Art Fromme, a 10-year veteran of the National League, led the PCL in ERA in 1916 (1.92 and a 23–14 record). Fromme again was strong in 1917 (21–19), while John Picus Quinn, a longtime major leaguer who was temporarily out of the bigs because of a flirtation with the Federal League, enjoyed an impressive season (24–20 with 409 innings pitched and a 2.36 ERA).

Although the circuit expanded to eight teams in 1919, Vernon began one of the great dynasties in PCL history, finishing first for three years in a row. In 1918 Vernon had a narrow lead over Los Angeles when the schedule was halted on July 14 by the "work or fight" order. But because of the abbreviated season, PCL directors mandated a best-of-nine playoff series between the Tigers and Angels. Los Angeles won, five games to two, claiming the championship, but the PCL Record Book acknowledges Vernon as the 1918 pennant winner.

The 1919 schedule was played in full, and Vernon edged Los Angeles in a dramatic closing-day doubleheader before an overflow crowd of 22,000 in Washington Park. But during the last two weeks of the season, rumors proliferated that opposing players had been bribed to insure Vernon the flag. It was the year of the "Black Sox," the tainted World Series that would result in the expulsion from baseball of eight players in 1920 for collusion with gamblers. PCL President William H. McCarthy beat Commissioner Kenesaw Mountain Landis by expelling Tiger first baseman Babe Borton (.305), along with other players, from the league for suspected activities in the scandal.

Vernon bounced back in 1920 with a third-straight first-place finish. Bill Essick had proved to be a skillful manager, deftly handling a stable of fine players. Californian Bob Meusel turned in a fine season in 1919 (.337) before launching a long career with the New York Yankees. Chester Chadbourne was consistent in the outfield (.288, .294 and .286 in the championship seasons), and outfielders Stump Edington (.302) and Ed High (.317) were in top form in 1919. John Mitchell was the shortstop and Albert De Vormer (.302 in 1918) was the catcher in all three pennant years. The aging Art Fromme turned in a final big season in 1919 (20–7), while Wheezer Dell was outstanding in 1919 (16–3) and 1920 (27–15). Happy Finneran (14–4 in 1919) and Frank Shellenback (18–12 in 1920) contributed good years, while Willis Mitchell (25–13) led the league in strikeouts in 1920.

There was a slow decline after the dynasty years, although the Tigers finished second in 1922. Outfield mainstays during the 1920s were Pete Schneider (.325 in 1921, .346 in 1922, .360 in 1923,

*Vernon Tigers, 1919 PCL champs. Silent film comedian Fatty Arbuckle (center in dark suit) was team president. Notable players included Happy Finneran (number 2), Bob Meusel (3), John Mitchell (6), Willis Mitchell (7), Wheezer Dell (9), Stump Edington (10), Ed High (11), Al DeVormer (13), Art Fromme (14), Chester Chadbourne (15), manager Bill Essick (19), and Gus Fisher (20).*

— Courtesy Ted Leach

and .328 in 1924), Ed High (.340 in 1923), and Chester Chadbourne (.317 in 1923). The catcher was an American League veteran, Truck Hannah (.305 in 1921, .346 in 1923, and .318 in 1924). In 1923 this hard-hitting crew traveled to Salt Lake City and hammered out a 35–11 victory over the Bees; Pete Schneider blasted five home runs and 14 RBIs, and almost uncorked a sixth four-bagger in his last turn at bat. There were 11 home runs in the game, a record the Tigers and Bees tied in a 1924 slugfest. The record stood until 1988, when Colorado Springs and Phoenix blasted 13 homers out of Spurgeon Stadium, compact home of the Sky Sox.

Tiger fans enjoyed several fine pitching performances during the postchampionship years. Wheezer Dell was 28–14 in 1921 and 23–17 the next year. Frank Shellenback was dependable season after season, and Ken Penner went 24–13 in 1924. There were four 20-game winners in 1922: Dell (23–17), Jess Doyle (20–15), Seattle Bill James (21–12), and Jakie May, who won the pitcher's Triple Crown (35–9, 238 strikeouts and a 1.84 ERA), leading the PCL in victories, strikeouts and ERA, as well as winning percentage (.795).

But the Tigers finished last in 1923 and 1925. Attendance was limited by the small population of Vernon, and not enough fans came out from Los Angeles. In 1925 Edward Maier, who had assumed leadership of the club after the death of his brother Peter, sold the franchise to San Francisco backers who established the Mission club. The PCL Tigers would prove to be Vernon's only venture in Organized Baseball. But Vernon had hosted one of the Coast League's most notable dynasties, and by the time the Tigers left for San Francisco, Wrigley Field — new home of the Angels and a minor league showcase for decades — had been built two miles to the west on Vernon Avenue.

| Year | Record | Pcg. | Finish |
|------|--------|------|--------|
| 1909 | 80-131 | .379 | Sixth |
| 1910 | 113-107 | .514 | Fourth |
| 1911 | 118-88 | .573 | Second |
| 1912 | 118-83 | .587 | Second |
| 1915 | 102-104 | .495 | Fourth |
| 1916 | 115-91 | .558 | Second |
| 1917 | 84-128 | .396 | Sixth |
| 1918 | 58-44 | .569 | First — lost playoff |
| 1919 | 111-70 | .613 | First |
| 1920 | 110-88 | .556 | First |
| 1921 | 96-90 | .516 | Sixth |
| 1922 | 123-76 | .618 | Second |
| 1923 | 77-122 | .387 | Eighth |
| 1924 | 97-104 | .483 | Sixth |
| 1925 | 80-120 | .400 | Eighth |

# Pacific Coast League Records

## ANNUAL STANDINGS

During 37 seasons of Coast League play, the team which compiled the best record over the regular schedule was declared champion. But in 1904, the PCL's second season, the first postseason playoff for the championship was staged, and another playoff series was held the next year. For the following two decades, however, the only playoff was conducted in the war season of 1918. There were playoff series from 1928 through 1931, then from 1935 through 1949 and 1951. From 1952 through 1962 the pennant was awarded to the club with the best season's record, but since 1963 a postseason playoff has been conducted annually. Playoff devices have included the Shaughnessy Plan, split-season winners, and East-West or North-South division winners. * indicates playoff winners.

| 1903 | | | | 1904 | | |
|---|---|---|---|---|---|---|
| Los Angeles | 133-78 | .630 | | Tacoma * | 130-94 | .580 |
| Sacramento | 105-105 | .500 | | Los Angeles | 119-97 | .551 |
| Seattle | 98-100 | .495 | | Seattle | 114-106 | .518 |
| San Francisco | 107-110 | .493 | | Oakland | 116-109 | .516 |
| Portland | 95-108 | .468 | | San Francisco | 101-114 | .469 |
| Oakland | 89-126 | .414 | | Portland | 79-136 | .368 |

318

## 1905

| | | |
|---|---|---|
| Los Angeles * | 120-94 | .561 |
| San Francisco | 125-100 | .556 |
| Tac-Seattle | 106-107 | .498 |
| Oakland | 103-119 | .464 |
| Portland | 94-110 | .461 |
| Seattle | 93-111 | .456 |

## 1906

| | | |
|---|---|---|
| Portland | 115-60 | .657 |
| Seattle | 99-83 | .544 |
| Los Angeles | 95-87 | .522 |
| San Francisco | 91-84 | .520 |
| Oakland | 77-110 | .411 |
| Fresno | 64-117 | .353 |

## 1907

| | | |
|---|---|---|
| Los Angeles | 115-74 | .608 |
| San Francisco | 104-99 | .515 |
| Oakland | 97-101 | .489 |
| Portland | 72-114 | .388 |

## 1908

| | | |
|---|---|---|
| Los Angeles | 110-78 | .585 |
| Portland | 95-90 | .514 |
| San Francisco | 100-104 | .490 |
| Oakland | 83-116 | .417 |

## 1909

| | | |
|---|---|---|
| San Francisco | 132-80 | .622 |
| Portland | 112-87 | .563 |
| Los Angeles | 118-97 | .549 |
| Sacramento | 97-107 | .475 |
| Oakland | 88-125 | .413 |
| Vernon | 80-131 | .379 |

## 1910

| | | |
|---|---|---|
| Portland | 114-87 | .567 |
| Oakland | 112-98 | .555 |
| San Francisco | 114-106 | .518 |
| Vernon | 113-107 | .514 |
| Los Angeles | 101-121 | .455 |
| Sacramento | 83-128 | .393 |

## 1911

| | | |
|---|---|---|
| Portland | 113-79 | .589 |
| Vernon | 118-88 | .573 |
| Oakland | 111-99 | .528 |
| Sacramento | 95-109 | .466 |

| | | |
|---|---|---|
| San Francisco | 95-112 | .459 |
| Los Angeles | 82-127 | .392 |

## 1912

| | | |
|---|---|---|
| Oakland | 120-83 | .591 |
| Vernon | 118-83 | .587 |
| Los Angeles | 110-93 | .542 |
| Portland | 85-100 | .459 |
| San Francisco | 89-115 | .436 |
| Sacramento | 73-121 | .376 |

## 1913

| | | |
|---|---|---|
| Portland | 109-86 | .571 |
| Sacramento | 103-94 | .523 |
| Venice | 107-102 | .512 |
| San Francisco | 104-103 | .502 |
| Los Angeles | 100-108 | .484 |
| Oakland | 90-120 | .429 |

## 1914

| | | |
|---|---|---|
| Portland | 113-84 | .573 |
| Los Angeles | 116-94 | .552 |
| San Francisco | 115-96 | .545 |
| Venice | 113-98 | .535 |
| Missions | 90-121 | .426 |
| Oakland | 79-133 | .372 |

## 1915

| | | |
|---|---|---|
| San Francisco | 118-89 | .570 |
| Salt Lake City | 108-89 | .548 |
| Los Angeles | 110-98 | .529 |
| Vernon | 102-104 | .495 |
| Oakland | 93-113 | .451 |
| Portland | 78-116 | .402 |

## 1916

| | | |
|---|---|---|
| Los Angeles | 119-79 | .601 |
| Vernon | 115-91 | .558 |
| Salt Lake City | 99-96 | .507 |
| San Francisco | 104-102 | .504 |
| Portland | 93-98 | .487 |
| Oakland | 72-136 | .346 |

## 1917

| | | |
|---|---|---|
| San Francisco | 119-93 | .561 |
| Los Angeles | 116-94 | .552 |
| Salt Lake City | 102-97 | .513 |
| Portland | 98-102 | .490 |
| Oakland | 103-108 | .488 |
| Vernon | 84-128 | .396 |

**1918**

| Vernon | 58-44 | .569 |
|---|---|---|
| Los Angeles * | 57-47 | .548 |
| San Francisco | 51-51 | .500 |
| Sacramento | 48-48 | .500 |
| Salt Lake City | 48-49 | .495 |
| Oakland | 40-63 | .388 |

**1919**

| Vernon | 111-70 | .613 |
|---|---|---|
| Los Angeles | 108-72 | .600 |
| Salt Lake City | 88-83 | .515 |
| Sacramento | 85-83 | .506 |
| Oakland | 86-96 | .473 |
| San Francisco | 84-94 | .473 |
| Portland | 78-96 | .448 |
| Seattle | 62-108 | .365 |

**1920**

| Vernon | 110-88 | .556 |
|---|---|---|
| Seattle | 102-91 | .528 |
| Los Angeles | 102-95 | .517 |
| San Francisco | 103-96 | .517 |
| Salt Lake City | 95-92 | .508 |
| Oakland | 95-103 | .480 |
| Sacramento | 89-109 | .449 |
| Portland | 81-103 | .440 |

**1921**

| Los Angeles | 108-80 | .574 |
|---|---|---|
| Sacramento | 105-80 | .568 |
| San Francisco | 106-82 | .564 |
| Seattle | 103-82 | .557 |
| Oakland | 101-85 | .543 |
| Vernon | 96-90 | .516 |
| Salt Lake City | 73-110 | .399 |
| Portland | 51-134 | .276 |

**1922**

| San Francisco | 127-72 | .638 |
|---|---|---|
| Vernon | 123-76 | .618 |
| Los Angeles | 111-88 | .558 |
| Salt Lake City | 95-106 | .473 |
| Seattle | 90-107 | .457 |
| Oakland | 88-112 | .446 |
| Portland | 87-112 | .437 |
| Sacramento | 76-124 | .380 |

**1923**

| San Francisco | 124-77 | .617 |
|---|---|---|
| Sacramento | 112-87 | .563 |
| Portland | 107-89 | .546 |
| Seattle | 99-97 | .505 |
| Salt Lake City | 94-105 | .472 |
| Los Angeles | 93-109 | .460 |
| Oakland | 91-111 | .450 |
| Vernon | 77-122 | .387 |

**1924**

| Seattle | 109-91 | .545 |
|---|---|---|
| Los Angeles | 107-92 | .538 |
| San Francisco | 108-93 | .537 |
| Oakland | 103-99 | .510 |
| Salt Lake City | 101-100 | .502 |
| Vernon | 97-104 | .483 |
| Portland | 88-110 | .444 |
| Sacramento | 88-112 | .440 |

**1925**

| San Francisco | 138-71 | .641 |
|---|---|---|
| Salt Lake City | 116-84 | .580 |
| Seattle | 103-91 | .531 |
| Los Angeles | 105-93 | .530 |
| Portland | 92-104 | .470 |
| Oakland | 88-112 | .442 |
| Sacramento | 82-119 | .408 |
| Vernon | 80-120 | .400 |

**1926**

| Los Angeles | 121-81 | .599 |
|---|---|---|
| Oakland | 111-92 | .547 |
| Mission | 106-94 | .530 |
| Portland | 100-101 | .498 |
| Sacramento | 99-102 | .493 |
| Hollywood | 94-107 | .468 |
| Seattle | 89-111 | .445 |
| San Francisco | 84-116 | .420 |

**1927**

| Oakland | 120-75 | .615 |
|---|---|---|
| San Francisco | 106-90 | .541 |
| Seattle | 98-92 | .516 |
| Sacramento | 100-95 | .513 |
| Portland | 95-95 | .500 |
| Hollywood | 92-104 | .469 |
| Mission | 86-110 | .439 |
| Los Angeles | 80-116 | .408 |

## 1928

| San Francisco * | 120-71 | .628 |
| Hollywood | 112-79 | .586 |
| Sacramento | 112-79 | .586 |
| Mission | 99-92 | .518 |
| Oakland | 91-100 | .476 |
| Los Angeles | 87-104 | .455 |
| Portland | 79-112 | .335 |

## 1929

| Mission | 123-78 | .612 |
| San Francisco | 114-87 | .567 |
| Hollywood * | 113-89 | .559 |
| Oakland | 111-91 | .549 |
| Los Angeles | 104-98 | .510 |
| Portland | 90-112 | .446 |
| Sacramento | 85-117 | .421 |
| Seattle | 67-135 | .332 |

## 1930

| Hollywood * | 119-81 | .595 |
| Los Angeles | 113-84 | .574 |
| Sacramento | 102-96 | .515 |
| San Francisco | 101-98 | .508 |
| Oakland | 97-103 | .485 |
| Seattle | 92-107 | .462 |
| Mission | 91-110 | .453 |
| Portland | 81-117 | .409 |

## 1931

| San Francisco | 107-80 | .572 |
| Hollywood | 104-83 | .556 |
| Portland | 100-87 | .535 |
| Los Angeles | 98-89 | .524 |
| Oakland | 86-101 | .460 |
| Sacramento | 86-101 | .460 |
| Mission | 84-103 | .449 |
| Seattle | 83-104 | .444 |

## 1932

| Portland | 111-78 | .587 |
| Hollywood | 106-83 | .561 |
| Sacramento | 101-88 | .534 |
| San Francisco | 96-90 | .516 |
| Los Angeles | 96-93 | .508 |
| Seattle | 90-95 | .486 |
| Oakland | 80-107 | .428 |
| Mission | 71-117 | .378 |

## 1933

| Los Angeles | 114-73 | .609 |
| Portland | 105-77 | .577 |
| Hollywood | 107-80 | .572 |
| Sacramento | 96-85 | .530 |
| Oakland | 93-92 | .502 |
| San Francisco | 81-106 | .433 |
| Mission | 79-108 | .422 |
| Seattle | 65-119 | .353 |

## 1934

| Los Angeles | 137-50 | .733 |
| Mission | 101-85 | .543 |
| Hollywood | 97-88 | .524 |
| San Francisco | 93-95 | .495 |
| Oakland | 80-98 | .449 |
| Seattle | 81-102 | .443 |
| Sacramento | 79-109 | .420 |
| Portland | 66-117 | .361 |

## 1935

| San Francisco * | 103-70 | .595 |
| Los Angeles | 98-76 | .563 |
| Oakland | 91-83 | .523 |
| Portland | 87-86 | .503 |
| Mission | 87-87 | .500 |
| Hollywood | 73-99 | .483 |
| Seattle | 80-93 | .462 |
| Sacramento | 75-100 | .429 |

## 1936

| Portland * | 96-79 | .549 |
| Oakland | 95-81 | .540 |
| San Diego | 95-81 | .540 |
| Seattle | 93-82 | .531 |
| Los Angeles | 88-88 | .500 |
| Mission | 88-88 | .500 |
| San Francisco | 83-93 | .472 |
| Sacramento | 65-111 | .369 |

## 1937

| Sacramento | 102-76 | .573 |
| San Francisco | 98-80 | .551 |
| San Diego * | 97-81 | .545 |
| Portland | 90-86 | .511 |
| Los Angeles | 90-88 | .506 |
| Seattle | 81-96 | .458 |
| Oakland | 79-98 | .446 |
| Mission | 73-105 | .410 |

**1938**

| | | |
|---|---|---|
| Los Angeles | 105-73 | .590 |
| Seattle | 100-75 | .571 |
| Sacramento * | 95-82 | .537 |
| San Francisco | 93-85 | .522 |
| San Diego | 92-85 | .520 |
| Portland | 79-86 | .451 |
| Hollywood | 79-99 | .444 |
| Oakland | 65-113 | .365 |

**1939**

| | | |
|---|---|---|
| Seattle | 101-73 | .580 |
| San Francisco | 97-78 | .554 |
| Los Angeles | 97-79 | .551 |
| Sacramento * | 88-88 | .500 |
| San Diego | 83-93 | .472 |
| Hollywood | 82-94 | .466 |
| Oakland | 78-98 | .443 |
| Portland | 75-93 | .434 |

**1940**

| | | |
|---|---|---|
| Seattle * | 112-66 | .629 |
| Los Angeles | 102-75 | .576 |
| Oakland | 94-84 | .528 |
| San Diego | 92-85 | .520 |
| Sacramento | 90-88 | .506 |
| Hollywood | 84-94 | .472 |
| San Francisco | 81-97 | .455 |
| Portland | 56-122 | .315 |

**1941**

| | | |
|---|---|---|
| Seattle * | 104-70 | .598 |
| Sacramento | 102-75 | .576 |
| San Diego | 101-76 | .571 |
| Hollywood | 85-91 | .483 |
| San Francisco | 81-95 | .460 |
| Oakland | 81-95 | .460 |
| Los Angeles | 72-98 | .424 |
| Portland | 71-97 | .423 |

**1942**

| | | |
|---|---|---|
| Sacramento | 105-73 | .590 |
| Los Angeles | 104-74 | .584 |
| Seattle * | 96-82 | .539 |
| San Diego | 91-87 | .511 |
| San Francisco | 88-90 | .490 |
| Hollywood | 85-92 | .480 |
| Portland | 75-103 | .421 |
| Oakland | 67-110 | .379 |

**1943**

| | | |
|---|---|---|
| Los Angeles | 110-45 | .710 |
| San Francisco * | 89-66 | .574 |
| Seattle | 85-70 | .548 |
| Portland | 79-76 | .510 |
| Hollywood | 73-82 | .471 |
| Oakland | 73-82 | .471 |
| San Diego | 70-85 | .455 |
| Sacramento | 41-114 | .265 |

**1944**

| | | |
|---|---|---|
| Los Angeles | 99-70 | .586 |
| Portland | 87-82 | .515 |
| San Francisco * | 86-83 | .509 |
| Oakland | 86-83 | .509 |
| Seattle | 84-85 | .497 |
| Hollywood | 83-86 | .491 |
| Sacramento | 76-93 | .450 |
| San Diego | 75-94 | .444 |

**1945**

| | | |
|---|---|---|
| Portland | 112-68 | .622 |
| Seattle | 105-78 | .574 |
| Sacramento | 95-85 | .528 |
| San Francisco * | 96-87 | .525 |
| Oakland | 90-93 | .492 |
| San Diego | 81-102 | .448 |
| Los Angeles | 76-107 | .415 |
| Hollywood | 73-110 | .399 |

**1946**

| | | |
|---|---|---|
| San Francisco * | 115-68 | .628 |
| Oakland | 111-72 | .607 |
| Hollywood | 95-88 | .519 |
| Los Angeles | 94-89 | .514 |
| Sacramento | 94-92 | .505 |
| San Diego | 78-108 | .419 |
| Portland | 74-109 | .404 |
| Seattle | 74-109 | .404 |

**1947**

| | | |
|---|---|---|
| Los Angeles * | 106-81 | .567 |
| San Francisco | 105-82 | .561 |
| Portland | 97-89 | .522 |
| Oakland | 96-90 | .516 |
| Seattle | 91-95 | .489 |
| Hollywood | 88-98 | .473 |
| Sacramento | 83-103 | .446 |
| San Diego | 79-107 | .425 |

### 1948

| | | |
|---|---|---|
| Oakland * | 114-74 | .606 |
| San Francisco | 112-76 | .596 |
| Los Angeles | 93-95 | .543 |
| Seattle | 93-95 | .495 |
| Portland | 89-99 | .473 |
| Hollywood | 84-104 | .447 |
| San Diego | 83-105 | .441 |
| Sacramento | 75-113 | .399 |

### 1949

| | | |
|---|---|---|
| Hollywood * | 109-78 | .583 |
| Oakland | 104-83 | .556 |
| Sacramento | 102-85 | .545 |
| San Diego | 96-92 | .510 |
| Seattle | 95-93 | .508 |
| Portland | 85-102 | .454 |
| San Francisco | 84-103 | .449 |
| Los Angeles | 74-113 | .395 |

### 1950

| | | |
|---|---|---|
| Oakland | 118-82 | .590 |
| San Diego | 114-86 | .570 |
| Hollywood | 104-96 | .520 |
| Portland | 101-99 | .505 |
| San Francisco | 100-100 | .500 |
| Seattle | 96-104 | .480 |
| Los Angeles | 86-114 | .430 |
| Sacramento | 81-119 | .405 |

### 1951

| | | |
|---|---|---|
| Seattle * | 99-68 | .593 |
| Hollywood | 93-74 | .557 |
| Los Angeles | 86-81 | .515 |
| Portland | 83-85 | .494 |
| Oakland | 80-88 | .476 |
| San Diego | 79-88 | .473 |
| Sacramento | 75-92 | .449 |
| San Francisco | 74-93 | .443 |

### 1952

| | | |
|---|---|---|
| Hollywood | 109-71 | .666 |
| Oakland | 104-76 | .578 |
| Seattle | 96-84 | .533 |
| Portland | 92-88 | .511 |
| San Diego | 88-92 | .489 |
| Los Angeles | 87-93 | .483 |
| San Francisco | 78-102 | .433 |
| Sacramento | 66-114 | .367 |

### 1953

| | | |
|---|---|---|
| Hollywood | 106-74 | .589 |
| Seattle | 98-82 | .544 |
| Los Angeles | 93-87 | .517 |
| Portland | 92-88 | .511 |
| San Francisco | 91-89 | .506 |
| San Diego | 88-92 | .489 |
| Oakland | 77-103 | .428 |
| Sacramento | 75-105 | .417 |

### 1954

| | | |
|---|---|---|
| San Diego | 102-67 | .604 |
| Hollywood | 101-68 | .598 |
| Oakland | 85-82 | .509 |
| San Francisco | 84-84 | .500 |
| Seattle | 77-85 | .475 |
| Los Angeles | 73-92 | .442 |
| Sacramento | 73-94 | .437 |
| Portland | 71-94 | .430 |

### 1955

| | | |
|---|---|---|
| Seattle | 95-77 | .552 |
| San Diego | 92-80 | .535 |
| Hollywood | 91-81 | .529 |
| Los Angeles | 91-81 | .529 |
| Portland | 86-86 | .500 |
| San Francisco | 80-92 | .465 |
| Oakland | 77-95 | .448 |
| Sacramento | 76-96 | .442 |

### 1956

| | | |
|---|---|---|
| Los Angeles | 107-61 | .637 |
| Seattle | 91-77 | .542 |
| Portland | 86-82 | .512 |
| Hollywood | 85-83 | .506 |
| Sacramento | 84-84 | .500 |
| San Francisco | 77-88 | .467 |
| San Diego | 72-96 | .429 |
| Vancouver | 67-98 | .406 |

### 1957

| | | |
|---|---|---|
| San Francisco | 101-67 | .601 |
| Vancouver | 97-70 | .581 |
| Hollywood | 94-74 | .560 |
| San Diego | 89-79 | .530 |
| Seattle | 87-80 | .521 |
| Los Angeles | 80-88 | .476 |
| Sacramento | 63-105 | .375 |
| Portland | 60-108 | .357 |

## 1958

| | | |
|---|---|---|
| Phoenix | 89-65 | .578 |
| San Diego | 84-69 | .549 |
| Vancouver | 79-73 | .520 |
| Portland | 78-76 | .506 |
| Salt Lake City | 77-77 | .500 |
| Sacramento | 71-83 | .461 |
| Spokane | 68-85 | .444 |
| Seattle | 68-86 | .442 |

## 1959

| | | |
|---|---|---|
| Salt Lake City | 85-69 | .552 |
| Vancouver | 82-69 | .543 |
| San Diego | 78-75 | .510 |
| Sacramento | 78-76 | .506 |
| Spokane | 77-77 | .500 |
| Portland | 75-77 | .493 |
| Seattle | 74-80 | .481 |
| Phoenix | 64-90 | .416 |

## 1960

| | | |
|---|---|---|
| Spokane | 92-61 | .601 |
| Tacoma | 81-73 | .526 |
| Salt Lake City | 80-73 | .523 |
| San Diego | 77-75 | .507 |
| Seattle | 77-75 | .507 |
| Sacramento | 73-81 | .474 |
| Vancouver | 68-84 | .447 |
| Portland | 64-90 | .416 |

## 1961

| | | |
|---|---|---|
| Tacoma | 97-57 | .630 |
| Vancouver | 87-67 | .565 |
| Seattle | 86-68 | .558 |
| San Diego | 72-82 | .468 |
| Portland | 71-83 | .461 |
| Hawaii | 68-86 | .442 |
| Spokane | 68-86 | .442 |
| Salt Lake City | 67-87 | .435 |

## 1962

| | | |
|---|---|---|
| San Diego | 93-61 | .604 |
| Salt Lake City | 81-73 | .526 |
| Tacoma | 81-73 | .526 |
| Seattle | 76-74 | .507 |
| Hawaii | 77-76 | .503 |
| Portland | 74-80 | .481 |
| Vancouver | 72-79 | .477 |
| Spokane | 58-96 | .377 |

## 1963

### NORTHERN DIVISION

| | | |
|---|---|---|
| Spokane | 98-60 | .620 |
| Hawaii | 81-77 | .513 |
| Tacoma | 79-79 | .500 |
| Portland | 73-84 | .465 |
| Seattle | 68-90 | .430 |

### SOUTHERN DIVISION

| | | |
|---|---|---|
| Oklahoma City * | 84-74 | .532 |
| San Diego | 83-74 | .529 |
| Dallas-Ft. Worth | 79-79 | .500 |
| Salt Lake City | 73-85 | .462 |
| Denver | 71-87 | .449 |

## 1964

### EASTERN DIVISION

| | | |
|---|---|---|
| Arkansas | 95-61 | .609 |
| Indianapolis | 89-69 | .563 |
| Oklahoma City | 88-70 | .557 |
| Denver | 80-78 | .508 |
| Salt Lake City | 58-98 | .372 |
| Dallas | 53-104 | .338 |

### WESTERN DIVISION

| | | |
|---|---|---|
| San Diego * | 91-67 | .576 |
| Portland | 90-68 | .570 |
| Spokane | 85-73 | .538 |
| Seattle | 81-75 | .519 |
| Tacoma | 73-82 | .471 |
| Hawaii | 60-98 | .380 |

## 1965

### EASTERN DIVISION

| | | |
|---|---|---|
| Oklahoma City * | 91-54 | .628 |
| Denver | 83-62 | .572 |
| San Diego | 70-78 | .473 |
| Indianapolis | 70-78 | .473 |
| Arkansas | 67-79 | .459 |
| Salt Lake City | 56-91 | .381 |

### WESTERN DIVISION

| | | |
|---|---|---|
| Portland | 81-67 | .547 |
| Seattle | 79-69 | .534 |
| Vancouver | 77-69 | .527 |
| Hawaii | 75-72 | .510 |
| Tacoma | 75-72 | .510 |
| Spokane | 57-90 | .388 |

## 1966

### EASTERN DIVISION

| | | |
|---|---|---|
| Tulsa | 85-62 | .578 |
| Phoenix | 81-67 | .547 |

| | | | | | | |
|---|---|---|---|---|---|---|
| Indianapolis | 80-68 | .541 | SOUTHERN DIVISION | | | |
| Denver | 79-68 | .537 | Eugene | 88-58 | .603 |
| San Diego | 72-75 | .490 | Phoenix | 75-71 | .514 |
| Oklahoma City | 59-89 | .399 | Hawaii | 74-72 | .507 |
| WESTERN DIVISION | | | Tucson | 60-86 | .411 |
| Seattle * | 83-65 | .561 | | | |
| Vancouver | 77-71 | .520 | **1970** | | |
| Spokane | 75-73 | .507 | NORTHERN DIVISION | | |
| Portland | 69-79 | .466 | Spokane * | 94-52 | .644 |
| Hawaii | 63-84 | .429 | Portland | 68-78 | .466 |
| Tacoma | 63-85 | .426 | Eugene | 66-80 | .452 |
| | | | Tacoma | 45-98 | .315 |
| **1967** | | | SOUTHERN DIVISION | | |
| EASTERN DIVISION | | | Hawaii | 98-48 | .671 |
| San Diego * | 85-63 | .574 | Phoenix | 85-61 | .582 |
| Indianapolis | 76-71 | .517 | Tucson | 81-65 | .555 |
| Phoenix | 75-72 | .510 | Salt Lake City | 44-99 | .308 |
| Oklahoma City | 74-74 | .500 | | | |
| Denver | 69-76 | .476 | **1971** | | |
| Tulsa | 65-79 | .451 | NORTHERN DIVISION | | |
| WESTERN DIVISION | | | Tacoma | 78-65 | .545 |
| Spokane | 80-68 | .541 | Portland | 71-71 | .500 |
| Portland | 79-69 | .534 | Spokane | 69-76 | .476 |
| Vancouver | 77-69 | .527 | Eugene | 66-79 | .455 |
| Tacoma | 73-75 | .493 | SOUTHERN DIVISION | | |
| Seattle | 69-79 | .466 | Salt Lake City * | 78-68 | .534 |
| Hawaii | 60-87 | .408 | Phoenix | 74-70 | .514 |
| | | | Hawaii | 73-73 | .500 |
| **1968** | | | Tucson | 69-76 | .476 |
| EASTERN DIVISION | | | | | |
| Tulsa * | 95-53 | .642 | **1972** | | |
| San Diego | 76-70 | .521 | EASTERN DIVISION | | |
| Phoenix | 76-71 | .517 | Albuquerque * | 92-56 | .622 |
| Denver | 73-72 | .503 | Phoenix | 81-76 | .547 |
| Indianapolis | 66-78 | .458 | Salt Lake City | 80-68 | .541 |
| Oklahoma City | 61-84 | .421 | Tucson | 60-88 | .405 |
| WESTERN DIVISION | | | WESTERN DIVISION | | |
| Spokane | 85-60 | .586 | Eugene | 79-69 | .534 |
| Hawaii | 78-69 | .531 | Hawaii | 74-74 | .500 |
| Portland | 72-72 | .500 | Tacoma | 65-83 | .439 |
| Seattle | 71-76 | .483 | Portland | 61-87 | .412 |
| Tacoma | 65-83 | .439 | | | |
| Vancouver | 58-88 | .397 | **1973** | | |
| | | | EASTERN DIVISION | | |
| **1969** | | | Tucson | 84-60 | .583 |
| | | | Salt Lake City | 79-65 | .549 |
| NORTHERN DIVISION | | | Phoenix | 70-73 | .490 |
| Tacoma * | 86-60 | .589 | Albuquerque | 62-82 | .431 |
| Spokane | 71-73 | .493 | WESTERN DIVISION | | |
| Vancouver | 71-73 | .493 | Spokane * | 81-63 | .563 |
| Portland | 57-89 | .390 | | | |

| | | |
|---|---|---|
| Hawaii | 70-74 | .486 |
| Tacoma | 65-79 | .451 |
| Eugene | 64-79 | .448 |

## 1974

### EASTERN DIVISION

| | | |
|---|---|---|
| Albuquerque | 76-66 | .535 |
| Phoenix | 75-69 | .521 |
| Salt Lake City | 69-73 | .486 |
| Tucson | 65-78 | .455 |

### WESTERN DIVISION

| | | |
|---|---|---|
| Spokane * | 78-64 | .549 |
| Tacoma | 75-66 | .532 |
| Hawaii | 67-77 | .465 |
| Sacramento | 66-78 | .458 |

## 1975

### EASTERN DIVISION

| | | |
|---|---|---|
| Salt Lake City | 80-64 | .556 |
| Tucson | 72-71 | .503 |
| Albuquerque | 71-73 | .493 |
| Phoenix | 66-77 | .462 |

### WESTERN DIVSION

| | | |
|---|---|---|
| Hawaii * | 88-56 | .611 |
| Tacoma | 73-69 | .514 |
| Spokane | 64-78 | .451 |
| Sacramento | 59-85 | .410 |

## 1976

### EASTERN DIVISION

| | | |
|---|---|---|
| Salt Lake City | 90-54 | .625 |
| Phoenix | 75-67 | .528 |
| Albuquerque | 66-78 | .458 |
| Tucson | 54-88 | .380 |

### WESTERN DIVISION

| | | |
|---|---|---|
| Hawaii * | 77-68 | .531 |
| Tacoma | 76-69 | .524 |
| Sacramento | 71-72 | .497 |
| Spokane | 65-78 | .455 |

## 1977

### EASTERN DIVISION

| | | |
|---|---|---|
| Phoenix * | 81-59 | .579 |
| Salt Lake City | 74-65 | .532 |
| Tucson | 65-73 | .471 |
| Albuquerque | 60-78 | .435 |

### WESTERN DIVISION

| | | |
|---|---|---|
| Hawaii | 79-67 | .541 |
| Spokane | 75-69 | .521 |

| | | |
|---|---|---|
| Tacoma | 68-75 | .476 |
| San Jose | 64-80 | .444 |

## 1978

### EASTERN DIVISION

| | | |
|---|---|---|
| Albuquerque * | 78-62 | .557 |
| Salt Lake City | 72-65 | .526 |
| Phoenix | 72-68 | .514 |
| Tucson | 69-71 | .493 |
| San Jose | 53-87 | .379 |

### WESTERN DIVISION

| | | |
|---|---|---|
| Tacoma * | 80-57 | .584 |
| Portland | 76-62 | .551 |
| Vancouver | 74-65 | .532 |
| Spokane | 64-75 | .460 |
| Hawaii | 56-82 | .406 |

## 1979

### NORTHERN DIVISION

| | | |
|---|---|---|
| Vancouver | 79-68 | .537 |
| Tacoma | 74-73 | .503 |
| Portland | 73-74 | .497 |
| Hawaii | 72-76 | .486 |
| Spokane | 68-79 | .463 |

### SOUTHERN DIVISION

| | | |
|---|---|---|
| Albuquerque | 86-62 | .581 |
| Salt Lake City * | 80-68 | .541 |
| Tucson | 74-74 | .500 |
| Ogden | 72-75 | .490 |
| Phoenix | 59-88 | .401 |

## 1980

### NORTHERN DIVISION

| | | |
|---|---|---|
| Hawaii | 79-60 | .568 |
| Vancouver | 76-65 | .539 |
| Tacoma | 74-74 | .500 |
| Portland | 69-76 | .476 |
| Spokane | 60-86 | .429 |

### SOUTHERN DIVISION

| | | |
|---|---|---|
| Tucson | 87-59 | .596 |
| Albuquerque * | 85-62 | .578 |
| Salt Lake City | 77-65 | .542 |
| Ogden | 59-83 | .415 |
| Phoenix | 53-95 | .358 |

## 1981

### NORTHERN DIVISION

| | | |
|---|---|---|
| Tacoma | 78-61 | .561 |
| Hawaii | 72-65 | .526 |
| Portland | 72-65 | .526 |

| Edmonton | 62-74 | .456 |
|---|---|---|
| Vancouver | 56-76 | .424 |
| Spokane | 56-84 | .400 |

SOUTHERN DIVISION

| Albuquerque * | 94-38 | .712 |
|---|---|---|
| Phoenix | 69-63 | .523 |
| Salt Lake City | 63-71 | .470 |
| Tucson | 57-82 | .410 |

**1982**

NORTHERN DIVISION

| Tacoma | 84-59 | .587 |
|---|---|---|
| Spokane | 78-65 | .545 |
| Vancouver | 72-72 | .500 |
| Edmonton | 70-74 | .486 |
| Portland | 65-79 | .451 |

SOUTHERN DIVISION

| Albuquerque * | 85-58 | .594 |
|---|---|---|
| Salt Lake City | 73-70 | .510 |
| Hawaii | 73-71 | .507 |
| Tucson | 59-83 | .415 |
| Phoenix | 58-86 | .403 |

**1983**

NORTHERN DIVISION

| Edmonton | 75-67 | .528 |
|---|---|---|
| Portland * | 75-67 | .528 |
| Salt Lake City | 67-75 | .472 |
| Tacoma | 65-77 | .458 |
| Vancouver | 60-80 | .429 |

SOUTHERN DIVISION

| Albuquerque | 85-58 | .594 |
|---|---|---|
| Las Vegas | 83-60 | .580 |
| Hawaii | 72-71 | .503 |
| Tucson | 68-74 | .479 |
| Phoenix | 61-82 | .427 |

**1984**

NORTHERN DIVISION

| Salt Lake City | 74-66 | .529 |
|---|---|---|
| Vancouver | 71-71 | .500 |
| Tacoma | 69-71 | .493 |
| Edmonton * | 69-73 | .486 |
| Portland | 62-78 | .443 |

SOUTHERN DIVISION

| Hawaii | 87-53 | .621 |
|---|---|---|
| Las Vegas | 71-65 | .522 |
| Tucson | 69-71 | .493 |
| Phoenix | 69-74 | .483 |
| Albuquerque | 62-81 | .434 |

**1985**

NORTHERN DIVISION

| Vancouver * | 79-64 | .552 |
|---|---|---|
| Calgary | 71-70 | .504 |
| Portland | 68-74 | .479 |
| Edmonton | 66-76 | .465 |
| Tacoma | 66-76 | .465 |

SOUTHERN DIVISION

| Hawaii | 84-59 | .587 |
|---|---|---|
| Phoenix | 80-62 | .563 |
| Albuquerque | 67-76 | .469 |
| Tucson | 65-75 | .464 |
| Las Vegas | 65-79 | .451 |

**1986**

NORTHERN DIVISION

| Vancouver | 85-53 | .616 |
|---|---|---|
| Tacoma | 72-72 | .500 |
| Edmonton | 68-73 | .482 |
| Portland | 68-73 | .482 |
| Calgary | 66-77 | .462 |

SOUTHERN DIVISION

| Phoenix | 81-61 | .570 |
|---|---|---|
| Las Vegas * | 80-62 | .563 |
| Tucson | 71-72 | .497 |
| Hawaii | 65-79 | .451 |
| Albuquerque | 54-88 | .380 |

**1987**

NORTHERN DIVISION

| Calgary | 84-57 | .596 |
|---|---|---|
| Tacoma | 78-65 | .545 |
| Vancouver | 72-72 | .500 |
| Edmonton | 69-74 | .483 |
| Portland | 45-96 | .319 |

SOUTHERN DIVISION

| Albuquerque * | 77-65 | .542 |
|---|---|---|
| Phoenix | 77-67 | .535 |
| Tucson | 75-67 | .528 |
| Las Vegas | 69-73 | .486 |
| Hawaii | 65-75 | .464 |

**1988**

NORTHERN DIVISION

| Vancouver | 85-57 | .599 |
|---|---|---|
| Portland | 76-66 | .535 |
| Calgary | 68-74 | .479 |
| Edmonton | 61-80 | .433 |
| Tacoma | 62-82 | .431 |

328 THE PACIFIC COAST LEAGUE

| SOUTHERN DIVISION | | | Tucson | 68-75 | .476 |
|---|---|---|---|---|---|
| Albuquerque | 86-56 | .606 | Phoenix | 67-76 | .469 |
| Las Vegas | 74-66 | .529 | Colorado Springs | 62-77 | .446 |

## PLAYOFF RESULTS

**1904** Tacoma defeated Los Angeles 5 games to 4 with 1 tie.

**1905** Los Angeles defeated Tacoma-Sacramento 5 games to 1.

**1918** Los Angeles defeated Vernon 5 games to 2.

**1928** San Francisco defeated Sacramento 4 games to 2.

**1929** Hollywood defeated Mission 4 games to 2.

**1930** Hollywood defeated Los Angeles 4 games to 1.

**1931** San Francisco defeated Hollywood 4 games to 0.

**1935** San Francisco defeated Los Angeles 4 games to 2.

**1936** Oakland defeated San Diego 4 games to 1. Portland defeated Seattle 4 games to 0. **FINALS:** Portland defeated Oakland 4 games to 1.

**1937** San Diego defeated Sacramento 4 games to 0. Portland defeated San Francisco 4 games to 0. **FINALS:** San Diego defeated Portland 4 games to 0.

**1938** Sacramento defeated Los Angeles 4 games to 1. San Francisco defeated Seattle 4 games to 1. **FINALS:** Sacramento defeated San Francisco 4 games to 1.

**1939** Los Angeles defeated Seattle 4 games to 2. Sacramento defeated San Francisco 4 games to 1. **FINALS:** Sacramento defeated Los Angeles 4 games to 2.

**1940** Seattle defeated Oakland 4 games to 1. Los Angeles defeated San Diego 4 games to 3. **FINALS:** Seattle defeated Los Angeles 4 games to 1.

**1941** Seattle defeated Hollywood 4 games to 3. Sacramento defeated San Diego 4 games to 0. **FINALS:** Seattle defeated Sacramento 4 games to 3.

**1942** Seattle defeated Sacramento 4 games to 1. Los Angeles defeated San Diego 4 games to 3. **FINALS:** Seattle defeated Los Angeles 4 games to 2.

**1943** Seattle defeated Los Angeles 4 games to 0. San Francisco defeated Portland 4 games to 2. **FINALS:** San Francisco defeated Seattle 4 games to 2.

**1944** Los Angeles defeated Portland 4 games to 2. San Francisco defeated Oakland 4 games to 1. **FINALS:** San Francisco defeated Los Angeles 4 games to 3.

**1945** Seattle defeated Portland 4 games to 3. San Francisco defeated Sacramento 4 games to 3. **FINALS:** San Francisco defeated Seattle 4 games to 2.

**1946** San Francisco defeated Hollywood 4 games to 0. Oakland defeated Los Angeles 4 games to 3. **FINALS:** San Francisco defeated Oakland 4 games to 2.

**1947** Los Angeles defeated San Francisco, 5–0, for first place. Los Angeles defeated Portland 4 games to 1. Oakland defeated San Francisco 4 games to 1. **FINALS:** Los Angeles defeated Oakland 4 games to 1.

**1948** Oakland defeated Los Angeles 4 games to 2. Seattle defeated San Francisco 4 games to 1. **FINALS:** Oakland defeated Seattle 4 games to 1.

**1949** Hollywood defeated Sacramento 4 games to 1. San Diego defeated Oakland 4 games to 3. **FINALS:** Hollywood defeated San Diego 4 games to 2.

**1951** Seattle defeated Los Angeles 2 games to 1. Hollywood defeated Portland 2 games to 0. **FINALS:** Seattle defeated Hollywood 3 games to 2.

**1954**  San Diego defeated Hollywood 7–2, for the pennant.
**1963**  Oklahoma City defeated Spokane 4 games to 3.
**1964**  San Diego defeated Arkansas 4 games to 3.
**1965**  Oklahoma City defeated Portland 4 games to 1.
**1966**  Seattle defeated Tulsa 4 games to 3.
**1967**  San Diego defeated Spokane 4 games to 2.
**1968**  Tulsa defeated Spokane 4 games to 1.
**1969**  Tacoma defeated Eugene 3 games to 2.
**1970**  Spokane defeated Hawaii 4 games to 0.
**1971**  Salt Lake City defeated Tacoma 3 games to 1.
**1972**  Albuquerque defeated Eugene 3 games to 1.
**1973**  Spokane defeated Tucson 3 games to 0.
**1974**  Spokane defeated Albuquerque 3 games to 0.
**1975**  Hawaii defeated Salt Lake City 4 games to 2.
**1976**  Hawaii defeated Salt Lake City 3 games to 2.
**1977**  Phoenix defeated Salt Lake City 3 games to 2.
**1978**  Albuquerque defeated Salt Lake City 3 games to 0. Tacoma-Portland were tied at 2 wins each when PCL president Roy Jackson declared the series ended by continuing rain and wet grounds. Albuquerque and Tacoma ruled co-champions.
**1979**  Hawaii defeated Vancouver 2 games to 1. Salt Lake City defeated Albuquerque 2 games to 0. **FINALS:** Salt lake City defeated Hawaii 3 games to 0.
**1980**  Hawaii defeated Vancouver 2 games to 1. Albuquerque defeated Tucson 2 games to 0. **FINALS:** Albuquerque defeated Hawaii 3 games to 2.
**1981**  Tacoma defeated Hawaii 2 games to 1. **FINALS:** Albuquerque defeated Tacoma 3 games to 0.
**1982**  Albuquerque defeated Salt Lake City 2 games to 0. Spokane defeated Tacoma 2 games to 1. **FINALS:** Albuquerque defeated Spokane 4 games to 2.
**1983**  Portland defeated Edmonton 3 games to 1. Albuquerque defeated Las Vegas 3 games to 2. **FINALS:** Portland defeated Albuquerque 3 games to 0.
**1984**  Hawaii defeated Las Vegas 3 games to 0. Edmonton defeated Salt Lake City 3 games to 2. **FINALS:** Edmonton defeated Hawaii 2 games to 0.
**1985**  Vancouver defeated Calgary 3 games to 0. Phoenix defeated Hawaii 3 games to 0. **FINALS:** Vancouver defeated Phoenix 3 games to 0.
**1986**  Las Vegas defeated Phoenix 3 games to 2. Vancouver defeated Tacoma 3 games to 0. **FINALS:** Las Vegas defeated Vancouver 3 games to 2.
**1987**  Albuquerque defeated Las Vegas 3 games to 0. Tacoma defeated Calgary 3 games to 2. **FINALS:** Albuquerque defeated Tacoma 3 games to 1.
**1988**  Vancouver defeated Portland 3 games to 0. Las Vegas defeated Albuquerque 3 games to 0. **FINALS:** Las Vegas defeated Vancouver 3 games to 1.

## ALL-STAR GAMES

In 1925 PCL President Harry Williams asked baseball writers to select an official All-Star Team. A tenth player — a utility man — was added to the nine best in 1928, along with additional pitchers in later years. These dream teams have been named regularly until the present day but in the 86-year history of the Coast League, PCL fans have had the opportunity to watch only 24 All-Star games.

Although the major leagues enjoyed immediate success with the first All-Star game in 1933, the Coast League would not stage a similar exhibition until 1941. All-Star squads were selected from the four northernmost clubs and the four southern teams. Attendance dropped severely during the war year of 1942, and no All-Star game was held in 1943. In 1944 and 1945 two North vs. South games were staged on the same day in different cities. In 1946 and 1947 a new format was tried: the team in first place on a given date would host the All-Star game, playing against a squad of stars selected from the other seven teams. This format would be utilized again in 1954, 1955, 1960, 1961 and 1963.

The North vs. South contests were resumed from 1948 through 1950, but no All-Star game was held from 1951 through 1953. All-Star games were staged from 1954 through 1963, and in 1962 PCL All-Stars defeated the Los Angeles Angels of the American League, 6–5. The PCL All-Star Game was discontinued for a decade beginning in 1964. In 1973 All-Star contests resumed, featuring teams from the Eastern and Western divisions, but attendance was poor and the series stopped after three years.

The last All-Star game to date was staged in 1975, although PCL players participated in the first Triple-A All-Star Game, held in 1988 at Buffalo's new Pilot Field. A financial and artistic success, the game featured star athletes from the PCL, International League, and American Association, aligned in the American League and National League teams from the top-level AL and NL farm clubs. The Triple-A All-Star Game was scheduled to be played in a Pacific Coast League city in 1990.

| Year | City | Results | Attendance |
|------|------|---------|-----------|
| 1941 | San Francisco | South 3, North 1 | 9,556 |
| 1942 | Hollywood | South 1, North 0 | 5,079 |
| 1944 | Hollywood | South 5, North 4 | 3,434 |
| 1944 | San Francisco | South 5, North 4 | 4,490 |
| 1945 | Los Angeles | South 3, North 1 | 6,735 |
| 1945 | Portland | North 13, South 3 | 4,550 |
| 1946 | San Francisco | San Francisco 3, All-Stars 0 | 13,307 |
| 1947 | Los Angeles | All-Stars 12, Los Angeles 2 | 19,851 |
| 1948 | San Francisco | South 6, North 2 | 14,210 |
| 1949 | Seattle | South 5, North 3 | 9,780 |
| 1950 | Sacramento | North 9, South 2 | 6,424 |
| 1954 | Hollywood | All-Stars 11, Hollywood 7 | 5,964 |
| 1955 | San Diego | All-Stars 7, San Diego 4 | 3,204 |
| 1956 | Portland | South 10, North 5 | 10,437 |
| 1957 | Los Angeles | North 3, South 1 | 6,417 |
| 1958 | Vancouver | South 13, North 4 | 8,349 |
| 1959 | San Diego | South 5, North 2 | 4,693 |
| 1960 | Spokane | Spokane 4, All-Stars 3 | 10,018 |

| 1961 | Seattle | All-Stars 5, Seattle 2 | 6,100 |
| 1962 | Portland | All-Stars 6, LA Angels 5 | 12,198 |
| 1963 | Spokane | All-Stars 4, Spokane 2 | 6,595 |
| 1973 | Albuquerque | West 9, East 6 | 3,197 |
| 1974 | Tacoma | East 8, West 1 | 1,871 |
| 1975 | Sacramento | East 10, West 2 | 3,200 |

## PRESIDENTS OF THE PACIFIC COAST LEAGUE

| 1903-1906 | Eugene F. Bert | 1944-1954 | Clarence H. Rowland |
| 1907-1909 | J. Cal Ewing | 1955 | Claire V. Goodwin |
| 1910-1911 | Judge Thomas F. Graham | 1956-1959 | Leslie M. O'Connor |
| 1912-1919 | Allan T. Baum | 1960-1968 | Dewey Soriano |
| 1920-1923 | William H. McCarthy | 1969-1973 | William B. McKechnie, Jr. |
| 1924-1931 | Harry A. Williams | 1974-1978 | Roy Jackson |
| 1932-1935 | Hyland H. Baggerly | 1979- | William S. Cutler |
| 1936-1943 | William C. Tuttle | | |

## BATTING CHAMPIONS

| 1903 | Harry Lumley, Sea. | .387 | 1932 | Ox Eckhardt, Miss. | .371 |
| 1904 | Emil Frisk, Sea. | .337 | 1933 | Ox Eckhardt, Miss. | .414 |
| 1905 | Kitty Brashear, LA | .303 | 1934 | Frank Demaree, LA | .383 |
| 1906 | Michael Mitchell, Pd. | .351 | 1935 | Ox Eckhardt, Miss. | .399 |
| 1907 | Truck Eagan, Oak. | .335 | 1936 | Joe Marty, SF | .359 |
| 1908 | Babe Danzig, Pd. | .298 | 1937 | Harlan Pool, Sea. | .334 |
| 1909 | Henry Melchior, SF | .298 | 1938 | Smead Jolley, Hol.-Oak. | .350 |
| 1910 | Hunky Shaw, SF | .281 | 1939 | Dom Dellessandro, SD | .368 |
| 1911 | Buddy Ryan, Pd. | .333 | 1940 | Lou Novikoff, LA | .363 |
| 1912 | Henry Heitmuller, LA | .335 | 1941 | John Moore, LA | .331 |
| 1913 | Henry Bayless, Ver. | .324 | 1942 | Ted Norbert, Pd. | .378 |
| 1914 | Harry Wolter, LA | .328 | 1943 | Andy Pafko, LA | .356 |
| 1915 | Harry Wolter, LA | .359 | 1944 | Les Scarsella, Oak. | .329 |
| 1916 | Duke Kenworthy, Oak. | .314 | 1945 | Jo Jo White, Sac. | .355 |
| 1917 | Maurice Rath, SLC | .341 | 1946 | Harvey Storey, LA-Pd. | .326 |
| 1918 | Art Griggs, Sac. | .378 | 1947 | Hillis Layne, Sea. | .367 |
| 1919 | Bill Rumler, SLC | .362 | 1948 | Gene Woodling, SF | .385 |
| 1920 | Earl Sheely, SLC | .371 | 1949 | Art Wilson, SD-Oak. | .348 |
| 1921 | Hack Miller, Oak. | .347 | 1950 | Frank Baumholtz, LA | .379 |
| 1922 | Paul Strand, SLC | .384 | 1951 | Jim Rivera, Sea. | .352 |
| 1923 | Paul Strand, SLC | .394 | 1952 | Robert Boyd, Sea. | .320 |
| 1924 | Duffy Lewis, SLC | .392 | 1953 | Robert Dillinger, Sac. | .366 |
| 1925 | Paul Waner, SF | .401 | 1954 | Harry Elliott, SD | .350 |
| 1926 | William Bagwell, Pd. | .391 | 1955 | George Metkovich, Oak. | .335 |
| 1927 | Smead Jolley, SF | .397 | 1956 | Steve Bilko, LA | .360 |
| 1928 | Smead Jolley, SF | .404 | 1957 | Ken Aspromonte, SF | .334 |
| 1929 | Ike Boone, Miss. | .407 | 1958 | Andre Rodgers, Phx. | .354 |
| 1930 | Earl Sheely, SF | .403 | 1959 | Tommy Davis, Spo. | .345 |
| 1931 | Ox Eckhardt, Miss. | .369 | 1960 | Willie Davis, Spo. | .346 |

| 1961 | Carlos Bernier, Haw. | .351 |
|------|----------------------|------|
| 1962 | Jesse Gonder, SD | .342 |
| 1963 | Chico Salmon, Den. | .325 |
| 1964 | Lou Klimchock, Den. | .334 |
| 1965 | Ted Uhlaender, Den. | .340 |
| 1966 | Walt Williams, Tulsa | .330 |
| 1967 | Cesar Gutierrez, Phx. | .322 |
| 1968 | James Hicks, Tulsa | .366 |
| 1969 | Angel Bravo, Tuc. | .342 |
| 1970 | Bobby Valentine, Spo. | .340 |
| 1971 | Tom Hutton, Spo. | .352 |
| 1972 | Von Joshua, Alb. | .337 |
| 1973 | Steve Ontiveros, Phx. | .357 |
| 1974 | Glenn Adams, Phx. | .352 |

| 1975 | Jerry Royster, Alb. | .333 |
|------|---------------------|------|
| 1976 | Paul Dade, SLC | .363 |
| 1977 | Don Cardoza, Alb. | .356 |
| 1978 | Jeff Leonard, Alb. | .365 |
| 1979 | Mickey Hatcher, Alb. | .371 |
| 1980 | Danny Heep, Tuc. | .343 |
| 1981 | Mike Marshall, Alb. | .373 |
| 1982 | Michael Wilson, Alb. | .378 |
| 1983 | Chris Smith, Phx. | .379 |
| 1984 | Anthony Brewer, Alb. | .357 |
| 1985 | John Kruk, LV | .351 |
| 1986 | Ty Gainey, Tuc. | .351 |
| 1987 | James Eppard, Edm. | .341 |
| 1988 | Edgar Martinez, Calg. | .363 |

## HOME RUN CHAMPIONS

| 1903 | Truck Eagan, Sac. | 13 |
|------|-------------------|-----|
| 1904 | Truck Eagan, Tac. | 25 |
| 1905 | Truck Eagan, Tac. | 21 |
| 1906 | Michael Mitchell, Pd. | 6 |
| 1907 | Walter Carlisle, LA | 14 |
| 1908 | Henry Heitmuller, Oak. | 12 |
| 1909 | Otis Johnson, Pd. | 13 |
| 1910 | Ping Bodie, SF | 30 |
| 1911 | Buddy Ryan, Pd. | 23 |
| 1912 | Bert Coy, Oak. | 19 |
| 1913 | Bert Coy, Oak. | 18 |
| 1914 | Ty Lober, Pd. | 9 |
| 1915 | Biff Schaller, SF | 20 |
| 1916 | Bunny Brief, SLC | 33 |
| 1917 | Ken Williams, Pd. | 24 |
| 1918 | Art Griggs, Sac. | 12 |
|      | Earl Sheely, SLC | 12 |
| 1919 | Earl Sheely, SLC | 28 |
| 1920 | Earl Sheely, SLC | 33 |
| 1921 | Paddy Siglin, SLC | 22 |
| 1922 | Paul Strand, SLC | 28 |
| 1923 | Paul Strand, SLC | 43 |
| 1924 | James Poole, Pd. | 38 |
| 1925 | Tony Lazzeri, SLC | 60 |
| 1926 | Elmer Smith, Pd. | 46 |
| 1927 | Elmer Smith, Pd. | 40 |
| 1928 | Smead Jolley, SF | 45 |
| 1929 | Ike Boone, Miss. | 55 |
| 1930 | David Barbee, Sea.-Hol. | 41 |
| 1931 | David Barbee, Hol. | 47 |
| 1932 | Fred Muller, Sea. | 38 |
| 1933 | Gene Lillard, LA | 43 |

| 1934 | Frank Demaree, LA | 45 |
|------|-------------------|-----|
| 1935 | Gene Lillard, LA | 56 |
| 1936 | Art Hunt, Sea. | 30 |
|      | Fred Muller, Sea. | 30 |
| 1937 | Art Hunt, Sea. | 39 |
| 1938 | Ted Norbert, SF | 30 |
| 1939 | Rip Collins, LA | 26 |
| 1940 | Lou Novikoff, LA | 41 |
| 1941 | Ted Norbert, Pd. | 20 |
| 1942 | Ted Norbert, Pd. | 28 |
| 1943 | John Ostrowski, LA | 21 |
| 1944 | Francis Kelleher, Hol. | 29 |
| 1945 | Ted Norbert, Sea. | 23 |
| 1946 | Loyd Christopher, LA | 26 |
| 1947 | Max West, SD | 43 |
| 1948 | Jack Graham, SD | 48 |
| 1949 | Max West, SD | 48 |
| 1950 | Francis Kelleher, Hol. | 40 |
| 1951 | Joe Gordon, Sac. | 43 |
| 1952 | Max West, LA | 35 |
| 1953 | Dale Long, Hol. | 35 |
| 1954 | James Marshall, Oak. | 31 |
| 1955 | Steve Bilko, LA | 37 |
| 1956 | Steve Bilko, LA | 55 |
| 1957 | Steve Bilko, LA | 56 |
| 1958 | James McDaniel, SLC | 37 |
| 1959 | Willie McCovey, Phx. | 29 |
| 1960 | R. C. Stevens, SLC | 37 |
| 1961 | Eugene Oliver, Pd. | 36 |
| 1962 | Stan Palys, Haw. | 33 |
| 1963 | Deron Johnson, SD | 33 |
| 1964 | Costen Shockley, Ark. | 36 |

| | | | | | | |
|------|------------------------|----|------|------------------------|----|
| 1965 | Dave Roberts, Ok. City | 38 | 1978 | Willie Aikens, SLC | 29 |
| 1966 | Tommy Murray, Ok. City | 26 | 1979 | Isaac Hampton, SLC | 30 |
| 1967 | Willie Kirkland, Haw. | 34 | 1980 | Tim Hosley, Ogd. | 26 |
| 1968 | Clarence Jones, Tac. | 24 | 1981 | Mike Marshall, Alb. | 34 |
| 1969 | Russ Nagelson, Pd. | 23 | 1982 | Ron Kittle, Edm. | 50 |
| 1970 | Joseph Lis, Eug. | 36 | 1983 | Sid Bream, Alb. | 32 |
| 1971 | Adrian Garrett, Tac. | 43 | | Kevin McReynolds, LV | 32 |
| 1972 | Tom Paciorek, Alb | 27 | 1984 | Rob Deer, Phx. | 31 |
| 1973 | Eugene Martin, Eug.-Haw. | 31 | 1985 | Danny Tartabull, Calg. | 43 |
| 1974 | Bill McNulty, Sac. | 55 | 1986 | Rich Lancellotti, Phx. | 31 |
| 1975 | Robert Hansen, Sac. | 29 | 1987 | David Hengel, Calg. | 23 |
| 1976 | Robert Gorinski, Tac. | 28 | 1988 | Luis Medina, Col. Spr. | 28 |
| 1977 | Dan Walton, Alb. | 42 | | | |

## RBI LEADERS

| | | | | | | |
|------|------------------------|-----|------|--------------------------|-----|
| 1922 | Paul Strand, SLC | 138 | 1954 | James Marshall, Oak. | 123 |
| 1923 | Paul Strand, SLC | 187 | 1955 | Earl Rapp, SD | 133 |
| 1924 | Bert Ellison, SF | 188 | 1956 | Steve Bilko, LA | 164 |
| 1925 | Tony Lazzeri, SLC | 222 | 1957 | Steve Bilko, LA | 140 |
| 1926 | Russ Arlett, Oak. | 140 | 1958 | James McDaniel, SLC | 100 |
| 1927 | Smead Jolley, SF | 163 | | Dusty Rhodes, Phx. | 100 |
| 1928 | Smead Jolley, SF | 188 | 1959 | Steve Bilko, Spo. | 92 |
| 1929 | Ike Boone, Miss. | 218 | | Willie McCovey, Phx. | 92 |
| 1930 | Earl Sheely, SF | 180 | 1960 | Harry Bright, SLC | 119 |
| 1931 | Ed Coleman, Pd. | 183 | 1961 | Harry Simpson, SD | 105 |
| 1932 | George Burns, Sea. | 140 | 1962 | Jesse Gonder, SD | 116 |
| 1933 | Joe DiMaggio, SF | 169 | 1963 | Billy Cowan, SLC | 120 |
| 1934 | Frank Demaree, LA | 173 | 1964 | Lou Klimchock, Den. | 112 |
| 1935 | Joe DiMaggio, SF | 154 | | Costen Shockley, Ark. | 112 |
| 1936 | Arthur Hunt, Sea. | 135 | 1965 | Andy Kosco, Den. | 116 |
| 1937 | Arthur Hunt, Sea. | 131 | 1966 | Ron Clark, Den. | 94 |
| 1938 | Ted Norbert, SF | 163 | | Richard Kenworthy, Ind. | 94 |
| 1939 | Rip Collins, LA | 128 | 1967 | Willie Kirkland, Haw. | 97 |
| 1940 | Lou Novikoff, LA | 171 | 1968 | Jose Laboy, Tulsa | 100 |
| 1941 | Froilan Fernandez, SF | 129 | 1969 | John Werhas, Haw. | 90 |
| 1942 | Kermit Lewis, SF | 115 | 1970 | Winston Llenas, Haw. | 108 |
| 1943 | Andy Pafko, LA | 118 | 1971 | Ron Cey, Spo. | 123 |
| 1944 | Francis Kelleher, Hol. | 121 | 1972 | Doug Howard, SLC | 109 |
| 1945 | Harold Patchett, Oak.-Sea. | 110 | 1973 | Eugene Martin, Eug.-Haw. | 106 |
| 1946 | Ferris Fain, SF | 112 | 1974 | William McNulty, Sac. | 135 |
| 1947 | Max West, SD | 124 | 1975 | Robert Hansen, Sac. | 102 |
| 1948 | Gus Zernial, Hol. | 156 | 1976 | Robert Gorinski, Tac. | 110 |
| 1949 | Max West, SD | 166 | 1977 | Dan Walton, Alb. | 122 |
| 1950 | Harry Simpson, SD | 156 | 1978 | Pedro Guerrero, Alb. | 116 |
| 1951 | Joe Gordon, Sac. | 136 | 1979 | Pedro Guerrero, Alb. | 103 |
| 1952 | Harold Gilbert, Oak. | 118 | 1980 | Alan Knicely, Tuc. | 105 |
| 1953 | Dale Long, Hol. | 116 | 1981 | Mike Marshall, Alb. | 137 |

| 1982 | Ron Kittle, Edm. | 144 | 1986 | Tim Pyznarski, LV | 119 |
| 1983 | Sid Bream, Alb. | 118 | 1987 | David Hengel, Calg. | 103 |
| 1984 | Rick Lancelotti, LV | 131 | 1988 | Rod Allen, Col. Spr. | 100 |
| 1985 | Danny Tartabull, Calg. | 109 | | | |

## STOLEN BASE LEADERS

| 1903 | Dan Shay, SF | 83 | 1943 | Oral Burnett, Sac. | 32 |
| 1904 | Robert Ganley, Oak. | 72 | 1944 | William Ramsey, Sac. | 45 |
| 1905 | Lawrence Schafly, Pd.-LA | 77 | 1945 | Gene Handley, Sac. | 56 |
| 1906 | John Kane, Sea. | 65 | 1946 | Ed Sauer, LA | 45 |
| 1907 | George Hildebrand, SF | 59 | 1947 | Ulysses Lipien, Hol. | 40 |
| 1908 | Rollie Zeider, SF | 93 | | Dain Clay, SD | 40 |
| 1910 | Ivan Howard, LA | 77 | 1948 | Jack Tobin, SF | 37 |
| 1911 | George Cutshaw, Oak. | 90 | 1949 | Art Wilson, SD-Oak. | 47 |
| 1912 | Bill Leard, Oak. | 80 | 1950 | Luis Marquez, Pd. | 38 |
| 1913 | James Johnston, SF | 124 | 1951 | Bob Boyd, Sac. | 41 |
| 1914 | W. K. Rodgers, Pd. | 71 | 1952 | Carlos Bernier, Hol. | 65 |
| 1915 | James Johnston, Oak. | 82 | 1953 | Tom Saffell, Hol. | 29 |
| 1916 | Bill Lane, Oak. | 56 | 1954 | Tom Saffell, Hol. | 48 |
| 1917 | Emil Meusel, LA | 69 | 1955 | Carlos Bernier, Hol. | 29 |
| 1918 | Charles Pick, SF | 55 | 1956 | Carlos Bernier, Hol. | 48 |
| 1919 | Bill Lane, Oak. | 59 | 1957 | Solomon Drake, Pd. | 36 |
| 1920 | Rod Murphy, Sea. | 63 | 1958 | Vada Pinson, Sea. | 37 |
| 1921 | Patsy McGaffigan, Sac. | 55 | 1959 | Marv Breeding, Van. | 27 |
| 1922 | Bill Lane, Sea. | 60 | 1960 | Willie Davis, Spo. | 30 |
| 1923 | Merlin Kopp, Sac. | 80 | 1961 | David Mann, Sea. | 33 |
| 1924 | Bill Lane, Sea. | 45 | 1962 | Hiraldo Ruiz, SD | 40 |
| 1925 | Bill Hunnefield, Pd. | 42 | 1963 | Hiraldo Ruiz, SD | 50 |
| 1926 | Evar Swanson, Miss. | 43 | 1964 | Jose Cardenal, Tac. | 40 |
| 1927 | Lefty O'Doul, SF | 40 | | Cesar Tovar, SD | 40 |
| 1928 | Evar Swanson, Miss. | 49 | 1965 | Fred Valentine, Haw. | 58 |
| 1929 | Fred Haney, LA | 56 | 1966 | Edwin Stroud, Ind. | 57 |
| 1930 | Fred Haney, LA | 52 | 1967 | David Nelson, Pd. | 29 |
| 1931 | Jigger Statz, LA | 45 | 1968 | Pat Kelly, Den. | 38 |
| 1932 | Art Garabaldi, SF | 49 | 1969 | Larry Bowa, Eug. | 48 |
| 1933 | Fred Haney, Hol. | 63 | 1970 | Doug Griffin, Haw. | 35 |
| 1934 | Fred Haney, Hol. | 71 | 1971 | Cleo James, Tac. | 37 |
| 1935 | Jigger Statz, LA | 53 | 1972 | Davey Lopes, Alb. | 48 |
| 1936 | Jigger Statz, LA | 43 | 1973 | John Rivers, SLC | 47 |
| 1937 | George Myatt, SD | 33 | 1974 | David Moates, Spo. | 42 |
| 1938 | Bernard Uhalt, Hol. | 32 | 1975 | William Almon, Haw. | 33 |
| 1939 | Jo Jo White, Sea. | 47 | | Jerry Royster, Alb. | 33 |
| 1940 | John Barrett, SF | 40 | 1976 | Glenn Burke, Alb. | 63 |
| 1941 | Don Gutteridge, Sac. | 46 | 1977 | Rafael Landestoy, Alb. | 56 |
| 1942 | Bernard Olsen, LA | 33 | 1978 | Rudy Law, Alb. | 79 |

| 1979 | Jose Mangual, SLC | 46 |
| 1980 | Kim Allen, Spo. | 84 |
| 1981 | Alan Wiggins, Haw. | 73 |
| 1982 | Gary Pettis, Spo. | 52 |
| 1983 | Scott Loucks, Tuc. | 71 |

| 1984 | Trench Davis, Haw. | 53 |
| 1985 | Mike Fieder, Van. | 61 |
| 1986 | Devon White, Edm. | 42 |
| 1987 | Donell Nixon, Calg. | 46 |
| 1988 | Eric Bullock, Pd. | 51 |

## .400 HITTERS

| 1933 | .414 | Ox Eckhardt, Miss. |
| 1929 | .407 | Ike Boone, Miss. |
| 1928 | .404 | Smead Jolley, SF |

| 1930 | .403 | Earl Sheely, SF |
| 1925 | .401 | Paul Waner, SF |

## 50 HOME RUNS

| 1925 | 60 | Tony Lazzeri, SLC |
| 1935 | 56 | Gene Lillard, LA |
| 1957 | 56 | Steve Bilko, LA |
| 1956 | 55 | Steve Bilko, LA |
| 1929 | 55 | Ike Boone, Miss. |

| 1974 | 55 | Bill McNulty, Sac. |
| 1974 | 51 | Gorman Thomas, Sac. |
| 1929 | 51 | Gus Suhr, SF |
| 1982 | 50 | Ron Kittle, Edm. |

## PITCHERS — MOST VICTORIES —

| 1903 | Doc Newton, LA | 35 |
| 1904 | Doc Newton, LA | 39 |
| 1905 | James Whalen, SF | 32 |
| 1906 | Rube Vickers, Sea. | 39 |
| 1907 | Dolly Gray, LA | 32 |
| 1908 | Robert Groom, Pd. | 29 |
| 1909 | Frank Browning, SF | 32 |
| 1910 | Cack Henley, SF | 34 |
| 1911 | William Steen, Pd. | 30 |
| 1912 | Harry Ables, Oak. | 25 |
| | Charles Chech, LA | 25 |
| 1913 | Skeeter Fanning, SF | 28 |
| 1914 | Irv Higginbotham, Pd. | 30 |
| 1915 | Lefty Williams, SLC | 33 |
| 1916 | Allen Sothoron, Pd. | 30 |
| 1917 | Eric Erickson, SF | 31 |
| 1918 | Doc Crandall, LA | 16 |
| | Walt Leverenz, SLC | 16 |
| 1919 | Doc Crandall, LA | 28 |
| 1920 | Russell Arlett, Oak. | 29 |
| 1921 | Wheezer Dell, Ver. | 28 |
| 1922 | Jackie May, Ver. | 35 |
| 1923 | Ray Kremer, Oak. | 25 |
| 1924 | Willis Mitchell, SF | 28 |
| 1925 | Clyde Barfoot, Ver. | 26 |

| 1926 | Bert Cole, Miss. | 29 |
| 1927 | George Boehler, Oak. | 22 |
| 1928 | W. H. Ruether, SF | 29 |
| 1929 | Frank Shellenback, Hol. | 26 |
| 1930 | Ed Baecht, LA | 26 |
| | Jimmy Zinn, SF | 26 |
| 1931 | Sam Gibson, SF | 28 |
| 1932 | Frank Shellenback, Hol. | 26 |
| 1933 | Buck Newsom, LA | 30 |
| 1934 | Fay Thomas, LA | 28 |
| 1935 | Walter Beck, Miss. | 23 |
| 1936 | George Custer, Pd. | 25 |
| 1937 | Adolph Liska, Pd. | 23 |
| 1938 | Fred Hutchinson, Sea. | 25 |
| 1939 | Hal Turpin, Sea. | 23 |
| 1940 | Dick Barrett, Sea. | 24 |
| 1941 | Yank Terry, SD | 26 |
| 1942 | Dick Barrett, Sea. | 27 |
| 1943 | Red Lynn, LA | 21 |
| 1944 | Marino Pieretti, Pd. | 26 |
| 1945 | Robert Joyce, SF | 31 |
| 1946 | Larry Jansen, SF | 30 |
| 1947 | Cliff Chambers, LA | 24 |
| 1948 | Red Lynn, LA | 19 |
| 1949 | Harold Saltzman, Pd. | 23 |

| | | | | | |
|---|---|---|---|---|---|
| | Guy Fletcher, Sea. | 23 | | Robert Garibaldi, Phx. | 13 |
| | George Woods, Hol. | 23 | | Jeff James, Eug. | 13 |
| 1950 | James Wilson, Sea. | 24 | | Fred Norman, Spo. | 13 |
| 1951 | Marv Grissom, Sea. | 20 | | Larry Staab, Spo. | 13 |
| | William Ayers, Oak. | 20 | 1970 | Dennis Bennett, Haw. | 18 |
| 1952 | Johnny Lindell, Hol. | 24 | | Jerry Stephenson, Spo. | 18 |
| 1953 | Allen Gettel, Oak. | 24 | 1971 | Richard Woodson, Pd. | 16 |
| 1954 | Roger Bowman, Hol. | 22 | 1972 | Mike Wallace, Eug. | 16 |
| 1955 | George Munger, Hol. | 23 | 1973 | Glenn Abbott, Tuc. | 18 |
| 1956 | Rene Valdes, Pd. | 22 | 1974 | Rex Hudson, Alb. | 16 |
| 1957 | Leo Kiely, SF | 21 | 1975 | Gary Ross, Haw. | 16 |
| 1958 | Marshall Bridges, Sac. | 16 | 1976 | Dennis Lewallyn, Alb. | 15 |
| | Art Fowler, Sea.-Spo. | 16 | | Ed Plank, Phx. | 15 |
| 1959 | Richard Hall, SLC | 18 | | Gary Wheelock, SLC | 15 |
| 1960 | Chester Nichols, Van. | 18 | 1977 | Mark Wiley, Haw. | 16 |
| 1961 | Ron Herbel, Tac. | 16 | 1978 | Eric Wilkins, Pd. | 15 |
| | Gaylord Perry, Tac. | 16 | 1979 | Mark Bomback, Van. | 22 |
| 1962 | Richard Egan, Haw. | 17 | 1980 | Ralph Botting, SLC | 15 |
| 1963 | Howard Reed, Spo. | 19 | | Gerald Hannahs, Alb. | 15 |
| 1964 | Robert Locker, Ind. | 16 | | Dennis Lewallyn, Alb. | 15 |
| | Ken Rowe, Spo. | 16 | | David Stewart, Alb. | 15 |
| 1965 | William Hands, Spo. | 17 | 1981 | Ted Power, Alb. | 18 |
| | Chris Zachary, Ok. City | 17 | 1982 | Odell Jones, Pd. | 16 |
| 1966 | Jimmy Ollom, Den. | 20 | 1983 | Rick Rodas, Alb. | 16 |
| 1967 | Howard Reed, Ok. City | 19 | 1984 | Mike Bielecki, Haw. | 19 |
| 1968 | Jerry Crider, Den. | 18 | 1985 | Bob Walk, Haw. | 16 |
| | Richard Robertson, Phx. | 18 | 1986 | Mark Grant, Phx. | 14 |
| | Charles Taylor, Tulsa | 18 | 1987 | Mike Campbell, Calg. | 15 |
| 1969 | Dennis Bennett, Haw. | 13 | 1988 | Bill Krueger, Alb. | 15 |

## PITCHERS — WINNING PERCENTAGE —

| | | | |
|---|---|---|---|
| 1903 | Doc Newton, LA | 35-12 | .745 |
| 1904 | Doc Newton, LA | 39-17 | .696 |
| 1905 | Dolly Gray, LA | 30-16 | .652 |
| 1906 | Rube Vickers, Sea. | 39-15 | .722 |
| 1907 | Dolly Gray, LA | 32-14 | .696 |
| 1908 | Walter Nagle, LA | 24-10 | .706 |
| 1909 | Cack Henley, SF | 31-10 | .756 |
| 1910 | John Lively, Oak. | 31-15 | .674 |
| 1911 | William Steen, Pd. | 30-15 | .667 |
| 1912 | William Malarkey, Oak. | 20-11 | .645 |
| 1913 | John Williams, Sac. | 17-7 | .708 |
| 1914 | John Ryan, LA | 29-10 | .686 |
| 1915 | Lefty Williams, SLC | 33-12 | .733 |
| 1916 | John Ryan, LA | 29-10 | .744 |
| 1917 | Brad Hogg, LA | 27-13 | .675 |
| 1918 | Tiny Levernenz, SLC | 16-5 | .762 |
| 1919 | Curly Brown, LA | 25-8 | .758 |

| 1920 | Ralph Stroud, SLC | 26-13 | .667 |
|------|-------------------|-------|------|
| 1921 | Art Reinhart, LA | 15-5 | .750 |
| 1922 | Jakie May, Ver. | 35-9 | .795 |
| 1923 | Harry Courtney, SF | 19-6 | .760 |
| 1924 | Vean Gregg, Sea. | 25-11 | .694 |
| 1925 | Doug McWeeney, SF | 20-5 | .800 |
| | Martin Griffin, SF | 16-4 | .800 |
| 1926 | Earl Hamilton, LA | 24-8 | .750 |
| 1927 | Pudgy Gould, Oak. | 17-5 | .773 |
| 1928 | Dutch Ruether, SF | 29-7 | .806 |
| 1929 | Frank Shellenback, Hol. | 26-12 | .684 |
| 1930 | Tony Freitas, Sac. | 19-6 | .760 |
| 1931 | Frank Shellenback, Hol. | 27-7 | .794 |
| 1932 | James de Shong, Sac. | 19-6 | .760 |
| 1933 | Richard Ward, LA | 25-9 | .735 |
| 1934 | Fay Thomas, LA | 28-4 | .875 |
| 1935 | Sam Gibson, SF | 22-4 | .846 |
| 1936 | William Ludolph, Oak. | 21-6 | .778 |
| 1937 | Sam Gibson, SF | 19-8 | .704 |
| 1938 | Fred Hutchinson, Sea. | 25-7 | .781 |
| 1939 | Julio Bonetti, LA | 20-5 | .800 |
| 1940 | Dick Barrett, Sea. | 24-5 | .828 |
| 1941 | Hal Turpin, Sea. | 20-6 | .769 |
| 1942 | Hal Turpin, Sea. | 23-9 | .719 |
| 1943 | Jodie Phipps, LA | 17-5 | .773 |
| 1944 | Manny Salvo, Oak. | 18-7 | .720 |
| 1945 | Robert Joyce, SF | 31-11 | .738 |
| 1946 | Larry Jansen, SF | 30-6 | .833 |
| 1947 | Robert Chesnes, SF | 22-8 | .733 |
| 1948 | William Werle, SF | 17-7 | .708 |
| 1949 | Herbert Karpel, Sea. | 14-6 | .700 |
| 1950 | James Wilson, Sea. | 24-11 | .686 |
| 1951 | Ben Wade, Hol. | 16-6 | .727 |
| | Skinny Brown, Sea. | 16-6 | .727 |
| 1952 | John Lindell, Hol. | 24-9 | .727 |
| 1953 | Royce Lint, Pd. | 22-10 | .688 |
| 1954 | William Wight, SD | 17-5 | .773 |
| 1955 | Lou Kretlow, Sea. | 14-3 | .824 |
| 1956 | Dave Hillman, LA | 21-7 | .750 |
| 1957 | William Abernathie, SF | 13-2 | .867 |
| 1958 | Robert Alexander, SD | 10-5 | .667 |
| 1959 | Richard Hall, SLC | 18-5 | .783 |
| 1960 | Chester Nichils, Van. | 18-6 | .750 |
| 1961 | Ron Herbel, Tac. | 16-5 | .762 |
| 1962 | Sam Ellis, SD | 12-6 | .667 |
| 1963 | Howard Reed, Spo. | 19-7 | .731 |
| 1964 | Luis Tiant, Pd. | 15-1 | .938 |
| 1965 | Thomas Kelley, Pd. | 16-3 | .842 |
| 1966 | Manly Johnston, Ind. | 18-7 | .720 |
| 1967 | William Fischer, Ind. | 12-4 | .750 |

|  | | | |
|---|---|---|---|
|  | Roberto Rodriguez, Van. | 12-4 | .750 |
|  | Gary Wagner, SD | 12-4 | .750 |
| 1968 | Pete Mikkelson, Tulsa | 16-4 | .800 |
| 1969 | Bo Belinsky, Haw. | 12-5 | .706 |
| 1970 | Robert O'Brien, Spo. | 13-3 | .813 |
| 1971 | Archie Reynolds, SLC | 13-6 | .684 |
| 1972 | Doug Rau, Alb. | 14-3 | .824 |
| 1973 | Richard Henninger, Spo. | 12-5 | .706 |
| 1974 | Rex Hudson, Alb. | 16-4 | .800 |
| 1975 | Butch Metzger, Haw. | 15-7 | .682 |
| 1976 | Mike Pazik, Tac. | 14-5 | .737 |
| 1977 | Greg Minton, Phx. | 14-6 | .700 |
| 1978 | Robert Kammeyer, Tac. | 12-2 | .857 |
| 1979 | Mark Bomback, Van. | 22-7 | .759 |
| 1980 | Dennis Lewallyn, Alb. | 15-2 | .882 |
| 1981 | Ted Power, Alb. | 18-3 | .857 |
| 1982 | Chris Codiroli, Tac. | 10-3 | .769 |
| 1983 | Rick Rodas, Alb. | 16-4 | .800 |
| 1984 | Mike Bielecki, Haw. | 19-3 | .864 |
| 1985 | Roger Mason, Phx. | 12-1 | .923 |
| 1986 | Mark Williamson, LV | 10-3 | .769 |
| 1987 | Mike Campbell, Calg. | 15-2 | .882 |
| 1988 | Bill Krueger, Alb. | 15-5 | .750 |

## PITCHERS — MOST STRIKEOUTS —

| | | | | | | |
|---|---|---|---|---|---|---|
| 1906 | Rube Vickers, Sea. | 409 | | 1932 | Fay Thomas, Oak. | 196 |
| 1910 | Vean Gregg, Pd. | 376 | | 1933 | Buck Newsom, LA | 212 |
| 1911 | Harry Sutor, SF | 339 | | 1934 | Fay Thomas, LA | 204 |
| 1912 | Harry Ables, Oak. | 303 | | 1935 | Walter Beck, Miss. | 202 |
| 1913 | Bill James, Pd. | 215 | | 1936 | George Custer, Pd. | 234 |
| 1914 | Ed Klepfer, Ven. | 212 | | 1937 | Manuel Salvo, SD | 196 |
| 1915 | Lefty Williams, SLC | 294 | | 1938 | Manuel Salvo, SD | 191 |
| 1916 | Paul Fittery, SLC | -203 | | 1939 | Tony Freitas, Sac. | 172 |
| 1917 | Eric Erickson, SF | 307 | | 1940 | Dick Barrett, Sea. | 164 |
| 1918 | John P. Quinn, Ver. | 99 | | 1941 | Yank Terry, SD | 172 |
| 1919 | Bill Piercy, Sac. | 163 | | 1942 | Dick Barrett, Sea. | 178 |
| 1920 | Willis Mitchell, Ver. | 161 | | 1943 | Frank Dasso, SD | 154 |
| 1921 | Paul Fittery, Sac. | 164 | | 1944 | Frank Dasso, SD | 253 |
| 1922 | Jakie May, Ver. | 238 | | 1945 | Vallie Eaves, SD | 187 |
| 1923 | John Mails, Oak. | 206 | | 1946 | Ed Erautt, Hol. | 234 |
| 1924 | George Boehler, Oak. | 216 | | 1947 | Cliff Chambers, LA | 175 |
| 1925 | George Boehler, Oak. | 278 | | 1948 | Cornelius Dempsey, SF | 171 |
| 1926 | James Elliott, Sea. | 203 | | 1949 | Cornelius Dempsey, SF | 164 |
| 1927 | George Boehler, Oak. | 160 | | 1950 | James Wilson, Sea. | 228 |
| 1928 | Elmer Jacobs, SF | 159 | | 1951 | Sam Jones, SD | 246 |
| 1929 | Howard Craighead, Oak. | 190 | | 1952 | Johnny Lindell, Hol. | 190 |
| 1930 | Fay Thomas, Sac. | 228 | | 1953 | Joe Hatten, LA | 152 |
| 1931 | Sam Gibson, SF | 204 | | 1954 | Tom Byrne, Sea. | 199 |

| 1955 | Robert Garber, Hol. | 199 | 1972 | Steve Luebber, Alb. | 199 |
| 1956 | Richard Drott, LA | 184 | 1973 | Dave Freisleben, Haw. | 206 |
| 1957 | James Grant, SD | 178 | 1974 | Clarence Metzger, Phx. | 148 |
| 1958 | Marshall Bridges, Sac. | 205 | 1975 | Greg Shanahan, Alb. | 147 |
| 1959 | Richard Stigman, SD | 181 | 1976 | Gary Wheelock, SLC | 138 |
| 1960 | Noel Mickelsen, Pd. | 156 | 1977 | Frank Ricelli, Phx. | 135 |
| 1961 | Sam McDowell, SLC | 156 | 1978 | Steve Mura, Haw. | 158 |
| 1962 | Richard Egan, SD | 201 | 1979 | Juan Berenguer, Tac. | 220 |
| 1963 | William Spanswick, Sea. | 209 | 1980 | Mickey Mahler, Pd. | 140 |
| 1964 | Albert Stanek, Tac. | 220 | 1981 | Odell Jones, Pd. | 135 |
| 1965 | Tom Kelley, Pd. | 190 | 1982 | Odell Jones, Pd. | 172 |
| 1966 | William Singer, Spo. | 217 | 1983 | Richard Rodas, Alb. | 157 |
| 1967 | Richard Robertson, Phx. | 184 | 1984 | Mike Bielecki, Haw. | 162 |
| 1968 | Richard Robertson, Phx. | 216 | 1985 | Jose Rijo, Tac. | 179 |
| 1969 | Jaff James, Eng. | 155 | 1986 | Robert Patterson, Haw. | 137 |
| 1970 | Darrell Brandon, Tuc. | 167 | 1987 | Tim Belcher, Tac. | 133 |
| 1971 | Richard Woodson, Pd. | 163 | 1988 | Erik Hanson, Calg. | 154 |

## PITCHERS — LOWEST EARNED RUN AVERAGE

| 1914 | Slim Love, LA | 1.56 | 1943 | Alpha Brazle, Sac. | 1.69 |
| 1915 | Slim Love, LA | 1.95 | 1944 | Clement Dreiseward, Sac. | 1.61 |
| 1916 | Art Fromme, Ver. | 1.92 | 1945 | Robert Joyce, SF | 2.17 |
| 1917 | Eric Erickson, SF | 1.93 | 1946 | Larry Jansen, SF | 1.57 |
| 1918 | Jack Quinn, Ver. | 1.65 | 1947 | Robert Chesnes, SF | 2.32 |
| 1919 | Curly Brown, LA | 2.03 | 1948 | Con Dempsey, SF | 2.10 |
| 1920 | Jim Scott, SF | 2.29 | 1949 | Willard Ramsdell, Hol. | 2.60 |
| 1921 | Vic Aldridge, LA | 2.16 | 1950 | Jack Salveson, Hol. | 2.84 |
| 1922 | Jackie May, Ver. | 1.84 | 1951 | James Davis, Sea. | 2.44 |
| 1923 | Vean Gregg, Sea. | 2.75 | 1952 | Red Adams, Pd. | 2.17 |
| 1924 | Doc Crandall, LA | 2.71 | 1953 | Memo Luna, SD | 2.67 |
| 1925 | Doug McWeeney, SF | 2.70 | 1954 | William Wight, SD | 1.93 |
| 1926 | Elmer Jacobs, LA | 2.20 | 1955 | Red Munger, Hol. | 1.85 |
| 1927 | John Miljus, Sea. | 2.36 | 1956 | Elmer Singleton, Sea. | 2.55 |
| 1928 | Elmer Jacobs, SF | 2.56 | 1957 | Morrie Martin, Van. | 1.90 |
| 1929 | Lefty Gomez, SF | 3.43 | 1958 | George Bamberger, Van. | 2.45 |
| 1930 | Edward Baecht, LA | 3.23 | 1959 | Richard Hall, SLC | 1.87 |
| 1931 | Sam Gibson, SF | 2.48 | 1960 | Don Rudolph, Sea. | 2.42 |
| 1932 | Curtis Davis, SF | 2.24 | 1961 | Ronald Piche, Van. | 2.26 |
| 1933 | William Ludolph, Oak. | 3.09 | 1962 | Gaylord Perry, Tac. | 2.48 |
| 1934 | Dutch Lieber, Miss. | 2.50 | 1963 | Samuel Ellis, SD | 2.62 |
| 1935 | Mike Meola, LA | 3.00 | 1964 | Bruce Howard, Ind. | 2.20 |
| 1936 | Lou Koupal, Sea. | 2.42 | 1965 | William Hands, Tac. | 2.19 |
| 1937 | Bill Shores, SF | 2.47 | 1966 | William Fischer, Ind. | 2.35 |
| 1938 | Fred Hutchinson, Sea. | 2.48 | 1967 | Bobby Locke, Sea. | 2.22 |
| 1939 | Sam Gibson, SF | 2.24 | 1968 | Pete Mikkelson, Tulsa | 1.91 |
| 1940 | Jack Salveson, Oak. | 2.30 | 1969 | James Colburn, Tac. | 2.28 |
| 1941 | Yank Terry, SD | 2.31 | 1970 | Jerry Stephenson, Spo. | 2.82 |
| 1942 | Dick Barrett, Sea. | 1.72 | 1971 | Jerry Crider, Haw. | 3.29 |

| 1972 | Richard Lange, SLC | 2.97 | 1980 | Dennis Lewallyn, Alb. | 2.13 |
|------|--------------------|------|------|----------------------|------|
| 1973 | Dave Freisleben, Haw. | 2.82 | 1981 | Robert Stoddard, Spo. | 2.90 |
| 1974 | Juan Veintidos, Tac. | 3.67 | 1982 | Chris Codiroli, Tac. | 1.90 |
| 1975 | Steve Luebber, Tac. | 2.39 | 1983 | Jose de Leon, Haw. | 3.04 |
| 1976 | Diego Segui, Haw. | 3.18 | 1984 | Bob Walk, Haw. | 2.26 |
| 1977 | Ed Bane, Tac. | 4.14 | 1985 | Bob Walk, Haw. | 2.65 |
| 1978 | Larry McCall, Tac. | 2.93 | 1986 | David Johnson, Haw. | 3.17 |
| 1979 | Mark Bomback, Van. | 2.56 | 1987 | Vicente Palacios, Van. | 2.58 |
|      |                    |      | 1988 | Bill Krueger, Alb. | 3.01 |

## 30-GAME WINNERS

| 1906 | 39-15 | Rube Vickers, Sea. | 1905 | 32-25 | James Whalen, SF |
|------|-------|-------------------|------|-------|------------------|
| 1904 | 39-17 | Doc Newton, LA | 1909 | 31-10 | Cack Henley, SF |
| 1922 | 35-9 | Jakie May, Ver. | 1945 | 31-11 | Robert Joyce, SF |
| 1903 | 35-12 | Doc Newton, LA | 1909 | 31-12 | William Tozer, LA |
| 1903 | 34-15 | James Hughes, Sea. | 1910 | 31-15 | John Lively, Oak. |
| 1904 | 34-15 | Robert Keefe, Tac. | 1917 | 31-15 | Eric Erickson, SF |
| 1910 | 34-19 | Cack Henley, SF | 1910 | 31-20 | Walter Moser, Oak. |
| 1915 | 33-12 | Lefty Williams, SLC | 1914 | 31-20 | Irv Higginbotham, Pd. |
| 1904 | 33-20 | James Buchanan, Oak. | 1946 | 30-6 | Larry Jansen, SF |
| 1907 | 32-14 | Dolly Gray, LA | 1911 | 30-15 | William Steen, Pd. |
| 1909 | 32-16 | Frank Browning, SF | 1915 | 30-15 | Spider Baum, SF |
| 1903 | 32-18 | Warren Hall, LA | 1905 | 30-16 | Dolly Gray, LA |
| 1910 | 32-18 | Vean Gregg, Pd. | 1916 | 30-17 | Allen Sothoron, Pd. |
| 1904 | 32-23 | James Whalen, SF | 1905 | 30-22 | Robert Keefe, Tac. |
| 1904 | 32-25 | Orval Overall, Tac. | | | |

## PITCHERS WITH MORE THAN 200 VICTORIES

| Name | Won | Lost | Pcg. | Name | Won | Lost | Pcg. |
|------|-----|------|------|------|-----|------|------|
| Frank Shellenback | 295 | 178 | .624 | Sam Gibson | 227 | 140 | .619 |
| Spider Baum | 261 | 235 | .526 | Herman Pillette | 226 | 235 | .491 |
| Harry Krause | 249 | 220 | .531 | Cack Henley | 215 | 171 | .557 |
| Dick Barrett | 234 | 168 | .582 | Rudolph Kallio | 205 | 210 | .496 |
| Doc Crandall | 230 | 151 | .604 | Jack Salveson | 204 | 166 | .551 |
| Tony Freitas | 228 | 175 | .566 | Harold Turpin | 203 | 158 | .562 |

## MOST VALUABLE PLAYERS

In 1927 the PCL underwrote a $1,000 cash prize to be awarded to the man selected by sportswriters as Most Valuable Player. San Francisco outfielder Lefty O'Doul won this award. From 1932 through 1947 *The Sporting News* selected the league's Most Valuable Player. Beginning in 1948 the Charles H. Graham Memorial Award was established to honor the PCL's Most Valuable Player. No MVP was designated in 1973 or in 1975 through 1979. The only men selected more than once were Oakland's Les Scarsella (1944 and 1946) and LA slugger Steve Bilko, who won three consecutive awards (1955, 1956, and 1957).

| | | | | |
|---|---|---|---|---|
| 1927 | Lefty O'Doul, OF, SF | | 1957 | Steve Bilko, 1B, LA |
| 1932 | Jigger Statz, OF, LA | | 1958 | Earl Averill, C, SD |
| 1933 | Buck Newsom, P,LA | | 1959 | Dick Hall, P, SLC |
| 1934 | Frank Demaree, OF, LA | | 1960 | Willie Davis, OF, Spo. |
| 1935 | Joe DiMaggio, OF, SF | | 1961 | Dick Phillips, IF-OF, Tac. |
| 1936 | Willie Ludolph, P, Oak. | | 1962 | Jesse Gonder, C, SD |
| 1937 | Art Garibaldi, 3B, Sac. | | 1963 | Billy Cowan, OF, SLC |
| 1938 | Fred Hutchinson, P, Sea. | | 1964 | Tony Perez, IF, SD |
| 1939 | Dom DiMaggio, OF, SF | | 1965 | David Roberts, OF, |
| 1940 | George Archie, 1B, Sea. | | | Okla. Cty. |
| 1941 | Yank Terry, P, SD | | 1966 | Duane Josephson, C, Ind. |
| 1942 | Ray Mueller, C, Sac. | | 1967 | Ricardo Joseph, 3B, SD |
| 1943 | Andy Pafko, OF, LA | | 1968 | Jim Hicks, OF, Tulsa |
| 1944 | Les Scarsella, OF-1B, Oak. | | 1969 | R. Dennis Doyle, 2B, Eug. |
| 1945 | Robert Joyce, P, SF | | 1970 | Bobby Valentine, SS, Spo. |
| 1946 | Les Scarsella, 1B, Oak. | | 1971 | Tom Hutton, 1B, Spo. |
| 1947 | Tony Lupien, 1B, Hol. | | 1972 | Tom Paciorek, 1B, Alb. |
| 1948 | Jack Graham, OF, SD | | 1974 | Tom Robson, OF-1B, Spo. |
| 1949 | Irv Noren, OF, Hol. | | 1980 | Dennis Lewallyn, P, Alb. |
| 1950 | George Metkovich, OF, Oak. | | 1981 | Mike Marshall, 1B, Alb. |
| 1951 | Jim Rivera, OF, Sea. | | 1982 | Ron Kittle, OF, Edm. |
| 1952 | John Lindell, P-OF, Hol. | | 1983 | Kevin McReynolds, OF, LV |
| 1953 | Dale Long, 1B, Hol. | | 1984 | Alejandro Sanchez, OF, Phx. |
| 1954 | Jack Phillips, IF, Hol. | | 1985 | Danny Tartabull, SS, Calg. |
| 1955 | Steve Bilko, 1B, LA | | 1986 | Tim Pyznarski, 1B, LV |
| 1956 | Steve Bilko, 1B, LA | | 1987 | Mike Campbell, P, Calg. |
| | | | 1988 | Sandy Alomar, Jr., C, LV |

## PACIFIC COAST LEAGUE HALL OF FAMERS
(Hall of Famers Who Have Played or Managed in the PCL)

Earl Averill (SF, 1926-28)
Dave Bancroft (Pd. 1912-14)
Mickey Cochrane (Pd. 1924)
Stan Coveleski (Pd. 1915)
Joe DiMaggio (SF, 1932-35)
Bobby Doerr (Hol., 1934-35; SD, 1936)
Lefty Gomez (SF, 1929)
Babe Herman (Oak., 1950)
Harry Heilmann (SF, 1915)
Harry Hooper (Miss., 1927)
Rogers Hornsby (Mgr. — Sea., 1951)
George Kelly (Oak., 1933)
Bob Lemon (SD, 1958; Mgr. — Honolulu, 1964;)
    (Sea., 1965-66; Sac., 1974)
Ernie Lombardi (Oak., 1926-30; Sac. — Oak., 1948)
Willie McCovey (Phx., 1958-59)

Mel Ott (Mgr. — Oak., 1951-52)
Satchell Paige (Pd., 1961)
Brooks Robinson (Van., 1959)
Warren Spahn (Tulsa, 1967; Mgr. — Tulsa, 1967-68)
Casey Stengel (Mgr. — Oak., 1946-48)
Dazzy Vance (Sac., 1919)
Arky Vaughan (SF, 1949)
Lloyd Waner (SF, 1925-26)
Paul Waner (SF, 1923-25)
Ted Williams (SD, 1936-37)

## LIFETIME RECORDS

| BEST LIFETIME HITTING RECORDS | | | | | |
|---|---|---|---|---|---|
| Years | Jigger Statz | 18 | RBIs | Buzz Arlett | 1,135 |
| Games | Jigger Statz | 2,790 | Stolen Bases | William Lane | 468 |
| Runs | Jigger Statz | 1,996 | | | |
| Hits | Jigger Statz | 3,356 | | | |
| Doubles | Jigger Statz | 595 | | | |
| Triples | Jigger Statz | 137 | | | |
| Home Runs | Buzz Arlett | 251 | | | |

| BEST LIFETIME PITCHING RECORDS | | |
|---|---|---|
| Years | Herman Pillette | 23 |
| Games | Herman Pillette | 708 |
| Victories | Frank Shellenback | 295 |
| Losses | Spider Baum | 235 |
| Strikeouts | Dick Barrett | 1,866 |

## SEASON RECORDS

### BEST INDIVIDUAL SEASON BATTING RECORDS

| | | |
|---|---|---|
| Games | William Dunleavy (Oak., 1905) | 227 |
| Average | Ox Eckhardt (Miss., 1933) | .414 |
| Runs | Tony Lazzeri (SLC, 1925) | 202 |
| Hits | Paul Strand (SLC, 1923) | 325 |
| Singles | Ox Eckhardt (Miss., 1933) | 231 |
| Doubles | Paul Waner (SF, 1925) | 75 |
| Triples | Willie Davis (Spo., 1960) | 26 |
| Home Runs | Tony Lazzeri (SLC, 1925) | 60 |
| Grand Slams | ERic Soderholm (Pd., 1971) | 4 |
| Extra Base Hits | Tony Lazzeri (SLC, 1925) 52 2Bs, 14 3Bs, 60 Hrs | 126 |
| Consecutive Hits | Mickey Heath (Hol., 1930) | 12 |
| | Ted Beard (Hol., 1953) | 12 |
| Hitting Streak (Games) | Joe DiMaggio (SF, 1933) | 61 |
| Consecutive Pinch Hits | Richard Smith (Hol., 1957) | 6 |
| | Jack Littrell (Sac., 1960) | 6 |
| RBIs | Tony Lazzeri (SLC, 1925) | 222 |
| Stolen Bases | James Johnston (SF, 1913) | 124 |
| Walks | Max West (SD, 1949) | 201 |

| Strikeouts | Greg Luzinski (Eug., 1971) | 167 |
|---|---|---|
| HBP | Charles Irwin (SF, 1903) | 23 |
| | George Wheeler (LA, 1903) | 23 |

## BEST INDIVIDUAL SEASON PITCHING RECORDS

| Games | Kenneth Rowe (Spo., 1964) | 88 |
|---|---|---|
| Complete Games | Cack Henley (SF, 1910) | 48 |
| Victories | Doc Newton (LA, 1904) | 39 |
| | Rube Vickers (Sea., 1906) | 39 |
| Losses | Isaac Butler (Pd., 1903 and 1904) | 31 |
| Winning Percentage | Luis Tiant (Pd., 1964, 15-1) | .938 |
| Lowest ERA | Slim Love (LA, 1914) | 1.56 |
| Most Innings | Rube Vickers (Sea., 1906) | 526 |
| Consecutive Wins | Frank Browning (SF, 1909) | 16 |
| | Fay Thomas (LA, 1933-34) | 22 |
| Shutouts | Vean Gregg (Pd., 1910) | 14 |
| Consecutive Shutout Innings | William Tozer (LA, 1905) | 44 |
| Strikeouts | Rube Vickers (Sea., 1906) | 408 |
| Walks | Oscar Graham (Oak., 1903) | 234 |

## 1989 Wrap-up Features Three No-Hitters

During the 1989 Season Albuquerque again posted the PCL's best record, then knocked off Colorado Springs in the playoff opener to win another Southern Division title. Vancouver swept Calgary in three games to claim the Northern Division, and downed Albuquerque in the finals, three games to one, to become the 1989 champs. Four clubs, Albuquerque, Calgary, Las Vegas and Tacoma, exceeded 300,000 in attendance.

For the second year in a row Las Vegas catcher Sandy Alomar (.306 with a league-leading 101 RBIs) was named Most Valuable Player. The batting champ was Calgary outfielder Bruce Fields (.351) and Colorado Springs third baseman Danny Gonzalez (.288 with 27 homers) won the home run crown, although Phoenix third sacker Matt Williams (.320 with 26 homers) probably would have won the title except for a callup to San Francisco — which forced him to play in the National League Championship Series and in the World Series! Vancouver fireballer Jeff Bittger (9–5, 2.12 ERA) posted the lowest ERA while Tacoma lefty Bryan Clark (15–7) rang up the most victories.

But the premier pitching performance of 1989 was turned in by Vancouver southpaw Tom Drees. On a frigid Tuesday night in Nat Bailey Stadium (there were only 289 shivering fans), May 23, 1989, the 26-year-old Drees fired a nine-inning no-hitter to defeat Calgary. On his next start five days later Drees did it again, tossing a seven-inning classic against Edmonton. In 1938 Johnny Vander Meer of the Cincinnati Reds won permanent fame by twirling back-to-back no-hitters, and righthander Bill Bell repeated the feat in 1952 for Bristol of the Class D Appalachian League, striking out 17 and 20 in consecutive nine-inning no-hitters. Incredibly, in another seven-inning game against Las Vegas on August 16, Drees used just 78 pitches to no-hit the Stars. The 5–0 victory gave Drees three no-hitters in a single season, a feat unprecedented in the upper levels of Organized Baseball. In 1952 Bill Bell threw a total of three no-hitters for Bristol, and in 1908 Walter "Smoke" Justis hurled four no-hitters in two months for the Lancaster Lanks of the Class D Ohio State League.

# Bibliography

## Books

An indispensable source of statistical and anecdotal information for a project of this nature is the Pacific Coast League section of the annual baseball guides. The library of the Baseball Hall of Fame in Cooperstown helpfully provided photocopies of this essential material from the following guides:

> *Reach Official American League Guide,* 1902–1938.
> *Spalding-Reach Official Base Ball Guide,* 1939–1940.
> *Official Baseball Record Book,* 1941.
> *1943 Baseball,* 1942.
> *Baseball Guide and Record Book,* 1943–1961.
> *Official Baseball Guide,* 1962–1986.

Other books containing pertinent information included:

Alou, Felipe, with Herm Weiskopf, *My Life and Baseball.* Waco, Texas: Word Books, 1967.

Bailey, Jim. *Arkansas Travelers, 79 Years of Baseball.* Little Rock: Arkansas Travelers Baseball Club, Inc., [1980].

Beverage, Richard. *The Angels, Los Angeles In The Pacific Coast League, 1919–1957.* Placentia, California: Deacon Press, 1981.

Beverage, Richard. *The Hollywood Stars, Baseball in Movieland, 1926–1957.* Placentia, California: Deacon Press, 1984.

Clough, Charles W., *et al. Fresno County In The 20th Century, From 1900 to the 1980s.* Vol. II. Fresno, California: Panorama West Books, 1986.

Creamer, Robert W. *Stengel, His Life and Times.* New York: Dell Publishing Co., Inc., 1984.

Foster, Mark S. *The Denver Bears From Sandlots to Sellouts.* Boulder, Colorado: Pruett Publishing Company, 1983.

Goldstein, Richard. *Spartan Seasons — How Baseball Survived the Second World War.* New York: Macmillan Publishing Co., Inc., 1980.

*A History of Baseball in the San Francisco Bay Area; San Francisco Giants Official 1985 Yearbook, Special Historical Edition.* San Francisco: Woodford Associates, 1985.

Humber, William. *Cheering for the Home Team, The Story of Baseball in Canada.* Ontario: The Boston Mills Press, 1983.

James, Bill. *The Bill James Historical Baseball Abstract*. New York: Villard Books, 1986.

Kiersh, Edward. *Where Have You Gone Vince DiMaggio?* New York: Bantam Books, 1983.

Lange, Fred W. *History of Baseball in California and Pacific Coast League, 1847–1938, Memories and Musings of and Old Time Baseball Player*. Oakland: n.p., 1938.

MacFarlane, Paul, ed. *Daguerreotypes of Great Stars of Baseball*. St. Louis: The Sporting News Publishing Co., 1981.

MacLean, Norman, ed. *Who's Who in Baseball 1986*. New York: Who's Who in Baseball, Inc., 1986.

Martin, Harry, and Caroline Kellogg. *Tacoma, A Pictorial History*. Virginia Beach Virginia: The Donning Company/Publisher, 1981.

Moore, Jack B. *Joe DiMaggio, Baseball's Yankee Clipper*. New York: Praeger Publishers, 1987.

Obojski, Robert. *Bush League, A History of Minor League Baseball*. New York: Macmillan Publishing Co., Inc., 1975.

Pourade, Richard F. *City of the Dream, The History of San Diego*. La Jolla, California: Copley Books, 1977.

Reichler, Joseph L., ed. *The Baseball Encyclopedia*. New York: Macmillan Publishing Co., Inc., 1988.

Reidenbaugh, Lowell. *Take Me Out To The Ball Park*. St. Louis: The Sporting News Publishing Co., 1983.

Reynolds, Edward Samuel. *Fifty Cartoons by "Tige" Reynolds*. Portland, Oregon: Metropolitan Press, Publishers, 1931.

Ritter, Lawrence S. *The Glory of Their Times*. New York: William Morrow and Company, Inc., 1984.

Ryan, Bob. *Wait Till I Make the Show, Baseball in the Minor Leagues*. Boston: Little, Brown and Company, 1974.

Society for American Baseball Research. *Minor League Baseball Stars*, Vol. I. Manhattan, Kansas: Ag Press, Inc., 1984.

Society for American Baseball Research. *Minor League Baseball Stars*, Vol. II. Manhattan, Kansas: Ag Press, Inc., 1985.

Stadler, Ken. *The Pacific Coast League, One Man's Memories, 1938–1957*. Los Angeles: Marbek Publications, 1984.

Sullivan, Neil J. *The Dodgers Move West*. New York and Oxford: Oxford University Press, 1987.

Thorn, John. *A Century of Baseball Lore*. New York: Hart Publishing Company, Inc., 1974.

Turkin, Hy, and S. C. Thompson. *The Official Encyclopedia of Baseball*. New York: A. S. Barnes and Company, 1956.

Tomlinson, Gerald. *The Baseball Research Handbook*. Kansas City: Society for American Baseball Research, 1988.

Torrence, Bruce T. *Hollywood: The First Hundred Years*. New York: New York Zoetrope, 1982.

Waddington, Gary. *The Seattle Rainiers 1938–1942*. Seattle: Gary Waddington, 1988.

Weiss, William J., ed. *1987 Pacific Coast League Record Book.* Tempe, Arizona: Pacific Coast Baseball League, 1987.
Williams, Ted, with John Underwood. *My Turn At Bat: The Story of My Life.* New York: Pocket Books, 1970.

## Game Programs and Media Guides

A great deal of information about the background of specific professional baseball clubs and their ballparks may be found in game programs, media guides and similar publications. Modern game programs frequently are in magazine format and contain historical articles and statistical information. Publications that I found to be of interest and use included:

*Albuquerque Dukes Media Guide.* 1988.
*Albuquerque Dukes Season Magazine.* 1988, 1987, 1986, 1985, 1984, 1983, 1982, 1981, and 1980.
*Calgary Cannons Fact Book.* 1988, 1987, 1986, and 1985.
*Calgary Cannons Magazine.* 1988.
*Canadians Illustrated.* 1988.
*Colorado Springs Sky Sox Magazine.* 1988.
*Edmonton Trappers Fact Book.* 1986.
*Edmonton Trappers Media Guide.* 1988 and 1985.
*Edmonton Trappers Scorebook Magazine.* 1984.
*Edmonton Trappers' Yearbook.* 1987.
*Las Vegas Stars Baseball '88, The Joys of Summer.* 1988.
*Padre Parade Sketchbook.* 1951.
*Portland Beavers Souvenir Program.* 1988.
*Salt Lake Trappers Souvenir Program.* 1988.
*Seattle Rainier Baseball Club Press Book.* 1949.
*Tacoma Tiger News.* 1988.
*Tacoma Tigers Media Guide.* 1988.
*Tacoma Yankees Pictorial Yearbook.* 1978.
*Tucson Toros Souvenir Program.* 1988.
*Tulsa Drillers Souvenir Program.* 1987 and 1986.

## Articles and Miscellaneous

Daniels, Stephen M. "The Hollywood Stars." *Baseball Research Journal* (1980), 155–163.
Franks, Joel. "Of Heroes and Boors: Early Bay-Area Baseball." *Baseball Research Journal* (1987), 45–47.
Gergen, Joe. "Will Postema's Apprenticeship Be Rewarded?" *The Sporting News* (August 1, 1988), 6.
Hyman, Lawrence J., and Dennis Desprots. "Willie McCovey, Interview." *Giants Magazine,* Vol. III, No. 3 (1988), 5–9.
Keller, Richard. "Bay Area Sports Hall of Fame." *Giants Magazine,* Vol. III, No. 3 (1988), 111–114.

Klink, Bill. "Coast League Dreams." *Sports History* (July 1988), 42–48.

Lang, Jack. "The Move West, Farewell to New York." *Giants Magazine*, Vol. III, No. 3 (1988), 87–90.

Melnick, Norman. "The Return of the Solons." *California Living Magazine* (July 7, 1974), 20–21 ff.

Nightingale, Dave. "A Batting Champion Gone to Pot." *The Sporting News* (May 16, 1988), 18–19.

*Rollie Truitt's Scrapbook, "56" Beavers,* Souvenir Edition, Vaughn Street to Multnomah Stadium, 1903–1956.

Runquist, Willie. "Dickshot Swat Streak Had Hollywood Streak." *Baseball Research Journal* (1985), 23–25.

Soulsberry, Charles. "Fifty Years of Baseball." *Oklahoma City Times* (long-running serial in 1940).

Schroeder, W. R. "The 1934 Los Angeles Angels." *Baseball Research Journal* (1977), 13–16.

Schroeder, W. R. The Pacific Coast League. Typescript available in the Seattle Public Library.

Spander, Art. "The Day the Majors Said Hello to California." *The Sporting News* (May 2, 1988), 14.

Tomlinson, Gerald. "A Minor-League Legend: Buzz Arlett, the 'Mightiest Oak.' " *Baseball Research Journal* (1988), 13–16.

Verrell, Gordon. "Pam Postema Still Paying Her Dues." *The Sporting News* (March 28, 1988), 36–37.

Weiss, William J. Final Official Pacific Coast League Averages, 1987 Season.

## Newspapers

*Albuquerque Journal* (1966, 1969).
*Arizona Daily Star,* Tucson (1950, 1983–84, 1986).
*Dallas Morning News* (1963–64).
*Edmonton Journal* (1981–87).
*Fort Worth Star-Telegram* (1963).
*Las Vegas Review Journal* (1986).
*Los Angeles Mirror* (1949–50).
*Los Angeles Times* (1949–50).
*Oakland Tribune* (1953, 1957, 1970, 1977, 1988).
*Oklahoma City Times* (1940).
*Oregon Journal,* Portland (1969, 1975–76, 1978, 1980).
*Pacific Coast Baseball News* (1947–50).
*Sacramento Bee* (1957).
*San Diego Union* (1948, 1951).
*San Francisco Chronicle* (1950).
*Seattle Post Intelligencer* (1949–50).
*Seattle Times* (1949–50).
*Tacoma News Tribune* (1959–88).
*Tacoma Times* (1924, 1937, 1953).

*Tulsa Tribune* (1949, 1958, 1974, 1979).
*Tulsa World* (1965, 1967, 1969, 1971, 1976, 1977, 1983).
*The Province,* Vancouver (1952, 1956, 1968–69, 1977–78, 1984, 1987–88).

## Local Baseball Files

The following libraries have files on local baseball teams or sports history. These files include newspaper clippings, old game programs, photographs, etc., and offer rich sources of information.

Albuquerque Public Library
Arizona Historical Society Library, Tucson
California State Library, Sacramento
Dallas Public Library
Edmonton Public Library
Eugene Public Library
Fort Worth Public Library
Fresno County Free Library, Fresno
Metropolitan Library System, Oklahoma City
Oakland Public Library
Oregon Historical Society, Portland
Sacramento City Library
San Francisco Public Library
San Jose Public Library
Seattle Public Library
Spokane Public Library
Tacoma Public Library
Tulsa Public Library
Vancouver Public Library

# Index

Due to the tendency of team names to change all teams are referred to by city only.

**A**

Aaron, Tommy, 193
Abbott, Glenn, 138, 139, 302
Abernathie, William, 113, 280
Ables, Harry, 21, 24, 26, 86, 234
Abner, Shawn, 218
Adams, Buster, 83, 258, 259
  Earl, 258
  Glenn, 140, 245
  Red, 169, 252
  Ricky, 292
Adcock, Joe, 130
Adduci, James, 155
Agee, Tommie, 215
Agnew, Sam "Slam," 42, 276, 277
Aguayo, Luis, 253
Aikens, Willie, 144, 266
Akerfelds, Darrell, 159, 298
Akin, Roy, 22, 24
Alameda, Louis, 60, 67
Alberson, Cliff, 95
Albert, Bill, 54
Albuquerque, 134, 137, 138, 140, 141, 143, 144, 145, 146, 148, 149, 150, 151, 152, 153, 154, 155, 158, 159, 160, 162, 164, 166, 179–185, 188, 200, 213, 217, 218, 219, 253, 266, 267, 292, 298, 303
Albuquerque, New Mexico, 136, 176, 291
Aldridge, Vic, 39, 223
Allen, Bob, 265
  Gracie, 207
  Kim, 149, 292
  Rod, 162, 190
All-Star Games, 329–331

Almada, Louis, 233
Almon, William, 212
Alomar, Rafael, 296
  Sandy, 162, 164, 219
Alou, Felipe, 122, 243
  Jesus, 296
  Matty, 121, 122, 296
Alvarez, Roselio, 122, 272
Alvis, Max, 265
Amelung, Ed, 185
Anderson, Bob, 112, 227, 228
  Dave, 150, 183
  Mike, 136, 200
Annual Standings, 318–328
Anton, Leroy, 236
Arbuckle, Fatty, 316
Archie, George, 76, 79, 287
Arlett, Russell "Buzz," 37–38, 40, 46, 48, 59, 235, 236
Arlington, Texas, 191, 201
Arnold, Chris, 212, 245
Arroyo, Luis, 111
Aspromonte, Ken, 113, 280
Atz, Jake, 12
Ault, Doug, 142, 261
Autry, Gene, 207
Averill, Earl, Jr., 115, 122
  Earl, Sr., 50, 51, 122, 276

**B**

Baecht, Ed, 60, 224
Baettie, Jim, 298
Bagwell, Bill, 46, 250
Bailey, Nat, 112, 307, 308, 309
Baker, Newton, 32
  Steve, 298
Ballou, Win, 68
Baltimore, 6, 235, 268, 308
Bamberger, George, 115, 308
Bancroft, Dave "Beauty," 27, 170

Bane, Eddie, 143, 297
Banks, George, 201
Barbee, Dave, 59, 61, 204
Barnes, Don, 81
  Rich, 197
Barrett, "Kewpie Doll" Dick, 70, 74, 76, 79, 80, 82, 96, 168, 287
Bartell, "Rowdy," 170
Bartimore, Tony, 209
Barton, Larry, 251
Basinski, Ed "Professor," 169
Bass, Randy, 194
Bassler, Johnny, 51, 59, 61, 63, 64, 67, 204, 205
Bateman, John, 242
Batting Champions, 331–332
Baum, Spider, 29, 30, 31, 169, 275, 312, 313
Baumholtz, Frank, 102, 226
Baver, Ray, 228
Baxes, Jim, 99, 207
Bayless, Dick, 312, 314
  Henry, 313
Beamon, Charles, 283
Beard, Ted, 107, 108, 162, 208
Bearden, Gene, 236
Beasley, B. L., 259
  Lewis, 142, 261, 302
Beattie, Jim, 144
Beaumont, Texas, 241
Beban, Bob, 200
Beck, Walter "Boom Boom," 68, 170
Bedore, Fred, 71, 251
Beers, Clarence, 259
Belcher, Tim, 159
Belinski, Bo, 131, 211
Bell, Juan, 185
Benevento, Rocky, 248

Bennett, Dennis, 134, 211
Benson, Arizona, 300
Berenguer, Juan, 146, 298
Berger, Fred, 250
  Wally, 52
Bernier, Carlos "The Comet,"
  105, 107, 109, 121, 170,
  208, 211, 265
Berra, Dale, 304
Berry, Henry, 314
  "Jittery" Joe, 169
Bert, Eugene F., 7, 13, 294
Bevacqua, Kurt, 292, 302
Bevington, Terry, 162, 310
Bichette, Dante, 198
Bidwell, C. S. H., 9
Bielecki, Mike, 154, 213
Bilko, "Stout" Steve, 110, 111,
  113, 116, 149, 150, 169,
  227, 228, 289
Birkbeck, Mike, 310
Birtsas, Tim, 159, 298
Bisbee, Arizona, 300
Bitker, Joe, 219
Bittiger, Jeff, 311
Blackerby, George, 250
Bladt, Dick, 132, 297
Blanco, Ozzie, 297
Blankenship, Lance, 164
Bodie, Ping, 29, 170, 275
Boehler, George, 44, 45, 46, 48,
  236
Boggio, Craig, 304
Bolack, Tom, 179
Bolger, Jim, 227, 228
  Joe, 112
Bomback, Mark, 145, 146, 309
Bond, Walt, 193, 265
Bonds, Barry, 214
Bonetti, Julio, 75, 81, 115, 226
Bonham, "Tiny," 169
Boone, Bob, 200
  Daniel, 266
  Ike, 46, 52, 55, 57, 230, 231,
  232
Boozer, John, 221
Borton, Babe, 36, 168, 312, 313,
  315
Bosetti, Richard, 298
Bosio, Chris, 310
Boston, 14, 40, 63, 70, 80, 106,
  232, 280
Boston, Massachusetts, 178
Botting, Paul, 148

Ralph, 182
Bowa, Larry, 132, 165, 199, 218
Bowman, Joe, 250
  Roger, 109, 208
Boyd, Bob, 99
Brackenridge, ———, 314
Bradley, Mark, 183
  Tom, 211
Bragan, Bobby, 107, 108, 109,
  207, 208
Braggs, Glenn, 155, 310
Brandon, Darrell, 301
Brannon, Otis, 59, 204, 205
Branom, Dudley, 48
Brantley, Mickey, 188
Brashear, Kitty, 10, 169, 222,
  314
Brassil, Tom, 219
Braun, Randy, 188
Bravo, Angel, 301
Bray, Wallace, 312
Brazill, Frank, 44, 45, 47, 250
Brazle, Alpha, 85, 259
Bream, Sid, 153, 184, 185
Breeden, Danny, 306
Breeding, Marv, 244, 308
Brenly, Bob, 245
Brennan, Bill, 164, 185
Brewer, Tony, 184, 185
Bridges, Marshall, 260
  Rocky, 245
  Tommy, 93–94, 97, 251, 252
Brief, Bunny, 30, 169, 263
Briggs, Dan, 143, 252
Bright, Harry, 121, 265
Briley, Greg, 189
Brinkman, Chuck, 302
Bristol, Dave, 125
Brock, Greg, 183
Brooklyn, 8, 33, 46, 48, 52, 72,
  90, 98, 99, 112, 227, 232,
  237, 251, 284
Brooklyn, New York, 289
Brower, Frank "Turkeyfoot,"
  43, 277
Brown, Curly, 33, 223
  Fred, 256, 294
  Hector "Skinny," 104, 169,
  287
  Jackie, 138, 292
  Joe E., 69
  Mike, 153, 159, 188, 197, 198
  Rogers, 218, 297
  Tom, 283

Browning, Frank, 16, 61, 275
Brucker, Earle, 251
Brumley, Mike, 162, 164, 219
Brunansky, Tom, 266
Bryant, Derek, 240, 283, 309
Brye, Steve, 137
Bucci, Mike, 303
Bucek, Michael, 167
Buchanan, James, 8, 234
Buckner, Bill, 291
Budaska, Mark, 240
Buffalo, 164
Bullock, Eric, 164, 253, 303
Burke, Glenn, 181
Burnett, Dick, 191
  Oral, 258
Burns, George, 63, 207, 232
Bush, "Bullet" Joe, 169
Butler, Isaac, 8
Butte, Montana, 2
Buxton, Ralph "Pine Tar," 95,
  170
Buzas, Joe, 89, 167, 253

C
Calderon, Ivan, 267
Calgary, 156, 157, 158, 159,
  161, 162, 164, 167, 174,
  186–189, 195, 310
Calgary, Canada, 147, 155, 187,
  189, 267
Campbell, Archie, 65, 205
  Gilly, 66, 67
  M., 66
  Mike, 159, 160, 188
Campisi, Sal, 130, 306
Candini, Mario, 106
Capp, Merlin, 256
Cardenal, Jose, 125, 296
Cardoza, Don, 143, 181
Carlisle, Walter, 14, 15, 22, 24,
  25, 314
Carlton, Steve, 306
Carlyle, Cleo, 54, 59, 61, 63,
  204, 205
Carroll, Dixie, 39
Carson, Al, 22
  Alex, 17, 21, 314
Cartwright, Ed, 202
Casey, Pat, 188
  Perle, 12, 255, 293
  Ray, 240
Caster, George, 251
Castle, Don, 138, 291, 292
Castleton, ———, 314

Cates, Eli, 10
Caughey, Wayne, 183
Cey, Ron, 136, 180, 291
Chadbourne, Chester, 34, 315, 316
Chambers, Al, 187
  Cliff, 94
Chance, Frank, 201
Chandler, Happy, 101
Chaplin, "Tiny" Jim, 72, 77, 169, 270
Charles, Ed, 121, 308
Chase, Hal, 8, 222
Chech, Charles, 24
Cheney, Ben, 295
Chesnes, Robert, 94, 278
Chicago, 30, 35, 37, 39, 46, 48, 79, 99, 127, 189, 196, 201, 223, 224, 230, 233, 250, 276, 301, 310
Chicago, Illinois, 178, 235
Chiffer, Floyd, 218
Christensen, Bruce, 266
  John, 164, 253
  Walter, 231
Christian, Joe, 191, 201
  Tyler, 17
Christiansen, Bruce, 135
Christopher, George, 280
  Joe, 265
  Loyd, 237
Churn, Chuck, 121
  Clarence, 289
Cias, Darryl, 298
Cincinnati, 1, 41, 110
Cissell, Bill, 48, 250
Clabaugh, Moose, 71, 251
Clark, Chris, 197, 198
  Dave, 190
  Jack, 142, 245
  Jerald, 219
  Robert, 145, 266
  Ron, 127, 193
  Roy, 306
Clendenin, Len, 221
Cleveland, 21, 42, 50, 99, 125, 131, 162, 189, 249, 252, 260, 271, 272, 298
Coachman, Bobby, 198
Coats, Bob, 228
Cobb, Bob, 114, 207, 209
Cochrane, Dave, 188
  Mickey, 44, 250
Cockrell, Alan, 164

Allen, 253
Codiroli, Chris, 150, 298
Colavito, Rocky, 111, 169
Colburn, James, 132, 297
Cole, Bert, 46, 53, 230, 231, 232
Coleman, Ed, 62, 250
Coles, Darnell, 187, 267
Colligan, Robert, 191
Collins, Rip, 75, 226
  Terry, 159, 162, 183, 185
Colorado Springs, 158, 159, 163, 164, 167, 189–190, 214, 316
Colorado Springs, Colorado, 174
Conde, Ramon, 120, 289
  Ray, 216
Connors, Chuck, 226
Cooper, Gary, 77, 207
  Wilbur, 49
Cora, Joey, 162, 164
Corbett, Hiram, 301
  Joe, 6
Corcoran, Tim, 154, 253
Corrales, Pat, 124, 216, 220, 306
Corsicana, 268
Coscarart, "Coffee Joe," 168
  Jose, 67
  Pete, 122
  Steve, 122
Courtney, Henry, 276
Coveleskie, Stan, 30
Cowan, Billy, 123, 265
Cox, Dick, 47
  Jeff, 240
Coy, Bert, 26, 27, 234
Cradall, Del, 182
Craghead, Howard, 53
Cramer, "Doc," 169
Crandall, Del, 144, 148, 150, 183
  Doc, 33, 39, 47, 53, 122, 223, 224
  Karl, 122
Cravath, Gavvy, 6, 14, 15
Crawford, "Wahoo" Sam, 33, 39, 170, 223
  Willie, 290
Crews, Tim, 185
Crider, Jerry, 194, 211
Crosby, Bing, 77, 207
Crosetti, Frank, 59, 61, 277
Crouch, John, 39

Crowder, Enoch, 32
Cruz, Cirilo, 142, 261, 297
  Henry, 143, 181
  Julio, 143, 212
Cubbage, Mike, 292
Custer, George, 71
Cutler, William S. (Bill), 137, 144, 145, 167
Cutshaw, George, 11, 22, 234
Cypret, Greg, 303
D
Dade, Paul, 141, 266
Dahlgren, Babe, 67, 233
Dallas, 125, 191–192, 201, 308
Dallas-Fort Worth, 123
Dallas-Fort Worth, Texas, 178
Dallas, Texas, 91, 120, 124
Danning, "Horse," 169
Danzig, Babe, 15, 168, 249
Dasso, Frank, 86, 272
Daviault, Ray, 296
Davis, Bryshear, 297
  Gerald, 218
  Glenn, 303
  Jacke, 124
  Jim, 104
  Joel, 311
  Mike, 298
  Piper, 228
  Red, 130, 132, 169, 243, 244, 295, 296
  Richard, 154, 253, 292
  Robert, 212
  Thomas O. "Tod," 170
  Tommy, 116, 289
  Trench, 213, 214
  Willie, 120, 289
Dean, James, 9
  Tommy, 290
DeBusschere, Dave, 215, 216
Deer, Rob, 245
DeJesus, Ivan, 140, 181
DeLeon, Jose, 213
Del Greco, Bobby "The Greek," 169
Dell, Wheezer, 33, 37, 39, 41, 170, 315, 316
Dellesandro, Dom, 75, 76, 270
Demaree, Frank, 65, 66, 67, 68, 225, 251
DeMerritt, Marty, 162
DeMille, Cecil B., 77, 207
Dempsey, Con, 94, 100, 278
  Pat, 240

Denver, 123, 124, 125, 126, 127,
   130, 131, 191, 192–195
Denver, Colorado, 91, 120, 192
Derks, John C., 265
Des Moines, 58, 90
Detore, George, 270
Detroit, 38, 42, 94, 97, 110, 193,
   251, 286
Devereaux, Mike, 162, 164, 166,
   185
DeVormer, Albert, 315, 316
DeWitt, John, 82
Diaz, Edgar, 155, 310
   Mario, 164, 188–189
   Mike, 214
Dickshot, Johnny, 206
Dillinger, Robert, 108, 260
Dillon, Pop, 6, 8, 10, 14, 15, 222
DiMaggio, Dominic, 72–73, 75,
   76, 122
   Joe, 57, 63, 64, 65, 67, 68, 69,
   72, 122, 277, 278
   Vince, 64, 72, 122, 204, 205,
   269, 277
Dinoso, Lino, 109, 208
Dittmar, Carl, 59, 65, 66, 67
Dittrich, John, 189
Doerr, Bobby, 70, 269
Donnelly, Sylvester, 83, 259
Donovan, Jack, 153
Doran, Billy, 303
Doyle, Charles, 255, 256, 294
   Dennis, 132, 199
   Jess, 40, 316
Drachman, Manny, 300
Drake, Solly, 252
Dreisewerd, Clem, 86, 259
Dressen, Charlie, 99, 102, 106,
   237, 238
Drew, Cameron, 162, 304
Driessen, Dan, 304
Drott, Dick, 228
Drumright, Keith, 298
Dubuc, Jean, 264
Dugdale, Dan, 285
Duncan, Mariano, 185
Dunn, "Dynamite," 169
Dupree, Mike, 143, 212
Duren, Ryne, 111, 307
Durst, Cedric, 205, 270

E
Eagan, Truck, 7, 8, 10, 14, 234,
   255, 293
Easter, Luke, 98, 270, 271

Easterly, Ted, 12
Eaves, Vallie, 88, 272
Eckhardt, Ox, 57, 62, 63, 64,
   67, 68, 169, 232
Edington, Stump, 170, 315, 316
Edmonton, 149, 150, 151, 152,
   153, 154, 155, 158, 164,
   167, 174, 175, 186, 190,
   195–198, 253, 267
Edmonton, Canada, 147, 178,
   196, 240
Edwards, Marshall, 310
Egan, Richard, 211
Eldred, Brick, 40, 44, 284
Elia, Lee, 215, 220, 221
Elliott, Harry, 109, 271
   James, 46
   Rowdy, 312
Ellis, Robert, 143, 252
   Sammy, 122, 123, 272
Ellison, Bert, 42, 44, 46, 276,
   277
Elmore, Dave, 214
   David, 189
El Paso, 179
Emery, Calvin, 199, 216
Encino, California, 68
English, Charles, 75, 84, 226
Eppard, James, 158, 161, 198
Epperly, A. P., 85
Erautt, Eddie, 206
Erickson, Eric, 31, 275
Essick, Bill, 315, 316
Estelle, Dick, 296
   Richard, 126
Estrada, Chuck, 308
   Manuel, 283
Etten, Nick, 95, 237
Eugene, 131, 132, 135, 136, 137,
   138, 180, 198–200, 212,
   297
Eugene, Oregon, 120, 239, 260
Evans, Bill, 264
   Rube, 168
Evansville, 138, 181
Everitt, Leon, 130, 290
Ewing, J. Cal, 7, 13, 14, 234
F
Fagan, Paul I., 90, 91, 101, 278,
   279, 280
Fahey, Bill, 291, 292
Fain, Ferris, 278, 279
Fairey, James, 212, 290
Fairly, Ron, 120

Fanning, Skeeter, 27, 30, 170,
   275
Fanzone, Carmen, 135, 297
Farley, Bob, 296
Federoff, Al, 271
Feider, Mike, 155
Felder, Mike, 310
Felske, John, 154, 253
Fenton, John, 48
Fernandez, Sid, 184
Ferrara, Al, 290
Ferrarese, Don, 238, 308
Ferris, Robert, 266
Fesler, Bob, 111
Fields, Bruce, 189
50 home runs, 335
Finley, Charles O., 238
Finn, Neal, 231
Finneran, "Happy" Joe, 33,
   170, 315, 316
Finney, Lou, 250
Fireovid, Steve, 218
Firova, Dan, 190
Fisher, Bill, 127, 216
   Bus, 249
   Eddie, 295
   Gus, 27, 316
   Mique, 7, 202, 255, 256, 293,
   294
Fittery, Paul, 30, 39, 256, 264
Fitzgerald, Jack, 22
   Mike, 31
Fitzpatrick, John, 250
Flannery, Tim, 213, 310
Flavin, John, 122, 272
Fleischaker, Herbert, 73, 233
Fletcher, Guy, 89, 99, 259
Florence, Arizona, 300
Flores, Jesse, 99
Fodge, Gene, 112, 228
Fondy, Dee, 104
Fort Worth, 112, 191, 200–201
Fort Worth, Texas, 120, 124
Foster, Alan, 130
   George, 245
   .400 hitters, 335
Fournier, Jack, 223
Fowler, Art, 194
Francona, Terry, 162, 190
Franklin, Murray, 108
Frazier, Foy, 62
Freary, Ralph, 12
Frederick, John, 71, 251, 263
Freese, Gene, 209, 228

George, 112
Freisleben, Dave, 138, 211
Freitas, Tony, 60, 61, 71, 74, 75, 77, 83, 257, 258, 259
French, Ray, 257
Fresno, 13, 201–202
Fresno, California, 2, 202
Frick, Emil, 7, 284
Fromme, Art, 30, 33, 314, 315, 316
Funk, Elias, 54, 204

**G**
Gainey, Ty, 155, 304
Gallagher, Dave, 311
Galvez, Balvino, 164, 253
Ganley, Robert, 234
Garber, Bob, 109, 209
Garcia, Alfonso, 253
 Ralph, 141
 Steve, 218
Garibaldi, Art, 71, 258
 Bob, 245
Garland, L., 66
 Lou, 225
Garms, Debs, 259
Garner, Phil, 139, 302
Garrett, Adrian, 135, 297
 Ray, 17
Garvey, Steve, 135
Gaspar, Rod, 141, 212
Gay, Fred "Hard Luck," 170
Geary, Robert "Speed," 42, 276, 277
Gehrman, Paul, 85
Gentile, Jim, 117
Gera, Bernice, 165
Gettel, Allen "Cowboy," 102, 108, 168, 237, 238
 "Two-Gun," 168
Gibson, Bob, 310
 Joel, 124, 220, 221
 "Sad" Sam, 62, 65, 67, 68, 72, 75, 76, 82, 170, 277, 278
Gigon, Norm, 124, 220, 221
Gilbert, "Tookie," 170
Gill, John Wesley, 251
Gillmore, William E., 9
Giusti, Dave, 123, 241
Gladden, Dan, 245
Gobel, Walt, 66
Gomez, Lefty, 53, 168
 Preston, 289
Gonder, Jesse, 122, 272

Gonzales, Tommy, 244
Goodwin, Danny, 240, 298
Gordon, Joe, 74, 104, 106, 113, 236, 259, 280, 281
 Si, 12
Gorinski, Bob, 142, 297
Gould, Albert "Pudgy," 48, 169
Graham, Charles E., 96, 255
 Charlie, 294
 Jack, 96, 102, 270, 271
 Oscar, 6
 Wayne, 124, 220, 221
Grandas, Robert, 240
Grant, Mark, 155, 246
 Mudcat, 272
Gray, Dolly, 6, 10, 14, 15, 223
 Lorenzo, 197
Green, Harry, 59
 Lenny, 308
Greenberg, Steve, 292
Gregg, Sylveanus Augustus, 19
 (*see also* Gregg, Vean)
 Vean, 20, 21, 44, 86, 249, 284
Gregory, Paul, 76
Gretzky, Wayne, 195
Griffin, Doug, 134, 211
 Martin, 277
Griggs, Art, 33, 40
Grissom, Marv, 104, 287
Groom, Robert, 249
Gross, Wayne, 302
Gudat, Marv, 65, 66, 67, 225
Guerrero, Pedro, 143, 144, 181, 182
Guillen, Ozzie, 154, 218
Gura, Larry, 135, 297
Gutierrez, Cesar, 130, 245
Gutteridge, Don, 80, 215, 258
Gwynn, Chris, 162, 164
 Tony, 213, 218
Gyselman, Dick "The Thin Man," 169, 286–287

**H**
Haas, "Mule," 169
Hague, Joe, 130, 306
Haines, Dennis, 283
Hall, Charles "Sea Lion," 10, 168, 284
 Dick, 265
 Russell, 11
 Warren, 6, 223
Haller, Tom, 295
Hall of Famers (Pacific Coast League), 341–342

Hamilton, Earl, 47, 223
 Jeff, 159, 185
Hampton, Isaac, 266
Hamric, Bert, 113
Handley, Gene, 89, 258, 259
 "Jeep," 170
Hands, Bill, 126, 296
Haney, Fred, 53, 59, 63, 64, 67, 99, 103, 105, 107, 205, 206, 207, 208, 224
 Larry, 302
Hanlon, Ned, 7
Hannah, Joe, 228
 Truck, 226, 316
Hannahs, Gerald, 148, 182
Hansen, Robert, 141, 260
Hardy, Carroll, 123, 241
 Jack, 311
Harkness, Fred, 17
 Specs, 312
Harmon, Charles, 265
Harper, Brian, 164, 253, 266, 298
 Tommy, 122, 272
Harrell, Ray, 86
Harrelson, Ken, 191
Harrington, Andy, 67
Harris, Greg, 162
 John, 145, 266
 Spencer, 76
Harrison, Charles, 241
Harrist, Earl "Irish," 169, 237
Hart, Mike, 303
Hartenstein, Charles, 212
Hartsfield, Robert, 212
 Roy, 290
Haslin, Mike, 270
Hatcher, Mickey, 144, 182
Hatten, Joe, 108
Hatton, Grady, 123, 241, 242
Haus, Bert, 237
Hawaii, 134, 135, 137, 138, 141, 142, 143, 144, 145, 146, 148, 149, 152, 154, 155, 159, 180, 182, 185, 189, 198, 217, 245, 246, 260, 266, 279, 290, 295
Hawkins, Andy, 213
Hayes, Charlie, 246
 "Fireball," 169
Heath, Mickey, 54, 59, 61, 107, 204, 208
 Tommy, 281
Heathcock, Jeff, 303, 304

Hebert, Preacher, 270
Wally, 80, 82
Heep, Danny, 149, 303
Heilmann, Harry, 29, 275
Heiser, Roy, 251
Heitmuller, Harry, 223
Helena, 3
Helena, Montana, 2
Helms, Tommy, 125
Helser, Joe, 88
Roy, 86
Henderson, Ed, 21, 249
Mike, 310
Rickey, 240
Hendryx, Tim, 43
Hengel, Dave, 158, 161, 188
Henkle, Ferdinand, 22
Henley, Cack, 16–17, 20, 275
Henninger, Richard, 138, 291
Henshaw, R., 66
Roy, 225
Herbel, Ron, 121, 295
Herman, Babe, 86, 206
Billy, 237
Herrmann, LeRoy, 65, 67
Hersh, Dave, 152
Hershiser, Orel, 153, 183, 184
Hess, ———, 314
Hetling, Gus, 24
Hickey, John, 7
Thomas J., 3
Hicks, Jim, 130, 215, 306
Higginbotham, Irv, 27, 249
Higgins, Pinky, 63, 250
High, "Bunny," 169
Ed, 315, 316
Hildebrand, George, 255, 275
Hill, Jess, 61, 204
Jesse, 58
Hillegas, Shawn, 158, 159, 185
Hiller, Chuck, 122, 296
Hillman, Dave, 112, 228
Hinshaw, George, 159, 164, 166, 185
Hisle, Larry, 137, 180
Hitt, Bruce, 312, 314
Hobaugh, Ed, 216
Hoffman, Fred, 231
Hogan, Hap, 21, 202, 312
Hogg, Brad, 223
Holder, Brooks, 236, 237
Holland, Robert, 60
Holle, Gary, 196, 197
Hollingsworth, Al, 258

Hollywood, 37, 48, 51, 52, 53, 54, 55, 58, 60, 61, 62, 63, 65, 67, 69, 70, 73, 77, 82, 83–84, 85, 87, 88, 90–91, 92, 93, 96, 99, 103, 104, 105, 107, 108, 109, 110, 111, 113, 114, 121, 203–209, 222, 224, 231, 233, 269, 271
Hollywood, California, 45, 68, 73, 86, 102, 264
Holman, Ernie, 269
Holms, Tommy, 272
Holsey, Tim, 240
Holton, Brian, 149, 183
Holtzman, Richard M., 304
Home Run Champions, 332–333
Honeywell, Ed, 295
Honolulu, 119, 174, 210–215
Honolulu, Hawaii, 121, 159, 178
Hooper, Harry, 47
Hooten, Burt, 135, 141
Hornsby, Rogers, 104, 287
Hosley, Tim, 283
Hosp, Frank, 15
Hough, Charlie, 135, 137, 180, 291
Houston, 191, 201, 241, 242, 301, 303, 304
Houston, Texas, 91
Howard, Bruce, 125, 216
Frank, 120
Ivan, 40
Howell, Dixie, 179
Jack, 198
Ken, 164, 185
Hoy, Dummy, 6, 169
Hudson, Rex, 140, 181
Hufft, Irvin, 59, 230, 231, 232
Hughes, Jim, 6, 220, 284
Hunt, Art, 65, 67, 70, 72, 285
Mike "Old Baggy Pants," 169
Huntz, Steve, 302
Hutchinson, Fred "The Iceman," 75, 111, 170, 286, 287
Hutto, Jim, 132, 199
Hutton, Tom, 130, 135, 136, 290, 291

I
Independence, 58
Indianapolis, 123, 125, 127, 130, 131, 215–216
Indianapolis, Indiana, 120, 178
Iott, "Hooks," 170

J
Jablonski, Ray, 201
Jackson, Roland, 126, 242
Roy, 144, 182, 298
Jacobs, Art, 250
Elmer, 47, 51, 223, 276
Forrest "Spook," 170
Ray, 59, 205
Jahn, Art, 47, 223
James, Bill, 26, 40, 249, 316
Cleo, 135, 290, 297
Dion, 310
Jeff, 130, 132, 199
Phil, 143, 245
Jansen, Larry, 91, 111, 278
Javier, Stan, 298
Jeffcoat, Mike, 155, 246
Jefferson, Stan, 164, 219
Jeffries, Jim, 10
Jenkins, Fergie, 126, 220
Jensen, "Swede," 169
Johnson, Alex, 124, 220, 221, 305
Ban, 7
"Chesty," 170
Dave, 214
Deron, 123
Frank, 244
Jerry, 212
Jimmy, 303
Lance, 164, 311
Randy, 155, 246
Robert, 62
Roy, 50, 51, 276, 298
Johnston, James, 30
Jimmy, 275
Manly, 127, 216
Johnstone, Jay, 302
Jolley, Smead, 49, 50, 51, 52, 54, 57, 65, 67, 68, 73, 205, 276
Jones, Chris, 303
Darryl, 297
Earl, 95
Jeff, 240
"Nippy," 170
Odell, 150, 253
Robert, 266, 292

Sad Sam, 272
Sherman, 295
T. F., 283
Jose, Felix, 299
Joseph, Ricardo, 127, 130, 191,
    308
Josephson, Duane, 127, 216
Joshua, Von, 136, 180
Joyce, Robert, 82, 85, 86, 88,
    278
Joyner, Wally, 156, 198
Jurak, Ed, 299
**K**
Kallio, Rudy, 250
Kamm, Willie, 43, 275
Kammeyer, Robert, 144, 298
Kampouris, Alex, 63
Kane, Sugar, 312, 314
Kansas City, 238
Kearney, Bob, 298
Keating, Ray, 51, 256
Keefe, Bobby, 293, 294
    Kevin, 181
    Robert, 8, 10
Keesey, James, 61, 250, 277
Kehoe, Stu, 167, 311
Kelleher, Frank, 85, 86, 99, 102,
    107, 108, 109, 207, 208
Kellert, Frank, 113, 280
Kelley, Anthony, 304
    Tom, 125, 252
Kelly, George "Highpockets,"
    106, 169
    Joe, 43
    Pat, 194
Kennedy, Duke, 234
    James, 143
    Junior, 245
    William, 121
Kenworthy, Duke, 28, 30, 31
Keough, Matt, 304
Kerr, Johnny, 51
Kerrigan, Bob, 109
Kiely, Leo, 113
Kilduff, Pete, 42, 276, 277
Kiley, Leo, 280
Killefer, "Reindeer" Bill, 169
    Wade, 223, 231, 284
Killilay, Jack, 234
Kim, Wendell, 246
Kindl, John, 305
King, Clyde, 130
    Kevin, 198
Kingery, Mike, 189

Kingman, Brian, 240
    Dave, 245, 246
Kirkland, Willie, 130, 211
Kittle, Ron, 149, 150, 151, 197
Klepfer, Ed, 312
Klimchock, Lou, 125, 193
Knicely, Alan, 149, 303
Knight, Goodwin, 280
Koegel, Pete, 200
Koehler, Pip, 256
Koenig, Mark, 233
Koentopp, Larry, 167, 217, 219
Koestner, Bob, 312
    Elmer, 21, 22, 249
Kosco, Andy, 126, 193
Kostro, Frank, 194
Koupal, Louis, 70, 250
Kowalchuk, Mel, 167, 195, 196
Krapp, Gene "Rubber," 19, 21,
    170, 249
Krause, Hal, 249
    Harry, 39, 40, 49, 236
    "Moose," 169
Krauss, Tim, 197
Krausse, Lew, 191
Kretlow, Lou, 110
Krol, Jack, 218
Kroll, Gary, 221
Krueger, Bill, 164, 185
Krug, Marty, 223, 224
Kruk, John, 155, 218
Kubski, Gil, 266
Kusick, Craig, 213
Kusnyer, Arthur, 135, 265
**L**
Laboy, Jose, 130, 305, 306
Lachemann, Rene, 282, 283
Lafayette, 306
Lake, Ed, 259
Lancellotti, Rick, 154, 155, 218,
    246
Landestoy, Rafael, 143, 181
Landis, Bill, 191
    Kenesaw Mountain, 35, 81,
    224, 315
Lane, Bill, 29, 30, 31, 33, 40, 44,
    45, 52, 54, 59, 70, 203, 205,
    206, 230, 235, 262–263,
    269, 284
Larsen, Don, 244
Lary, Lyn, 51
Lasorda, Tommy, 135, 136,
    180, 291
Las Vegas, 121, 148, 153, 154,

    155, 158, 159, 162, 164,
    165, 167, 184, 185, 198,
    216–219, 310, 311
Las Vegas, Nevada, 174, 177,
    292
Lavagetto, Cookie, 95, 106, 236
Law, Rudy, 144, 149, 181, 183
Lawrence, "Highpockets" Bill,
    169
Laws, Brick, 236, 237
Layne, Hillis, 93, 95–96
    Tony, 287
Lazzeri, Tony, 37, 44, 45, 264
Leard, Bill, 26, 27, 234
Lee, "Deadly" Dudley, 51, 58,
    170
Lefebvre, Jim, 246
Lelivelt, Jack, 63, 66, 75, 76,
    224, 225, 226, 285
LeMay, Dick, 306
Lemon, Bob, 127, 128, 260, 287
Leonard, Jeff, 144, 181, 245
Leverenz, Tiny, 33, 264
Levey, Jim, 67
Lewallyn, Dennis, 181
Lewis, Duffy, 40, 44, 263
    James, 154
Lezcano, Sixto, 139, 260
Lifetime Records, 342
Lillard, Gene, 65, 66, 67, 68, 75,
    83, 225, 226, 258
Lindell, Johnny, 105, 107, 208
Lint, Royce, 252
Lis, Joe, 199, 200
Liska, Ad, 71, 86, 88, 97, 111,
    251
Little Rock, 124, 219–221
Little Rock, Arkansas, 120
Littrell, Jack, 121
Lively, John, 20, 234
Llenas, Winston, 134, 135, 211
Llewallyn, Dennis, 148, 182
Lober, Ty, 27
Locke, Lawrence, 221
Locker, Bob, 216
    Robert, 125
Lockman, Whitey, 130, 132,
    296, 297
Lodigiani, Dario, 95, 236, 237
Lohrke, "Lucky" Jack, 170
Lollar, Sherm, 139, 302
Loman, Doug, 310
Lombardi, Ernie "Schnoz," 59,
    95, 169, 236

Long, Dale, 108, 208
  Robert, 149
Lopes, Davey, 137, 180
Lopez, Carlos, 141, 266
Los Angeles, 5, 6, 7, 8, 10, 11,
  12, 13, 14, 15, 17, 19, 20,
  22, 27, 28, 30, 32, 37, 38,
  39, 40, 42, 46, 47, 51, 53,
  57, 58, 59, 62, 65, 66, 68,
  70, 71, 74, 75, 78, 79, 81,
  82, 83, 84, 85, 87, 89, 92,
  93, 94, 95, 96, 98, 104, 106,
  108, 110, 111, 112, 113,
  114, 118, 132, 136, 179,
  183, 195, 196, 222–229,
  233, 236, 237, 256, 258,
  294, 314, 315, 317
Los Angeles, California, 3, 16,
  21, 24, 31, 36, 41, 45, 52,
  54, 55, 101, 107, 171, 178,
  203, 209, 274, 287, 289,
  312, 313
Loucks, Scott, 153, 303
Louisville, 45
Love, Slim, 28, 223
Lown, "Turk," 169
Lubratich, Steve, 150, 197, 292
Luby, Hugh, 76
Lucchesi, Frank, 124, 132, 199,
  219–220, 221
Ludolph, Wee Willie, 70, 169,
  236
Luebber, Steve, 137, 141, 297
Lugo, Urbano, 164
Lumley, Harry, 6, 284
Lupien, Tony, 93, 206
Luzinski, Greg, 136, 200
Lynch, Ed, 159
Lynn, Red, 85, 95, 107, 169,
  208
Lysander, Richard, 240

**M**
McCall, Larry, 144, 297
McCann, Ernest, 44
McCarthy, Jack, 9
  William H., 35, 36, 45, 315
McCovey, Willie, 115, 116, 117,
  243, 295
McCredie, W. W., 249
  Walter, 14, 19, 26, 248, 249
McDaniel, Jim, 265
  O. C., 230–231
McDaniels, Booker, 98
McDermott, Terry, 181

McDonald, George, 270
McDonnell, ———, 314
McDowell, "Sudden" Sam,
  121, 125, 169
McGaffigan, Patsy, 256
McGaha, Mel, 242
McGuire, Mickey, 302
McGwire, Mark, 298
Mack, Connie, 250, 265
  Shane, 162, 219
Mackanin, Pete, 292
McKeon, Jack, 191, 201
McKernan, Pat, 167, 182, 185
McKinney, Rich, 302
McLaughlin, George, 255, 256,
  294
  James, 51
McLean, Larry, 12
McNulty, Bill, 139, 260
McQuaid, H., 231
McRae, Hal, 216
McReynolds, Kevin, 153, 217
McWeeney, Doug "Buzz," 43,
  276, 277
McWilliams, George, 272
Madlock, Bill, 138, 291
Maggart, Harl, 36
  Vess, 263
Mahler, Mickey, 253
Maier, Edward, 317
  Peter, 26, 29, 312, 314
Mails, Walter, 51
Makanin, Pete, 140
Malarkey, William, 24, 27, 234
Maldonado, Candy, 149, 183
Malmud, Bernard, 82
Mandish, George, 259
Mangual, Jose, 145, 266
Manhattan Island, New York,
  13
Mann, Red, 169
Mansfield, Jayne, 207
Manuel, Charles, 140, 181
Maranda, Georges, 296
Marichal, Juan, 121, 295
Marquez, Edwin, 198
  Luis, 252
Marshall, Jim, 238, 297, 308,
  309
Mike, 149, 151, 153, 183
Martin, Billy, 95, 130, 194, 237
  Eugene, 138
  Gene, 212
  Hershel, 236

Morrie, 113, 307
  Pepper, 80, 83, 258, 259
Martinez, Edgar, 158, 162, 188
Mason, Roger, 155, 246
Matuszek, Len, 154, 253
Mauch, Gene, 112, 227, 228
Maxvill, Dal, 215
May, Jakie, 39, 41, 316
  Lee, 126
Mayo, Eddie, 75, 81, 82
Mays, Carl "Sub," 170
  Willie, 124
Mazeroski, Bill, 111, 209
Medina, Luis, 162, 164, 190
Melchior, Henry, 15, 16, 275
Melendez, Francisco, 155, 162,
  246
Meloan, Paul, 312, 313
Melton, Cliff "Ears," 169
  Dave, 102
  "Mountain Music," 169
Menke, Dennis, 296
Meola, E., 66
Mercer, Tommy, 191
Mesner, Steve, 259, 270
Metkovich, George "Catfish,"
  102, 169, 234, 237, 238
Metzger, Butch, 212
  Clarence, 141
  George, 22
Meusel, Bob, 32, 204, 315, 316
  Emil "Irish," 32, 169, 223
Mickelsen, Noel, 252
Mikkelson, Pete, 130, 306
Miley, Sammy, 265
Miller, Darrell, 197, 198
  Dots, 39
  Frank, 20, 21
  Hack, 234
  John, 290
  Lemmie, 153, 184, 185
Milwaukee, 193, 287, 292, 310
Milwaukee, Wisconsin, 106
Minneapolis, 70
Minnesota, 191, 194, 201, 253
Minoso, Minnie, 98–99, 102,
  215, 271
Minton, Greg, 143, 245
Mission, 88
Mission-San Francisco, 230–
  233
Mitchell, Bobby, 182, 183
  Clarence, 67
  John, 315, 316

Mike, 13, 14, 248
Robert, 145
Willis, 37, 42, 276, 277, 315, 316
Moates, David, 140, 291, 292
Modesto, 257
Moeller, Joe, 130, 290
Mohler, Kid, 17
Monroe, J. A., 232, 250
Montaserio, Juan, 197
Monteagudo, Aurelio, 191
Monterey, California, 28
Montreal, 98, 186
Montreal, Canada, 289
Monzo, Vince, 73
Moore, Charles, 22
Dave, 183
James, 250
Johnny, 59, 82, 85
Kelvin, 240, 298
Morales, Jose, 302
Moreno, Jose, 213
Morgan, Nick, Jr., 210
Morley, Jim, 7, 294
Moser, Walter, 20, 234
Moses, John, 187, 188
Moskau, Paul, 167
Moss, Les, 215
Most Valuable Players, 340–341
Mota, Manny, 122, 296
Moulder, Glen, 103
Mueller, Ray, 83, 258, 259
Muller, Fred, 63, 70, 285
"Old Scrapiron," 170
Mulligan, Ed, 43, 231, 277
Mullinks, Rance, 145, 266
Munger, Red, 109, 169, 208, 209
Murdock, Wilbur, 12
Murphy, Foghorn, 274
Murray, Dan, 31
Tom, 242
Muskowitz, ——, 21

**N**

Naccarato, Stan, 152, 167, 299
Nagelson, Russ, 252
Nagle, Walter, 15, 16
Nance, Clyde, 54
Narron, Jerry, 150, 197, 292
Nash, Charles, 216
Nelson, Dave, 252
E., 66
Emmitt, 225

Gerald, 241
M. A., 231
Mel, 289
"Six O'Clock," 168
"Slim," 168
Ness, Jack, 28
Nettles, Craig, 131, 194
New Orleans, Louisiana, 306
Newsom, Buck, 65, 88, 225
Newsome, Dick, 270
Newton, Doc, 6, 7, 12, 13, 169, 222
New York, 13, 32, 43, 51, 59, 62, 68, 76, 90, 91, 95, 113, 193, 236, 237, 243, 251–252, 275–276, 277, 279, 280, 297, 315
New York, New York, 178
Nichols, Chester, 308
Niekro, Phil, 125, 193
Nixon, Donell, 158, 161, 188
Noble, Ray, 237
Noga, George, 215
Norbert, Ted, 74, 75, 76, 82, 84, 85, 89, 251
Nordyke, Lou, 256
Noren, Irv, 99, 207, 211
Norman, Fred, 290
Nossek, Joe, 201
Nottle, Ed, 298
Novikoff, Lou "The Mad Russian," 78–79, 92, 93, 169, 226
Nyman, Chris, 197

**O**

Oakland, 1, 5, 6, 8, 10, 11, 12, 13, 14, 15, 16, 17, 20, 21, 22, 24, 25, 26, 27, 28, 30, 31, 34, 37, 38, 39, 40, 42, 44, 46, 48, 49, 51, 52, 53, 59, 62, 63, 64, 70, 73, 76, 79, 84, 85, 91, 92, 94, 95, 96, 98, 99, 102, 105, 106, 108, 112, 118, 196, 233–239, 240, 251, 255, 261, 271, 278, 282, 283, 298, 301, 302, 309
Oakland, California, 2, 3, 10, 21, 26, 32, 33, 142, 178, 235, 274
Oana, Prince Henry, 62, 250, 277
O'Berry, Mike, 197
O'Brien, Robert, 135, 291

O'Connell, Jimmy, 43, 275
O'Donnell, George "Ezra," 107, 168, 208
O'Doul, Lefty, 39, 45, 47, 70, 72, 74, 76, 90–91, 94, 106, 109, 168, 238, 263, 271, 279, 280, 281, 307
Ogden, 149, 195, 196, 239–240
Ogden, Utah, 144, 261, 283
Oglesby, Jim, 65, 66, 67, 68, 225
O'Hara, William, 11
Oklahoma City, 123, 124, 125, 131, 191, 241–243
Oklahoma City, Oklahoma, 120
Oldfield, Barney, 10
Oliva, Pedro, 191, 201
Oliver, Bob, 194
Eugene, 252
Harry, 221
Ollom, Jim, 127, 194
O'Malley, Walter, 112, 227, 228, 289
O'Neill, John, 87, 251
Ontiveros, Steve, 138, 245
Orengo, Joe, 258
Orr, Billy, 31
Ortiz, Jose, 297, 301
Osborn, Don, 85
Osenbaugh, Roger, 113
Osteen, Claude, 115
Ostrowski, John, 85
Ott, Mel, 237
Ouelette, Phil, 164
Outen, William, 233
Overall, Orval, 8
Overy, Mike, 266
Owen, Marvin, 251
Ozark, Danny, 123, 290

**P**

Paciorek, Jim, 310
Tom, 136, 180, 291
Padgett, Don, 237
Pafko, Andy, 84, 226
Pagan, Jose, 116, 121, 240, 244
Page, Vance, 65, 205
Palacios, Vicente, 159
Palica, Ervin, 308
Pall, Donn, 164, 311
Palys, Stan, 211
Papkin, Max, 157
Parker, Bill, 266
Russ, 167, 186, 189, 195, 267
William, 135

Pasley, Kevin, 181
Patchett, Harold, 270
Pate, Bob, 303
Patterson, ——, 314
  Bob, 214
  Dave, 183
  Ken, 311
  Mike, 240
  Reggie, 197
Pazik, Mike, 297
Pearson, Albie, 111, 114, 281
Peckinpaugh, Roger, 24, 249
Pena, Alejandro, 183
  Tony, 149, 253
Penner, Ken, 316
Perconte, Jack, 185
  John, 145, 149, 182, 183
Perez, Atanasio, 272
  Tony, 125
Perezchica, Tony, 162, 246
Perkins, Brod, 213, 303
Perlman, Jon, 155, 158, 159, 246
Pernoll, Hub, 25
Perry, Gaylord, 121, 122, 296
  "Little Buffalo," 169
Peterson, Adam, 311
  Carl, 271, 308
Pettis, Gary, 150, 153
Pettit, Paul "Pills," 168
Philadelphia, 13, 27, 38, 41, 90, 124, 125, 137, 199, 200, 219, 250, 257, 264, 279
Philadelphia, Pennsylvania, 178
Phillips, Adolfo, 124, 221
  Dick, 121, 212
  Jack, 109
Phipps, Jodie, 85
Phoenix, 115, 116, 117, 119, 127, 130, 131, 138, 140, 142, 143, 152, 153, 155, 158, 159, 162, 167, 182, 212, 218, 243–247, 295, 310, 316
Phoenix, Arizona, 114, 121, 126, 165, 187, 205, 244, 300
Piche, Ron, 308
Pickrel, Clarence "Snake Eyes," 169
Piercy, "Wild Bill," 33, 170
Pieretti, Marino, 86, 251
Pillette, Duane, 88, 97, 122
  Herman "Old Folks," 38, 46, 53, 67, 88, 97, 122, 170,

230, 231, 232
Pinelli, Babe, 53, 63
Piniella, Lou, 131, 252
Pinson, Vada, 115
Pippen, Henry "Cotton," 169
Pitchers (Lowest Earned Run Average), 339–340
Pitchers (More than 200 Victories), 340
Pitchers (Most Strikeouts), 338–339
Pitchers (Most Victories), 335–336
Pitchers (Winning Percentage), 336–338
Pittsburgh, 105, 107, 207, 208, 209
Pizarro, Juan, 134, 297
Pladson, Gordon, 303
Plank, Ed, 143, 245
Playoff Results, 328–329
Plummer, Bill, 188
Pocklington, Peter, 149, 195
Polidor, Gus, 198
Polonia, Luis, 299
Ponce, Carlos, 155, 310
  Tony, 108
Pool, Harlan, 236, 285
Poole, James, 44, 249
Portland, 8, 10, 11, 12, 13, 14, 15, 17, 19, 20, 21, 22, 23, 24, 25, 26, 27, 30, 31, 32, 33, 34, 36, 39, 40, 41, 42, 44, 46, 47, 49, 54, 60, 62, 63, 64, 71, 72, 82, 86, 87, 88, 89, 94, 97, 99, 106, 109, 111, 121, 122, 125, 126, 129, 130, 131, 132, 135, 136, 137, 138, 144, 149, 150, 152, 154, 164, 167, 174, 181, 184, 197, 202, 247–255, 256, 270, 274, 278, 291, 311, 314
Portland, Oregon, 2, 3, 10, 48, 52, 91, 120, 140, 143, 178, 196, 203
Posedel, Barnacle Bill, 71, 72, 169, 251
Postema, Pam, 165
Powell, Putt, 22
  William, 207
Power, Ted, 149, 182, 183
Prescott, George, 211, 243, 244
Presidents of Pacific Coast

League, 331
Presley, Jim, 267
Prim, Ray, 75, 82, 85, 226
Prough, Bill, 30, 256
Pulford, Burt, 88, 251
Pulido, Alfonso, 154, 213
Pulliam, H. C., 7
Purkey, Bob, 209
Putnam, Pat, 302, 303
Pyznarski, Tim, 155, 218

**Q**
Queen, Mel, 109, 208
Quilici, Frank, 127
Quinn, Jack, 33
  John Picus, 314
  "Whimpy," 170

**R**
Rabb, John, 189
Rabe, Charles, 113
Rader, Doug, 213
Raffensberger, Ken, 85
Raft, George, 207
Raimondi, Billy, 95
Raines, Tim, 194
Rajsich, Gary, 303
Rakow, Ed, 289
Raleigh, ——, 314
  John, 312
Ramsdell, Willard, 99, 207
Ramsey, Bill, 258
Randall, Bobby, 181
  Robert, 140
  Sap, 164
Ranew, Merritt, 308
Rapp, Earl, 102, 109, 237, 271
Rapps, William, 26
Raschi, Vic, 251
Rath, Maurice, 31
  Morrie, 263
Rau, Doug, 137, 180
Ray, Johnny, 303
  Larry, 303
Rayford, Floyd, 266
RBI Leaders, 333–334
Ready, Randy, 310
Reed, Howard, 123, 242, 290
Reese, Jimmy, 38, 51, 65, 66, 67, 270
  Rich, 193
Reinhart, Art, 39, 223
Reuschel, Rick, 214
Reynolds, Archie, 297
  Don, 143, 212
  Harold, 154, 187, 188

Ken, 199
Tom, 135, 265
Tommie, 141
Rhiel, William, 60
Rhodes, Dusty, 243
Rhyne, Hal, 42, 50, 276, 277
Rice, Del, 135
Ricelli, Frank, 245
Richards, Eugene, 141, 212
Ricketts, David, 306
Rickey, Branch, 99
Rijo, Jose, 298
Ritchey, John, 98
Rivera, German, 153, 184
Jim, 287
John, 138
Jungle Jim, 104
Rivers, John, 135
Mickey, 265, 266
Roberts, Bip, 164, 218, 219
David, 126, 241
Robertson, Richard, 131, 245
Robinson, Bill, 137, 200
Brooks, 308
Bruce, 309
Jackie, 98
Robson, Tom, 140, 292
Rocco, Mike, 94
Rochester, 111
Rodas, Rich, 153, 183, 184
Rodgers, Andre, 115, 116, 243
"Rawmeat" Bill, 168
W. K., 27, 31, 249
William, 40
Rodriguez, Edwin, 218
Roberto, 135, 297
Roenicke, Ron, 155, 183
Rohwer, Ray, 40, 44, 45, 48, 284
Rollings, Bill, 306
Russ, 54, 204
Rolph, James, Jr., 10
Roosevelt, Franklin Delano, 83
Theodore, 192
Root, Charlie, 45, 83, 86, 206, 223
Rosario, Santiago, 308
Rosen, Al, 99, 271
Rosenberg, Henry, 232, 233
Ross, Gary, 141, 212
Rowe, Ken, 125, 290
Rowen, Rob, 202
Rowland, Clarence "Pants," 89, 93

Royster, Jerry, 141, 181
Ruby, Harry, 69
Ruess, Wild Bill, 25
Ruether, Dutch, 50, 51, 67, 169, 276
Ruiz, Hiraldo, 122, 123
Rumler, Bill, 33, 36, 54, 58, 204, 263
Russell, Rip, 75, 84, 85, 169
Ruth, Babe, 32, 36, 37, 38, 45
Ryal, Mark, 198
Ryan, Buddy, 21, 31, 249
Jack, 28, 30
John, 223

**S**
Sacramento, 5, 6, 7, 9, 12, 16, 17, 20, 21, 22, 26, 28, 30, 31, 32, 33, 37, 39, 45, 48, 51, 60, 61, 63, 71, 72, 74, 75, 77, 79, 80, 82, 83, 84, 86, 88, 94, 96, 99, 104, 106, 108, 113, 116, 119, 121, 128, 139, 141, 142, 144, 159, 174, 230, 255–262, 270, 281, 293, 294, 295, 313
Sacramento, California, 1, 2, 3, 5, 10, 58, 91, 102, 120, 138, 200, 202, 240, 282
Sadowski, Ted, 201
Saffell, Tom, 107, 109, 117, 208
St. Louis, 32, 39, 58, 68, 77, 81, 107, 186, 221, 225, 227, 259, 264, 284, 294, 305
St. Louis, Missouri, 178
St. Paul, 45
Sakata, Lenn, 145, 309
Salmon, Chico, 123, 193
Salt Lake City, 30, 31, 33, 36, 37, 39, 40, 44, 49, 59, 70, 90, 115, 116, 117, 118, 121, 122, 123, 126, 127, 134, 135, 138, 141, 143, 144, 145, 146, 148, 152, 153, 155, 159, 181, 182, 183, 186, 195, 197, 203, 210, 212, 213, 227, 230, 262–268, 269, 272, 279, 297, 303, 309, 316
Salt Lake City, Utah, 29, 41, 45, 114, 120, 209, 263
Saltzman, Harold, 99–100, 252
Salveson, Jack, 82, 102, 207
Salvo, Manuel, 72, 74, 270, 272
Sample, Billy, 303

Samuel, Juan, 253
Sanchez, Alejandro, 245
Sand, Harry, 31
Sanders, "Bones," 169
San Diego, 6, 37, 38, 71, 72, 74, 75, 82, 84, 86, 88, 91, 93, 96, 98, 99, 102, 106, 107, 109, 110, 115, 116, 122, 123, 125, 126, 127, 128, 129, 130, 153, 174, 208, 213, 220, 238, 258, 269– 274
San Diego, California, 54, 70, 120, 131, 178, 205, 221
Sands, Henry, 39
Sandt, Tommy, 213
Saner, Ed, 103
Sanford, Fred, 106
San Francisco, 1, 7, 8, 9, 10, 12, 13, 14, 15, 16, 17, 19, 20, 21, 22, 26, 27, 29, 30, 31, 33, 34, 36, 37, 39, 41, 42, 43, 44, 45, 48, 50, 51, 52, 53, 54, 57, 58, 59, 60, 61, 62, 63, 65, 67, 68, 70, 72, 74, 75, 78, 81, 82, 84, 85, 88, 92, 94, 95, 96, 100, 102, 104, 108, 114, 118, 122, 132, 171, 172, 173, 209, 238, 244, 246, 256, 261, 263, 274–282, 279, 280, 283, 296, 308, 317
San Francisco, California, 1, 2, 3, 6, 10, 24, 28, 32, 33, 35, 49, 55, 73, 80, 86, 90–91, 101, 106, 113, 142, 178, 202, 203, 204, 222, 230, 233, 234, 243, 260, 281, 282
San Jose, 144, 282–284
San Jose, California, 2, 142, 240, 261
Santa Cruz, California, 2
Santa Fe, New Mexico, 179
Santiago, Benito, 218
Sarni, Bill, 84, 85
Sauer, Ed, 95
Savage, Ted, 305
Sax, Dave, 184
Scarsella, Les, 85, 91, 234, 236, 237
Schaefer, ———, 314
Schaller, Biff, 31
Schallock, Art, 238
Schang, Robert, 256

Scheffing, Bob, 227, 228
Schlafly, Larry, 10
Schmees, George, 207
Schmidt, Bill, 258, 259
Mike, 137, 200
Schneider, Paul, 188
Pete, 40, 41, 53, 162, 263, 315, 316
Schroder, Robert, 244
Schu, Rick, 155
Schuler, David, 266
Schulmerich, Wes, 59, 224
Schulte, "Ham," 170
Schuster, "Broadway" Bill, 81, 170
"Buffalo" Bill, 169
Sciosia, Mike, 144, 182
Sconiers, Daryl, 150, 266, 292
Scott, Jim "Death Valley," 43, 276
John, 141, 212
Pete, 231
Season Records, 342–343
Seaton, Tom, 21, 23, 36, 249
Seats, Tom, 77, 86, 278
Seattle, 6, 7, 8, 10, 11, 12, 13, 14, 17, 33, 37, 40, 42, 44, 46, 49, 53, 59, 60, 62, 63, 64, 67, 70, 72, 74, 75, 76, 77, 78, 79, 80, 81, 82, 84, 85, 86, 88, 89, 91, 92, 93, 94, 95, 97, 99, 103, 106, 110, 111, 113, 115, 121, 123, 127, 128, 130, 143, 174, 183, 186, 188, 202, 206, 227, 230, 235, 250–251, 258, 266, 267, 283, 284–289, 292, 299, 306, 307, 308
Seattle, Washington, 2, 3, 45, 52, 120, 131, 143, 178, 203
Secrist, Don, 216
See, Larry, 159, 185
Segui, Diego, 141, 212
Severeid, Hank, 54, 59, 61, 204
Severns, Billy, 145, 309
Sexton, Jimmy, 298, 303
Michael H., 3
Shanz, Charles, 99
Sharperson, Mike, 164, 185
Shaughnessy Plan, 57, 68, 71, 102, 103, 226, 318
Shaw, Hunky, 15, 19, 169, 275
Shay, Dan, 6, 275

Shea, Frank, 236
John, 276
Sheehan, "Minnie Mouse," 169
Tom, 12, 65, 205
Sheehand, Bill, 294
Sheely, Bud, 122
Earl, 33, 37, 51, 59, 60, 122, 169, 250, 256, 263, 276
Shellenback, Frank, 30, 37, 53, 54, 55, 58, 61, 63, 65, 70, 74, 203, 204, 205, 315, 316
Jim, 138, 291–292
Sherlock, Jack, 231
Shields, Charles, 10, 135, 141
Shinn, William, 28
Shirley, Bart, 290
Shockley, Costen, 124, 125, 220, 221
Shone, Frank, 251
Shores, Bill, 250
Sick, Emil, 75, 97, 285, 286, 287
Siglin, Paddy, 39
Silverio, Tomas, 135, 211, 265
Simmons, "Mysterious" Tom, 170
Todd, 158, 164, 218, 219
Simpson, Harry, 99, 102, 271
Joe, 143, 181
"Suitcase," 170
Singer, Bill, 290
Singleton, Elmer, 106, 110, 111
Sisler, Dick, 109, 271
Siwacki, Bill, 183
Skidmore, Rod, 132, 297
Skinner, Bob, 130, 272
Skurski, Audy, 103
Slade, Gordon, 231
Slagle, Roger, 144, 298
Smajstria, Craig, 304
Smith, A. Ray, 305, 306
Billy, 303
Bobby, 310
C. Arnholt, 271
Casey, 36
Charles, 120, 289
Chris, 153, 245
Dick, 113, 121, 209
Elmer, 46, 47, 48, 250
Garry, 297
Greg, 218
Indian, 31
Ira, 77
Keith, 142, 261
Milton, 271

Ray, 218
Red, 40
Roy, 164, 253
"Scooter," 170
Steve, 218
Snyder, Ray, 81
Soderholm, Eric, 136
Solomon, Eddie, 181
Soriano, Dewey, 308
Sorrell, Bill, 220, 221
Sothoron, Allen, 30, 249
Souchak, Steve, 102
Spackman, Alice, 248
Spahn, Warren, 130, 306
Spanswick, Bill, 123
Spargo, Harvey, 279
Speake, Bob, 112, 117, 228
Speaker, Tris, 22
Speer, Floyd, 95
Spies, Harry, 6
Spiezio, Ed, 306
Spokane, 110, 115, 116, 117, 121, 123, 125, 129, 130, 134, 135, 136, 138, 140, 141, 144, 149, 150, 152, 153, 183, 210, 211, 217, 241, 252, 272, 289–293, 298, 302, 306
Spokane, Washington, 2, 114, 120
Sposito, Gustavo, 290
Staab, Larry, 290
Stachie, Marv, 215
Stainback, Tuck, 65, 225
Standridge, Pete, 223
Stanek, Al, 125, 296
Stanwyck, Barbara, 77, 207
Statz, Arnold "Jigger," 38, 39, 47, 59, 62, 63, 65, 66, 67, 68, 75, 170, 223, 224
Steels, James, 218
Steen, Bill, 19, 21, 23, 249
Steevens, Morris, 124, 220, 221
Steinbacher, Harry, 85
Steirer, Rick, 197
Stengel, Casey, 91, 94, 95, 170, 236, 237
Stephenson, Jerry, 135, 291
Stevens, R. C., 121, 265
Stewart, Dave, 148, 182
Ed, 270
"Gabby," 170
Harry, 22, 314
Stigman, Richard, 116, 271

Stimes, Craig, 213
Stinson, ——, 314
Stockton, 61, 222, 257
Stockton, California, 2
Stolen Base Leaders, 334–335
Stone, Jeff, 155
Marvin, 246
Stoneham, Horace, 113
Storey, Harvey, 76, 97, 251
Strahler, Mike, 135, 291
Strand, Paul, 40, 41, 48, 250, 263, 264
Strange, Alan, 76, 205
Lee, 191, 201
Striker, Jake, 117
Strom, Brent, 303
Stroud, Ed "The Creeper," 127, 170, 216
Ralph "Sailor," 169, 256, 264
Stuart, Dick, 115, 209, 265
Dick "Iron Glove," 169
Dick "Socko," 169
Stubbs, Franklin, 155, 185
Stubing, Moose, 197, 292
Sturdy, Maurice, 259
Suhr, Gus, 49, 50, 52, 249, 276
Sullivan, Charles, 286
Joe, 65, 67, 205
Summers, John, 302
Sunday, Billy, 222
Surhoff, B. J., 155, 310
Sutcliffe, Rich, 144
Rick, 181
Sutor, Harry, 21, 275
Swanson, Evar, 46, 51, 230
Sweeney, Bill, 71, 84, 85, 251
Sweet, Richard, 143, 212, 302

**T**
Tabb, Jerry, 283, 309
Tacoma, 3, 7, 8, 9, 10, 11, 119, 120, 121, 122, 124, 125, 126, 130, 132, 135, 141, 142, 143, 144, 146, 149, 150, 152, 155, 159, 162, 164, 167, 171, 172, 173, 181, 182, 183, 187, 199, 202, 211, 260, 265, 266, 289, 292, 293–299, 310
Tacoma-Sacramento, 14
Tacoma, Washington, 2, 116, 121, 127, 140, 244, 248, 255, 277
Tagi, Atushi, 202
Taitt, Doug, 205

Tanner, Chuck, 134, 211
Tappe, Elvin, 228
Tartabull, Danny, 154, 155, 157, 187, 267
Taylor, Charles, 130, 306
Robert, 77, 207
Terry, 188
Tellman, Tom, 213
Terry, Yank, 80, 270, 272
Thielman, John, 6, 20
30-Game Winners, 340
Thomas, Bill, 293, 294
Fay "Scow," 61, 65, 66, 68, 75, 169, 225, 226
Gorman, 139, 260
Tom, 255
Thompson, Averett, 259
Rupert, 270
Thorpe, Jim, 250
Thurston, Hollis, 50, 51, 276
Tiant, Luis, 125, 149, 196, 252
Tidewater, 138, 181
Tiefenthaler, Verle, 121, 296
Tillman, Kerry, 218
Tingley, Ron, 190
Tobik, Dave, 187
Tobin, Jack, 32
Tolan, Bobby, 306
Toliver, Fred, 253
Tolman, Tim, 303
Tombstone, 300
Tomlin, Dave, 214
Toms, Tom, 245
Toner, Red, 169
Toothman, Ken, 265
Torre, Frank, 308
Torve, Kelvin, 164, 253
Tovar, Cesar, 125, 191, 201
Townsend, ——, 255
Tozer, William, 10, 17, 113, 223
Tracy, Jim, 303
Trebelhorn, Tom, 310
Trillo, Manny, 138, 139, 302
Trower, "Jeep," 170
Tsitouris, John, 122, 130, 272
Tucson, 131, 138, 139, 148, 149, 152, 153, 155, 164, 174, 182, 198, 291, 300–304
Tucson, Arizona, 120, 178, 188, 303
Tulsa, 126, 127, 130, 131, 221, 287, 305–306
Tulsa, Oklahoma, 120, 305
Tunnell, Lee, 214

Turner, Jim, 58, 204
John, 141, 212
Turpin, Hal, 76, 79, 80, 82, 287
Tuttle, William C., 68, 73, 81

**U**
Uecker, Bob, 193
Uhalt, Frenchy, 63, 73, 85, 169, 206, 235
Uhlaender, Ted, 126, 193

**V**
Valdes, Rene, 111, 252
Valdespino, Hilario, 193
Valenti, Jack, 208
Valentine, Bobby, 135, 136, 212, 291
Fred, 126, 211
Valla, Gene, 42, 46, 276, 277
Valle, Dave, 187, 188
Van Buren, Ed, 21
Vance, Dazzy, 33
Vancouver, 91, 111, 112, 115, 121, 123, 125, 127, 129, 130, 135, 145, 146, 149, 152, 155, 158, 159, 162, 164, 167, 174, 177, 185, 187, 190, 212, 218, 219, 238, 246, 265, 295, 307–312
Vancouver, Canada, 117, 120, 143
Van Fleet, Red, 169
Van Haltren, George, 8
Vanni, Edo, 76
Vaughns, Clarence, 200
Veeck, Bill, 107
Veintidos, Juan, 297
Venice, 28, 30, 171, 203, 222, 312–313
Venice, California, 26, 29, 312, 314
Ventura, 108
Vergez, John, 53
Vernon, 16, 19, 21, 22, 25, 26, 30, 32, 33, 34, 36, 37, 39, 40, 41, 42, 44, 45, 70, 79, 88, 171, 203, 222, 223, 230, 262, 263, 313–317
Mickey, 130
Vernon, California, 24, 29, 312, 313
Vickers, Rube, 13, 168, 284
Vinci, Louri, 51, 256
Vinson, Charles, 135, 211, 265

Vitt, Oscar, 61, 203, 205
Vitter, Joe, 73
**W**
Waco, 24
Wade, Ben, 207
 Gale, 228
Wagner, Gary, 130
 Leon, 115
Waitkus, Eddie, 82
Waits, Mike, 138, 291, 292
 Rick, 310
Walk, Bob, 154, 155, 213
Walker, Bill, 75
Wallace, Dave, 185
 Mike, 137, 200
Walsh, Ed, Jr., 64
 Jim, 107
Walters, Ken, 272
Walton, Dan, 140, 143, 181
Waner, Lloyd, 43
 Paul, 43, 45, 46, 276, 277
Ward, Dick, 65, 66, 74, 75, 225
Washington, 6, 112, 192
 LaRue, 302
 Ron, 181
Wasiak, Stan, 140
Wasinger, Mark, 218
Waslewski, Gary, 302
Watsonville, California, 2
Webb, Earl, 52
Webber, Les, 76
Weekly, Johnny, 241
Weis, Art, 223
Wellman, Brad, 159, 185
Welsh, Jim, 284
Werhas, Johnny, 211, 290
Werle, Bill, 94, 279
 "Bugs," 170
Werth, Dennis, 297
West, Max, 93, 99, 106, 227,
 233, 270, 271
Westerzill, "Tex," 170
Westmoreland, Claude, 143

Wetzel, Buzz, 205
Whalen, James, 8, 10, 113, 275
Wheeler, George, 11, 20
Wheelock, Gary, 141, 266
Whitacre, Fred, 167, 214
White, Devon, 198
 Doc, 169, 312
 Jo Jo, 76, 79, 88, 95, 259, 286
 Roy, 290
Wichita, 189, 218
Wicker, Kemp, 259
Wiggins, Alan, 149, 213
Wiggs, Long Jim, 16, 169
Wight, Bill, 109, 271
Wilber, Del, 140, 291
Wiley, Mark, 143, 212, 297
Wilhoit, Joe, 40, 263, 312
Wilkie, Aldon, 95
Wilkins, Eric, 143, 252
Willett, ———, 314
Williams, D. R., 201
 Denny, 54
 Dibrell, 258
 Eddie, 190
 Esther, 10
 Guy, 276, 277
 Henry, 51
 Jimy, 146, 266
 John, 28, 256
 Kenneth, 249
 Lefty, 30, 168, 264
 Mark, 283
 Matt, 162
 Reggie, 190
 Richard, 303
 Ted, 69, 70, 269, 270
 Walt, 127, 305
Williamson, Mark, 218
Wills, Bump, 142, 261
 Frank, 187
 Maury, 115
Wilson, Artie, 98, 99, 237
 Gary, 303

Mike, 150, 155
 Tack, 183, 184, 198, 246
Winder, Ray, 219, 220
Windsor, "Duke," 169
Winnipeg, Canada, 164, 304
Wise, K. C. "Casey," 170, 228
Wissel, Richard, 200
Witt, Red, 169
Wolter, Harry, 28, 223
Woodall, Larry, 67
Woodard, Mike, 155, 164, 246,
 311
Woodling, Gene, 94, 278
Woods, Gary, 303
 Pinky, 99, 207
Woodson, Richard, 136, 137,
 252
 Tracy, 162, 164, 185
Wren, Christine, 165
Wright, Al, 67
 Richard, 149
 Wayne, 47, 223
Wrigley, Phil, 81
 William K., 39
 William K., Jr., 224
**Y**
Yelle, Archie, 42
Yellowhorse, "Chief" Moses,
 256
York, Tony, 94
Yost, Ned, 310
Young, Cy, 123
Yuill, Bill, 304
Yuma, Arizona, 159, 163, 189
**Z**
Zachary, Chris, 125–126, 242
Zahn, Geoff, 180
Zeider, Rollie, 275
Zernial, Gus, 96, 206
 "Ozark Ike," 170
Zimmer, Don, 130, 215
Zinn, Jimmy, 60
Zinssar, Charles, 11